STUDY GUIDE WITH READINGS
TO ACCOMPANY PAPALIA AND OLDS

T5-DHH-764

PSYCHOLOGY

VIRGINIA NICHOLS QUINN
Northern Virginia Community College

JOLYNE SHIELDS DAUGHTRY
California State University, Fresno

McGRAW-HILL BOOK COMPANY

New York	Lisbon	Panama
St. Louis	London	Paris
San Francisco	Madrid	San Juan
Auckland	Mexico	São Paulo
Bogotá	Milan	Singapore
Caracas	Montreal	Sydney
Colorado Springs	New Delhi	Tokyo
Hamburg	Oklahoma City	Toronto

SECOND EDITION

STUDY GUIDE WITH READINGS TO ACCOMPANY
PAPALIA AND OLDS: PSYCHOLOGY, 2/E

Copyright © 1988 by McGraw-Hill, Inc. All rights reserved. Printed in
the United States of America. Except as permitted under the United States
Copyright Act of 1976, no part of this publication may be reproduced
or distributed in any form or by any means, or stored in a data base or
retrieval system, without the prior written permission of the publisher.

1234567890 SEMSEM 89321098

ISBN 0-07-048535-6

This book was set by Archetype, Inc. The editors were Rhona Robbin,
James D. Anker, and Susan Gamer; the designer was Joan O'Connor; the
production supervisor was Diane Renda. Drawings were done by Fine
Line Illustrations, Inc. Semline, Inc. was printer and binder.

STUDY GUIDE WITH READINGS
TO ACCOMPANY PAPALIA AND OLDS

PSYCHOLOGY

CONTENTS

List of Readings
Preface
Study Tips
Tips for Writing Term Papers

PART I: PSCYHOLOGY AS A SCIENCE
 1. Introduction to Psychology

PART II: BIOLOGICAL FOUNDATIONS OF BEHAVIOR
 2. Biology and Behavior
 3. Sensation and Perception
 4. States of Consciousness

PART III: LEARNING, MEMORY, AND COGNITIVE PROCESSES
 5. Learning
 6. Memory
 7. Intelligence
 8. Language and Thought

PART IV: LIFE-SPAN DEVELOPMENTAL PSYCHOLOGY
 9. Early Development
10. Development from Adolescence On

PART V: MOTIVATION, EMOTION, AND SEXUALITY
11. Motivation and Emotion
12. Sexuality and Gender Roles

PART VI: PERSONALITY, ABNORMALITY, AND HEALTH
13. Theories and Assessment of Personality
14. Abnormal Psychology
15. Therapy
16. Health Psychology

PART VII: SOCIAL PSYCHOLOGY
17. Social Influence
18. Interpersonal Attraction and Relationships

APPENDIX: STATISTICS

LIST OF READINGS

1. Arthur Wiens, ""Defining Quality for Consumers" (1987). Emanuel Donchin, "Should There Be Uniform Standards of Quality for Graduate Education in All Fields of Psychology?"

2. Matt Clark and David Gelman with Mariana Gosnell, Mary Hager, and Barbara Schuler, ""The Power of Hormones" (1987)

3. Herschel W. Leibowitz, "Grade Crossing Accidents and Human Factors Engineering" (1985)

4. Isabel Abrams, "Beyond Night and Day" (1986)

5. Robert J. Trotter, "Stop Blaming Yourself" (1987)

6. Sharon Begley with Karen Springen, Susan Katz, Mary Hager, and Elizabeth Jones, "Memory" (1986)

7. Robert J. Trotter, "Profile: Robert J. Sternberg—Three Heads Are Better Than One" (1986)

8. Laura Berk, "Private Speech: Learning Out Loud" (1986)

9. Daniel Goleman, "Terror's Children: Mending Mental Wounds" (1987)

10. Jeff Meer, "The Reason of Age" (1986)

11. Connie Zweig, "The Big Thrill" (1987)

12. Elizabeth Stark, "Young, Innocent and Pregnant" (1986)

13. Daniel Goleman, "Major Personality Study Finds That Traits Are Mostly Inherited" (1986)

14. Sally Squires, "In Schizophrenia, a Virus Is Suspected" (1987)

15. Roger Kramer and Ira Weiner, "Psychiatry on the Borderline" (1983)

16. Ruth Elizabeth Borgman, "Lone Dangers" (1987)

17. Janice Gibson and Mike Haritos-Fatouros, "The Education of a Torturer" (1986)

18. Robert J. Trotter, "The Three Faces of Love" (1986)

PREFACE

Dear Student:

This *Study Guide with Readings* has been prepared to help you learn psychology and apply your knowledge. It contains "Study Tips," "Tips for Writing Term Papers," and 18 chapter guides. If possible, please read "Study Tips" before your course begins. Both "Study Tips" and "Term Paper Tips" will probably be useful in other courses as well as in psychology.

Each chapter of this study guide corresponds to a chapter in your text, Papalia and Olds: *Psychology,* and follows the same format:

CHAPTER OUTLINE	A detailed outline of the topics in the chapter is presented.
LEARNING OBJECTIVES	The objectives outline the major skills you should acquire as a result of your in-depth study of the chapter.
KEY CONCEPTS	Important concepts in the chapter are summarized here.
TERMS TO KNOW	This section lists the terms you need to be able to define and describe and gives page references in your text so that you can check your understanding of each term.
SELF-TEST	These tests--in two formats, multiple-choice and matching--allow you to check how well you have mastered important concepts in the chapter.
APPLICATION EXERCISES	This section provides you with several opportunities to actively practice, summarize, and apply your understanding of some of the most important concepts in the chapter. Feedback is provided in the "Answers" section at the end of the chapter.
READING EXERCISE	A relevant article or excerpt presents additional information or applies important concepts presented in the text. Questions follow each article.
ANSWERS	This section provides answers to the multiple-choice and matching tests, application exercises, and reading questions.

We hope that you will actively use this *Study Guide with Readings* and that learning psychology will be an enjoyable and rewarding experience.

Virginia Nichols Quinn
Jolyne Shields Daughtry

One of the most important skills you can learn in college is how to manage your time to study for success. Successful students are not necessarily the most intelligent; often they are students who simply have learned organizational skills and self-discipline. At some point most of us experience the frustration and stress of feeling that there is too much to accomplish and too little time. In truth, there rarely is enough time to do everything. But if you set your priorities and plan ahead to budget your time, you will experience less stress, frustration, and guilt, and your academic performance will improve.

PLANNING AHEAD

To budget your time properly, you need to make long-range plans (for the entire term), short-range plans (for each week), and immediate plans (for each day). You will need to develop a term calendar, a weekly calendar, and a daily list of activities. It is wise to inform your family, friends, and roommates of your plans so that they will cooperate and help you keep to your schedule.

Long-Range Plans: Your Term Calendar

Buy or make a calendar that provides a large space for each day of the entire term. You will use this calendar to plot and plan your entire semester. First, mark vacations and holidays so that your blocks of free time will be obvious. As soon as you receive course outlines from your instructors, fill in key dates for tests, midterms, deadlines for assignments and term papers, and final examinations. Next, add major social events for the semester--perhaps a few concerts, extracurricular events, dances, lectures, and sports competitions. Then add deadlines that you set for yourself. You should break long or complex assignments into segments. For example, you probably should set your own deadlines for paper or report outlines and for completing review work before tests. When setting personal deadlines, give yourself some space before the official deadline so that you are not constantly feeling time pressures. This also allows you some spontaneity should the person of your dreams invite you, or accept your invitation, to the event of the season. Use some method of distinguishing fixed dates from deadlines that you've assigned yourself; use different color inks or print fixed deadlines and use script for personal deadlines. Your term calendar might resemble Figure 1.

SEPTEMBER

S	M	T	W	Th	F	S
1	2	3	4	5	6	7
8	9	10	11	12	13 Complete review for history	14
15	16	17 HISTORY QUIZ	18	19	20 Outline English paper	21
22	23 Complete Math review	24	25 MATH TEST	26	27 ENGLISH PAPER DUE	28
29	30					

OCTOBER

S	M	T	W	Th	F	S
		1 Complete biology review	2 Outline English paper	3 BIOLOGY TEST	4 Complete English review	5 8 P.M. DR. PAPALIA LECTURE
6	7 ENGLISH MIDTERM	8	9	10	11	12
13	14 Complete Math review	15	16 MATH TEST	17 Complete review for history	18 ENGLISH PAPER DUE	19 "THE GROUP" ROCK CONCERT 9 P.M.
20	21 Complete psych review	22 HISTORY QUIZ	23 PSYC MIDTERM	24	25	26
27	28	29	30	31 HALLOWEEN PARTY		

NOVEMBER

S	M	T	W	Th	F	S
					1 Complete review for history	2
3	4	5 HISTORY QUIZ Complete biology review	6	7 BIOLOGY TEST	8 Outline English paper	9 HOMECOMING FOOTBALL 2pm DANCE 9pm
10	11 Outline history term paper	12	13 Outline English term paper	14	15 ENGLISH PAPER DUE	16
17	18 Complete Math review	19	20 MATH TEST	21 1st draft English term paper	22	23 1st draft history term paper
24	25 Complete review for history	26 HISTORY QUIZ	27 ← THANKS	28 GIVING B	29 REAK Complete English term paper	30 → Complete history term paper

DECEMBER

S	M	T	W	Th	F	S
1	2 ENGLISH TERM PAPER DUE	3	4 Complete biology lab report	5 HISTORY TERM PAPER DUE	6 Complete English review	7 Complete Math review
8	9 Complete history review	10 Complete Psyc review	11 Complete biology review	12 BIOLOGY LAB REPORT DUE	13	14
15	16 ENGLISH FINAL	17 MATH FINAL HISTORY FINAL	18	19 PSYC FINAL	20 BIOLOGY FINAL	21 ←
22 ←	23 HO	24 LIDAY	25 VA	26 CATION	27	28 →
29	30	31 →				

Figure 1

When you complete your term calendar, you will have a clear picture of your entire semester. Hang this calendar in a conspicuous place, perhaps over your desk or on your closet door.

Short-Range Plans: Your Weekly Calendar

Once you have completed your term calendar, you are in a good position to plan each week. You know which tests and paper deadlines you will face each week. Sunday might be a good day to develop your weekly plan. Again, you want to begin by filling in fixed obligations: class times, work hours, and commuting time. It's a good idea to print these to remind yourself they cannot be moved and will remain constant throughout the semester.

As you begin to fill in study times, consider the time of day when you are most efficient. If you usually feel groggy after lunch, be sure to give yourself a break then. Plan to study when you are feeling motivated and are likely to be productive. Your study hours should be consistent from week to week, and your schedule should allow you time to review the material immediately before each class and to check your notes after class. Schedule study times for your most difficult subjects first. Be sure to insert the times of leisure activities, television specials, or social visits and also leave yourself some free time for the unexpected! The weekly calendar below (Figure 2) is an example of a schedule for a student taking 16 credit hours, commuting 15 minutes each way, and working 6 hours each week.

Time	MON	TUES	WED	THURS	FRI	SAT
7–8	←		Breakfast / Commute			→
8–9	Study English	HISTORY	Study English	HISTORY	Study English	
9–10	ENGLISH	↓	ENGLISH	Study biology	ENGLISH	Breakfast/Commute
10–11	Study Psyc	Study biology	Study psyc	Study biology lab	Study psyc	JOB
11–12	PSYC	BIOLOGY	PSYC	BIOLOGY	PSYC	↓
12–1	Lunch	↓	Lunch	Lunch	Lunch	Lunch
1–2	Study Math	Lunch	Study Math	BIOLOGY	Study Math	Study Psyc
2–3	MATH	Free Time	MATH	LAB	MATH	Study English
3–4	Swim	Swim	Free Time	↓	Swim	Study Math
4–5	Study history	Study English	Study history	Study English	Free time	Free time
5–6	↓	Study Psyc	↓	Study Psyc	↓	↓
6–7	←		Commute / dinner			→
7–8	Free Time	JOB	Study biology	JOB	Free time	Free time
8–9	Study biology	↓	↓	↓	↓	↓
9–10	↓	Study Math	Free Time			
10–11	Unwind	→			→	↓
11–12						

Figure 2

Remember that your schedule will vary slightly from week to week. For example, during the week of midterms, you will probably spend some of your free time studying. Conversely, the week after midterms or after you have finished a major paper, you may need more free time to relax. However, if you are faithful to your weekly study schedule, heavy cramming will be unnecessary and you can face examinations with less stress.

Immediate Plans: Your Daily List of Activities

If you function well at night, you may want to take 15 or 20 minutes before bedtime to plan the next day; otherwise, save the planning until morning. Your daily list of activities will be a simple checklist of what you hope to accomplish. Once more, you may wish to distinguish essential from nonessential (but desirable) items by using print or cursive script. Figure 3 shows a typical daily list.

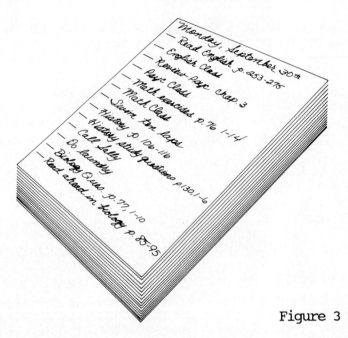

Figure 3

As you accomplish each item on your checklist, cross it off. Items that remain should be transferred to your schedule for the next day. If you are successful in completing all your goals, reward yourself at the end of the day. Your reward should vary; it might be a favorite dessert, a few minutes of listening to a favorite album, a hot bath or shower, a television special, a stroll for an ice cream cone, or relaxing with a magazine--anything that truly pleases you.

STUDY HABITS

Once you have your schedule organized, you are ready to sit down and study. But where? Just as you should be consistent in your scheduling, you should be consistent in your choice of study places. It is important to use a convenient place. If you have only 1 hour between classes, a nearby empty classroom might be a better spot than a library that requires a 15-minute walk each way. Cafeterias, student lounges, and other noisy places tend to have too many distractions that will interrupt your concentration.

If you plan to study in your room, it is wise to remove all distracting clutter and close your door. Use a straight chair that you reserve for study only, rather than an easy chair or bed that might induce sleep. Avoid distracting noises from television, radio, and stereo sets. If you must be surrounded by sound, try soft background music that will cover other noises.

Before you sit in your "study chair," assemble everything you will need. Most people need a few minutes to unwind and settle down for studying. Use this time to gather highlighters and pens and to sharpen pencils. Set up your books, notes, notepaper, and reference material. Then set a goal to accomplish before you take a break--perhaps a chapter or a unit within a chapter.

Having informed your friends of your schedule, you should be free from surprise visits and telephone calls. If you find that your mind starts to wander before you reach your goal, take a break. Do a few exercises, drink a glass of water, and return to your study resolved to concentrate. When you think you really have mastered the material, go over it one more time. Overlearning is the enemy of forgetting.

This *Study Guide with Readings* should help you concentrate on psychology. Begin your study session by turning to the appropriate chapter in this guide and check the sections "Chapter Outline" and "Learning Objectives." You will then have a general sense of the content of the chapter and the skills you will be expected to develop.

Next, begin reading the chapter in your text, following along with the "Key Concepts" section of this guide. Check off each concept as you read about it in the text. You may wish to write into the margin of this guide additional information or examples from the text.

When you finish reading a section, define the words listed in the "Key Terms" section. Use your own words at first and then refine your definition by checking the text page indicated or the text Glossary.

After you have read the entire chapter and feel you understand the key concepts and can define the key terms, you are ready to complete the "Self-Test" section and respond to the accompanying application exercises. Compare your answers with those suggested in the "Answers" section.

Reading the articles that are included in each chapter should enhance your understanding of the chapter content. These readings supplement material covered in the textbook.

If you follow this procedure, you can feel confident and well prepared as you go to class.

In courses that do not have study guides, you should follow the same general procedure. Scan each chapter for major headings. As you begin reading, take notes on key concepts and key terms. When you have finished your reading, test yourself on the key concepts and terms. Review areas where you are having difficulty. Avoid passive reading; if you are taking notes and using highlighters, it will be easier to concentrate.

IN CLASS

Class attendance is critical to success in college. Even if an instructor does not call the roll or penalize you for absence, you will indeed suffer if you do not attend class. The importance of class attendance cannot be overemphasized. In addition to finding out what your instructor considers important and what is likely to appear on an examination, you will also hear announcements of changed course requirements. On the first day of class be sure to exchange names and phone numbers with at least one other person so that you will have access to notes and announcements should you be forced to miss class.

For each session, arrive a few minutes before class and select a seat in the front of the room (where there are fewer distractions). Instructors often make key points or important announcements at the beginning of class; therefore, you don't want to be late.

If you are fully prepared for class, you will understand the lecture and be able to take intelligent notes. Pay attention to the instructor's train of thought and write down an outline of general ideas on only one side of a page so that you can fill in details after class when you have more time. Chances are, anything that is written on the blackboard or on a chart is important and worth noting. Also take notes on films, slides, demonstrations, experiments, and class discussions.

If you are uncertain in class, ask questions. Keeping active will enhance your learning. If you are shy about speaking out in class, at least maintain eye contact with your instructor. Teachers look for cues from students. If you nod agreement when you fully understand an explanation, the teacher will be relieved and move on. Similarly, a simple frown will help an instructor realize that another example of a concept is needed. As a result, your teacher will be more effective and your learning will be enhanced.

IMMEDIATELY AFTER CLASS

Fill in details on your notes while the information is still within easy recall. If possible, work with a friend and compare notes. It is useful to repeat and hear the information once again. Compare your lecture notes with your text. Highlight or underline concepts in your text that were emphasized in class and write additional notes in the margin of your book.

REVIEWING FOR AN EXAMINATION

Find out the nature of the examination. Knowing whether you are reviewing for a multiple-choice test or an essay test will be helpful. Ask your instructor if previous examinations are available. Try to predict the questions that are likely to appear on the test. A few nights before, get together with friends who are taking the same course. Share ideas and quiz each other on concepts from the text, study guide, and class notes. If you have been studying regularly, cramming will not be necessary. Review your class notes along with sections of your text that have been highlighted or underlined. Read notes you have written in margins. Review the chapter summaries in your text and check the "Key Concepts" and "Key Terms" sections in this study guide. Rest well the night before your examination; many people do not perform well when they lose necessary sleep.

TAKING AN EXAMINATION

Try to arrive at the test room early so that you can select a seat and make yourself comfortable. When you receive your examination, be certain you have all pages. Check the front and back of each page and read the directions carefully. If necessary, reread the directions several times and ask for clarification if you still feel uncertain. On essay tests, decide how to budget your time for each question. On objective tests, first answer only those questions you feel certain about. Often information presented later in the test will help you answer a question you had skipped. Before you hand in your examination, be sure you have answered all questions.

AFTER THE EXAMINATION

Review the test items you missed and refer to your text and class notes. Determine which questions were from the text and which were from lectures. Determine whether you missed more lecture questions or more text questions, to find out your weaker area. Be certain you know the correct responses. If you feel uncertain, contact your instructor. You should feel confident before proceeding to new studies.

Good study habits require self-discipline. The steps that have been described here apply to other courses as well as to psychology. If you develop good study techniques, you will not only learn more, you will be more organized, feel less stress, and, we hope, be happier!

TIPS FOR WRITING TERM PAPERS

Most papers assigned in introductory psychology courses are library research papers. Writing a library research paper can be painless and even enjoyable if you follow some simple guidelines.

CHOOSING YOUR TOPIC

Allow yourself enough time to choose a suitable topic. This means selecting a topic far enough in advance so that you can change your mind if for some reason it turns out to be unsuitable. Pick a topic that interests you. If a stimulating topic does not readily come to mind, skim the chapters of your textbook that seem most interesting to get ideas. You might also think in terms of a topic that has personal relevance. For example, if you suffer from test anxiety, techniques for dealing with this problem might be an interesting subject to pursue. Be certain your topic is narrow enough to treat adequately in your paper. You may, for example, be interested in the area of interpersonal attraction. This subject, however, would be far too broad for a research paper. You would need to narrow your focus in some way, selecting perhaps the role played by physical attractiveness in selection of a marriage partner.

Make sure that there is adequate literature on the topic you plan to write about. (*Literature* refers to the body of writing that has been done on a topic.) Avoid topics that have not been investigated by enough researchers to generate a reasonable body of literature. If you can't find enough material on your first choice of topics, you might explore the literature available on a closely related area. Be certain that your topic is not too difficult. The literature on certain topics may not be comprehensible to you as a beginning psychology student. To make sure your topic is narrow enough, that it's been written about sufficiently, and that it's not too difficult, you will have to do some preliminary scanning of the relevant literature.

DOING LIBRARY RESEARCH

After you have selected an appropriate topic, your next step is to locate, read, and take notes on books, journal articles, and other references relevant to your topic. To find books on your topic, you should use the library's card catalog. To locate journal articles, your best reference is *Psychological Abstracts*, which contains subject and author indices for hundreds of journals and other documents as well. It also contains a summary of each article indexed.

As you read the material you have located, you should take two types of notes: source notes and content notes. Taking source notes simply means recording on a separate card the facts of publication about each work you read. You will use these cards later to make up the list of references for your paper. If you number each source card, you can avoid rewriting publication facts on content cards. A source card for a book with one author would look like Figure 4.

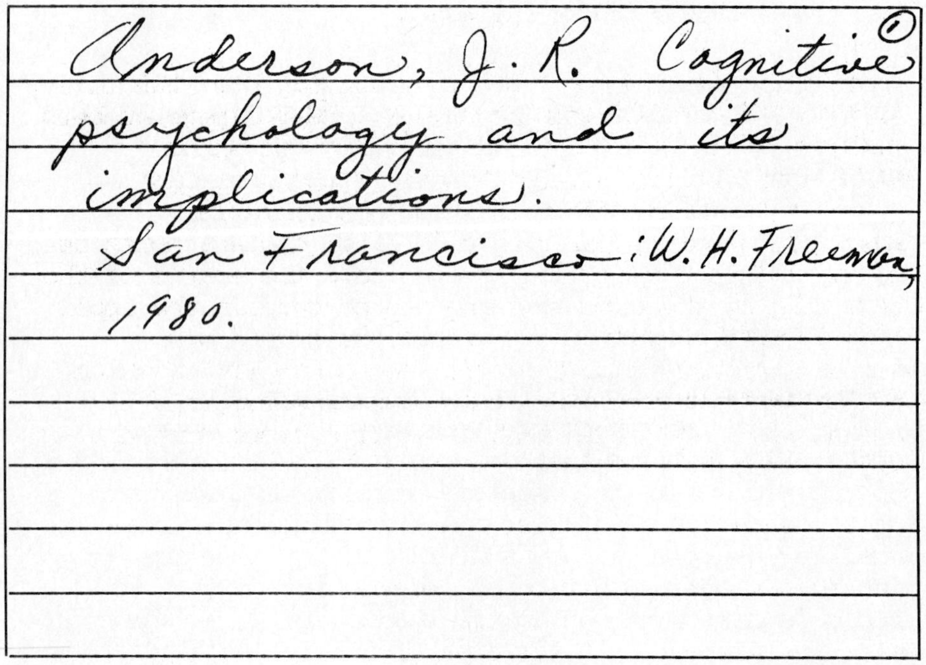

Anderson, J. R. Cognitive
psychology and its
implications.
San Francisco: W. H. Freeman,
1980.

Figure 4

Note that this card lists the name of the author (last name first), the title of the book, the city of publication, the publisher, and the date of publication.

A card for a journal article with one author would look like Figure 5.

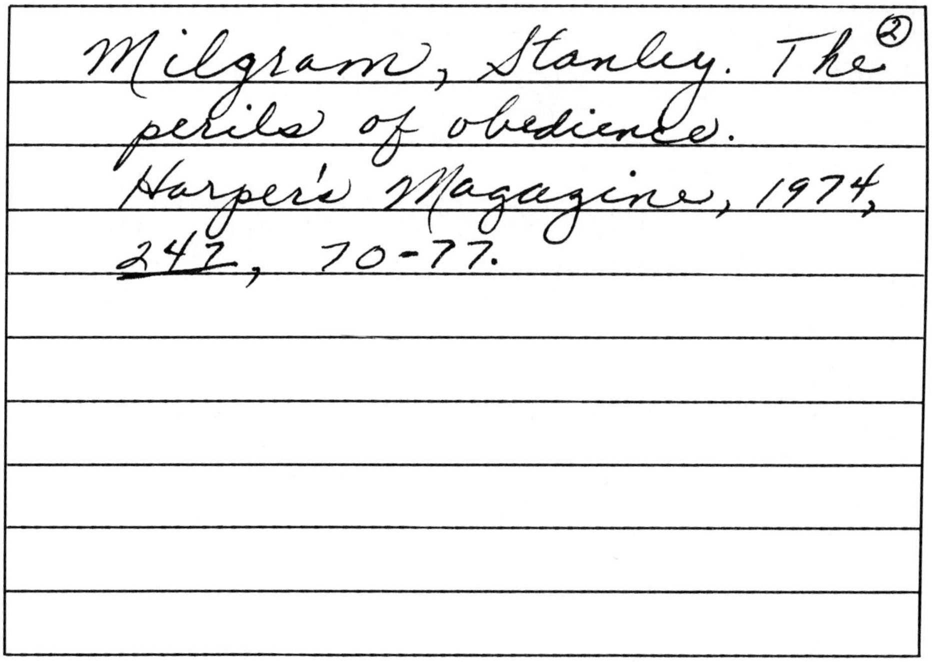

Milgram, Stanley. The ②
perils of obedience.
Harper's Magazine, 1974,
242, 70-77.

Figure 5

Note that this card lists the author's name, the title of the article, the name of the journal, the year of publication, the volume number, and the page numbers of the article. For further guidelines on documenting sources, you should consult the most recent edition of the *Publication Manual of the American Psychological Association,* which can be found in most college libraries.

In addition to source notes, you should also take detailed content notes on the documents you read. On each content card, you can indicate the source of the information by placing the number of the corresponding source card in the upper right-hand corner along with the appropriate page number. You should also indicate the aspect of your main topic (in other words, the subtopic) to which this card relates. Use content cards to summarize, paraphrase, quote, and comment on the material you read. A typical content card for a paper on the meaning of dreams might look like Figure 6.

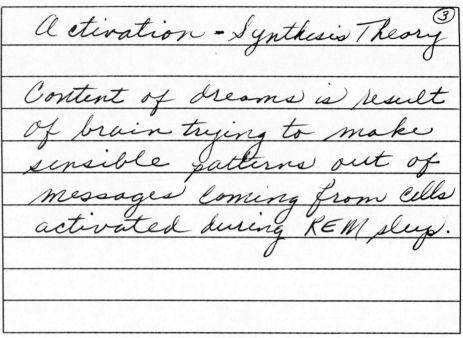

Activation - Synthesis Theory ③

Content of dreams is result of brain trying to make sensible patterns out of messages coming from cells activated during REM sleep.

Figure 6

During the process of reading and taking notes, you must formulate the main thesis, or main idea, of your paper.

OUTLINING YOUR PAPER

The preparation of an outline takes time, but it is well worth the effort. In fact, it is very difficult to write a logically organized paper of any length without the help of an outline.

Use the subtopic headings on your content cards to assemble all the material you have on each subtopic. At this point you may decide to eliminate certain subtopics because they are irrelevant or because you don't have enough information on the subject. Decide which subtopics will be major divisions of your paper and which will be minor divisions. Decide on some principle of organization and stick to this principle as you organize your cards. Finally, write your outline, using either key words, incomplete sentences, or complete sentences. In addition to the major and minor subdivisions derived from your content cards, you will need an introductory section and a concluding section.

WRITING YOUR PAPER

Use your outline and your content notes to aid you in writing your paper. You will probably need to write two drafts of the paper. In the first draft, focus on setting your ideas down in a clear and organized fashion. Keep in mind that you are writing to support your own thesis, or main idea, not simply to report what you have read. In the final draft, make sure that your paper is free from mechanical errors and as polished as you can make it.

You should pay special attention to two mechanical aspects of writing psychology papers. First, psychology papers contain a reference list at the end of the paper. The list contains only the works mentioned in the paper and is arranged alphabetically by authors' last names. Second, sources are not identified in footnotes. Instead, they are indicated in the text itself using the author-date method. In other words, the last name of the author and the year of publication of the work you are citing are inserted in the text of your paper, as shown in the following examples:

A 3-day-old baby can tell his or her mother's voice from a stranger's (DeCasper and Fifer, 1980). Brown (1973) discusses syntactic skill in terms of mean length of utterance.

For a more detailed explanation of how references are cited in psychology papers, you can consult the previously mentioned *Publication Manual of the American Psychological Association.*

SUMMARY

If you observe the following guidelines, you will simplify the task of writing a library research paper in psychology. Pick a topic that is personally interesting, narrow enough to write about adequately, sufficiently treated in the literature, and not too difficult for you to handle. Record all the necessary publication facts about the documents you need on source cards. Take detailed content notes as you read. Formulate a main thesis, or main idea, for your paper. Use your content notes to help you write an outline which differentiates between major and minor ideas and is logically organized. Finally, write at least two drafts of your paper, focusing first on the clear expression of ideas, then on mechanics and on polishing your prose.

MICRO STUDYGUIDE TO ACCOMPANY

PAPALIA-OLDS: *PSYCHOLOGY*, 2d ed.

FOR ONLY $12.95

MICRO STUDYGUIDE--Computerized Interactive Study Guide

This computerized interactive study guide makes learning and studying easier and helps you prepare for exams more efficiently.

MICRO STUDYGUIDE is a computer program designed to help you learn the most in the least time by working with a computer in a tutorial relationship. The program leads you through the basics of the course material, providing interactive questions and self-scoring tests.

MICRO STUDYGUIDE is easy to use--three keystrokes are all you need to get started.

If you don't own a computer, ask your instructor where you can use one on campus.

To order, complete the order form below, clip along the dotted line, and mail to:

Soft Productions, Inc.
100 Center Professional Bldg.
Mishawaka, IN 46544

Important: Be sure to indicate the type of computer disk you want and your method of payment.

- -

Papalia-Olds: *Psychology,* 2d ed.   MICRO STUDYGUIDE Order Form

Name _____   School _____

Address _____   Major _____

_____   Circle College Year   SR   JR
City   State   Zip
                                                                       SO   FR

Please send me MICRO STUDYGUIDE for the computer circled:

          Apple II   IBM PC

Method of payment enclosed:
                    VISA   MASTERCARD   PERSONAL CHECK

Account No. _____   Expiration Date _____

Signature _____   (Required for charges)

Chapter 1:

INTRODUCTION TO PSYCHOLOGY

CHAPTER OUTLINE

I. What is psychology?

II. What are the goals of psychology?

III. How this book presents the study of psychology
   A. We celebrate the human being
   B. We are practical
   C. We view psychology as a dynamic science
   D. We present a picture of psychology on a wide canvas

IV. How psychology has evolved
   A. A brief history of psychology
   B. Schools of thought in psychology
      1. Structuralism
      2. Functionalism
      3. Gestalt psychology
      4. Psychoanalysis
      5. Behaviorism
      6. Humanistic psychology
      7. Cognitive psychology

V. Contemporary psychology
   A. Areas of specialization in psychology
      1. Clinical psychology
      2. Counseling psychology
      3. Personality psychology
      4. Educational and school psychology
      5. Experimental psychology
      6. Physiological psychology
      7. Development psychology
      8. Health psychology
      9. Social psychology
      10. Psychometrics
      11. Industrial and organizational psychology
      12. Engineering psychology
      13. Some other specialties
   B. How psychologists study behavior
      1. Theories, hypotheses, and research
      2. Who takes part in psychological research?
         a. Subjects
            (1) College students
            (2) Animals
         b. Sampling
      3. Basic and applied research

      4. Research methods
        a. Correlation research
        b. Case histories
        c. Surveys
        d. Interviews
        e. Naturalistic observation
        f. Experiments
          (1) A laboratory experiment
          (2) A field experiment
          (3) Strengths and weaknesses of the experimental method
   C. Ethics in psychological research

Boxes
    Psychology in your life: Tips on more effective studying
    Psychology in your life: Preparing for a career in psychology
    In the forefront: Ethics in animal research

LEARNING OBJECTIVES

After you study Chapter 1, you should be able to do the tasks outlined in the following objectives.

1. Define *psychology* and specify its focus.
2. Identify techniques to improve retention when studying.
3. Describe the major emphasis of structuralism and functionalism.
4. Describe the major emphasis and principles of gestalt psychology, psychoanalysis, and behaviorism.
5. Specify the focus of humanistic psychology and cognitive psychology.
6. List the responsibilities of psychologists with specific specializations.
7. Recognize the importance of sample selection in psychological research.
8. Describe the methods used in case histories, surveys, naturalistic observation, and experiments.
9. Distinguish between correlation and causation.
10. Specify the unique properties of experiments and the importance of experimental controls.
11. Compare the methodology in laboratory experiments and field experiments.
12. Identify the basic rules of ethics required by the American Psychological Association (APA).

KEY CONCEPTS

As you read Chapter 1 in your text, look for each of the following concepts. You should understand each concept.

1. Focus of Psychology

Psychology is the scientific study of human behavior and mental processes. Behavior includes both external actions and internal thoughts and feelings. Psychologists describe, explain, predict, and modify behavior.

2. More Effective Studying

The SQ3R method can be used to improve retention. The steps in this method are survey, question, read, recite, and review. Other techniques for improving retention include personalizing material, using visual images, forcing yourself to concentrate, studying difficult items either first or last, and allotting extra time.

3. Origins of Psychology

Psychology's earliest roots were in philosophy. Psychology as a science began a little more than 100 years ago, when psychological researchers discovered important functions of the nervous system and raised questions about sensation and perception.

4. Early Approaches to Psychology

Under the leadership of Wilhelm Wundt, *structuralism* explored the basic structure of the mind. Structuralists' methods included simple experiments and analytic introspection. *Functionalism,* led by John Dewey and William James, extended the scope of psychology to the functions and uses of the mind. Functionalists introduced such scientific research methods as mental tests, questionnaires, and objective observations.

5. Gestalt Psychology

The basic gestalt assumption is that the whole is greater than the sum of its parts. Therefore, gestalt psychologists stress the importance of the wholeness of mind. They are concerned with the integration of behavior and focus much of their research on perception. The phi phenomenon, the perception of apparent motion when there is none, was of great interest to gestalt psychologists.

6. Psychoanalysis

According to Freud, unconscious impulses are responsible for most behavior. Most of these unconscious impulses stem from sexual energy. Scientific methods are of little or no use to psychoanalytic theory, since the unconscious can be neither measured nor observed scientifically.

7. Behaviorism

Behaviorists believe that psychology should focus strictly on observable behavior and use scientific methods to study changes in behavior. They believe that changes in behavior result primarily from operant conditioning, that is, reinforcements or rewards for desired changes. Behaviorists are not concerned with inner thoughts and feelings.

8. Humanistic Psychology

Humanism focuses on the uniqueness of each individual and stresses the importance of personal experiences and emotions. Humanistic psychologists believe that people should understand their own individual feelings and choices and determine their own self-directions. Humanists believe that people should develop their full potential using their own free will and making their own choices.

9. Cognitive Psychology

Cognitive psychologists are concerned with mental processes. The most recent perspective in psychology, cognitive psychology has been using experiments to study perception, memory, thought patterns, and mental organization.

10. Specializations in Psychology

Although many people believe that all psychologists analyze thoughts and treat abnormal behavior, these responsibilities usually fall within the specialization of clinical psychology. Other specializations in psychology include counseling, educational psychology, school psychology, experimental psychology, physiological psychology, developmental psychology, personality psychology, social psychology, psychometrics, industrial psychology, engineering psychology, comparative psychology, psycholinguistics, and quantitative psychology.

11. Subjects in Psychological Research

College students are used more frequently in psychological research than any other group. Although college students are suited for some studies, research results based solely on a sample of white, middle-class 18- to 22-year-olds cannot be generalized to the entire population. Animals are sometimes used in psychological research because psychologists can control their entire environment without ethical concerns. However, caution must be used in generalizing these findings to humans. In choosing samples of humans for research, every member of the population should have a chance of being selected. Stratified samples are most accurate because they give proportional representation to important group classifications within the population.

12. Correlational Methods

Correlation is the study of the relationship between two variables. Correlation is *not* the same as causation. Although survey findings may report high positive or negative correlations between two variables, this does not prove that one factor is causing the other. While this may be the case, there may also be one or more underlying factors causing the relationship.

13. Other Research Methods

There are four basic research methods in psychology: (1) case histories, in-depth studies of individuals; (2) surveys, including questionnaires and interviews; (3) naturalistic observations without intervention on the part of the observer; and (4) experiments.

14. Experiments

The experiment is the only method that can determine whether one factor *causes* another. A properly designed experiment requires control of all variables except the one factor being tested. Caution must be used to be sure that conditions are identical for subjects in the experimental and control groups. The use of the double-blind technique and placebos can help control intervening factors.

15. Laboratory Experiments versus Field Experiments

Laboratory experiments permit psychologists to exercise more control over intervening variables; however, psychologists cannot be certain that the results will hold in real-life situations. Field experiments permit testing real-life situations, but for ethical reasons the experimental conditions cannot be as well controlled.

16. Ethics in Psychological Research

The American Psychological Association has established standards for all psychologists conducting research to ensure that all subjects are protected from physical and mental harm. Psychologists must receive informed consent from participants, avoid deception, permit subjects to withdraw at any time, ensure each subject's right to privacy, assume full responsibility for the ethical behavior of staff members, and correct any undesirable experimental effects on the subjects.

Behavior   (p. 5)

Mental processes   (p. 5)

TERMS TO KNOW

Define each of the terms listed. You can check your definitions in the text Glossary or on the text pages listed in parentheses.

SQ3R method   (p. 6)

Psychology	(p. 5)	Analytic introspection	(p. 10)
Scientific method	(p. 5)	Structuralism	(p. 11)
Description	(p. 5)	Functionalism	(p. 12)
Explanation	(p. 5)	Gestalt	(p. 12)
Prediction	(p. 5)	Phi phenomenon	(p. 13)
Modification	(p. 5)	Psychoanalysis	(p. 13)

Behaviorism (p. 14)   Personality psychologists (p. 17)

Conditioning (p. 14)   Educational psychologists (p. 18)

Humanistic psychology (p. 15)   School psychologists (p. 18)

Cognitive psychology (p. 15)   Experimental psychologists (p. 18)

Stroop effect (p. 15)   Physiological psychologists (p. 18)

Clinical psychologists (p. 17)   Developmental psychologists (p. 19)

Abnormal psychology (p. 17)   Health psychologists (p. 19)

Psychiatrist (p. 17)   Social psychology (p. 19)

Counseling psychologists (p. 17)   Applied social psychologists (p. 19)

Psychometric psychologists   (p. 19)   Data   (p. 20)

Industrial and organizational   Population   (p. 22)
psychologists   (p. 20)

Engineering psychologists   (p. 20)   Samples   (p. 22)

Comparative psychology   (p. 20)   Random sample   (p. 23)

Psycholinguistics   (p. 20)   Stratified sample   (p. 23)

Quantitative psychology   (p. 20)   Basic research   (p. 23)

Theory   (p. 20)   Applied research   (p. 23)

Hypothesis   (p. 20)   Correlation   (p. 23)

Research   (p. 20)   Variables   (p. 23)

Positive correlation	(p. 23)	Dependent variable	(p. 26)
Negative correlation	(p. 23)	Experimental group	(p. 26)
Correlation coefficient	(p. 24)	Control group	(p. 26)
Case history; case study	(p. 24)	Treatment	(p. 28)
Survey methods	(p. 25)	Laboratory experiment	(p. 28)
Standardized	(p. 25)	Field experiment	(p. 29)
Naturalistic observation	(p. 26)	Replicate	(p. 29)
Psychological experiment	(p. 26)	Experimenter bias	(p. 29)
Independent variable	(p. 26)	Single-blind technique	(p. 29)

Double-blind technique   (p. 29)

Placebo   (p. 29)

SELF-TEST

Multiple-Choice

Choose the one best response to each question. An answer key is provided at the end of this chapter.

1. Psychology is the science of human

   a. behavior and mental processes
   b. perception
   c. knowledge
   d. activity

2. What method was used by structuralists to understand conscious experiences?

   a. Experimentation
   b. Perception
   c. Introspection
   d. Intuition

3. Functional psychologists broadened the scope of psychology to include a person's ability to adapt to the environment. As a result, which aspect of psychology did functionalists emphasize?

   a. Perception
   b. Education
   c. Therapy
   d. Physiology

4. What area of content would the gestalt school of psychology emphasize?

   a. Patterns of organization in perception
   b. Our adjustment to the environment
   c. Analysis of individual thought
   d. Ethical concerns and personal responsibility

5. What is the major area of concern for psychoanalysis?

   a. Motivation
   b. The unconscious
   c. Differences in perception
   d. Problem-solving processes

6. A psychologist is mainly interested in a person's observable responses, rather than his or her mental processes. What viewpoint does this psychologist probably hold?

   a. Psychoanalytic
   b. Structuralist
   c. Gestalt
   d. Behaviorist

7. A woman believes that psychology should focus on helping people use their own free will to determine their self-directions. Which perspective of psychology shares this woman's view?

   a. Psychoanalysis
   b. Humanistic psychology
   c. Gestalt psychology
   d. Behaviorism

8. What is stressed in the cognitive perspective of psychology?

   a. Active processing of information
   b. Personal emotions such as love, hate, and fear
   c. Stimulus-response relationships
   d. Introspective reports

9. Which type of psychologist would probably treat an individual suffering from severe depression?

   a. Experimental psychologist
   b. Social psychologist
   c. Psychometric psychologist
   d. Clinical psychologist

10. You wish to determine the average intelligence of all college students in the United States. Which of the following would give you the best sample?

    a. Choosing only healthy students
    b. Choosing at least 50 percent of the population
    c. Choosing only students between the ages of 18 and 22
    d. Choosing students representative of the entire population

11. A researcher decides to take a telephone poll to determine the average educational level of people in a community. What is wrong with this survey technique?

    a. The sample will be too large.
    b. The sample is not representative.
    c. The sample will be stratified.
    d. The technique does not include a control group.

12. Assume that a researcher found a high negative correlation between educational level and ability to bowl. What can be concluded from this?

    a. Education causes poor bowling ability.
    b. The higher a person's educational level, the more likely that person is to be a good bowler.

    c. The higher a person's educational ability, the less likely that person is to be a good bowler.
    d. There is no relationship between educational level and ability to bowl.

13. Imagine that you are a psychologist. You must find out as much as possible about a psychological problem of one individual. Which method is best to use?

    a. Experimental method
    b. Naturalistic observation
    c. Survey method
    d. Individual case study

14. A psychologist wishes to study how mentally retarded children are treated when placed in classrooms with children of average intelligence. What research method would the psychologist probably use?

    a. Naturalistic-observation method
    b. Case-history method
    c. Experimental method
    d. Correlational analysis

15. What is the purpose of naturalistic-observation technique in psychology?

    a. To find causes of behavior
    b. To change behavior
    c. To record behavior
    d. To make inferences from behavior

16. What is the main purpose of a psychological experiment?

    a. To record behavior
    b. To change behavior
    c. To survey unusual behavior
    d. To find causes of behavior

17. In an experiment to study the effects of a tranquilizer on anxiety levels, what is the tranquilizer?

    a. Independent variable
    b. Dependent variable
    c. Placebo
    d. Deceptive control

18. How does the double-blind feature improve the design of an experiment?

    a. It ensures stratification in sampling.
    b. It prevents most of the subjects from seeing the experimenter bias.
    c. It prevents the experimental group from seeing the control group.
    d. It helps prevent experimenter bias.

19. Why are placebos often used in psychological experiments?

    a. To ensure that the experimental group will perform better than the control group
    b. To equalize conditions in the experimental and control groups
    c. To reward subjects who participate in experiments
    d. To calm subjects who may be anxious

20. Why has the American Psychological Association established ethical guidelines for psychological research?

    a. To protect psychologists from being sued
    b. To protect subjects in experiments
    c. To ensure that all psychologists maintain the same theoretical viewpoint
    d. To allow psychologists to make private and personal information available to the public

Matching

Match each name in column A with a descriptive phrase in column B. The same phrase in column B may be used for more than one name.

Column A

_____ 1. Gustav Fechner

_____ 2. William James

_____ 3. G. Stanley Hall

_____ 4. Wilhelm Wundt

_____ 5. John Dewey

Column B

a. Held the world's first professorship in psychology
b. Began the behaviorist movement
c. A functionalist who taught the first psychology course at Harvard and wrote the classic text, *The Principles of Psychology*
d. A current behaviorist who has promoted the use of operant conditioning and teaching machines
e. A humanist who believes that psychology should include the study of personal feelings and attitudes which are not necessarily measurable

_____ 6. James McKeen Cattell
_____ 7. Edward Tichener

_____ 8. John B. Watson

_____ 9. B. F. Skinner

_____ 10. Sigmund Freud

_____ 11. Abraham Maslow

_____ 12. Carl Rogers

f. Began the psychoanalytic movement
g. Established the first American psychology laboratory at Johns Hopkins University and later became the first president of the American Psychological Association
h. A structuralist who started the first laboratory for psychological research and is often referred to as the "father of psychology"
i. A student of Wundt who brought structuralism to the United States
j. A German physicist who studied psychological experiences
k. A functionalist leader in American education and the founder of school psychology

APPLICATION EXERCISES

These application exercises will test your understanding of and ability to apply the material you have read in your text. Suggested answers are provided at the end of the chapter so that you can check your responses.

1. When completed, Table 1-1 will summarize the information related to the seven major schools of thought in psychology discussed in your text. The first view, structuralism, has been done for you; complete the remainder of the table.

Table 1-1 Seven Schools of Thought in Psychology

School of Psychology	Time Period	Basic Belief	Techniques Used
Structuralism	Late nineteenth century to early twentieth century	The structure of mind is of prime importance	Analytic introspection, reaction-time experiments
Functionalism			
Gestalt psychology			
Psychoanalysis			
Behaviorism			
Humanistic psychology			
Cognitive psychology			

2. Your text describes the following 13 specializations in psychology:

   Clinical psychology
   Counseling psychology
   Personality psychology
   Educational psychology
   School psychology
   Experimental psychology
   Physiological psychology
   Developmental psychology
   Health psychology
   Social psychology
   Psychometric psychology
   Industrial psychology
   Engineering psychology

   Although there may be some overlap in focus, most psychologists within each of these specializations handle rather specific issues. Listed below are 13 issues being handled by psychologists. For each, indicate the likely specialization of the psychologist.

   a. Determining the age at which children can first detect color differences

   _____

   b. Treating a woman who refuses to eat _____

   c. Finding ways to overcome prejudice in a community

   _____

   d. Finding techniques to improve reading levels in elementary school children

   _____

   e. Helping a child from a foreign country adjust to a new school

   _____

   f. Designing an airplane control panel that will be most efficient for pilots

   _____

   g. Designing a test to measure intellectual strengths

   _____

   h. Determining whether rats learn faster when they have been frustrated _____

   _____

   i. Finding the nature of speech disorders in the victims of strokes _____

   _____

   j. Testing college students for individual vocational interests

   _____

   _____

   k. Improving the production level of workers at a factory

   _____

   _____

   l. Studying why people develop different types of humor

   _____

   m. Writing a newspaper column on how to cope with stress in order to avoid heart disease.

   _____

3. There are five basic research methods in psychology:

   Correlational research
   Case histories
   Surveys (including questionnaires and interviews)
   Naturalistic observations
   Experiments

   Five research questions follow. For each, select the one method most suited for the problem. Briefly give one reason it should be used or one reason the other methods are not appropriate.

a. You need to determine whether students in your psychology course find the course useful.
Method _____
Reasons _____
_____
_____

b. You need to find the reasons why a young boy is afraid of other children.
Method _____
Reasons _____
_____
_____

c. You need to determine whether eating a good breakfast will improve children's scores on an arithmetic test.
Method _____
Reasons _____
_____
_____

d. You need to find out how the average person behaves when confronted with a child crying for help.
Method _____
Reasons _____
_____
_____

e. You want to find out whether there is a relationship between high school grades and college grades.
Method _____
Reasons _____
_____
_____

4. Your text describes a laboratory experiment on imitation of aggressive behavior. In this experiment the *independent variable* was seeing an aggressive or nonaggressive adult. The *dependent variable* was the children's aggressive or nonaggressive behavior at the end of the experiment. The experimental method studies that relationship between the independent and dependent variables.

Do you remember the field experiment described in your text? The researchers wanted to find out whether giving older people opportunities for decision making and self-determination could improve their alertness and general spirits. In this experiment, what were the independent and dependent variables?

a. Independent variable _____
_____

b. Dependent variable _____
_____

5. A well-designed experiment requires considerable planning. Each variable must be carefully controlled. If the experiment is well planned, the researcher can be confident that the results of the experiment did, in fact, occur because of changes in the independent variable.

Aspects of an experiment that need to be precisely controlled include:

a. Random assignment of subjects to the experimental and control groups
b. Similar treatment of the experimental and control groups
c. Control over variables that might interfere with the results
d. Care to avoid experimenter bias

Read the fictitious experiment described below. There are clearly many problems in its design. As you read, consider the key aspects for good design and critique the design of this experiment.

The Effects of Vitamin A on Short-Term Memory

Hypothesis: Vitamin A improves short-term memory.

Subjects: Subjects for the experiment were 100 student volunteers at a southeastern dental school. There were 60 males and 40 females. All females were assigned to the experimental group. The control group consisted of 50 males.

Method: All subjects were assigned to the same room. The experimenter served each member of the experimental group a vitamin A tablet along with a fruit-punch drink to "wash it down." The experimenter instructed the control group to sit in the back of the room. This group was not permitted any beverage or vitamins.

After an hour, both groups were given 50 seconds to memorize the following list of nonsense syllables:

CIX	WIH	CAH
LAJ	VOM	DUP
BEF	ZUP	JEK

The list of nonsense syllables was then removed from view. Both groups were told to write down all the nonsense syllables they remembered.

Results: None of the members of the control group remembered more than five nonsense syllables. All members of the experimental group retained all nine nonsense syllables.

Conclusion: Vitamin A causes an increase in ability to remember nonsense syllables.

What is wrong with each of the following aspects of the experiment?

a. Assignment of subjects to the experimental and control groups

_____
_____
_____

b. Treatment of the experimental and control groups

_____
_____
_____

c. Control over other variables that might interfere

_____
_____
_____

d. Experimenter bias

_____
_____
_____

6. Assume that you have volunteered to participate in a psychological experiment. On the basis of the ethical guidelines established by the American Psychological Association, you expect the researcher to conform to certain standards of conduct. Review the list below and check those items that represent reasonable expectations based on the principles of the ethical guidelines for research.

_____ You will know the general nature of your type of participation in the experiment before it begins.

_____ You can withdraw from the experiment at any time.

_____ You will know whether you are assigned to the experimental group or control group.

_____ You will be protected from physical harm.

_____ You are entitled to the names and addresses of other subjects in the experiment.

_____ Your test scores will be kept confidential.

READING EXERCISE

In the following articles from the *APA Monitor,* two psychologists, Arthur Wiens and Emanuel Donchin, take opposing positions in the controversy over uniform standards for graduate education in psychology. The first article is by Wiens, the second by Donchin.

Defining Quality for Consumers

The Carnegie Forum's Task Force on Teaching as a Profession asserted that the 1980s will be remembered for an outpouring of concern for the quality of education. The task force called for new standards of excellence in teaching and suggested that teaching make the transition from "occupation" to "profession." As a true profession, it would codify the knowledge and the specific expertise required by its practitioners and require that those who wish to practice the profession of teaching with the sanction of its members demonstrate that they have a command of the needed knowledge and the ability to apply it. That is, the leading members of the profession would decide what professionals in that area need to know and be able to do.

The concerns of many different educators center around similar issues: *what* is being taught; that it *is* being taught; and how *well* it is being taught.

During the past decade, many concerned with the education and practice of professional psychology have suggested that our most consequential efforts would: (1) define for ourselves and for the public the nature of basic educational preparation in professional psychology; (2) assure the public, our students, and ourselves that such educational preparation aspires to the highest standards of educational excellence; and (3) establish quality control concepts and

Copyright (c) 1987, American Psychological Association. Reprinted by permission of authors.

procedures to monitor the education and practice of professional psychologists.

I have been asked to discuss specifically whether all graduate programs should be accredited to ensure that all meet comparable standards of content and quality. My answer is "yes."

First, all professions must ultimately control entry to their professions through educational standards and a minimum core curriculum. Psychology students and the public have a right to assurance that psychologists have mastered the basic science knowledge that will be the foundation for subsequent careers in research, teaching, or professional practice. Fortunately, over the past decade representatives of the American Psychological Association, American Association of State Psychology Boards, and the National Register of Health Service Providers in Psychology have reached an essential consensus on the minimum educational requirements for a doctoral degree in psychology—completion of a generic core of study in psychology designed to distinguish psychologists from non-psychologists.

There is a fascination among some psychologist-educators about how psychologists differ one from the other and how easily, therefore, we fit into new hybrids of study, e.g., neurosciences, cognitive sciences, or industrial-organizational sciences. By contrast, Arthur Staats of the University of Hawaii has suggested that we should not pursue isolated paths; but instead see how our theory construction could bridge and unite our various fields of study. He asserts that with a unifying framework, psychology could enter into the first rank of sciences. Without a clear definition of our educational standards, we run the risk of losing our individual professional identity, and ultimately, our individual departments or schools. One educational model that would assure all psychologists a common background would be to have all students, within the first two years of graduate education, acquire the scientific knowledge base common to both research and practice. Subsequent differentiation in education and training would reflect the separate career goals of researchers and practitioners. (It can be noted that the separateness of research and practice careers seems to be blurring with the development of hybrids within psychology, e.g., applied developmental psychology, applied social psychology, geropsychology, behavioral medicine, and health psychology.)

Second, accreditation for all programs should be designed to include assurances that students in a program are, in fact, completing specified requirements. The work of the APA Task Force on Education and Credentialing showed that there is often a major divergence between stated program requirements and actual program compliance as reflected on graduates' transcripts. This observation has also been made by APA site visitors on accreditation visits. Such programs may not exercise internal controls, compliance procedures, or administrative monitoring over the educational curriculum that a graduate student actually pursues.

Third, there is the issue of how well a defined curriculum is being taught. In a sense, this is the issue of maintaining standards rather than bowing to sympathy for have-not programs or programs that want to establish their own individual rules. Such evaluation determines whether programs have the faculties and teaching resources to do a good job of teaching the courses they offer. Curriculum evaluation would include analysis of the degree to which courses actually matched the presumed content, e.g., whether the content of a course in "psychological measurement" provided practice in psychological testing rather than explanation of the fundamentals of psychometric theory.

True departmental accountability for program content and quality means being accountable to an external accreditation agency. As a profession, we must be sure that accreditation does not give misleading impressions of quality of training but truly defines a level of quality for consumers--our students and society.

Should There Be Uniform Standards of Quality for Graduate Education in All Fields of Psychology?

Radically different visions of Psychology and of the academic enterprise underlie the radically different views of accreditation expressed in the present exchange. The question before us is whether "all graduate programs should be accredited to ensure that all meet comparable standards of content and quality." Dr. Wiens's answer is steadfastly affirmative, mine is as firmly negative. The dispute derives, I believe, from the very different assumptions we bring to the discussion. We differ in our view of Psychology, we differ on the purposes of graduate education and we differ on utility of the accreditation process as an arbiter of quality.

Two perceptions of Psychology clash

in this dialogue. Psychology can be viewed as a scientific discipline or it can be regarded as a profession. Other scientific disciplines have spawned professions. Physics, as an example, begat Engineering; Physiology is among the progenitors of Medicine. Yet, the relationship between the parent discipline and its professional progeny in Psychology is rather unique. The profession is striving to specify, and control, the educational process in the discipline. It is difficult to imagine the American Medical Association assuming control over the training of future physiologists. It is unlikely that departments of physics will take their curricular cues from bodies engaged in the accreditation of engineering schools. Psychology, however, is a discipline which shares a name with one of its many professional descendants. Moreover, disciplinary training often takes place in departments that offer professional training as well. These circumstances emphasize a superficial identity between these two forms of Psychology. Many whose orientation is largely professional are led by this seeming identity to mold the educational process of the discipline in the shape of what has come to serve as the Professional Training Model in the USA. Yet, Disciplinary and Professional Psychology are different in purpose, and as a result are different in their practices. There is therefore little, if any, reason to impose the standards of one on the other.

In the context of the present discussion one of the most critical differences between professional and disciplinary training is in the degree to which the trainee must obtain certification, registration or licensing from a regulatory authority. Such authorities normally assume that a well-defined "body of knowledge" is among the accouterments of the Professional. The training of Professionals is seen, in part, as the process of imparting this body of

knowledge to the novice. The regulatory authority is responsible for assuring those calling upon the professional for service that the practitioner has acquired the necessary knowledge and skills. Accreditation of training programs is, at least in part, designed to confirm the expertise of the graduates of the accredited programs. As the regulatory and accreditor bodies naturally operate within the framework of the legal system, with litigation an ever present component of professional life, the regulators must measure their actions by the degree to which they will withstand scrutiny by courts of law. This inevitably introduces a measure of rigidity that is an inescapable concomitant of careful, and precise, specifications.

The security provided to professional training by requiring the accreditation of training programs is purchased at a cost. Programs seeking accreditation are forced to continually satisfy external criteria imposed by the regulatory apparatus. While it is possible to conceive of benign forms of accreditation, the form in which accreditation is implemented by the APA is probably the more common version of the process. When our department is visited by accreditation committees we encounter a group of creative, and highly competent, academics that are forced by their role as a site-visit team to behave as committed bureaucrats. How else can they behave? Their task is, in true bureaucratic fashion, to determine if the actions taken by our clinical division, and by the department, conform to a litigation-proof check list. Even if the site-visitors and the accreditation committee see the wisdom of deviations from the check list, and even if the reviewers have full trust in our faculty, they feel bound to follow "the process."

My experience with the accreditation process make me somewhat doubtful of the validity of the professional training model even for those preparing for practice in the so called "real world." My reluctance is due to an acute sensitivity I have developed to the educational, and professional, costs that such training entails. The rigidity of professional curricula (be they for lawyers, physicians, or psychologists) and the difficulty with which they adapt to emergent needs are well known, well documented, and often bemoaned. Those responsible for professional training must make their own cost-benefit analysis. The psychological community interested in preparing professionals for certification, or licensing, will make its own choices. I do maintain, however, that for those of us who are training Psychologists in the broad, disciplinary, sense of the term the imposition of the professional training model is abhorrent, because it would have disastrous effects on the quality of the training we can provide.

It is critical to note that a significant segment of the community of clinical psychologists does not espouse the professional model. For example, the Clinical Division in our own department (which has been accredited since the inception of accreditation by APA, though with increasing difficulty as the process rigidifies) continues to view itself without difficulty as a scientist-practitioner program. We train students, of whom about half become researchers and scholars, and about half become primarily practitioners (usually in public rather than private mental health settings). We view our clinical training as consistent with the disciplinary attitudes that obtains elsewhere in our department. The clinical faculty share with the rest of the department a belief that the best way to assure competence among those who practice is to assess the individual practitioners, not the programs. They do not wish, as the APA's accreditation mechanism is increasingly inclined, to burden their program in ways that may deter students from training with us merely because

they do not wish to fit the mold for psychologists prepared by the accreditation committee.

Our vision of Psychology as a discipline sees the primary role of the psychologist as a creator of new knowledge, rather than as a user of existing knowledge. The current body of knowledge is important and its acquisition is a necessary component of the training of a psychologist. However, this body of knowledge is viewed largely as a source of questions and puzzles rather than as the fountainhead of action. We wish to develop in the psychologists we train the ability to ask questions. We want them to acquire the facility to discriminate between useful, fruitful questions and sterile and premature questions. We hope they have the creative capacity to develop innovative answers to these questions. Above all we wish to assure that they have the courage and the acumen to continually assume that their observations require further checking, their models further validation and their theories further corroboration.

There is no prescription for quality training in this domain. No periodic examination of the degree to which we conform to some formula would assure that we train first-rate psychologists within the framework of this set of goals. It is not that quality cannot be a goal. Indeed, quality is of primary importance. However, it is the mission of the University rather than of the professional association to monitor the quality of the training. Training in a discipline is the mission of a community of scholars, rather than of "those who practice the profession of teaching." The community of scholars, organized as a university, exercises quality control over its constituents that is more detailed and demanding than an accreditation mechanism will ever provide. Accreditation, after all, is limited in its scope to periodic checks by a remote organization. It is all too often forgotten by proponents of accreditation how detailed is the evaluation of academic programs in a proper university. As the head of the department of psychology in our university I must continually document to the college and the university the excellence of our programs. Every faculty member we hire is evaluated before hiring, and prior to promotion, by several committees. These committees examine in great detail all aspects of the individual's performance. We evaluate in detail, annually, the performance of each member of the faculty on several different dimensions. Each course we offer, each change we make in our curriculum, is reviewed by several departmental and university committees. Moreover, in the competition for resources we must endlessly justify our quality as scholars and as teachers. Given this background of intensive, ceaseless and merciless evaluation the contribution of the accreditation process is so paltry that it borders on the superfluous.

In summary, then, I see little value, and much that is harmful, in a universal accreditation system which will be applied to "all fields of psychology."

Such a system is inherently conservative. It is likely to be sluggish in its response to new knowledge. An elaborate, and costly, bureaucracy will be necessary to enforce this unwonted uniformity. These costs will be generated with no visible advantage. There is little, if any, evidence that a universal accreditation system will enhance quality. Moreover, given the existing mechanisms for quality assurance in universities it is difficult to see the need for this system. Psychology has reached a position of much pride on our campuses. There is considerable demand for training in Psychology at all levels. There are many indicators of our success as a discipline, not the least of which is the very high demand for our graduates. They are admired for their critical percipience and for their problem solving ability. They are prized for their ability to address problems in novel and creative ways. We have arrived at our present position while maintaining a true academic, discipline oriented, paradigm. It is very difficult to see why we should renounce our successes and accept the deadly hand of the accreditation process.

QUESTIONS

Answer the following questions and then compare your responses with the suggested answers at the end of this chapter.

1. What type of educational model for psychologists is proposed by Wiens?

2. Why does Donchin oppose uniform standards?

3. In the articles presented, Emanuel Donchin is responding to Arthur Wiens. On the basis of the arguments stated in Wiens's article, how would you expect him to react to Donchin's position?

ANSWERS

Correct Answers to Self-Test Exercises

Multiple-Choice

1. a	8. a	15. c
2. c	9. d	16. d
3. b	10. d	17. a
4. a	11. b	18. d
5. b	12. c	19. b
6. d	13. d	20. b
7. b	14. a	

Matching

1. j	8. b
2. c	9. d
3. g	10. f
4. h	11. e
5. k	12. e
6. a	
7. i	

Suggested Answers to Application Exercises

1. Compare your completed chart with Table 1-2 in your text.

2. a. Developmental psychology
   b. Clinical psychology
   c. Social psychology
   d. Educational psychology
   e. School psychology
   f. Engineering psychology
   g. Psychometric psychology
   h. Experimental psychology
   i. Physiological psychology
   j. Counseling psychology
   k. Industrial psychology
   l. Personality psychology
   m. Health psychology

3. a. Survey. You could probably gain this information from questionnaires or interviews. Case histories would require too much time, and naturalistic observation could be misleading. Since you are not testing a hypothesis, there would be no need for an experiment.
   b. Case history. You need an in-depth study of the boy to gain additional information about his fear. Naturalistic observation would not be as useful, since you already know he fears other children. Experiments and surveys could not provide information on the boy's fear.
   c. Experiment. Since you are interested in the cause-effect relationship of two variables, you must test your hypothesis. The experimental method is the only technique that can clearly find causes of relationships.
   d. Naturalistic observation. You would want to observe the behavior without the person's knowledge. Case studies, surveys, and experiments would be necessary.
   e. Correlational research. You need to compute a correlation coefficient to determine if there is a positive or negative relationship.

4. a. Independent variable: opportunities for decision making and self-determination
   b. Dependent variable: alertness and general happiness

5. a. The assignment of all females to the experimental group prevents the two groups from having proportionate representation of the sexes. This makes it

difficult to compare the two groups in an experimental situation.

b. The two groups were treated quite differently. Control-group members were assigned seats in the back of the room and were not permitted the beverages and vitamins given to the experimental group.

c. Both the location of seats in the classroom and the drinking of beverages could have affected the performance of the experimental and control groups. Both of these variables could have been controlled if the experimenter had used random seating and provided beverages and placebo pills to the control group.

d. The researcher knew which students were in the experimental and control groups, and this information may have influenced his or her tone of voice and attitudes toward the two groups. The experiment would have better control with the double-blind feature, with neither the subjects nor the experimenter knowing who was assigned to the experimental and control groups.

6. You should have checked the following items:

   ____ You will know the general nature of your type of participation in the experiment before it begins.
   ____ You can withdraw from the experiment at any time.
   ____ You will be protected from physical harm.
   ____ Your test scores will be kept confidential.

Suggested Answers to Reading Questions

1. Wiens recommends a common program in scientific research and practice during the first two years of graduate school for all psychology students. He also believes that programs should be checked to be certain that all students are completing their specified requirements. Finally, he maintains that curriculum evaluation should include a check on course content.

2. Donchin differentiates between the discipline and the profession of psychology and feels the profession should not dictate to the discipline. He views accreditation as bureaucratic and rigid, and believes psychology should be exploring new knowledge rather than using old knowledge. Donchin maintains that universities should exercise their own quality control rather than rely on the superficial observations of outsiders.

3. Wiens would probably strongly disagree with Donchin, noting that there needs to be a check on the quality of education. He would argue that as a profession, psychology must have some standards for minimum entry.

Chapter 2:

BIOLOGY AND BEHAVIOR

CHAPTER OUTLINE

I. The nervous system
  A. How the nervous system is studied
    1. The pseudoscience of phrenology
    2. Surgery: Destroying a part of the brain
    3. Electrical and chemical stimulation of the living brain
    4. Modern techniques
      a. Electroencephalography (EEG)
      b. Computerized axial tomography (CAT)
      c. Positron emission tomography (PET)
      d. Magnetic resonance imaging (MRI)
  B. How the nervous system works
    1. Cells: The basis of all behavior
    2. Electrical and chemical activity: Keys to communication
    3. Neurotransmitters: Chemical messengers
      a. Action at the synapse: Neurotransmitters at work
      b. What are neurotransmitters?
  C. Components of the nervous system
    1. An overview
    2. The spinal cord
      a. Structure and functions of the spinal cord
      b. Reflexes and the spinal cord
    3. The peripheral nervous system
      a. Somatic nervous system
      b. Autonomic nervous system
        (1) Sympathetic functions
        (2) Parasympathetic functions
        (3) How the sympathetic and parasympathetic systems work together
        (4) How the brain activates the autonomic nervous system
    4. The brain
      a. Structures of the brain
        (1) Brain stem
        (2) Reticular formation
        (3) Cerebellum
        (4) Cerebrum
        (5) Hypothalamus
        (6) Thalamus
        (7) Basal ganglia
        (8) Limbic system
        (9) Cerebral cortex
      b. "Left" and "right" brains: hemisphere lateralizations
        (1) Research and its implications
        (2) How damage to the left hemisphere affects language
        (3) Functions of the right hemisphere

II. The endocrine system
    A. Endocrine glands
    B. Neural-endocrine interactions
Boxes
    In the forefront: Alzheimer's disease
    Psychology in your life: Sex, handedness, and your brain
    In the forefront: Brain-tissue grafts in people and animals

LEARNING OBJECTIVES

After you study Chapter 2, you should be able to do the tasks outlined in the following objectives.

1. Criticize phrenology and describe the methods used for studying the brain.

2. Describe the cells in the nervous system and their activity.

3. Specify three characteristics of neurotransmitters and recognize potential problems.

4. Describe the role of the spinal cord.

5. Identify the two main divisions of the nervous system and their components.

6. Identify the types of nerves in the peripheral nervous system.

7. Explain the functioning of the somatic nervous system and the autonomic nervous system.

8. Identify the three main parts of the brain and the roles of their components.

9. Describe the role of the reticular formation, the hypothalamus, the limbic system, and the cerebral cortex.

10. Distinguish between the roles of the left and right hemispheres of the brain.

11. Describe the role of the hypothalamus in coordinating the autonomic nervous system and the endocrine system.

KEY CONCEPTS

As you read Chapter 2 in your text, look for each of the following concepts. You should understand each concept.

1. Phrenology

Phrenology was based on the concept that personality and abilities are based on bumps on various sections of the skull. Although this approach was quickly discredited, it did raise the question of whether specific parts of the brain have specialized functions.

2. Methods for Studying the Brain

A number of modern methods have replaced older techniques that required surgery for analysis of brain functions. Among the modern techniques are electroencephalography (EEG), computerized axial tomography (CAT), positron emission tomography (PET), and magnetic resonance imaging (MRI).

3. Cells in the Nervous System

The nervous system has two types of cells: neurons and glial cells. Neurons receive and relay information throughout the body. All neurons are composed of a cell body with a nucleus, and all have dendrites. Most neurons have an axon. Some glial cells provide a covering for neurons, some remove dead nerve cells, some prevent toxins from entering the brain, and some support neurons in other ways.

4. Nervous System Activity

A neuron receives impulses from other neurons through its dendrites and cell body and transmits information down its axon. Impulses travel faster on axons that are covered with a myelin sheath. Since myelinization continues to develop until a person is about 10 years old and dendrites continue to grow during childhood, children's abilities improve steadily. In old age dendrites shrivel, allowing less communication among neurons. Communication occurs at a junction, or space, called a synapse, where the axon of one neuron comes close to the dendrites of another neuron. When an impulse reaches the end of an axon, a chemical transmitter substance is released into the synapse. Receptors from the adjacent neuron then "catch" the chemical.

5. Neurotransmitters

There are three characteristics of neurotransmitters: (1) they are released by neurons, (2) they generate excitatory or inhibitory currents, and (3) they can be broken down by enzymes that occur naturally in the brain. Problems with neurotransmitters may lead to a number of disorders, including schizophrenia, Parkinson's disease, and Alzheimer's disease. Psychoactive drugs can either speed up or slow down the effects of neurotransmitters.

6. Divisions of the Nervous System

The nervous system has two main divisions: the central nervous system (CNS) and the peripheral nervous system (PNS). The CNS consists of the brain and spinal cord. The PNS consists of sensory and motor nerves.

7. Spinal Cord

The spinal cord is part of the central nervous system. It acts as a relay in bringing sensory information to the brain and motor information from the brain to the muscles. Information from the neck down is channeled through the spinal cord. The spinal cord is also involved in the control of reflexes.

8. Peripheral Nervous System

The peripheral nervous system has two types of nerves, sensory nerves and motor nerves. Motor nerves can be part of either of the two subdivisions of the peripheral nervous system.

9. Somatic Nervous System

The somatic nervous system, a subdivision of the peripheral nervous system, controls reflex actions and voluntary actions. Some muscles work cooperatively, while others work in opposition.

10. Autonomic Nervous System

The autonomic nervous system controls involuntary life-support processes. The two parts of the autonomic nervous system are the sympathetic division and the parasympathetic division. The sympathetic division works to expand energy, while the parasympathetic division increases the body's supply of stored energy.

11. Brain Stem

The three parts of the brain are the brain stem, the cerebellum, and the cerebrum. The brain stem controls sensory inputs above the neck, involuntary motor activity, and levels of sleep and arousal.

12. Cerebellum

The cerebellum is responsible for the coordination of motor activity, posture, and balance.

13. Cerebrum

The cerebrum is the most highly developed part of the brain and has many functions, including control of the endocrine system, control of bodily movements, memory, thinking, and problem solving. The cerebrum includes the hypothalamus, the thalamus, the basal ganglia, the limbic system, and the cerebral cortex.

14. Thalamus and Basal Ganglia

The thalamus not only acts as a relay for vision, hearing, and pain but is also involved in memory for language. The basal ganglia are located near the thalamus and help to control bodily movements.

15. Limbic System

The limbic system mediates extreme emotions by balancing opposite emotional states. The limbic system is also involved in memory.

16. Cerebral Cortex

The cerebral cortex is responsible for complex human perception and thought. For purposes of study, the brain is divided into right and left hemispheres. Each hemisphere is then divided into areas, or lobes. Specific functions have been identified with each lobe. Each hemisphere controls separate functions. The hemispheres communicate through the corpus callosum.

17. Left and Right Hemispheres

Although language is usually controlled by the left hemisphere, the right hemisphere has some control, and, in a few cases, overall control of language is in both hemispheres. Damage to specific areas of the cortex can produce related disturbances. It is generally believed that the right hemisphere is more involved in artistic, musical, and creative thought. However, the distinction is not clear. Injuries in young children have suggested that the hemispheres can switch functions until about age 5.

18. Endocrine System

The hypothalamus acts as coordinator between the autonomic nervous system and the endocrine system. The pituitary gland controls the glands in the endocrine system.

TERMS TO KNOW

Define each of the terms listed. You can check your definitions in the text Glossary or on the text pages listed in parentheses.

Nervous system (p. 40) Computerized axial tomography (CAT) (p. 43)

Phrenology (p. 40) Positron emission tomography (PET) (p. 43)

Lesions (p. 41) Magnetic resonance imaging (MRI) (p. 43)

Psychosurgery (p. 41) Neurons (p. 43)

Electrical stimulation (p. 41) Sensory (afferent) neurons (p. 43)

Electrodes (p. 41) Motor (efferent) neurons (p. 43)

Cannula (p. 41) Interneurons (p. 43)

Noninvasive techniques (p. 41) Glial cells (p. 44)

Electroencephalography (EEG) (p. 41) Myelin (p. 44)

Dendrites   (p. 44)   Synapses   (p. 47)

Axon   (p. 44)   Neurotransmitter   (p. 47)

Resting membrane   Synaptic cleft   (p. 47)
potential (RMP)   (p. 44)

Action potential (AP)   (p. 45)   Synaptic vesicles   (p. 47)

Threshold   (p. 45)   Receptor site   (p. 47)

Axon hillock   (p. 45)   Neurotransmitters that excite   (p. 48)

Axon terminal   (p. 45)   Neurotransmitters that inhibit (p. 48)

Myelin nodes   (p. 45)   Dopamine   (p. 49)

Myelinization   (p. 45)   Serotonin   (p. 49)

Norepinephrine	(p. 49)	Nerves	(p. 51)
Endorphins	(p. 50)	Sensory nerves	(p. 51)
Parkinson's disease	(p. 50)	Motor nerves	(p. 51)
Phenothiazines	(p. 50)	Spinal cord	(p. 51)
Alzheimer's disease	(p. 47)	Reflex	(p. 52)
Acetylcholine	(p. 50)	Patellar reflex	(p. 52)
Psychoactive drugs	(p. 50)	Voluntary control	(p. 52)
Central nervous system (CNS)	(p. 51)	Involuntary control	(p. 52)
Peripheral nervous system (PNS)	(p. 51)	Somatic nervous system	(p. 53)

Striated muscles   (p. 53)   Hypothalamus   (p. 55)

Antagonistic muscles   (p. 53)   Homeostasis   (p. 55)

Synergistic muscles   (p. 53)   Brain stem   (p. 56)

Autonomic nervous system   (p. 53)   Reticular formation   (p. 56)

Cardiac muscles   (p. 53)   Ascending reticular
                                           activation system   (p. 56)

Smooth muscles   (p. 53)   Cerebellum   (p. 56)

Sympathetic division   (p. 54)   Cerebrum   (p. 57)

Parasympathetic division   (p. 55)   Hypothalamus   (p. 57)

Belladonna   (p. 55)   Thalamus   (p. 58)

Basal ganglia   (p. 58)   Hemispheres   (p. 59)

Limbic system   (p. 58)   Frontal lobe   (p. 59)

Septal area   (p. 58)   Temporal lobe   (p. 59)

Hippocampus   (p. 58)   Parietal lobe   (p. 59)

Amygdala   (p. 58)   Occipital lobe   (p. 59)

Amygdalectomy   (p. 58)   Primary cortex   (p. 61)

Korsakoff's syndrome   (p. 58)   Primary somatosensory cortex   (p. 61)

Cerebral cortex   (p. 58)   Primary sensory cortex   (p. 61)

Association cortex   (p. 59)   Hemispheric lateralization   (p. 63)

Asymmetry of the brain (p. 63)   Wernicke's area (p. 65)

Corpus callosum (p. 63)   Adrenal gland (p. 67)

Planum temporale (p. 64)   Chimeric stimuli (p. 67)

Disconnection syndrome (p. 65)   Endocrine system (p. 68)

Stroke (p. 65)   Hormones (p. 68)

Aphasia (p. 65)   Pituitary (p. 69)

Broca's area (p. 65)   Anterior pituitary (p. 69)

Motor aphasia (p. 65)   Posterior pituitary (p. 69)

Sensory aphasia (p. 65)   Luteinizing-hormone-releasing hormone (LHRH) (p. 69)

Luteinizing hormone (LH)   (p. 69)

Vasopressin   (p. 69)

Adrenalin   (p. 69)

Estrogen   (p. 69)

Testosterone   (p. 69)

Oxytocin   (p. 69)

Neural-endocrine interactions   (p. 70)

Let-down reflex   (p. 70)

Prolactin   (p. 70)

Activational effect   (p. 70)

Organizational effect   (p. 70)

Androgens   (p. 70)

SELF-TEST

Multiple-Choice

Choose the one best response to each question. An answer key is provided at the end of this chapter.

1. What is the basic purpose of the nervous system?

   a. To control the endocrine system
   b. To repair neurons
   c. To regulate the hippocampus
   d. To process information

2. What is the purpose of an electroencephalogram (EEG)?

   a. To measure the activity of a single neuron
   b. To stimulate specific sections of the brain for research
   c. To record electrical activity over wide regions of the brain
   d. To measure electrical changes during periods of emotion and stress

3. Which of the following describes one function of glial cells?

   a. Growing dendrites
   b. Producing transmitter substances

c. Providing a covering for neurons
d. Producing new neuron cells

4. What is the function of the dendrites of a neuron?

a. To pass on signals to the axons of other neurons
b. To pick up signals from other neurons
c. To release neurochemical transmitter substances
d. To provide necessary energy to sustain the neuron

5. There is a place where the axonal terminals of one neuron come close to the dendrites of another neuron and transmitter substances may be released. What is this space called?

a. Glia
b. Soma
c. Synapse
d. Myelin

6. A man has been diagnosed as having Parkinson's disease. What is his problem?

a. He has an insufficient supply of dopamine.
b. He has an excess of dopamine.
c. He has an insufficient supply of acetylcholine.
d. He has an excess of acetylcholine.

7. What are the two main divisions of the nervous system?

a. Sympathetic nervous system and parasympathetic nervous system
b. Autonomic nervous system and somatic nervous system
c. Central nervous system and peripheral nervous system
d. Endocrine system and spinal cord

8. Which part of the central nervous system is involved in simple reflexes?

a. Limbic system
b. Hypothalamus
c. Spinal cord
d. Cerebral cortex

9. Which type(s) of nerves is (are) responsible for allowing you to read this question and write a response?

a. Sensory nerves
b. Motor nerves
c. Sensory and motor nerves
d. Involuntary nerves

10. What are the two main divisions of the peripheral nervous system?

a. Central nervous system and endocrine system
b. Somatic nervous system and autonomic nervous system
c. Antagonistic division and synergistic system
d. Sympathetic system and parasympathetic system

11. One part of the peripheral nervous system primarily serves voluntary muscles. What is this part called?

a. Somatic nervous system
b. Autonomic nervous system
c. Sympathetic nervous system
d. Parasympathetic nervous system

12. Someone has just come up behind you and accidentally startled you. Which of the following structures is primarily responsible for the resulting increase in your heart rate?

a. Cerebellum
b. Hippocampus
c. Sympathetic nervous system
d. Spinal cord

13. Which of the following is most directly involved in wakefulness and sleep?

a. Corpus callosum
b. Hypothalamus
c. Reticular formation
d. Cerebellum

14. A tightrope walker was injured in a fall and some brain damage is suspected. Which of the following would be most detrimental to her balancing ability?

    a. Damage to the cerebellum
    b. Damage to the pituitary gland
    c. Damage to the hypothalamus
    d. Damage to the hippocampus

15. Which part of the motor system would be in control as a tightrope walker balanced during a complicated routine?

    a. Spinal cord
    b. Brain stem
    c. Cerebrum
    d. Limbic system

16. Which of the following has an important role in both your nervous system and your endocrine system?

    a. Cerebellum
    b. Spinal cord
    c. Hypothalamus
    d. Thalamus

17. Just as you are about to drive into the last available parking space at a restaurant, a man pulls his car around a corner and grabs the spot. Which of the following is probably responsible for the annoyance you feel?

    a. Reticular formation
    b. Hypothalamus
    c. Hippocampus
    d. Corpus callosum

18. What is one of the apparent functions of the limbic system?

    a. It controls basic reflexes below the neck.
    b. It maintains body posture and balance.
    c. It appears to be involved in memory storage.
    d. It determines higher cognitive processes.

19. What is the major difference between human brains and the brains of lower animals?

    a. Humans have a smaller cerebral cortex.
    b. Humans have a larger cerebral cortex.
    c. Animals do not have a corpus callosum.
    d. Humans do not have a corpus callosum.

20. Which portion of the brain is primarily involved with vision?

    a. Prefrontal cortex
    b. Temporal lobes
    c. Premotor cortex
    d. Occipital lobe

21. Assume that four people aged 4, 24, 34, and 64 were in accidents and suffered damage to the left hemisphere of the brain. All have impaired speech. Which person is most likely to recover speech functioning?

    a. 4-year-old
    b. 24-year-old
    c. 34-year-old
    d. 64-year-old

22. If you had undergone a split-brain operation, what would be the result?

a. You would have difficulty speaking.
b. You would have a loss of balance.
c. Your left hand may not know what the right hand is doing.
d. There would be no change in your behavior and you would be completely normal.

23. What has Sperry's split-brain research revealed about the role of the corpus callosum?

a. The corpus callosum connects the right and left hemispheres, allowing exchange of information.
b. The corpus callosum is located between the right and left hemispheres and blocks the exchange of information.
c. The corpus callosum controls the endocrine system.
d. The corpus callosum dominates the right hemisphere.

24. The hypothalamus regulates eating, body temperature, and sexuality. Which of the following has a close functional connection with the hypothalamus?

a. Pituitary gland
b. Spinal cord
c. Cerebellum
d. Occipital lobe

25. Why is the pituitary gland called the *master gland*?

a. It controls the memory of language.
b. It controls the central nervous system.
c. It permits communication between the left and right hemispheres of the brain.
d. It secretes hormones that control the activity of many other endocrine glands.

Matching

Match each name in column A with a descriptive phrase in column B.

Column A

_____ 1. Brain stem

_____ 2. Reticular formation
_____ 3. Cerebellum

_____ 4. Cerebrum

_____ 5. Hypothalamus
_____ 6. Thalamus

_____ 7. Basal ganglia
_____ 8. Limbic system

_____ 9. Cerebral cortex
_____ 10. Amygdala

_____ 11. Septum

Column B

a. Transmits sensory inputs to appropriate areas of the cortex
b. Damage will result in tremors
c. Receives sensory information from areas above the neck
d. Grey matter that surrounds the brain
e. Damage causes rage
f. Part of both the central nervous system and the endocrine system
g. Controls levels of arousal
h. Most highly developed part of the brain
i. Stimulation causes rage
j. Large collection of cell bodies involved in bodily movements
k. Set of structures that mediate and balance emotional states

APPLICATION EXERCISES

These application exercises will test your understanding of and ability to apply the material you have read in your text. Suggested answers are provided at the end of the chapter so that you can check your responses.

1. A neuron is a basic building block in the nervous system and provides communication within the system. Each neuron is made up of a cell body, dendrites extending from the cell body, an axon (sometimes covered by a *myelin sheath*), and axon terminals. Label each part of the neuron indicated in Figure 2-1.

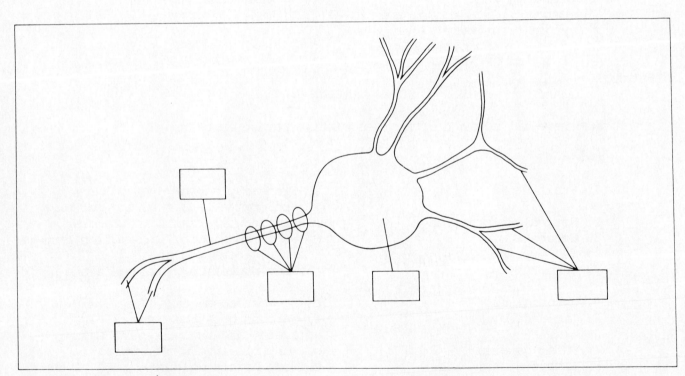

Figure 2-1

2. Neurons communicate with each other in a place called a synapse. The synapse is the space between the axon terminals of one neuron and the dendrites of another neuron. The terminals and the dendrites never really touch. Explain how the neurons pass impulses to each other

without actually touching each
other.

_____
_____
_____
_____
_____

3. The nervous system has several
    components. Figure 2-2 shows a
    simplified diagram of the nervous
    system, specifying the relationship
    between the components and at least
    one function of each component.
    Complete the diagram by labeling
    each component in the appropriate
    space.

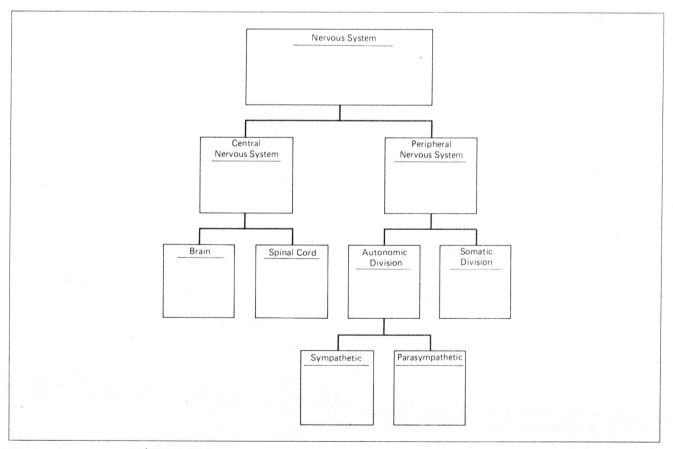

Figure 2-2

4. Although all the structures (parts of the brain and spinal cord) of the nervous system work together, each structure has one or more specialized functions. In each of the following examples, parts of the nervous system must be activated. Indicate which structure would play a primary role and specify how the structure would react.

a. Someone tickles the sole of your foot and your toes automatically curl.

Structure _____

Role _____
_____

b. As you are lying on the beach, someone races by and sprays sand in your eyes. You find yourself blinking.

Structure _____

Role _____
_____

c. You are performing intricate steps in a ballet and are trying to balance yourself on one toe.

Structure _____

Role _____
_____

d. You are in a sound sleep and are suddenly awakened.

Structure _____

Role _____
_____

e. You have just finished devouring a delicious meal and feel completely full and satisfied.

Structure _____

Role _____
_____

5. For purposes of study, the cerebral cortex has been divided into two hemispheres (right and left) connected by the corpus callosum and four lobes (frontal, temporal, parietal, and occipital). Although there is coordination and interaction among these areas of the cerebral cortex, damage to any of these parts can result in specific disturbances. Read each of the disturbances listed below and indicate the area or areas of the cortex that are most likely damaged or impaired.

a. A man is suffering from motor aphasia and cannot name common objects.

_____

b. A woman can write well but cannot read what she has written.

_____

c. A woman believes that her right arm does not exist.

_____

d. A man speaks at length but makes no sense. Further, he doesn't seem to understand other people.

_____

6. The nervous system and endocrine system work together in governing our behavior. One structure of the nervous system also functions in

the endocrine system, and one structure in the endocrine system also functions in the nervous system. Name these two structures, and in your own words describe their dual roles.

_____
_____
_____
_____
_____
_____

READING EXERCISE

The following article from *Newsweek on Health* describes recent research on hormones. Hormones are now believed to have a far more profound effect on human behavior than had been previously realized.

The Power of Hormones

The pituitary secretes two hormones: human-growth hormone, which helps make basketball stars, and oxytocin, which may prompt women who have had children to act like mother hens the rest of their lives. The testes put out testosterone, and increased levels may push men over the edge to a life of crime or sexual aberration. The adrenals unleash adrenaline, preparing the body to wrestle a woolly mammoth or stand up to the boss; they also pour out cortisol, which plays a role in anorexia, depression and shyness.

To understand this helter-skelter of activity, think of the human body as a hotel switchboard lit up by a constant stream of room-service orders and complaint calls: "Can you lower the temperature in this room?" "Would you send up a couple of cheeseburgers,

Copyright (c) 1987, Newsweek, Inc. All rights reserved. Reprinted by permission.

please?" The mediators of this ceaseless biological babble--the messengers rushing from cell to cell to satisfy all requests--are powerful molecules called hormones. Named after the Greek word *hormon* (to set in motion), these ubiquitous chemical substances act, in ways still somewhat mysterious, to maintain the exquisite balance of being.

Even that, however, doesn't begin to describe the frenzy of biochemical business going on in the human "hotel." Scientists who once thought hormones behaved like mere bellhops now know they can sometimes act like managers, security guards, cleaning personnel--even guests--all talking to each other. That hormones govern every aspect of human experience from growth and development to reproduction, metabolism and moods has long been known. But researchers are just beginning to fathom the full range of what they do and how they work.

"Everything is kept in perfect balance by hormones not only for normal maintenance and survival but in response to anything that comes along--physical insult, mental stress, physical exertion, a thought process," says Dr. Bert O'Malley, chairman of cell biology at Baylor College of Medicine and a former president of the Endocrine Society.

As recently as 1970, only about 20 human hormones had been identified; now researchers think there may be as many as 200. No longer seen just as substances produced by specific glands to perform specific functions, hormones are now defined as "anything produced by one cell that can get to another cell by any means and change what it does," says Wylie Vale, head of the peptide-biology lab at the Salk Institute in La Jolla, Calif. As a result, says Dr. Sidney Ingbar of Harvard Medical School, "our idea of what a hormone is is changing . . . the lines between hormones and other body chemicals are blurring."

In particular, endocrinology (the study of hormones) is merging with neuroscience--the study of the brain and central nervous system. It was only in the mid-1970s that researchers determined that the brain itself is a gland, secreting its own hormones and reacting to others. The breakthrough came with the discovery in the brain of hormones called opiates--pain blockers that some say account for a runner's "high" and may explain how mystics can walk over beds of hot coals without flinching. Since then scientists have identified at least 45 separate hormones in the brain, many of which perform different tasks elsewhere in the body. The hormone CCK (cholecystokinin), for instance, is released in the intestine when fats and proteins pass there from the stomach. But it also seems to act as an appetite suppressant in the brain, signaling that the stomach is full. Researchers are exploring the possibility that genetically obese people may have inborn defects in CCK.

Indeed, much current research is centered not just on identifying new hormones but on deciphering their precise functions. And virtually every advance at the research level has led to practical applications. Only a few years ago scientists discovered that the heart, too, makes its own hormone-- a powerful substance that can markedly reduce blood volume, relax blood vessels and increase excretion of salt. Already auriculin, a drug based on the hormone, is being tested on humans by California Biotechnology Inc., and preliminary studies show that it may be effective in treating congestive heart failure and kidney malfunction.

The dawn of genetic engineering is speeding still more discoveries in hormone research and treatment. Recombinant DNA, in which genes are inserted into bacteria to produce natural substances, "has allowed the production of hormones in unlimited amounts," says Hugh Niall, director of protein biochemistry at Genentech in South San Francisco. "There's been an enormous impact on understanding how the body works."

Researchers now know, too, that hormones are present in the immune system, in fact, governing how it communicates within itself and within the brain. Their ever-expanding knowledge is giving them fresh insights into hypertension, heart disease and growth disorders, and could hold out hope for treatment of Alzheimer's disease and AIDS. It is also allowing doctors to intervene in the most intricate human processes--using hormone therapy to treat breast cancer, diabetes and depression, for example, developing low-risk contraceptives and new treatments for infertility. Last year's Nobel Prize for medicine was awarded to biochemist Stanley Cohen and biologist Rita Levi-Montalcini for their work with hormonelike growth factors that may unlock the fundamental processes of cancer. "We now have a conceptual framework for how cancer is caused," says Charles Stiles of the Dana-Farber Cancer Institute. "We know that cancer is a cellular disorder of growth or differentiation and that hormones regulate both."

In short, hormone research has plugged scientists into the incredibly busy switchboard of the brain-body axis, though each new discovery also seems to bring new challenges. A look at what is known--and just being explored--in the body's complex chemical world:

The Chemistry of Mood and Madness

The frustration we feel when caught in a traffic jam. The way the body tenses when walking down a dark alley. The loss of appetite and inability to sleep that come before a dreaded task. Though some social scientists may never be convinced, molecular biologists see increasing evidence that hormones explain our moods and emotions--the essence of the way we are. Depression and anxiety, for example, can be the first symptoms of endocrine disorders. "These aren't purely psychological processes," says Bruce McEwen, head of the neuroendocrinology lab at New York's Rockefeller University. "They can change nerve cells and affect hormones."

Nowhere is the complex interplay more evident than in the way the body handles stress. The familiar "fight or flight" reaction evolved when our primitive ancestors encountered a large marauding animal and had to flee for their lives or face bloody combat. In preparation, the body undergoes an explosively swift series of events. The heart beats faster. Blood surges to the muscles, preparing them for action. Oxygen and nutrients speed to the brain, making the mind focused and alert. Under longer-term strains, anything from a traumatic operation to a malicious boss, the body responds with a stress "cascade." The

hypothalamus releases a substance called CRH (corticotropin-releasing hormone), which prompts the pituitary to secrete ACTH (adrenocorticotropic hormone), which prompts the adrenal glands to produce cortisol, increasing blood sugar and speeding up the metabolism. At the same time, cortisol suppresses the immune system.

That was all well and necessary in the face of a raging tiger. But when the threat is merely a scowl from the boss, the whole sequence is called into action inappropriately. Mild stress can sharpen alertness, but in heavier measure and for prolonged periods, it can set things awry. When suppressed, the immune system, for example, which may have shielded the ancient warrior from an inflammation of a wound, only makes modern man more susceptible to diseases. Students taking exams tend to be more vulnerable to respiratory infections, for example; bereaved people often become ill.

Some of the same stress hormones help to dampen the cascade and return the brain and body to their normal state. But prolonged stress can suppress growth, diminish the sex drive and reduce output of reproductive hormones. In studies at the National Institutes of Health, endocrinologist Dr. George Chrousos and psychiatrist Dr. Philip Gold have also found stress linked to depression and to the eating disorder known as anorexia nervosa, both conditions marked by the secretion of large amounts of cortisol. The stress hormones are involved in a wide range of other human disorders--from upper respiratory infections to cancers and memory loss. Even Alzheimer's disease may be aggravated by brain-cell loss brought on by stress-released hormones.

At the Salk Institute in La Jolla, biologist Vale and his colleagues have developed an agent that could modify the harmful effects of stress. It works by reducing the release of CRH, which in turn reduces levels of ACTH, which produces the familiar adrenaline rush.

So far, testing has been confined to animals, but the potential is huge.

Indeed, researchers are finding that the body's reaction to stress can influence even more subtle forms of behavior. In a recent study of 108 normal, upper-middle-class teens, researchers found that those who matured late and had adjustment problems had higher levels of cortisol. Monitoring 50 children over a period of 21 months, Harvard psychologist Jerome Kagan also found that those who were shy had higher levels of cortisol than those who were assertive, indicating that the shy children might be overreacting biochemically to challenging situations.

Scientists are just beginning to uncover other hormonal links to how we behave. Thomas Insel of the National Institute of Mental Health has found that oxytocin, the pituitary hormone that stimulates release of a mother's milk just after she gives birth, is also involved in the mothering instinct. It initiates licking and affectionate cuddling in animals, for example, and the effect may last for years. Present in humans as well, oxytocin may explain why a mother responds so forcefully to a baby's cry in the night—even after her own children have grown.

Hormones have long been implicated in PMS, premenstrual syndrome, but it is an area where doctors, as a rule, tread cautiously. As many as 90 percent of women experience some of the symptoms—including depression, anxiety, fatigue, irritability and eruptions of acne shortly before their menstrual periods. According to one new theory, acute sufferers may have an abnormal sensitivity to the body's natural opiates, which decline just before menstruation. Since opiates serve as a natural narcotic, PMS sufferers in effect may be experiencing drug withdrawal. Meanwhile, investigators at the Biopsychiatry Center in New Jersey reported last

December that 51 of 54 PMS patients showed some evidence of thyroid disorder; when 34 of them were given a thyroid hormone called thyroxine, all 34 reported "complete" relief.

Hormones may also be involved in criminal behavior in men. In a recent study of 89 male prison inmates, Georgia State University social psychologist James R. Dabbs Jr. found that those with higher concentrations of the "male" sex hormone testosterone had more often been convicted of violent crimes. Since testosterone levels usually peak between the ages of 16 and 18, the finding may help explain why men of that age are on the verge of their most crime-prone years.

Testosterone not only increases the tendency toward aggression and physical activity, it also spurs the sex drive and the capacity to act on it. In some cases, judges have offered men found guilty of aberrant sexual behavior— exhibitionists, rapists and child molesters—the chance to take a testosterone-blocking drug instead of staying in jail. The drug, cyproterone acetate, has allowed some to bring their behavior under control and return to normal life.

Researchers are also zeroing in on the role of hormones in psychiatric illnesses. Scientists have noted, for example, that depressed people who try to commit suicide tend to have higher levels of cortisol than other people. One study at Yale by Dr. Earl Giller Jr. and Dr. John W. Mason found that suicidal patients also had a high ratio of adrenaline to noradrenaline, a similar hormone found mostly in the brain. Together the two findings could allow clinicians to screen for patients who are particularly likely to harm themselves. The researchers also found that paranoid schizophrenics and manic-depressives have distinctive chemical profiles—the manic-depressives have higher levels of cortisol, noradrenaline and thyroxine but lower levels of testosterone. Armed with similar information, doctors may someday be able to draw up complete hormonal profiles of psychiatric patients to be used for diagnosis.

Sex, Fertility, and Life Span

To think of hormones is to think of sex. It's the sudden flood of sex hormones pouring into the bloodstream that makes puberty the watershed it is in everyone's life. Girls menstruate, boys get embarrassing erections—and everyone gets acne. The process starts with a master hormone called Gn-RH (gonadotropin-releasing hormone) released in the hypothalamus that signals the pituitary to secrete other hormones known as LH and FSH. In women, those hormones signal the ovaries to produce estrogen; in men, they tell the testes to make testosterone, which helps regulate the production of sperm. Sex hormones also exert influence on the body far beyond sex, affecting the brain, the liver, the salivary glands, the muscles and skin. "So much of how we function and how we age has to do with reproductive hormones," says Bardin.

Indeed, sex hormones account for major differences between men and women in how long they live and the way they die. "Men were designed for short, nasty, brutal lives," says Dr. Estelle Ramey of Georgetown University Medical School. "Women are designed for long, miserable ones." One explanation lies in evolution. Nature gives females a hormonal edge during the reproductive years, when more women than men are needed to perpetuate the species. Estrogen helps a woman's liver prevent the accumulation of cholesterol and makes her blood vessels more resilient to stress. Men are designed to protect women: the possibility for injury may be one reason his blood clots faster than hers—and why he has a greater risk of an early heart attack. But the female edge disappears with menopause. When estrogen production stops, she becomes prone to heart disease and the crippling wasting of bones known as osteoporosis.

Once conception has occurred, the woman's body secretes more sex hormones than at any other time. Hormones increase her blood volume, facilitating the flow of nutrients to the fetus. They also dampen her immune system so she won't reject the embryo as foreign tissue. Prolactin, released by the pituitary, stimulates the production of mother's milk. Progesterone, produced by the ovaries, prepares the lining of the uterus for implantation of the developing egg. Researchers think insufficient progesterone may be one reason why at least half of all fertilized eggs are lost in the first two weeks of pregnancy—before the woman even knows she is pregnant.

Given the complex biochemical interactions necessary for conception and pregnancy, it's no wonder hormone therapy holds the key to contraception. The Pill, the most effective contraceptive yet developed (excluding sterilization), is made up of a synthetic estrogen and progestin; their presence in the bloodstream fools the pituitary into thinking the user is pregnant, halting ovulation. French researchers recently devised a "once a month" pill, RU 486, that blocks the action of progesterone and prevents implantation of the fertilized egg.

Within the past year researchers have finally isolated a previously suspected hormone called inhibin, which may form the basis for a male contraceptive. Inhibin blocks the secretion of FSH, the follicle-stimulating hormone that causes the egg to mature in the female and sperm to be produced by the male. The main stumbling block to creating a male contraceptive is the vast difference between the two sexes in the way eggs and sperm are produced. "If you stopped 95 percent of a female's ovulations you would, for all practical purposes, make her infertile," says Dr. Jean Wilson of the University of Texas Health Science

Center. "If you knocked out 95 percent of a male's sperm production, he'd be just as fertile as before."

Greater understanding of sex hormones has also led to new treatment of infertility. Therapies involving Gn-RH can help stimulate sperm production and ovulation and help eggs mature. Genentech in South San Francisco is working with a hormone it calls activin, which seems to promote FSH and could one day be useful in helping women who do not ovulate.

The sex hormones that subside with age can cause serious disruptions in the body. The withdrawal of estrogen after menopause is often so detrimental to women that doctors now commonly administer replacement doses, helping alleviate such unpleasant symptoms as hot flashes and vaginal dryness and possibly staving off osteoporosis. Estrogen replacement can increase the possibility of cancer, but administering it in conjunction with progesterone virtually eliminates the risk.

Aging is not kind, hormonally, to men, either. Researchers think reduced levels of testosterone may be responsible not only for impotence but also for depression and lethargy. Direct-replacement therapy may increase the risk of prostate cancer and cardiovascular disease, so researchers are looking for new ways of administering it. At the same time, exposure to testosterone over a lifetime can cause the prostate to grow, blocking the urinary tract; researchers have developed a drug that in effect inhibits the hormone's action and could be an alternative to surgery.

Giants, Dwarfs, and Cancer Cells

A pro basketball team is a sports fan's delight, but to endocrinologists it also provides dramatic evidence of hormonal differences. Human-growth hormone, GH, is produced by the pituitary and is the master regulator of growth throughout childhood and puberty. Too much could make for seven-foot centers; too little could create dwarfs. Until recently, GH supplements had to be extracted from the pituitaries of human cadavers and were in short supply. But since 1985 genetic engineering has allowed GH to be made in vast quantities, and therein lies a potential dilemma. Should short children with low GH concentrations be administered growth hormone? And what about those just a bit below average whose parents associate stature with success?

Prescribing growth hormone can be risky. While stimulating elongation of the bones, it also speeds their maturation. As a result, children given supplements "may just run the developmental program faster," warns Dr. Gordon Cutler of the National Institute of Child Health and Human Development, and may end up just as short as they would normally. Too much GH can also theoretically cause some forms of diabetes and in rare cases make the thigh bone slip out of its pelvic socket, which occurs when bones grow too fast.

While GH stimulates the growth of the entire body, hormonelike growth factors stimulate the growth of particular kinds of cells. As such, they may play a role in human cancers. Stiles and his associates at the Dana-Farber Cancer Institute are now looking for substances that might *inhibit* growth factors by altering the genes involved in their synthesis and action. In particular, they are studying PDGF, platelet-derived growth factor, which stimulates certain cells to divide and form scar tissue and may encourage other cells to divide inappropriately, contributing to the growth of a cancer. "What we're asking is whether, in nature, there is not only an accelerator but a brake pedal as well," he explains. "In endocrinology, for every yin there is a yang."

Hormone research has already paid off dramatically in the treatment of breast cancer, a disease that takes the lives of some 38,000 American women each year. Years ago it was learned that estrogen can fuel the growth of tumors in some women, and removal of the pituitary, ovaries or adrenal glands (which also produce estrogen) became a standard therapy. But gland removal is drastic treatment. Without the adrenals, for example, patients must take cortisone for the rest of their lives, since without the cortical hormones produced by the adrenals, patients could not endure any kind of stress and would die.

A New Definition of Human Disease

Diabetes is by far the most common serious hormonal disorder, afflicting 11 million Americans. Perhaps half of all patients with hormone disorders suffer from it, with long-term implications that include blindness, kidney failure and a greatly increased risk of heart disease and strokes. All this because, among other things, the body doesn't have enough of the hormone insulin or can't properly use the insulin it has. One of the greatest challenges in endocrinology today is to find ways to deliver it in the exquisitely regulated ways the body needs. Once extracted from the pancreas of cattle or pigs, insulin can now be produced through gene splicing and in forms more compatible with the human body. Researchers are studying ways to spur insulin-producing cells, called beta cells, that remain in a patient's pancreas to multiply.

But "the hottest thing to come down the pike," says Dr. Daniel Porte Jr., president of the American Diabetes Association, is the effort to stimulate other cells in the body to produce insulin as needed. Every cell in the body contains exactly the same genes, so if the beta cells in the pancreas don't produce insulin, maybe the insulin genes in cells in other parts of the body could be "turned on" to produce the hormone instead. Tremendous research efforts are being focused on identifying the network of gene regulators within cells. "Once we know about them," says William J. Rutter, director of the Hormone Research Institute at the University of California, San Francisco, "it'll have great impact not only on efforts to cure diabetes but on regenerating other tissues and extending their functional life."

A similar excitement exists in the field of immunology, which researchers now believe is tightly linked with endocrinology. Biochemist Alan Goldstein of George Washington University School of Medicine has found that thymosins, a family of hormones produced by the thymus gland, hold sway over the entire immune system. The knowledge has prompted a new definition of disease, associating it with too little or too much hormone, and Goldstein predicts that will lead to a new field of therapy he calls "immunopharmacology."

Goldstein himself used immunopharmacology several years ago in treating Heather, a young California girl born without a thymus gland who suffered severe immune deficiency. Doses of thymosins helped her to produce fully active white blood cells. More recently, researchers at the University of Wisconsin administered thymic hormones to a group of elderly patients who could not respond to influenza vaccine and found that it enabled them to produce antibodies. Scientists are also planning to see if thymosins will help restore the devastated immune systems of AIDS victims.

The galloping pace of hormone research will undoubtedly unlock still more secrets of the human body. Some researchers even envision the day, perhaps within a generation, when people can take "cocktails" of hormones, allowing them to live longer, healthier and more active lives. That may bring new ethical dilemmas: How long do we want to live? To what extent do we want to regulate behavior? "We have to rethink the role of hormones throughout life and provide a background against which decisions can be made," says the Population Council's Bardin. We can only begin to fathom the possibilities, just as scientists have only begun to explore the infinite complexities in every gland, every tissue and every cell that make up the biochemical yin and yang of life.

QUESTIONS

Answer the following questions and then compare your responses with the suggested answers at the end of this chapter.

1. How has the concept of hormones changed in the past 30 years?

2. What is the relationship between hormones and mood?

3. How has recent research on hormones affected the concept of human disease?

ANSWERS

Correct Answers to Self-Test Exercises

Multiple-Choice				Matching			
1.	d	14.	a	1.	c	7.	j
2.	c	15.	c	2.	g	8.	k
3.	c	16.	c	3.	b	9.	d
4.	b	17.	b	4.	h	10.	i
5.	c	18.	c	5.	f	11.	e
6.	a	19.	b	6.	a		
7.	c	20.	d				
8.	c	21.	a				
9.	c	22.	c				
10.	b	23.	a				
11.	a	24.	a				
12.	c	25.	d				
13.	c						

**Suggested Answers to Application
Exercises**

1. See Figure 2-3.

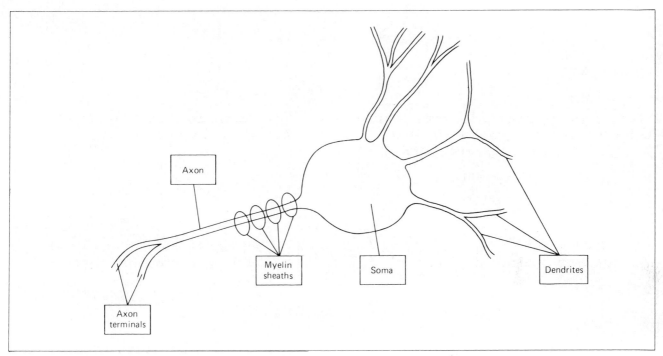

Figure 2-3

2. Transmitter substances or neurotransmitters are released into the synapse. The synaptic vesicles squirt these chemicals into the space, and receptor sites on the receiving dendrites "catch" the chemical.

3. See Figure 2-4 (page 50).

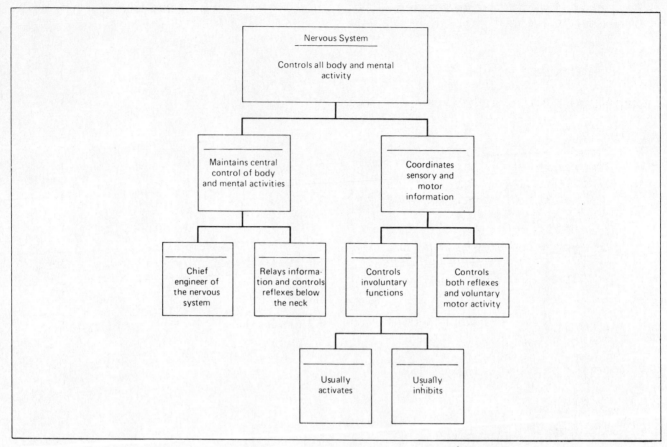

Figure 2-4

4. a. Spinal cord. The toe-curling behavior occurred involuntarily and is therefore a reflex. The sensory input of tickling was relayed to the spinal cord where motor neurons were activated and toe curling resulted.

b. Brain stem. Your blinking is a reflexive behavior, but since it occurs above the neck, coordination of sensory and motor neurons must occur in the brain stem rather than the spinal cord.

c. Cerebellum. The cerebellum would coordinate the motor activity in your feet and help you maintain your balance while you were on only one toe.

d. Reticular formation. The ascending reticular activation system would activate the cerebral cortex.

e. Hypothalamus. The hypothalamus may have recognized your hunger and you ate. The hypothalamus is now maintaining your homeostasis, making you feel full.

5. a. Damage to the left frontal lobe (Broca's area)

b. Damage to the left visual cortex and corpus callosum

c. Damage to the association area of the left parietal lobe

d. Damage to the left posterior temporal area (Wernicke's area)

6. Although part of the nervous system, the *hypothalamus* also functions in the endocrine system. The hypothalamus coordinates the two systems and controls the secretion of hormones. The *pituitary gland* is part of the

endocrine system, controlling the activity of all other glands. But

the posterior pituitary is made up of nerve tissue and is part of the nervous system.

Suggested Answers to Reading Questions

1. In 1979 only 20 hormones were known; currently, almost 200 have been identified. Hormones had been defined as substances produced by specific glands, but the definition has now expanded to include all cell-produced substances that move to other cells and cause changes. The brain and heart have been found to produce hormones.

2. Depression and anxiety can be caused by hormone disorders. Hormones are produced in times of stress; the resulting production of cortisol can suppress growth and diminish sex drive. Hormones have also been related to PMS in women and aggressive criminal behavior in men.

3. In addition to diseases that are known to be caused by hormone deficiency (for example, diabetes), hormones are now believed to affect the immune system. Thymosins have been found to aid the production of white cells and antibodies.

Chapter 3:

SENSATION AND PERCEPTION

CHAPTER OUTLINE

I. Psychophysics: How our senses work
   A. Sensory thresholds
      1. Absolute threshold
      2. Difference threshold
   B. Adaptation

II. Physiology: The senses
   A. Vision
      1. What we see
      2. How we see: The anatomy of the eye
      3. How we see: Beyond the retina
         a. Retinal ganglion cells and their receptive fields
         b. Visual cortex
      4. Adaptation to light and dark
      5. Color vision
         a. Trichromatic theory of color vision
         b. Opponent-process theory of color vision
         c. Color deficiency
   B. Hearing
      1. What we hear
         a. Loudness
         b. Pitch
         c. Timbre
      2. How we hear: The anatomy of the ear
         a. How we hear sounds of different frequencies: Place versus frequency theory
         b. How we can tell where sound comes from
      3. Hearing loss
   C. The skin senses
      1. Pressure
      2. Pain
   D. The chemical senses
      1. Smell (olfaction)
      2. Taste (gustation)

III. Perception: How the brain organizes sensory information
   A. Gestalt laws of perceptual organization
   B. Bottom-up and top-down processing in perception
      1. Word-superiority effect
      2. Phonemic restoration effect
   C. Attention

      D. Perceptual constancy
         1. Size constancy
         2. Shape constancy
         3. Brightness constancy
         4. Color constancy
      E. Depth perception
      F. Visual illusions
      G. The role of experience

Boxes
    Psychology in your life: Common vision problems
    In the forefront: Perception of biological motion

LEARNING OBJECTIVES

After you study Chapter 3, you should be able to do the tasks outlined in the following objectives.

1. Distinguish between sensation and perception.

2. Identify two types of thresholds and explain signal-detection theory.

3. Describe adaptation.

4. Describe the structure and functioning of the eye and identify common vision problems.

5. Describe the structure and functioning of the ear and identify common hearing problems.

6. Identify the functions of the skin senses.

7. Recognize the relationship between the senses of smell and taste and describe the physical characteristics of these two senses.

8. Describe five gestalt laws of perceptual organization.

9. Distinguish between bottom-up and top-down processing.

10. Explain the role of attention.

11. Describe six forms of perceptual constancy.

12. Explain the principles of depth perception involving the use of binocular and monocular cues and recognize the role of experience.

13. Cite research on the perception of biological motion.

KEY CONCEPTS

As you read Chapter 3 in your text, look for each of the following concepts. You should understand each concept.

1. Sensation and Perceptions

Sensation is information brought to us by our sensory organs, and perception is the organization and interpretation of this information.

2. Thresholds

The absolute threshold is the smallest intensity of a stimulus that can be perceived. Absolute threshold is related to background stimuli. The smallest difference between two stimuli that can be perceived is called the difference threshold, or jnd (just noticeable difference). Weber developed a ratio formula for jnd based on intensity.

3. Adaptation

We adapt to stimuli that are constant and become insensitive unless we specifically direct our attention to them.

4. Eye

The eye sees light energy in the form of light waves. Light passes through the cornea, enters the pupil (a small hole), and passes through the lens, which focuses the light into a clear image. This image is then projected on the retina.

5. Retina

The retina is the most important and most complicated part of the eye. It contains photoreceptor cells (rods and cones). Cones, located near the fovea, are responsible for color vision and fine details. Rods are on the edges of the cornea and are responsible for peripheral vision and vision in dim light. There are no photoreceptors in the optic disk, known as a blind spot.

6. Common Vision Problems

Among the most common vision problems are nearsightedness, farsightedness, astigmatism, strabismus, amblyopia, stereoblindness, presbyopia, cataracts, night blindness, cornea damage, and glaucoma.

7. Receptive Fields

Specific objects that we see stimulate individual ganglion cells. The brain determines which cells are active and locates the image in space. The cells respond to specific areas in the retina, called receptive fields. The ganglion cells encode retinal images, which are interpreted in the brain.

8. Light and Dark Adaptation

Light adaptation is a faster process than dark adaptation.

9. Color Vision

There are two explanations of how we see color: the trichromatic theory and the opponent-process theory. According to the trichromatic theory, our visual system has three color mechanisms (one for red, one for green, and one for blue). The combined output from these color mechanisms allows us to see all colors. The opponent-process theory is based on positive and negative afterimages. Color vision is affected by negative afterimages; after looking at a color, we tend to see the opposite color. Both theories are used in explaining color deficiency.

10. Hearing

Hearing is based on sound waves (repetitive changes in air pressure). The height of the sound waves determines loudness, and the number of cycles in the sound wave determines the pitch. Sound waves enter the outer ear and pass through the middle ear to the inner ear. Hair cells in the inner ear move in response to the sound waves and pass these impulses to the brain. Two theories explain how we determine the pitch of sound: place theory and frequency theory. Place theory explains our hearing of higher-pitched sounds; frequency theory explains our hearing of lower-pitched sounds. We locate sound by determining differences in intensity and time in reaching our right and left ears.

11. Hearing Loss

Hearing loss may be caused by damage to the hair cells of the cochlea or auditory nerve, by a bone defect in the middle ear, or by a ruptured eardrum.

12. Skin Senses

The skin senses include senses of temperature, pressure, and pain. It is generally believed that we have "pain pathways," which cross in the spinal cord. The brain controls pain through the production of endorphins. Physical exertion, fear, and stress activate the production of endorphins and minimize pain. Acupuncture, hypnosis, and placebos are also known to block pain.

13. Smell (Olfaction)

Odors enter the nasal cavity as molecules, either through the nostrils or from the back of the mouth. Hairlike projections in the nasal cavity catch the molecules and send electric signals to the olfactory bulb for processing. The signals are then relayed to the brain. Research has found that although we can distinguish between different smells, we have difficulty giving them appropriate names.

14. Taste (Gustation)

The senses of taste and smell interact and are closely related. We have receptors (taste buds) for four sensations: sweet, salty, sour, and bitter. Some food preferences are hereditary and others are learned.

15. Gestalt Laws of Perceptual Organization

Gestalt laws are based on how we tend to organize sensory information. They include the law of contiguity, the law of proximity, the law of similarity, and the law of closure. Another law deals with the perception of figure and ground.

16. Bottom-Up and Top-Down Processing

Two processes are involved in recognizing patterns: bottom-up processing and top-down processing. Bottom-up processing requires putting individual elements together to form a pattern. Top-down processing emphasizes recognizing an overall concept or pattern on the basis of our expectations and knowledge. The importance of top-down processing is seen in the word-superiority effect and the phonemic restoration effect.

17. Attention

Attention is a state of focused mental activity. Since we cannot attend to every stimulus, we are usually selective and ignore some stimuli. We divide our attention when we need to focus on more than one activity at the same time.

18. Perceptual Constancy

Although conditions in the environment can vary the appearance of objects, we use cues to identify those conditions and can compensate for them.

19. Depth Perception

Our judgment of depth is based on binocular cues and monocular cues. Binocular cues are the result of both eyes working together, each eye seeing

the object from a slightly different
view. Monocular cues, which can be
received with only one eye, include
size, motion parallax, partial overlap,
texture gradients, linear and
atmospheric perspective, and shading.

✗ Psychophysics   (p. 77)

✗ Absolute threshold   (p. 77)

20. Experience and Depth Perception

Cultural differences account for some
variations in perception. Early
experience can influence our ability to
see horizontal and vertical lines.

✗ Signal-detection theory   (p. 77)

21. Perception of Biological Motion

Biological motion is the pattern of
movements used by living organisms.
Researchers have found that it is easy
to identify the differences in familiar
movements such as walking, jogging, and
dancing as well as differences between
the movements of males and females.

✗ Difference threshold   (p. 78)

✗ Just noticeable difference
(jnd)   (p. 78)

TERMS TO KNOW

✗ Weber's law   (p. 78)

Define each of the terms listed. You
can check your definitions in the text
Glossary or on the text pages listed in
parentheses.

✗ Stimulus   (p. 77)   ✗ Adaptation   (p. 78)

✗ Sensation   (p. 77)   ✗ Visual capture   (p. 79)

✗ Perception   (p. 77)   ✗ Cornea   (p. 80)

Sclera   (p. 80)   Optic disk   (p. 81)

Pupil   (p. 80)   Fovea   (p. 83)

Iris   (p. 80)   Nearsightedness (myopia)   (p. 82)

Lens   (p. 81)   Farsightedness (hypermetropia) (p. 82)

Retina   (p. 81)   Astigmatism   (p. 82)

Accommodation   (p. 81)   Strabismus   (p. 82)

Rods   (p. 81)   Amblyopia   (p. 82)

Cones   (p. 81)   Stereoblindness   (p. 83)

Ganglion cells   (p. 81)   Presbyopia   (p. 83)

Cataract   (p. 83)   Wavelength   (p. 85)

Night blindness   (p. 83)   Intensity   (p. 85)

Cornea damage   (p. 83)   Trichromatic theory   (p. 86)

Glaucoma   (p. 83)   Purity   (p. 86)

Receptive field   (p. 84)   Complementary colors   (p. 86)

Visual cortex   (p. 84)   Afterimage   (p. 87)

Simple cells   (p. 84)   Opponent-process theory   (p. 88)

Complex cells   (p. 84)   Positive afterimage   (p. 88)

Hypercomplex cells   (p. 84)   Negative afterimage   (p. 88)

Color deficiency   (p. 89)   Malleus   (p. 91)

Decibels (dB)   (p. 90)   Incus   (p. 91)

Hertz (Hz)   (p. 90)   Stapes   (p. 91)

Pitch   (p. 90)   Oval window   (p. 91)

Timbre   (p. 90)   Inner ear   (p. 91)

Pinna   (p. 91)   Cochlea   (p. 91)

Middle ear   (p. 91)   Basilar membrane   (p. 91)

Auditory meatus   (p. 91)   Hair cells   (p. 91)

Tympanic membrane   (p. 91)   Cilia   (p. 91)

Place theory   (p. 92)   Enkephalin   (p. 95)

Frequency theory   (p. 92)   Acupuncture   (p. 96)

Tinnitus   (p. 93)   Placebos   (p. 96)

Sensorineural hearing loss   (p. 93)   Hypnosis   (p. 96)

Presbycusis   (p. 93)   Olfaction   (p. 96)

Conductive deafness   (p. 94)   Olfactory mucosa   (p. 97)

Skin senses   (p. 94)   Gustation   (p. 98)

Two-point-discrimination   Taste buds   (p. 98)
threshold   (p. 95)

Endorphins   (p. 95)   Papillae   (p. 98)

Phenylthiocarbamide (PTC) (p. 100) Top-down processing (p. 102)

Gestalt psychology (p. 100) Word-superiority effect (p. 103)

Gestalt laws (p. 100) Phonemic restoration effect (p. 103)

Law of contiguity (p. 100) Attention (p. 103)

Law of proximity (p. 100) Selective attention (p. 103)

Law of similarity (p. 100) Divided attention (p. 103)

Law of closure (p. 100) Shadowing technique (p. 104)

Figure-ground (p. 102) Dichotic listening (p. 104)

Bottom-up processing (p. 102) Perceptual constancy (p. 104)

Unconscious-inference theory (p. 104)   Binocular disparity   (p. 107)

Ecological theory   (p. 104)   Stereopsis   (p. 107)

Ames room   (p. 105)   Stereomotion   (p. 107)

Size constancy   (p. 105)   Monocular cues   (p. 107)

Shape constancy   (p. 106)   Size   (p. 107)

Brightness constancy   (p. 106)   Motion parallax   (p. 107)

Color constancy   (p. 106)   Partial overlap   (p. 108)

Depth perception   (p. 106)   Texture gradients   (p. 108)

Binocular cues   (p. 107)   Linear perspective (convergence
                                         of parallel lines)   (p. 108)

Atmospheric perspective (p. 108)

Shading (p. 108)

Illusions (p. 111)

Mueller-Lyer illusion (p. 109)

Ponzo illusion (p. 109)

Moon illusion (p. 111)

Theory of misapplied constancy (p. 111)

Critical period (p. 112)

Biological motion (p. 112)

SELF-TEST

Multiple-Choice

Choose the one best response to each question. An answer key is provided at the end of this chapter.

1. While tasting a cookie, you recognize the familiar flavor of cinnamon. What is this process of sensation and interpretation called?

    a. Perception
    b. Absolute threshold
    c. Weber's law
    d. Proprioceptive sense

2. What does the Weber fraction indicate?

    a. Effects of intensity on human judgment
    b. Differences in ability to dark-adapt
    c. Effect of constancy on illusions
    d. Differences in cone activity in color vision

3. Which of the following best describes visual accommodation?

    a. Changes in the size of the cornea
    b. Changes in the shape of the lens
    c. Changes in the role of rods
    d. Changes in the weight of the iris

4. Which part of the eye is most helpful in permitting us to see in a dark room?

    a. Iris
    b. Cornea
    c. Cones
    d. Rods

5. What is the best time to correct the visual problem of strabismus?

a. Before age 5
b. Between ages 5 and 7
c. After age 12
d. After middle age

6. Each ganglion cell responds to a specific area within the retina. What is this specific area called?

    a. Fovea
    b. Blind spot
    c. Receptive field
    d. Cornea

7. On a dark night a car with bright lights approaches you and passes by. Why are there potentially dangerous moments after this occurs?

    a. You had to light-adapt as the car was approaching. Additional time is required for rods to take over and reach their maximum functioning.
    b. You had to light-adapt as the car was approaching, and this could temporarily impair peripheral vision.
    c. Negative afterimages occur after light adaptation. This will make it impossible for you to determine correct color for at least 1 hour.
    d. You are more susceptible to illusions when you are required to light- and dark-adapt.

8. According to trichromatic theory, how do three types of cones in the eye produce a color wavelength which is sent to the brain?

    a. Outputs from each of the three types of cones are combined.
    b. Outputs from each of the three types of cones are processed by rods.

c. Outputs from the strongest set of cones are sent to the brain, while outputs of the other types are ignored.
    d. Only outputs that produce an after-image are sent to the brain.

9. If you suffered from the most common form of color deficiency, which of the following colors would be seen as shades of grey?

    a. Blue and yellow
    b. White and black
    c. Red and green
    d. Orange and purple

10. Which of the following sounds is easiest to locate if you are blindfolded?

    a. Sound directly in front of you
    b. Sound directly behind you
    c. Sound directly above you
    d. Sound to your right

11. A teenaged boy is afflicted with tinnitus and hears a continuous ringing. What is probably causing his problem?

    a. Hair cells in the cochlea or auditory nerve have been damaged.
    b. His eardrum has been ruptured.
    c. He has a bone defect in his middle ear.
    d. He has hearing in only one ear and is suffering from a monaural buzz.

12. Which of the following persons is least likely to feel the pain if jabbed in the arm with a stick?

    a. A woman who has just awakened
    b. A man who is relaxing in an easy chair
    c. A woman who just jogged 2 miles
    d. A man who is tired after a long automobile drive

13. Imagine that you are taking cherry-flavored medicine while you have a heavy cold. Why might the medicine seem tasteless?

    a. Your taste buds are blocked when you have a cold.
    b. Your sense of smell is blocked, and smell interacts with taste.
    c. All senses are impaired when you have a cold.
    d. Nerve endings are numbed by viruses.

14. If you relied only on your taste buds, which of the following qualities could you detect in a seasoned steak?

    a. Aroma
    b. Chewy
    c. Peppery
    d. Salty

15. What principle does the following figure illustrate?

    a. Proximity
    b. Closure
    c. Similarity
    d. Figure-ground

16. Imagine that you are waiting at a train station and see a vague black rectangle with a large white light approaching on the track in the distance. Although you cannot see any specific features, you perceive this as your train. What type of processing did you use?

    a. Closure
    b. Bottom-up
    c. Top-down
    d. Accommodation

17. Which of the following situations provides an example of dichotic listening?

    a. A man is walking and hears his name called.
    b. While conversing with a group at a coctail party, a woman nibbles on some hors d'oeuvres.
    c. A man eavesdrops on a conversation in a foreign language.
    d. A student listening to her professor's lecture hears her name spoken by a student on her right.

18. A large mug 10 feet away may project an image on the retina which is no larger than a 2-ounce shot glass 1 foot away. Despite the similar size of the images on the retina, the mug is perceived as much larger. What is this characteristic of perception called?

    a. Retinal disparity
    b. Atmospheric perspective
    c. Size constancy
    d. Motion parallax

19. How are partial overlap, motion parallax, shading, and texture gradients alike?

    a. They are binocular effects that require the coordination of both eyes.
    b. They are monocular cues for depth perception.
    c. They are techniques for organization in a figure-ground perspective.
    d. They are methods for determining color deficiency.

20. Why is it relatively easy to distinguish between the walking movements of males and females?

a. Men have a lower center of movement.
b. Men walk faster.
c. Women take larger strides.
d. Women use a limping movement.

Matching

Match each disorder in column A with a descriptive phrase in column B.

Column A	Column B
_____ 1. Glaucoma	a. Inborn defect in eye muscles, resulting in monocular vision
_____ 2. Myopia	b. Inability to see in dim light caused by either a lack of vitamin A or a retinal disease
_____ 3. Hypermetropia	c. Limitations in vision along horizontal and vertical axes
_____ 4. Presbyopia	d. Hearing impairment caused by the blocking of sound waves before they reach the cochlea
_____ 5. Astigmatism	e. Continuous ringing or hissing sound
_____ 6. Amblyopia	f. Eye disease caused by an increase in pressure and resulting in a smaller field of vision
_____ 7. Strabismus	g. Visual information from one eye is not received by the brain.
_____ 8. Stereoblindness	h. Caused by damage to hair cells in the cochlea or auditory nerve
_____ 9. Cornea damage	i. Nearsightedness caused by an elongated eyeball
_____ 10. Cataract	j. Farsightedness caused by a loss of elasticity in the lens that affects people past middle age
_____ 11. Night blindness	k. Hearing loss that results when hair cells die off in old age
_____ 12. Tinnitus	l. Loss of transparency in the lens, causing an eventual loss of vision
_____ 13. Sensorineural hearing loss	m. Farsightedness caused by a shortened eyeball
_____ 14. Presbycusis	n. Inability to perceive depth, caused by retinal disparity
_____ 15. Conductive deafness	o. Injury that can be corrected by a transplant

APPLICATION EXERCISES

These application exercises will test your understanding of and ability to apply the material you have read in your text. Suggested answers are provided at the end of the chapter so that you can check your responses.

1. The major structures of the eye are the sclera, the cornea, the anterior chamber, the posterior chamber, the pupil, the iris, the lens, the vitreous humor, and the retina, including the optic disk and fovea. Label each of these structures, as indicated in Figure 3-1.

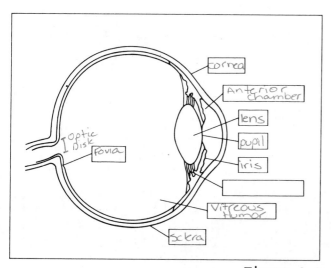

Figure 3-1

2. How is your peripheral vision? Try this exercise. Face directly ahead and place a book in your right hand. Stretch your right arm horizontally to the side. Without moving your head, see what you can read out of the corner of your eye.

   Most likely you can see the book but cannot read the detailed print. From what you have learned from your text about the functions of rods and cones, describe why you had difficulty distinguishing detail from the corner of your eye.

   _____
   _____
   _____
   _____

3. Read the following scenario and on the basis of your knowledge of light and dark adaptation, explain what has occurred.

   A man is in a dimly lit restaurant enjoying a juicy steak with an exceptionally subtle and delicious sauce. He feels he cannot leave the restaurant without complimenting the chef. He asks his waiter to show him to the kitchen. Although the restaurant is lit only by candles, he has no difficulty negotiating the many turns and stairs to the kitchen. As he enters the brightly lit kitchen, he rubs his eyes and feels shocked by the light. After about 10 minutes of conversing with the chef, he is no longer bothered by the brightness. He then leaves to join his friends at his table. As he walks back to his table he feels blinded by the darkness, bumping into walls and tripping on steps.

   _____
   _____
   _____
   _____

4. A man describes himself as color-deficient, yet he has no difficulty seeing blue and yellow. Explain how this is possible according to trichromatic theory and opponent-process theory.

   Trichromatic theory _____

   _____
   _____
   _____

   Opponent-process theory _____

_____
_____
_____

5. There are two primary physical characteristics of sound: intensity and frequency. Use Table 3-1 to summarize how we perceive and measure these characteristics.

Table 3-1 Physical Characteristics of Sound

Physical Characteristic	Perception	Measuring Unit
Intensity (height of sound waves)		
Frequency (number of cycles or changes in the wave)		

6. Our ability to locate the source of sound is dependent on (1) which ear the sound reaches first and (2) differences in intensity in the sound as it reaches each ear. Imagine that you are driving in traffic and suddenly hear a loud siren. At first you cannot determine the location of the sound. What might you do to help locate the sound?

_____
_____
_____
_____

7. Four gestalt principles, or laws, are the law of continuity, the law of proximity, the law of similarity, and the law of closure.

Continuity involves continuing in the direction suggested by the stimulus. Proximity involves organizing our perception according to elements close to each other. Similarity involves organizing our perception according to elements similar in appearance. Closure involves completing an incomplete figure. For each of the following figures (Figures 3-2, 3-3, 3-4, and 3-5), identify which gestalt law is influencing your perception and describe what you see as a result.

a.

Figure 3-2

Principle _____
Perception _____
_____

b.

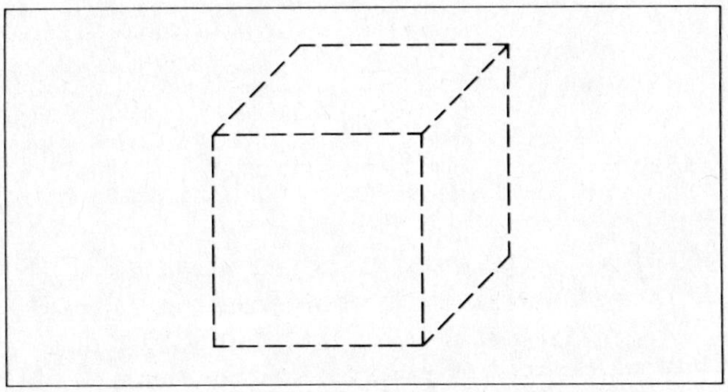

Figure 3-3

Principle _____
Perception _____
_____

c.

d.

Figure 3-4

Principle _____

Perception _____

_____

Figure 3-5

Principle _____

Perception _____

_____

8.

"It's me—Alice! Alice Terkleman! Your wife of 22 years!
You just don't recognize me because I'm out of context."

FROM "MARITAL BLITZ," BY JACK ZIEGLER

Figure 3-6 Source: "Marital Blitz" by Jack Ziegler. Copyright (c) 1987 by Jack
Zeigler, Warner Books, Inc.

Notice Figure 3-6. If Alice Terkleman is correct, why might her husband have difficulty using top-down processing to recognize her? _____

_____

_____

How could her husband use bottom-up processing to be certain that this is his wife? _____

_____

_____

9. Your text identified seven monocular cues for the perception of depth: size, motion parallax, partial overlap, texture gradients, linear and atmospheric perspective, and shading. Study Figure 3-7 and indicate which of these seven monocular cues are present.

_____

_____

_____

Figure 3-7

READING EXERCISE

Human factors engineering is an interdisciplinary study of the interaction of people and machines; human perception is a key factor in this study. In the following article from *American Scientist,* Herschel Leibowitz describes the sensory and perceptual principles that contribute to accidents at railroad crossings.

Grade Crossing Accidents and Human Factors Engineering

Advances in technology during the past four decades have resulted in the development of a new discipline referred to as human factors engineering. As machines have become more complex, their safe and efficient operation depends progressively on the interaction between them and their human operators. An early historical example is the development of the airplane. As airplanes were able to fly at faster speeds and as increasingly complex controls as well as communications and navigation equipment were developed, the demands on pilots became so great that errors and accidents were occurring with greater frequency. By analyzing the nature of these errors in the context of human sensory, perceptual, memory, and cognitive capacities, engineers were

Reprinted with permission of *American Scientist,* copyright (c) 1985.

able to redesign the controls and instruments to provide a better match with pilots' capabilities (Chapanis et al., 1949).

The pioneer work in aviation has served as a model of human factors engineering. Any system in which humans use complex equipment should be designed taking into consideration the capabilities as well as the limitations of the human operator. In some cases, the equipment is modified either to eliminate the human operator by automation, as is often feasible for predictable and routine tasks, or to reduce the possibility of error by more compatible design or by training procedures. Consideration of the inherent limitations of humans as well as our unique capabilities plays an essential role in explaining the basis of accidents and making the relationship between human operator and machine safe and productive.

Human factors engineering is by its very nature strongly interdisciplinary, involving cooperation among engineers, physiologists, and psychologists as well as other behavioral scientists. Although the early work was primarily in aviation, developments in technology have broadened the scope of the discipline. It is commonplace to find human engineering considerations in almost any situation in which humans use equipment or machinery as diverse as telephones, automobiles, nuclear power plants, and computers.

The objective of the present paper is to analyze the problem of collisions between vehicles and trains in the light of relevant human factors principles and to suggest ways in which our knowledge of behavioral, sensory, and perceptual principles can help us to understand and ameliorate the problem.

The Problem

Collisions between trains and vehicles are responsible for approximately 650 fatalities annually in the United States (*Rail-Highway Crossing Bull.*, 1983). The number of grade crossing accidents, currently more than 7,000 annually, is large in relation to the number of trains in operation (27,000 locomotives). Virtually every crossing is protected either by an active warning system, including lights, bells, and gates, or by a crossbuck, which reminds us that we are in a danger zone and should stop, look, and listen. Trains are required by law to sound their horns as they approach a crossing, and the locomotive headlights are routinely activated even during daylight. The locomotives themselves are large, approximately 3 m wide by 4.5 m or more high. Advance information is often provided by signs situated at the side of the road and by warnings painted directly on the pavement.

Analysis of accidents reveals that in most cases there was clear warning of the train's approach and adequate visibility, but for some unexplained reason, the driver of the vehicle chose to cross the track and was killed or seriously injured. Conversations with train crews indicate that this behavior is not unusual. Some motorists will ignore the warning and attempt to beat the train. This is, of course, a risky decision. Although their braking systems are very efficient, trains require an extended stopping distance because of their immense weight. A locomotive traveling alone on a flat grade at 48 km/hr (30 mph) requires almost 185 m to come to a complete halt. If the train's speed is higher or it is pulling a load, the stopping distance will be increased. A 100-car freight train may require 2 km or more to stop after full application of the emergency brakes. As a consequence of the vast differences in weights, the vehicle and passengers are at particular risk in any collision with a train.

Figure 3-8 Despite the obvious danger, many motorists will ignore warnings at a railroad grade crossing and attempt to beat a train. The perceived risk is low; balanced against it is the uncertainty of how long it might take the train to clear the crossing. An active warning system such as that shown here is designed to accommodate the fastest train and the slowest vehicle, and thus encourages motorists to decide for themselves whether they can make it before the train actually reaches the crossing. Usually the vehicle does beat the train, reinforcing the inclination to try again. (Photo courtesy of Association of American Railroads.)

Driver Behavior

In view of the obvious hazard of an approaching train, why do motorists attempt to cross the tracks? Closer examination of both the crossing environment and the bases for a driver's decision suggests several possible reasons.

Railroad safety engineers are faced with an inherent dilemma. Signal systems protecting grade crossings must be designed so that the lights, bells, and gates are activated in sufficient time to accommodate the fastest train, the slowest motorist, and the worst weather. In engineering terms, the system is designed anticipating the "worst case." This concept is analogous to the procedure in civil engineering for specifying the design loading weight for a bridge. The maximum weight the bridge could conceivably be required to support is estimated, and this value is multiplied by a safety factor. However, unlike the estimation of a safe loading weight for a bridge, allowance of a safety margin in the design of railroad signaling systems can have an undesirable effect on the behavior of drivers. When the warning activation time is designed for the worst case, it will be excessive for the majority of drivers under most conditions. In many cases, it is safe to proceed across the tracks even though the signals have been activated. This encourages motorists to ignore the official warnings and to judge for themselves whether it is safe to proceed.

As motorists, we are typically impatient. Most of us have had personal experiences with drivers who do not come to a complete halt at stop signs or who accelerate to cross an intersection just before or even after the light has changed. We expect the automobile to save time in our daily lives, and we drive accordingly.

This tendency is exaggerated at grade crossings. Although we know approximately how long we will be delayed if we stop for a red traffic light, there is much more uncertainty at a grade crossing. It is not unusual for a freight train to block an intersection for as long as 10 to 15 minutes. In some communities, trains will couple and uncouple cars in urban areas, blocking traffic for an indeterminate period of time. The uncertainty about the length of the potential delay is further encouragement to ignore official warnings and try to beat the train. Although difficult to justify, this behavior is perhaps understandable in view of the disruptive effect of unanticipated delays, particularly when we are driving in our home communities.

The fact that in most cases we can safely ignore official warnings contributes to the danger. Faced with a decision to evaluate the risk of crossing the tracks versus the inconvenience of stopping, we unconsciously weigh the advantages and disadvantages of the alternative courses of action. Whenever we decide not to wait and are successful in crossing safely, our behavior is rewarded and reinforced. The result of such reinforcement is to increase our self-confidence and to increase the probability that we will make the same decision again in the future.

The concept of perceived risk is helpful in analyzing this behavior (Fischhoff et al., 1981). Many decisions are based on a comparison between the inconvenience of a particular course of action and the perceived risk of the alternative. Although traffic accidents are a major cause of death and injury, the perceived risk on the highway is apparently so low that drivers will assume the risk of an accident rather than be inconvenienced by obeying grade crossing and traffic signals, fastening seat belts, or complying with posted speed limits. The low perceived risk may be a consequence of the fact that the probability of injury or death on a given day for a given individual is in fact extremely low.

The perceived risk of colliding with a train is probably reduced still further by the low frequency of trains at some crossings. There is some evidence that we tend to ignore infrequent dangers and assume that they could not possibly happen to us on a given occasion. A train may not be encountered at some crossings over a period of years. When crossbucks and other warning signs remain in place even after a track is no longer in use, the dangerous tendency to disregard official warnings is encouraged.

This analysis, which has been couched largely in terms of driver behavior at grade crossings protected by active systems, suggests that for a variety of reasons drivers will ignore the official warnings and decide for themselves whether to attempt to cross. Of the approximately 225,000 public grade crossings in North America, 50,000 are protected by active devices, while the remainder have only a passive crossbuck. For crossings protected only by crossbucks, the decision to wait or attempt a crossing must be based on the driver's estimate of the safe time interval. In effect, the sensory and perceptual mechanisms on which decisions are based are critical, either because drivers disregard information from an active protection system or because there is no other basis for making a decision.

Sensory and Perceptual Factors

Although information regarding the driver's own vehicle is usually accurate and under the driver's control, judgment of train speed and distance, which is essential in determining the safe time interval, is subject to several systematic biases. These biases--the illusion of velocity and size, the illusion of perspective, and the deceptive geometry of collisions--can mislead the driver into assuming that the safe time interval for crossing the tracks is longer than is actually the case.

The illusion of velocity and size arises from the fact that, the larger the object, the more slowly it appears to be moving. This can be observed at airports by noting the apparent landing speeds of different-sized jet planes. Although they have approximately the same velocities, the larger aircraft appear to be traveling more slowly. This illusion is extremely compelling, even to experienced pilots, who are well aware of the actual velocities.

Figure 3-9

Also contributing to the incidence of collisions at grade crossings are biases that affect a motorist's perception of the distance of a train from the crossing and the speed at which it is moving. The illusion of velocity and size makes a large object such as a train engine appear to be moving more slowly than it really is. The illusion of perspective makes a train appear to be farther away than it really is. The increase of the expansion pattern--a phenomenon called *looming*--is slow at the distance at which a motorist's decision is usually made and thus adds to the overestimation of the safe time interval for crossing the tracks. (Photo courtesy of Association of American Railroads.)

This inverse relationship between apparent velocity and size has been attributed to the relative contribution of the two systems subserving smooth eye movements, which may be activated either reflexively or voluntarily (Post and Leibowitz, in press). The reflexive system, or optokinetic nystagmus, is activated by moving contours and serves to prevent degradation of vision from retinal image motion when the observer is moving. These reflex eye movements have no conscious concomitants. The second system maintains objects of interest on the fovea of a (usually stationary) observer by means of voluntary "pursuit" eye movements. Unlike the reflexive system, activation of the voluntary system does have conscious correlates. The effort required to make a pursuit eye movement is determined by the actual velocity of the object being tracked and in turn determines the apparent velocity of the object. The effort depends also on the extent of the object's contour. The more moving the contour in the direction orthogonal to the eye movement, the greater the contribution of the reflexive system, the less the effort required by the voluntary system, and the slower the apparent velocity. The net result is that, for equal actual velocities, the larger the object, the slower the perceived velocity.

Motorists are experienced at judging the velocities of other vehicles and may not be aware that a large train which appears to be moving at a given velocity is in fact traveling much faster. This illusion would contribute to overestimation of the safe time interval for crossing the tracks.

The illusion of perspective involves learned responses to monocular cues to depth, two-dimensional cues that can be appreciated with one eye. The perception of size and distance is not innate, but rather is learned as a consequence of perceptual and perceptual-motor experience. With such experience, which does not fully mature until adolescence, we learn to appreciate the significance of the monocular cues. For example, the decreasing visual angles subtended by a uniform texture, by trees or telephone poles, or by the apparent convergence of parallel contours from roads or railroad tracks all become associated with distance (Gregory, 1978). These cues operate unconsciously to signal depth relationships in the environment and in drawings and photographs. Several of the cues are typically present when a motorist views an oncoming train, e.g., the tracks, the ties, and the ballast or stone in the vicinity of the tracks. In some cases rows of telephone poles or trees may also be visible. The effect of such monocular cues would be expected to increase the perceived distance of the train and would thus also contribute to overestimation of the safe time interval.

The deceptive geometry of collisions is created by the fact that, if two objects traveling in straight lines at constant velocities are on a collision course, their positions relative to each other in the visual field remain constant. There is no lateral motion, and thus the principal cue to velocity is the increase in size of the visual angle subtended or the expansion pattern, a phenomenon sometimes referred to as "looming" (Schiff 1965). The rate of increase of the expansion pattern is not linear but rather is described by a hyperbolic function. For distant objects, the rate of change in the expansion pattern is low. As the distance decreases, the visual angle subtended increases at an accelerated rate. At the distance at which a motorist's decision is usually made, the expansion pattern is increasing slowly, indicating that the approaching train is traveling at a slower speed than is actually the case. The result is an overestimation of the safe time interval.

It is important to point out that,

by unconsciously biasing the motorist's estimation of the safe time interval, all three of these factors--the inverse relationship between velocity and size, the illusion of perspective, and the rate of change of the expansion pattern--serve to increase unjustifiable confidence in the ability to judge the time remaining before the train reaches the crossing and influence the motorist's critical decision to wait or attempt to cross.

Role of the Train Crew

Train crews are well aware of the dangers, but they face a particularly difficult task when approaching a grade crossing. This I learned when I was given the opportunity to ride in the cab of a locomotive through the city of Memphis, over a section of track crossed by a series of roads carrying heavy local traffic. A moving vehicle on the tracks does not ordinarily represent a danger because, except in the rare cases in which the vehicle stalls, it will clear the tracks before the arrival of the train. More typically, the critical decisions must be made with respect to vehicles while they are approaching the crossing.

The complexity of the perceptual and decision-making processes and the distances at which a braking decision must be made pose difficulties for the train crew. In addition to the distance required to stop after the brakes have been activated, which is rarely less than 185 m, the time required for the engineer to perceive, decide, and act must be taken into consideration. Decision-making time increases with uncertainty. If every time a vehicle was observed in the vicinity of the tracks the emergency brake were activated, the decision-making time would be relatively short. However, since braking when approaching a grade crossing is effective and appropriate only under special circumstances,

uncertainty is increased and the decision-making time is lengthened.

In the literature on automobiles, a reasonable estimate of the average time needed to react to unexpected events is 2.5 seconds (Summala, 1981). A vehicle moving at 48 km/hr--13.4 m/sec--will travel 30.5 m or more while the decision is being made and before the brakes are activated. Thus, for a locomotive traveling at this speed which is not pulling a load, the minimum distance at which the engineer can recognize a hazard and stop the train is in excess of 215 m. Of course, if the speed is higher or the locomotive is pulling a load, this distance will be lengthened. Automobile drivers can decelerate quickly in response to traffic and can also change direction rapidly. The train cannot change direction, and its deceleration time is significantly longer than that of an automobile.

The complexity of the crew's task is illustrated by analysis of the frequently encountered situation in which the engineer must decide whether the train and vehicle are on a collision course. As pointed out above, the principal cue for estimating the velocity of a vehicle on a collision course is the rate of change of its expansion pattern, which is a nonlinear function of the closing distance. This is a particularly difficult task when the viewing distance is large, because the image of the vehicle is small and the rate of change of its expansion pattern is low. In addition, at most urban grade crossings, approaching vehicles are visible from the locomotive for only a limited time, which exacerbates the task of the engineer and in many situations precludes the possibility of preventive action.

Even when the approaching vehicle is visible at a sufficient distance so that effective braking of the train would be possible, the engineer has no way of knowing whether the vehicle will stop, increase or decrease speed, or even possibly change course. The many possible courses of action of the vehicle and the fact that in most cases the driver's behavior is appropriate have the effect of increasing the uncertainty, which in turn prolongs the engineer's decision-making time. In addition, the engineer must be alert to the possibility of vehicles approaching from two or more directions simultaneously. The only options available to the engineer are to sound the horn continuously (the normal pattern when approaching an intersection is two longs, a short, and a long) and to activate the brakes.

From the point of view of perception and decision-making, the task of the engineer in most situations is beyond the limits of human capability. In human factors engineering, it is recognized that in some situations, humans simply do not have the sensory and perceptual skills necessary to perform certain tasks. The train crews play a valuable role in avoiding grade crossing accidents by maintaining the braking system in good working order, by reducing speed at dangerous intersections, and by braking for stalled or moving vehicles when there is adequate time to avoid a collision. However, it is clear that because of the distances at which critical decisions must be made, the limited view of approaching vehicles, the many possible parameters of vehicle movement, and the time required to decelerate a train, the crew is often powerless to avoid a collision when the driver of the vehicle overestimates the time remaining before the train arrives at the crossing.

Possible Solutions

There are a variety of measures which could be taken to reduce the possibility of collisions between vehicles and trains (Sonefeld, 1980). The most effective techniques are to separate tracks and highways by

overpasses or bridges, or to construct barriers to prevent vehicle movement, but these are not economically feasible as a general procedure in the United States. It is possible to activate the lights and bells at grade crossings so that they more accurately indicate the arrival time of a train, and this should have a salutary long-term effect on driver behavior. Procedures designed to apprise the public of the dangers at grade crossings have already proved effective, as indicated by the reduction of almost 50% in the death rate following the initiation of the Operation Lifesaver program of the National Safety Council.

To the extent that unjustified confidence of drivers in their ability to judge accurately the safe time interval is a causative factor, any procedure to reduce this self-confidence would be effective. In addition to dissemination of information through the public media and driver education, the effect of campaigns against the abuse of alcohol should also prove useful. Alcohol unjustifiably increases self-confidence and would therefore be expected to exacerbate any tendency to attempt to beat trains as well as the tendency to overestimate the safe time interval. More vigilant law enforcement may be useful not only with respect to alcohol but in increasing driver awareness of the dangers at grade crossings and modifying driver behavior.

If the assumption that misjudgment of vehicle velocity contributes to the underestimation of the safe time interval at grade crossings is correct, it would be interesting to determine whether the perceived velocity of large objects could be increased. For example, it may be feasible to minimize the contribution of reflexive smooth eye movements by means of special markings or lights on locomotives. Such studies would also contribute to our understanding of the role of the oculomotor system in the perception of movement.

The choice among the various possible measures and their effective implementation will be facilitated by our understanding of the underlying causes of grade crossing accidents. The role of the human factors engineer is to assist those responsible for instituting ameliorative procedures by providing insights or suggestions which derive from the behavioral sciences. Effective human factors engineering is based on a multidisciplinary approach in which the behavioral sciences may be expected to play a more prominent role as a consequence of advances in technology and the increasing demands on human operators.

References

Chapanis, A., W. R. Garner, and C. T. Morgan. 1949. *Applied Experimental Psychology.* Wiley.

Fischhoff, B., S. Lichtenstein, P. Slovic, S. L. Derby, and R. L. Keeney. 1981. *Acceptable Risk.* Cambridge Univ. Press.

Gregory, R. 1978. *Eye and Brain,* 3rd ed. World Univ. Library.

Post, R. B., and H. W. Leibowitz. In press. A revised analysis of the role of efference in motion perception. *Perception.*

Rail-Highway Crossing Accident/Incident and Inventory Bulletin No. 5. 1983. Washington: Fed. Railroad Admin.

Schiff, W. 1965. The perception of impending collision: A study of visually directed avoidant behavior. *Psych. Mono.* 79, no. 604.

Sonefeld, O. F. 1980. Railroad-highway grade crossings: Not just an engineering problem. *Transp. Res. News* 91:7-9.

Summala, H. 1981. Driver/vehicle response latencies. *Human Factors* 23:683-92.

QUESTIONS

Answer the following questions and then compare your responses with the suggested answers at the end of this chapter.

1. How does the "worst-case" design of railroad-crossing-signal systems affect motorists?

2. What percentage of public grade crossings have only a passive crossbuck and rely totally on driver perception?

3. What are the three illusions that commonly mislead drivers and cause accidents at railroad intersections?

4. List four factors that complicate the train crew's ability to avoid danger at intersections.

ANSWERS

Correct Answers to Self-Test Exercises

Multiple-Choice

1.	a	8.	a	15.	b
2.	a	9.	c	16.	c
3.	b	10.	d	17.	d
4.	d	11.	a	18.	c
5.	a	12.	c	19.	b
6.	c	13.	b	20.	a
7.	a	14.	d		

Matching

1.	f	9.	o	
2.	i	10.	l	
3.	m	11.	b	
4.	j	12.	e	
5.	c	13.	h	
6.	g	14.	k	
7.	a	15.	d	
8.	n			

Suggested Answers to Application Exercises

1. See Figure 3-10.

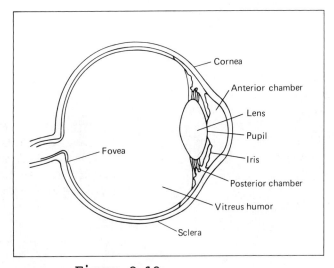

Figure 3-10

2. The cones of your eye are responsible for the ability to see fine detail and are located in the center of the retina. The periphery of the retina contains rods, which do not have the ability to see detail. You were looking at the book primarily with your rods and could not distinguish the details.

3. Since the man had finished his dinner, he probably had been in the restaurant for more than 30 minutes. Both his rods and cones had totally adapted to the darkness. When he entered the kitchen, he had to light-adapt. Light adaptation is a faster process than dark adaptation, and he probably had fully adapted to the kitchen lights by the time he completed his conversation with the chef. As he reentered the restaurant area, he had to readapt to the darkness and had difficulty seeing.

4. According to trichromatic theory, there are three mechanisms for color (one for red, one for green, and one for blue). There are specific kinds of cones which work most effectively with each of these colors. The man apparently lacks cones with visual pigments for red and for green but has cones with visual pigments for yellow.

   According to the opponent-process theory, each of the three basic colors operates in opposition to its complementary color. Red would be seen when red cells were excited and green cells inhibited. Green would be seen when green cells were excited and red cells inhibited. If red and green cones are lacking or do not perform appropriately, the result would be red-green color deficiency. Yellow-blue vision would not be affected.

5. Table 3-2

Physical Characteristics of Sound

Physical Characteristic	Perception	Measuring Unit
Intensity (height of sound waves)	Loudness	Decibels
Frequency (number of cycles or changes in the wave)	Pitch	Hertz

6. You might move your head to the left and right and try to see which ear is receiving more volume or hearing the sound first. When the sound is directly to the right or left of you it will be easiest to detect.

7. a. Law of proximity. You tend to see pairs of boats rather than an entire line.
   b. Law of closure. Even though the figure is incomplete, you tend to see a complete cube.
   c. Law of continuity. Although parts of the house are blocked by trees and shrubs, you tend to see the whole house.
   d. Law of similarity. You tend to see vertical rows of similar objects rather than horizontal rows of different objects.

8. It seems that Alice's husband is dining with another woman and did not expect to see Alice at the restaurant. Since top-down processing is based on expectations, he would have difficulty.

   He could use bottom-up

processing by checking the color of her eyes, the shape of her nose, and similar specific features. However, this is more time-consuming and might explain his initial delay in recognizing his wife.

9. You should have identified the following monocular depth cues: (1) size, (2) partial overlap, (3) texture gradients, (4) linear perspective, and (5) atmospheric perspective.

Suggested Answers to Reading Questions

1. The system is designed to accommodate the slowest-moving car and the fastest-moving train. In many cases, it is safe to cross the intersection and motorists take the risk rather than face a possible delay. Motorists who cross safely are then positively reinforced and are likely to attempt crossing again.

2. Only 50,000 of the 225,000 have active devices (22 percent). Thus 78 percent of the crossings are relying on driver perception.

3. a. Illusion of velocity and size
   b. Illusion of perspective
   c. Deceptive geometry of collision

4. a. A long distance is required for stopping.
   b. The train cannot change direction.
   c. The viewing distance is limited.
   d. There is uncertainty as to whether the crossing vehicle will stop, increase or decrease speed, or change direction.

Chapter 4:

STATES OF
CONSCIOUSNESS

CHAPTER OUTLINE

I. What is consciousness?

II. The normal state of consciousness versus altered states
   A. Characteristics of altered states of consciousness
      1. Alterations in thinking
      2. Disturbed time sense
      3. Loss of control
      4. Change in emotional expression
      5. Change in body image
      6. Perceptual distortions
      7. Change in meaning or significance
      8. Sense of the indescribable
      9. Feelings of rejuvenation
      10. Hypersuggestibility
   B. Bringing on altered states

III. Sleep
   A. Aspects of sleep
      1. Stages and kinds of sleep
         a. Non-REM sleep
         b. REM sleep
      2. Characteristics of sleep
      3. Circadian rhythms
      4. Why we sleep
         a. What causes sleep?
         b. Functions of sleep
         c. Functions of REM sleep
         d. Sleep deprivation
         e. Can we learn to sleep less?
      5. What is your sleep profile?
         a. How long do you sleep?
         b. Do you need more sleep at certain times in your life?
         c. How soundly do you sleep?
   B. Dreaming
      1. Criteria of dreaming
      2. Patterns of dreaming
         a. What is a typical night of dreaming like?
         b. Is it possible that I never dream?
         c. Why don't I remember my dreams?
         d. How much time do my dreams really take?
         e. Do objective aspects of my environment during sleep affect the
            content of my dreams?
      3. Content of dreams

        4. Why we dream
            a. Fulfilling wishes and guarding sleep
            b. Resolving personal issues and solving everyday problems
            c. Maintaining sleep during psychological activation of the brain
    C. Sleep disorders
        1. Narcolepsy
        2. Insomnia
        3. Sleep apnea
        4. Night terrors (pavor nocturnus)
        5. Nightmares

IV. Meditation

 V. Hypnosis
    A. What is hypnosis?
    B. Who can be hypnotized?
    C. How can we explain hypnosis?
        1. Split-consciousness (neodisassociation) theory
        2. Cognitive-behavioral theory
    D. Is hypnosis safe?

VI. Drugs
    A. Stimulants
        1. Caffeine
        2. Nicotine
        3. Amphetamines
        4. Cocaine
    B. Hallucinogens
        1. Marijuana
        2. LSD
        3. PCP
    C. Depressants
        1. Alcohol
        2. Sedatives and tranquilizers
        3. Narcotics

Boxes
    In the forefront: Flow states
    Psychology in your life: Sleep throughout the life span
    Psychology in your life: Suggestions for poor sleepers
    Psychology in your life: Practical applications of hypnosis

LEARNING OBJECTIVES

After you study Chapter 4, you should be able to do the tasks outlined in the following objectives.

1. Distinguish between the normal state of consciousness and altered states of consciousness.

2. Cite 10 common characteristics of altered states of consciousness.

3. Describe five methods for inducing an altered state.

4. Describe what happens during REM and NREM sleep.

5. Explain what circadian rhythms are and how they affect sleep patterns.

6. Describe several different viewpoints on the function of sleep.

7. Describe the effects of sleep deprivation.

8. Summarize three basic explanations of why people dream.

9. Describe the following sleep disorders: narcolepsy, insomnia, sleep apnea, night terrors, and nightmares.

10. Discuss the research controversy concerning meditation.

11. Define *hypnosis*.

12. Explain four current views on hypnosis.

13. Describe the following drugs or classes of drugs in terms of their effect on consciousness and their other short-term and long-term effects: caffeine, nicotine, alcohol, marijuana, amphetamines, cocaine, sedatives, hallucinogens, and narcotics.

KEY CONCEPTS

As you read Chapter 4 in your text, look for each of the following concepts. You should understand each concept.

1. Definition of Consciousness

No universally agreed-upon definition exists for the elusive phenomenon of consciousness. The working definition used in your text is *our awareness of ourselves and of the world around us.*

2. Normal State versus Altered States of Consciousness (ASCs)

When we experience a qualitative change from our normal, everyday waking state of consciousness, we are in an altered state. The concept of normality varies among individuals, cultures, and historical eras.

3. Characteristics of ASCs

Altered states of consciousness commonly involve changes in our thinking, time sense, emotional expression, body image, and perceptions. An altered state may also cause us to lose self-control, to gain real or imagined insights, to undergo experiences which we later cannot describe, and to be unusually susceptible to the suggestions of others.

4. Inducing Altered States

Altered states may be brought on by understimulation or overstimulation of the senses, mental concentration, passivity, or physiological factors.

5. Flow States

Flow states are conditions of intense concentration during which a task is performed with little or no awareness of time or external distractions. Peak performances occur during these states, along with a sense of euphoria.

6. Stages and Kinds of Sleep

There are two basic types of sleep: REM (rapid-eye-movement) sleep and NREM (non-rapid-eye-movement) sleep. These two types of sleep are distinguished by different brain-wave patterns, levels of breathing, heart rates, and dream patterns. NREM sleep occurs in four stages, in which sleep becomes progressively deeper. Once we have descended into stage 4 sleep, we climb back through stages 3, 2, and 1. At this point, we enter REM sleep. This cycle is repeated throughout the night.

7. Circadian Rhythms

These rhythms govern our sleeping-waking schedule. If permitted to set our own schedules, most of us would drift into a 25-hour day. The consequences of tampering with circadian rhythms can be severe.

8. Unanswered Questions about Sleep

Researchers do not know for certain why we sleep or what causes us to sleep. They have determined, however, that we cannot do without sleep.

9. Effects of Sleep Deprivation

For human beings, the physiological effects of moderate sleep deprivation are not dramatic. Our ability to function is also not severely impaired by lack of sleep. However, prolonged lack of sleep makes certain tasks more difficult to carry out and causes confusion, disorientation, and irritability.

10. Sleep throughout the Life Cycle

Sleep patterns change throughout life. From infancy to old age, we all experience changes in the number of hours we sleep, the percentage of time we spend in REM sleep and the various stages of NREM sleep, and the number of times we wake up each night.

11. Individual Sleep Patterns

Some people typically sleep more than other people do. Although clinical observations suggest that short sleepers tend to be "high-drive" people and long sleepers "depressed," research has not demonstrated this difference. The need for sleep varies according to life circumstances for about one out of three people. In times of stress or depression, these people need more sleep. People vary concerning the ease with which they fall asleep and stay asleep. There is some evidence to indicate that "poor" sleepers have more emotional problems than "good" sleepers have. People also vary in the soundness of their sleep. Sound sleepers are less apt to be awakened by noise or other stimuli than light sleepers are.

12. Definition of Dreaming

A *dream* is a mental experience that occurs during sleep, consisting of vivid, usually visual, and often hallucinatory images.

13. How Researchers Detect Dreaming

Four signs alert researchers to the fact that someone is dreaming: a typical brain-wave EEG of an emergent stage 1 pattern, an increase in pulse and breathing rates, the lack of body movement, and the appearance of rapid eye movements.

14. How Much Do We Dream?

We typically experience four to six periods of dreaming each night, for a total of 1 to 2 hours of dream time.

15. Why Dreams Are Forgotten

All of us dream every night, but we usually forget our dreams. Explanations for forgetting dreams include repression, distractions upon awakening, and individual differences in visual memory. Yet another explanation is that our forgetting is due to state-dependent amnesia. According to one of the most recently proposed explanations, dreaming is a way of erasing unnecessary information; consequently, dreams are meant to be forgotten.

16. Content of Dreams

Most dreams take place in familiar settings and involve people with whom we are emotionally involved. Apprehension is the most common emotion experienced in dreams. Hostile acts are found in dreams more often than friendly acts.

17. Purpose of Dreaming

While we do not have conclusive evidence to explain why we dream, many explanations have been proposed. Sigmund Freud felt that dreams allow us to express repressed wishes and that they also guard our sleep. Alfred Adler thought that dreams help us work out solutions to real-life problems. Carl Jung believed that dreams make us aware of suppressed aspects of ourselves. A somewhat more matter-of-fact view of dreams is that they provide opportunities to rehearse things we know we will be doing in the future. Finally, a physiological view of dreaming suggests that the content of our dreams is determined by electrical activity in the brain and has no particular significance. According to this view, dreaming helps us to maintain sleep.

18. Narcolepsy

People suffering from this sleep disorder have an uncontrollable need to sleep for brief periods, usually during the day. These experiences are accompanied by loss of muscle tone and sometimes by hallucinations.

19. Insomnia

Insomniacs have trouble getting to sleep or staying asleep. There is no simple cure for insomnia, which has a wide variety of causes, ranging from poor health to emotional problems.

20. Sleep Apnea

This disorder is characterized by loud snoring, poor sleep at night, extreme sleepiness during the day, and periods when breathing stops during sleep. Treatment may include a surgical opening of the windpipe that can be closed during the day.

21. Night Terrors

This disorder, which is common among young children, involves episodes in which a child wakes up suddenly in panic but goes quickly back to sleep. These episodes usually go away without treatment of any kind.

22. Nightmares

If a child has persistent nightmares that cause daytime anxiety, he or she may be under too much stress. Repetitive themes in nightmares may be related to a specific problem the dreamer is having difficulty solving.

23. Meditation

Currently, there is no precise definition of the meditative state. A variety of techniques are used in meditating. The question of therapeutic benefits is a controversial one.

24. Definition of Hypnosis

Because it has been difficult to identify physiological differences between hypnotized and unhypnotized people, the definition of hypnosis is controversial. Your text defines hypnosis as a *procedure practiced by a person with special skills who is able to induce in a subject a condition of heightened suggestivity in which the subject's perceptions have changed along lines suggested by the practitioner.*

25. Hypnotizability

About 5 to 10 percent of the population cannot be hypnotized at all; about 15 percent can be hypnotized very easily. Physiological, psychological, and genetic differences may all relate to the fact that some people are highly hypnotizable.

26. Two Views on Hypnosis

According to neodisassociation theory, various aspects of a person's consciousness may become separated under hypnosis so that the person is functioning on more than one level of awareness. Cognitive-behavioral theorists believe that the hypnotic state depends on a subject's willingness to think or imagine along the lines suggested by the hypnotist.

27. Uses of Hypnosis

Hypnosis has been used to treat a variety of ailments. The most successful use of hypnosis has been in the treatment of pain. Hypnosis has also been used on witnesses to crimes to help them remember the incidents they have seen. However, this is a highly controversial practice because hypnosis may contaminate memory.

28. Is Hypnosis Safe?

The U.S. Department of Health and Human Services has listed hypnosis as a potentially stressful procedure, but the results of one research study indicated that hypnosis was no more stressful to college students than many of their ordinary daily activities.

29. Widespread Use of Drugs

Most adults regularly take one or more psychoactive, or mind-altering, drugs. These drugs range from caffeine and nicotine to LSD and heroin.

30. Caffeine

Caffeine is a commonly ingested stimulant which raises heart rate, breathing rate, and blood pressure. In large doses, it can cause a variety of ailments, ranging from restlessness to headaches or diarrhea.

31. Nicotine

Nicotine, which is contained in cigarettes, cigars, and pipe tobacco, is an addictive stimulant which increases blood pressure and heart rate. Cigarette smoking is the major cause of death from many types of cancer.

32. Amphetamines

Amphetamines are strong stimulants. People may take amphetamines to increase their powers of concentration, to stay awake, to feel energetic, to suppress hunger, or simply to feel good. Abuse of amphetamines can lead to weight loss and malnutrition, pain in muscles and joints, a feeling of paralysis, and amphetamine psychosis.

33. Cocaine

The use of cocaine has increased alarmingly in recent years, along with related medical emergencies and deaths. Acting on the central nervous system, cocaine produces feelings of euphoria and excitement. While users may not become addicted physically, they can become addicted psychologically.

34. Marijuana

The mind-altering component of marijuana is THC. The common short-term effects of smoking marijuana include increased heart rate and sometimes blood pressure, reddened eyes, dry mouth and throat, altered sense of time, and mood changes. The long-term effects of smoking marijuana are unknown. Marijuana has several therapeutic uses.

35. LSD (Lysergic Acid Diethylamide)

LSD is a hallucinogen which some people take to enhance their creativity or to achieve spiritual visions. Negative effects of LSD may include distressing flashbacks and the impairment of memory, attention span, and ability to think abstractly. Heavy users may also suffer organic brain damage.

36. PCP (Phencyclidine)

PCP is a hallucinogen which is also a stimulant, a depressant, and a painkiller. It is used, illegally, for mood elevation, relaxation, stimulation, and heightened sensitivity. Its negative effects may include memory and speech problems, depression, anxiety, paranoia, violent behavior, hallucinations, convulsions, depersonalization, poor coordination, numbness, psychosis, and even death.

37. Alcohol

Alcohol is a central-nervous-system depressant with varying effects. Small amounts of alcohol may either tranquilize or stimulate, but large amounts tranquilize most people. In sufficient quantity, alcohol dulls sensation, impairs judgment, memory, and muscular coordination, and eventually causes unconsciousness. Uncontrolled or insufficiently controlled drinking is a problem for about 10 million Americans; thus abuse of alcohol is the country's number 1 drug problem.

38. Sedatives and Tranquilizers

Sedatives and tranquilizers have a calming effect and bring on sleep. Sedatives may be taken to counteract the effects of amphetamines or to relieve anxiety. Abuse can impair memory and judgment and lead to coma or even death.

39. Heroin and Other Narcotics

Narcotics are depressants which relieve pain and induce sleep. Heroin, a highly addictive narcotic, produces feelings of euphoria, contentment, and safety. When heroin addicts are deprived of the drug, they suffer severe withdrawal symptoms. Treatment of heroin addiction may include substituting a less harmful narcotic, methadone, or providing the addict with group therapy and peer support in a residential treatment center.

TERMS TO KNOW

Define each of the terms listed. You can check your definitions in the text Glossary or on the text pages listed in parentheses.

Consciousness   (p. 119)   Narcolepsy   (p. 135)

Altered state of   Insomnia   (p. 135)
consciousness (ASC)   (p. 119)

Electroencephalograph (EEG)   (p. 122)   Sleep apnea   (p. 136)

Electromyograph   (p. 123)   Night terrors   (p. 137)

Electrooculograph   (p. 123)   Nightmares   (p. 137)

REM sleep   (p. 123)   Tryptophan   (p. 137)

NREM sleep   (p. 123)   Meditation   (p. 138)

Circadian rhythms   (p. 126)   Transcendental meditation   (p. 138)

REM rebound   (p. 127)   Mantra   (p. 138)

Hypnosis   (p. 139)   Caffeine   (p. 144)

Neodisassociation theory of   Nicotine   (p. 144)
hypnosis   (p. 140)

Cognitive-behavioral theory   Amphetamines   (p. 145)
of hypnosis   (p. 141)

Drug   (p. 143)   Cocaine   (p. 145)

Drug abuse   (p. 143)   Hallucinogens   (p. 147)

Physiological dependence   (p. 143)   Marijuana   (p. 147)

Psychoactive   (p. 143)   LSD   (p. 148)

Psychological dependence   (p. 144)   PCP   (p. 148)

Stimulant   (p. 144)   Alcohol   (p. 149)

Sedatives and tranquilizers   (p. 149)

Narcotics   (p. 152)

Opium   (p. 152)

Morphine   (p. 152)

Heroin   (p. 152)

Methadone   (p. 152)

SELF-TEST

Multiple-Choice

Choose the one best response to each question. An answer key is provided at the end of this chapter.

1. According to the psychologist John B. Watson and his followers, the study of psychology is scientific only if it focuses on which of the following?

   a. Consciousness
   b. "The perception of what passes in a man's own mind."
   c. Observable, measurable behaviors
   d. Consciousness and behavior

2. Which of the following conditions characterizes an altered state of consciousness?

   a. Being aware of mental functions that do not operate in your usual state
   b. Seeing things that you usually do not perceive
   c. Being more preoccupied than usual with internal sensations
   d. All of the above

3. Imagine that you experience varying degrees of change in concentrating, paying attention, remembering, and exercising judgment. Which of the following ASC characteristics would apply to you?

   a. Body image change
   b. Disturbed time sense
   c. Loss of control
   d. Alterations in thinking

4. Reading, writing, and problem solving are examples of which of the following methods of inducing altered states of consciousness?

   a. Repetition
   b. Mental concentration
   c. Barrage of stimulation
   d. Passivity

5. Flow states are typically characterized by which of the following conditions?

   a. Rapid eye movements
   b. Intense concentration
   c. Drowsiness
   d. Exhaustion

6. What does the electroencephalograph measure?

    a. Eye movements
    b. Pulse
    c. Muscle movements
    d. Brain waves

7. In what stage of sleep are we most likely to dream?

    a. REM sleep
    b. Stage 1
    c. Stage 3
    d. Stage 4

8. The amount of sleep we need during a typical day is governed by which of the following?

    a. Alpha rhythms
    b. Wave frequency
    c. Beta rhythms
    d. Circadian rhythms

9. Which of the following conditions resulted from the Bonnet (1985) sleep study involving repeated awakenings?

    a. Increase in sleep drunkenness
    b. Increase in stage 3 sleep
    c. Increase in body movement
    d. Decrease in stage 1 sleep

10. When freed from the constraints of schedules and alarm clocks, most humans drift into a day containing how many hours?

    a. 23
    b. 28
    c. 25
    d. 24

11. Why do we sleep?

    a. Research on this question is still inconclusive.
    b. To restore ourselves psychologically

    c. To restore ourselves physiologically
    d. To prevent exhaustion

12. If you had a classmate who often fell asleep while eating lunch or while giving oral reports, he or she might be suffering from which of the following sleep disorders?

    a. Sleep apnea
    b. Narcolepsy
    c. Pavor nocturnus
    d. REM rebound

13. If you have difficulty getting to sleep and staying asleep, which of the following suggestions would the sleep experts most likely make?

    a. Drink a cup of hot chocolate before bedtime.
    b. Vary your bedtime schedule.
    c. Eat a small bowl of spaghetti before bedtime.
    d. Drink a bottle of wine before bedtime.

14. If you had a dream that you were swimming naked up and down the watery aisles of a supermarket, which of the following explanations would be most accurate?

    a. You were fulfilling a repressed wish.
    b. You were "rehearsing" for a future anxiety-laden event.
    c. Your brain was discharging random bursts of electrical activity.
    d. Research on this question is still inconclusive.

15. Adults who are easily hypnotized usually demonstrate which of the following psychological characteristics?

    a. They are able to set aside ordinary reality.
    b. They seldom engaged in fantasy as children.

c. They are more likely to suffer from serious psychiatric disturbances.

d. They tend to be gullible.

16. Which of the following reflects the American Medical Association's position on the use of hypnosis in criminal trials?

a. It recommends use of hypnosis in court only if a skilled psychiatrist is involved.

b. It recommends hypnosis in the investigative stages only.

c. It believes that hypnosis should not be used to produce investigative leads.

d. It has declined to take a position on such a controversial issue.

17. Assume that you are a hypnotist and want to specialize in treatments that have a fair probability of success. Which of the following ailments would you logically choose?

a. Alcoholism
b. Obesity
c. Cigarette dependence
d. Pain

18. If you wanted to relieve stress without resorting to drugs, you could try which of the following?

a. Smoke a few cigarettes.
b. Meditate.
c. Drink a few beers.
d. Drink a cup of warm tea.

19. Which of the following drugs is used to treat such ailments as asthma, glaucoma (eye disorder), seizures, and the nauseating side effects of chemotherapy?

a. Methadone
b. Morphine
c. Amphetamines
d. Marijuana

20. This country's number 1 drug problem is which of the following?

a. Nicotine
b. Alcohol
c. Caffeine
d. Amphetamines

21. If you had a hyperactive child, which of the following drugs would your doctor probably prescribe to lengthen attention span and control restlessness?

a. Caffeine
b. Barbiturates
c. Amphetamines
d. Tranquilizers

22. Which of the following drugs is used heavily by many professionals who do not fit the typical profile of drug abusers?

a. Methadone
b. Cocaine
c. Morphine
d. Heroin

23. Imagine that you have a friend who hasn't used any drugs for over a year but suddenly, without injesting anything, is seized with tremors, chills, and nausea. Vivid images of a scolding at the hands of a third-grade teacher have driven your friend cowering into a corner. What drug is capable of triggering such delayed effects?

a. Amphetamine
b. STP
c. LSD
d. Cocaine

24. Over the past 10 years, what has been the pattern of marijuana use among high school seniors?

a. The percentage of smokers has increased.

b. The percentage of smokers has remained relatively constant.

c. The percentage of smokers has decreased.

d. Conflicting data leave the question unresolved.

25. Narcotics fall under which of the following classifications?

    a. Depressants
    b. Hallucinogens
    c. Stimulants
    d. Sedatives

Matching

Match each name in column A with a descriptive phrase in column B.

Column A	Column B
_____ 1. Heroin	a. Taken by dieters to suppress the appetite
_____ 2. Barbiturates	b. Increasingly used illicit drug that acts on the central nervous system to produce feelings of euphoria and excitement
_____ 3. Hallucinogens	c. Central-nervous-system depressant that is this country's number 1 drug problem
_____ 4. Cocaine	d. Causes physical addiction with severe withdrawal symptoms within 12 to 16 hours after the last dose; accounts for 90 percent of narcotic abuse in the United States
_____ 5. PCP	e. Noted for the imaginary visual, auditory, and tactile sensations produced
_____ 6. Methadone	f. The most dangerous aspect of this street drug is its utter unpredictability.
_____ 7. Morphine	g. Painkiller frequently administered to injured soldiers in the Civil War and World War I
_____ 8. Alcohol	h. Overdoses of this kind of drug account for nearly one-third of accidental drug-related deaths—particularly dangerous when taken with alcohol.
_____ 9. Opium	i. Early in this century, this pain reliever was a common ingredient in over-the-counter medicines for coughs, diarrhea, and numerous other ailments.
_____ 10. Amphetamines	j. Addictive narcotic used to treat prior addiction to heroin

APPLICATION EXERCISES

These application exercises will test your understanding of and ability to apply the material you have read in your text. Suggested answers are provided at the end of the chapter so that you can check your responses.

1. Your text describes 10 characteristics which are common to many altered states of consciousness. After reviewing these characteristics, see if you can identify how five of them are illustrated in the scenario which follows.

    Chris and her friend Beth have been smoking marijuana. When the phone rings, Chris jumps up from her chair, amazed at the loudness of the ring. It's Chris's boyfriend on the phone. He says that he'll be late in coming over because he has to meet a bus.

    "Meet a bus?" Chris says in a perplexed tone of voice. "That's really weird." Chris imagines that her boyfriend is going to be introduced to a bus.

    Chris and Beth decide to watch the late news on television. The local weather reporter is just announcing that tomorrow will be hot and humid. The two young women look at each other and burst out laughing. During the rest of the forecast, they laugh until their sides hurt. Following the newscast, they develop a severe case of the "munchies." They put some frozen chocolate-chip cookies into the oven and go back to the living room to play an album while the cookies bake. The refrain of the first song on the album is "I'm so ordinary, I'm so ordinary." Beth excitedly tells Chris to turn down the volume.

    "Chris, something has suddenly become clear to me. I've found the key to my identity. I feel that for the first time in my life I know what I am—I'm ordinary!"

    Chris interrupts Beth's monologue when she jumps up screaming, "The cookies—they were supposed to bake for 10 minutes. They must have been in for half an hour."

    When they run to the kitchen and open the oven door, they are amazed to see that the cookies aren't even brown. The clock on the wall indicates that they've been baking for only 2 minutes.

    Characteristics illustrated _____
    _____
    _____
    _____
    _____
    _____
    _____
    _____
    _____
    _____

2. There are a variety of ways in which an altered state of consciousness can be induced. Explain why the persons described in the following situations might experience an altered state of consciousness.

    a. A mathematician has been working on a new proof for 8 hours without taking a break. _____
    _____
    _____

    b. A fraternity member has been alternately drinking beer and coffee for 48 hours as his fraternity attempts to set the campus record for the longest party. _____
    _____
    _____

c. A teenager is sitting in the third row at a heavy-metal concert. _____ _____

d. A woman has been continuously floating on her back in a swimming pool for 30 minutes. _____ _____

e. A man has been driving alone for 6 hours on an interstate highway through the desert. _____ _____ _____

3. Imagine that you are a sleep expert who gives advice to poor sleepers. The following people come to you for your expert opinion, telling you what they generally do to ensure a good night's sleep. Indicate for each case whether the person is practicing a good sleep habit or a poor sleep habit, and explain your reasoning.

Case a. My wife and I share a bottle of white wine every night before we retire.
____ Good habit ____ Poor habit

Why? _____ _____

Case b. I jog just before going to bed each night.
____ Good habit ____ Poor habit

Why? _____ _____

Case c. I eat a handful of chocolate kisses before I go to bed.

____ Good habit ____ Bad habit

Why? _____ _____

Case d. I drink a small vanilla milkshake late at night.

____ Good habit ____ Bad habit

Why? _____ _____

Case e. I swim or play tennis every day before lunch.

____ Good habit ____ Bad habit

Why? _____ _____

4. Dream researchers have learned a great deal about dreaming. They have determined not only when we dream and how often but also what we typically dream about. On the basis of what you have read about the usual content of dreams, indicate which member of the following pairs of dreams contains the most typical dream content.

a. ____ Dream in which the setting is someone's living room *or*
   ____ Dream which is set on an exotic tropical island

b. ____ Dream in which you are alone *or*
   ____ Dream involving other people

c. ____ Dream about your father *or*
   ____ Dream about your dentist

d. ____ Dream about going to a party *or*
   ____ Dream about doing laundry

e. ____ Dream in which you float up to receive an award *or*
   ____ Dream in which you walk up to receive an award

f. ____ Dream in which you have a
friendly chat with a
cabdriver *or*
____ Dream in which you yell at
a cabdriver

5. Assume that a hypnotist suggests to
a 30-year-old hypnotized man that
he is only 5 years old. A large
tricycle is brought forward and the
subject is told he can ride it if
he wishes. The subject climbs onto
the tricycle and happily speeds
around the room. Explain this
episode from the following points
of view on hypnosis.

a. Neodisassociation theory _____

_____
_____
_____
_____

b. Cognitive-behavioral theory ___

_____
_____
_____
_____

6. Your text describes some important
characteristics of a number of
psychoactive drugs. After reviewing
these characteristics, identify the
drug indicated in each of the
following descriptions.

a. This drug is sometimes thought
of as a stimulant, but it is
actually a central-nervous-
system depressant. Large amounts
of this drug interfere with many
human functions, including the
ability to exercise good
judgment.

Drug indicated _____

b. This drug is often used to
attain feelings of euphoria and
heightened powers of perception.
While it is not physically
addictive, some users develop a
psychological dependence on it.
Its mind-altering component is
THC.

Drug indicated _____

c. One out of every four people
over the age of 17 uses this
drug six or more times a day.
Most use it for mental or
physical stimulation. In large
doses it can cause headaches,
diarrhea, and a variety of other
maladies.

Drug indicated _____

d. This drug is a hallucinogen
taken by some people who believe
it will increase their
creativity. It may produce
organic brain damage in some
heavy users. In the 1950s it was
used in psychotherapy, but its
legal use was subsequently
restricted.

Drug indicated _____

e. This drug is an expensive and
fashionable stimulant which
produces feelings of euphoria
and excitement. Small doses may
lead to sudden death. It is not
physically addictive, but users
become psychologically dependent
on it.

Drug indicated _____

READING EXERCISE

Recent research at the NASA space laboratories is uncovering some surprising information regarding the role of our circadian rhythms. In the following article from *Space World,* Isabel S. Abrams describes some of these findings.

Beyond Night and Day

When Shuttle astronauts orbit the Earth, sunrise is quickly followed by sunset, with a new day dawning every 90 minutes. The human body, though, operates naturally on a circadian rhythm synchronized to the Earth's 24-hour cycle of daylight and darkness. Does a 90-minute cycle cause sleepiness and poor astronaut performance? How do circadian rhythms affect astronaut health? NASA is trying to find out.

Dr. Charles Winget, a research scientist in the Biomedical Research Division at NASA's Ames Research Center outside San Francisco, is conducting biological rhythm studies in a simulated space environment to discover what might happen to astronauts during long missions in space.

Like all known living things, human beings are adapted to the 24-hour light-dark cycle. They are diurnal--more active in daytime, when body temperature and most body functions peak. These peaks and troughs in body rhythms are controlled internally, but they are synchronized to cues in the environment. As a result, shift workers who switch from daylight to nighttime hours and travelers who cross many time zones suffer desynchronization, a condition in which body timing is out of synchrony with the environment. According to Winget, this desynchrony or jet lag can cause problems for astronauts orbiting the Earth.

To minimize desynchrony on Space Shuttle missions, NASA tries to keep the astronauts on Houston time during a

Reprinted from *Space World* Magazine. Copyright 1986 by the author, Isabel S. Abrams.

space flight. Since Houston is where mission control is located and where the Shuttle crew normally work and live, things go easier for both the ground technicians and the astronauts. But something usually happens during a mission that requires the crew to depart from the planned work-rest schedule, and this is when circadian rhythms are disrupted.

Judging from what happens to shift workers, Winget predicts the main problem for astronauts would probably be loss of sleep. They might also develop gastrointestinal problems such as diarrhea, constipation or malaise. At a much later date, other problems such as ulcers might show up. Some astronauts deal with the jet lag quickly and resynchronize their scheduling. Others take longer.

To find out what might happen in orbit, Winget simulated weightlessness by doing biological rhythm studies using subjects on complete bedrest. Some of his bedrest experiments ran as long as 56 days, but Winget found seven to nine days were quite adequate for most tests. The Soviets have done bedrest studies up to 105 days.

During the studies, the bedridden subjects had their heads tilted down at an angle of five to nine degrees to duplicate the fullness of the head that astronauts experience in microgravity. Because fluids have a tendency to move to the upper part of the torso in weightlessness, "Cardiovascular deconditioning, or pooling of the blood in the upper torso, is one of the major problems of space flight," explains Winget.

The studies on bedrest patients encompassed psychological and performance tests as well as physiological data. "Virtually every body function shows a circadian rhythm," says Winget. In fact, he says, high blood pressure is being redefined based on the findings in circadian rhythm experiments. "Systolic or diastolic blood pressure taken at one time of day may be reported as normal blood pressure. But that is not necessarily true. It depends on what time of day the blood pressure reading was taken, whether you are male or female, whether you've just come in from the East Coast or West Coast, or whether you are a shift worker. Because there are many parameters that affect the circadian rhythms, there is no such thing as a mean or correct blood pressure. It will vary throughout the day."

Winget believes that knowledge of biological rhythms should cause physicians to redefine other standards as well—heartbeat, respiration and other body functions—by taking into consideration the daily fluctuations of diurnal rhythms.

Because body systems are "up" during daylight hours and "down" at night, space flight planners take the biological clock into consideration. Shuttle crew schedules are designed so astronauts can operate at peak performance. However, if a task needs to be done in the middle of the night, astronauts are trained—and highly motivated—to do it.

Winget found that in both men and women, most body functions peak at the body temperature peak, between 2:00 and 4:00 p.m. The actual wave form—the peaks and valleys in circadian rhythms—appear the same in men and women. Nevertheless, Winget found circadian rhythms do vary according to gender. In women, the heart rate rhythm at any time of day is always higher than it is for men. The same is true of body temperature and many other physiological functions. Women, for example, have a body temperature minimum very early in the morning and

so do men. "But," says Winget, "the male low is lower than the female low, and the female high is higher than the male high."

Both men and women are more active during daylight than darkness. But early risers, or larks, have different body rhythms from night owls. "Larks and owls can be either male or female," says Winget. "A lark peaks earlier in the day. Owls peak later."

Thus far, early bird and night owl astronauts have worked well together on the Space Shuttle, which is to be expected because astronauts are highly trained and the missions have been relatively short. "Of course, we do have the problem of space sickness, which is somewhat similar to motion sickness," says Winget. "We can't say that is due to jet lag or internal desynchronization. Thus far, we've been up relatively short periods of time, but as we move on to the next era of space exploration, the Space Station, we will be up 90 days or more. Then we will have to make circadian rhythms more of a consideration."

During the biological rhythm experiments, Winget found that about 60 percent of the group seemed to have fairly stable circadian rhythms. He also found that certain individuals affect others' rhythms. "We call it social entrainment, and we don't know why it happens," he says. "It would be very interesting to figure out why one person either slows down or speeds up another's rhythms. Then we could isolate the compound, or whatever it is, and use it to treat such things as jet lag and shift work problems."

The least affected personalities when it comes to entrainment are people who rise early in the morning. "Larks are usually locked into their circadian rhythm, so they are pretty stable and have trouble adjusting to shift work," says Winget. "Owls are inclined to have more labile rhythms and adjust to shift work more easily."

Would an individual who influences other people's biological rhythms have a more dominating personality? "Probably. But this is not easy to predict ahead of time," says Winget. "When we do studies involving social psychology, we may be able to predict what personality type would be detrimental to work-rest scheduling during space missions."

People with circadian desynchrony or jet lag seem to be at risk for a variety of performance problems. Although Shuttle astronauts are kept on Houston time, their 90-minute days might cause them to become tired and vulnerable to accidents, depression, and errors. Astronauts, however, are a very select group, so Winget believes they are probably less affected than the average population.

When shift workers go from one shift to the other there is more absenteeism, more errors in the work they do, and more friction between individuals on the job. According to Winget, a change from standard time to daylight savings time, or back again, causes an increase in automobile accidents, absenteeism on the job and in schools, and more errors on tests given in schools. After the time shift, a high percentage of people don't sleep as well for three or four days. Even a one hour time change is therefore significant.

If desynchronization affects the immune system, this would cause astronauts to be susceptible to infections. The Soviets have reported an increase in colds and viral infections in cosmonauts. Many people catch cold after they fly across time zones, but this may be attributable to the dry atmosphere of an airplane, which could cause mucus membranes in nasal passages to dry out and make people more susceptible to infection. It is not clear whether susceptibility to infection is brought on by desynchronization.

To provide greater understanding of biological rhythms, plants have been studied in space. "We've found changes in circadian periods in plants that orbit the Earth," says Winget. "Plant and animal research can aid us in finding out the basic mechanisms of the bioclock. Then, presumably, we would have spinoffs into agriculture and even to human research."

Winget's research on circadian rhythms has brought quite a few surprises. When the bedrest experiments began, the scientists thought that getting up and lying down set the rhythms. "It was a surprise that it wasn't that way," says Winget. It was clear that circadian rhythms were intrinsic, controlled by a biological clock within the body rather than being set by environmental cues. Winget was surprised about the impact of social interaction, and at just how important light-dark cycles are for humans--in performance, fatigue and sleep disorders, as well as in psychological disorders such as depression. "The picture is very complicated, but light and circadian rhythms seem to be the basis for most physiological phenomena."

"It takes about 16 hours of light and 8 hours of darkness for the biological clock to work at its optimum," claims Winget. "Not only that, it takes a minimum light intensity and a certain spectrum of light. Yellow light won't do. You need a total spectrum of colors such as white light, or sunlight," he says. "In fact, if you are depressed, illuminating your home or office with broad spectrum lights may help. Or you can take a walk in the sunshine."

Sunlight, or any other light, is received mainly through the eyes, but also through the skull. The light has an effect on the pineal gland which, in turn, affects the secretion of melatonin, a chemical involved in fatigue and sleep. In other words, the number of hours of daylight and darkness affect the amount of melatonin and, therefore, the daily wake-sleep cycle.

Understanding the effects of circadian rhythms can help prevent sleepiness in orbit. It can also lead to down-to-Earth medical benefits. "By knowing when to give a drug, we will achieve the same effect from a lower dose of a pharmacological compound," says Winget. "Treatment of certain kinds of mental disorders like schizophrenia or depression will be done by regulating the light-dark cycles. These spinoffs are probably even more significant than what we talk of in the space program."

QUESTIONS

Answer the following questions and then compare your responses with the suggested answers at the end of this chapter.

1. What body functions seem to be affected by our daily biological rhythms?

2. What is social entrainment?

3. Explain the relationship between light and our circadian rhythms.

ANSWERS

Correct Answers to Self-Test Exercises

Multiple-Choice

1. c	10. c	18. b			
2. d	11. a	19. d			
3. d	12. b	20. b			
4. b	13. c	21. c			
5. b	14. d	22. b			
6. d	15. b	23. c			
7. a	16. b	24. c			
8. d	17. d	25. a			
9. a					

Matching

1. d	6. j
2. h	7. g
3. e	8. c
4. b	9. i
5. f	10. a

Suggested Answers to Application Exercises

1. The five characteristics illustrated in the scenario are as follows:

   Perceptual distortion. The ring of the phone sounds much louder to Chris than usual.

   Alterations in thinking. Chris is confused by her boyfriend's simple assertion that he is going to meet a bus.

   Change in emotional expression. Chris and Beth find an ordinary weather forecast hilariously funny.

   Change in meaning or significance. Beth thinks she has attained a profound insight concerning her own identity when she comes to the conclusion that she is ordinary.

   Disturbed time sense. Chris thinks that the cookies have been baking for 30 minutes when, in fact, they've been in the oven for only 2 minutes.

2. a. The intense mental concentration required to work on a mathematical proof for 8 hours could conceivably induce an altered state of consciousness.
   b. The physiological changes which would be brought about by consuming large amounts of beer and coffee over a 48-hour period without sleep would undoubtedly produce an altered state of consciousness.
   c. The barrage of stimulation at a heavy-metal concert, which would probably include deafening music, dazzling lights, and a frenzied crowd, might produce an altered state of consciousness.
   d. The passivity and muscular relaxation involved in floating around a swimming pool for an extended period of time could result in an altered state of consciousness.
   e. The monotony, restricted movement, and solitude which would characterize a long drive through the desert on an interstate highway might alter a person's consciousness.

3. Case a. This is a poor habit. While drinking a large quantity of white wine may help the man fall asleep, he is likely to wake up when the sedating effect of the wine wears off.

   Case b. Jogging just before bedtime is a poor habit. This person should avoid stimulating activities like jogging at this time of night.

   Case c. This is a poor habit. Chocolate contains the stimulant caffeine.

   Case d. Drinking a vanilla milkshake late at night is a good habit as far as going to sleep is concerned. (Let's hope the person is not on a diet!) Milk, sweets, pasta, bread, and rice all contain an ingredient which induces sleep.

   Case e. This is a good habit. Exercise such as swimming or playing tennis early in the day helps a person sleep well at night.

4. a. Dream in which the setting is someone's living room
   b. Dream involving other people
   c. Dream about your father
   d. Dream about going to a party
   e. Dream in which you walk up to receive an award
   f. Dream in which you yell at a cabdriver

5. a. Neodisassociation theory would explain this episode in terms of the subject's ability to function on more than one level of awareness. The hypnosis is allowing the subject to focus his attention entirely on the hypnotic suggestion that he is only 5 years old. The part of his consciousness which is aware that he is, in fact, a grown man has become separated or dissociated.
    b. Cognitive-behavioral theorists would point out that the subject is not doing anything that an unhypnotized person could not do. The subject in this study is simply demonstrating his readiness to think and act imaginatively along the lines suggested by the hypnotist.

6. a. Alcohol
    b. Marijuana
    c. Caffeine
    d. LSD
    e. Cocaine

Suggested Answers to Reading Questions

1. According to studies of bedridden patients, all our body functions are influenced by circadian rhythms. Blood pressure, for example, depends on the time of day the reading is taken. Heartbeat and respiration also fluctuate with our biological clock.

2. Winget's experiments reveal that people are capable of speeding up or slowing down the circadian rhythms of others. This phenomenon is referred to as *social entrainment*.

3. The light-dark cycles were found to have a strong impact on performance, fatigue, sleep disorders, and psychological disorders. In order for our natural rhythms to function most effectively, we need about 16 hours of light and 8 hours of darkness each day. Depression can be related to the amount of light one receives.

Chapter 5:

LEARNING

CHAPTER OUTLINE

I. What is learning?

II. Associative learning
    A. Classical conditioning
        1. Pavlov and his dogs
        2. Can people be conditioned?
            a. Little Albert
            b. Overcoming fears
    B. Operant conditioning
        1. Thorndike: His cats and his law of effect
        2. Skinner: Principles derived from the "Skinner box"
        3. A note on animal studies
        4. Aspects of operant conditioning
            a. Reinforcement
                (1) Timing of reinforcement
                (2) Schedules of reinforcement
            b. Superstitious behavior
            c. Shaping
            d. Biological influences on learning
            e. Generalization and discrimination
            f. Extinction
            g. Spontaneous recovery
            h. Punishment
                (1) How punishment works--or doesn't work
                (2) Problems with punishment

III. Cognitive perspectives on learning
    A. Thought processes in associative learning
    B. Latent learning
    C. Cognitive maps
    D. Observational learning
        1. How observational learning occurs
        2. Self-reinforcement

IV. Practical insights into learning
    A. Biofeedback
        1. What biofeedback does
        2. Evaluating biofeedback
    B. Learned helplessness
        1. What is learned helplessness?
        2. Preventing learned helplessness

Boxes
    In the forefront: The medical potential of classical conditioning
    In the forefront: Using operant conditioning to encourage use of seat belts
    Psychology in your life: How to teach an animal

LEARNING OBJECTIVES

After you study Chapter 5, you should be able to do the tasks outlined in the following objectives.

1. Define learning.

2. Describe classical conditioning.

3. Explain the process of extinction.

4. Describe operant conditioning.

5. Explain how the four basic schedules of partial reinforcement affect rate of response and resistance to extinction.

6. Describe the technique of shaping.

7. Explain how the phenomena of generalization and discrimination apply to operant as well as classical conditioning.

8. Describe three factors that determine the effectiveness of punishment.

9. Discuss problems with the use of punishment.

10. Describe latent learning.

11. Describe observational learning.

12. Define biofeedback and explain why it is difficult to evaluate its effectiveness.

13. Discuss ways of preventing learned helplessness.

KEY CONCEPTS

As you read Chapter 5 in your text, look for each of the following concepts. You should understand each concept.

1. Definition of Learning

Learning is often, but not always, reflected in a relatively permanent change in behavior. Instinct, reflexes, and abilities and skills which result from maturation are not learned.

2. Classical Conditioning

Classical conditioning is a type of associative learning in which an organism learns to make a reflex response to some stimulus that was previously neutral. This type of learning occurs when an unconditioned stimulus is repeatedly paired with a neutral stimulus.

3. Timing in Classical Conditioning

Conditioning is affected by the period of time between the presentation of the neutral stimulus and the presentation of the unconditioned stimulus. Generally, the most effective time to present the neutral stimulus is just before and overlapping with the presentation of the unconditioned stimulus.

4. Extinction and Spontaneous Recovery

After classical conditioning has taken place, if the conditioned stimulus is repeatedly presented without the unconditioned stimulus, the organism will usually stop making the conditioned response. However, the organism may begin making the conditioned response at some later time without having had any new conditioning trials.

5. Generalization and Discrimination

After being conditioned to respond to one stimulus, an organism may make the same response to similar stimuli. On the other hand, an organism may also learn to distinguish between very similar stimuli, responding to one but not the other.

6. Psychotherapeutic Use of Classical Conditioning

Anxieties may be learned. Classical conditioning may be used to help a person overcome phobias (irrational fears) and habits like excessive drinking or smoking.

7. Operant Conditioning

Like classical conditioning, operant conditioning is a type of associative learning. In operant conditioning, positive or negative reinforcement following a certain behavior influences the likelihood that the behavior will occur again.

8. Schedules of Reinforcement

In operant conditioning, reinforcement can be given according to different schedules or patterns. Organisms respond differently to the various patterns of reinforcement.

9. Shaping

The technique of shaping is used to teach animals or people to make responses that they have never made before. In animals, however, instinctive behavior is sometimes more powerful than learned behavior.

10. Generalization and Discrimination in Operant Conditioning

The phenomena of generalization and discrimination apply to operant as well as classical conditioning. Generalization allows organisms to benefit from prior learning. Discrimination makes it possible for organisms to respond appropriately to different stimuli.

11. Punishment

Punishment attempts to decrease the tendency to behave in a certain way. Factors such as timing, consistency, and the availability of an alternative reinforced response determine the effectiveness of punishment.

12. Cognitive Perspectives on Learning

Cognitive psychologists view learning as more than the result of external forces acting on an organism. They view learning as being an internal, cognitive process as well.

13. Latent Learning

Learning is not always reflected in performance. An organism may not display what it has learned until it has a purpose for doing so.

14. Observational Learning

Learning based on the observation and imitation of models is called *observational learning.* In other words, we do not have to learn everything through direct experience. Psychologists who emphasize the role of observation are adherents of social-learning theory.

15. Controlling Our Own Behavior

From the cognitive point of view people can and, to some extent, do control their own behavior. We develop new ways of behaving by rewarding and punishing ourselves.

16. Biofeedback

Biofeedback helps people monitor their body signals with the aim of controlling various bodily processes. While its effectiveness is debatable, it does heighten consciousness in stressful situations and aids in the reduction of tension.

17. Learned Helplessness

Learned helplessness is a condition that has been observed in both animals and people. It is the result of being unable to control important events in one's environment.

TERMS TO KNOW

Define each of the terms listed. You can check your definitions in the text Glossary or on the text pages listed in parentheses.

Instinct	(p. 159)
Reflex	(p. 159)
Learning	(p. 159)
Maturation	(p. 159)
Habituation	(p. 160)
Associative learning	(p. 160)
Cognitive learning	(p. 160)
Classical (Pavlovian) conditioning	(p. 160)
Neutral stimulus	(p. 160)

Conditioned stimulus (CS) (p. 160)   Operant (instrumental)
                                       conditioning   (p. 160)

Conditioned response (CR) (p. 160)   Unconditioned stimulus (UCS) (p. 162)

Interstimulus interval   (p. 160)   Unconditioned response (UCR) (p. 162)

Delayed relationship   (p. 162)   Counterconditioning   (p. 166)

Trace relationship   (p. 162)   Trial-and-error learning   (p. 168)

Extinction   (p. 160)   Law of effect   (p. 168)

Spontaneous recovery   (p. 160)   Law of exercise   (p. 168)

Stimulus generalization   (p. 160)   Reinforcement   (p. 168)

Discrimination   (p. 160)   Operant   (p. 168)

Positive reinforcement   (p. 169)   Fixed-interval schedule   (p. 171)

Negative reinforcement   (p. 169)   Variable-interval schedule   (p. 171)

Primary reinforcer   (p. 169)   Fixed-ratio schedule   (p. 171)

Secondary reinforcer   (p. 169)   Variable-ratio schedule   (p. 171)

Schedules of reinforcement   (p. 170)   Superstitious behavior   (p. 172)

Continuous reinforcement   (p. 170)   Shaping   (p. 174)

Intermittent (partial)   Instinctive drift   (p. 176)
reinforcement   (p. 170)

Interval schedule   Stimulus control   (p. 176)
of reinforcement   (p. 171)

Ratio schedule   Punishment   (p. 177)
of reinforcement   (p. 171)

Aversive stimulus (p. 177)

Latent learning (p. 180)

Cognitive maps (p. 181)

Observational learning (p. 181)

Social-learning theory (p. 181)

Modeling (p. 182)

Self-reinforcement (p. 183)

Biofeedback (p. 183)

Learned helplessness (p. 186)

SELF-TEST

Multiple-Choice

Choose the one best response to each question. An answer key is provided at the end of this chapter.

1. Which of the following is a reflex?

   a. Waving your hand in response to a friend's wave
   b. Jerking your finger away after accidentally touching a hot iron
   c. Crying at a sad movie
   d. Smiling when someone smiles at you

2. What is the relationship between learning and performance?

   a. They are identical.
   b. They are not related.
   c. Learning can often be deduced from performance.
   d. Learning can always be deduced from performance.

3. In classical conditioning, when is the most effective time to present the neutral stimulus?

   a. Just before the unconditioned stimulus (UCS) but *not* overlapping with it
   b. Just before the UCS and overlapping with it
   c. At exactly the same time as the UCS
   d. After the UCS

4. What process would make it possible for a person to cook using a gas stove when he or she had learned to cook on an electric stove?

   a. Generalization
   b. Simultaneous conditioning
   c. Backward conditioning
   d. Extinction

5. In the experiment with little Albert described in your text, what was the unconditioned stimulus?

   a. Loud noise
   b. White rat
   c. Dog
   d. Rabbit

6. Which of the following statements is true of classical and operant conditioning?

   a. Both involve some type of reflex behavior.
   b. Both involve positive reinforcement.
   c. Both involve forming new associations between a stimulus and a response.
   d. Both involve learning that a particular behavior will result in a reward or escape from punishment.

7. In backward conditioning, what is presented first?

   a. Demonstration of the desired response
   b. Punishment
   c. Unconditioned stimulus
   d. Conditioned stimulus

8. Assume that a loud, annoying buzzer, which is activated in your car as soon as you turn the key, stops when you buckle your seat belt. What is the buzzer?

   a. Operant
   b. Positive reinforcer
   c. Negative reinforcer
   d. Neutral stimulus

9. Which of the following could be a primary reinforcer?

   a. Letter of commendation
   b. Merit badge
   c. Trophy
   d. Piece of candy

10. Every time you put a penny in a gum machine, you receive a piece of gum. Which type of reinforcement schedule does this represent?

    a. Continuous
    b. Fixed-interval
    c. Fixed-ratio
    d. Variable-ratio

11. A teenage girl who has to read *Silas Marner* in one weekend allows herself a 10-minute telephone call every time she completes 50 pages of the novel. What schedule of reinforcement has she set up for herself?

    a. Continuous
    b. Fixed-interval
    c. Fixed-ratio
    d. Variable-ratio

12. If you want to extinguish a behavior that has previously been reinforced, which past schedule of reinforcement would make your task the most difficult?

    a. Continuous
    b. Fixed-ratio
    c. Fixed-interval
    d. Variable-ratio

13. Imagine that a young child has a series of painful injections given by a doctor wearing a white coat. Later the child cries at the sight of a druggist, who is also wearing a white coat. What type of learning has probably taken place?

    a. Classical conditioning
    b. Operant conditioning
    c. Latent learning
    d. Observational learning

14. If you want to teach your dog to hop on one foot--something that it has never done before--what approach would probably be most effective?

a. Punishment
b. Shaping
c. Modeling
d. Persuasion

15. What happens in the process of extinction?

   a. A behavior is learned because it has been negatively reinforced.
   b. A behavior is learned because it has been positively reinforced.
   c. A behavior stops because it has been punished.
   d. A behavior stops because it is no longer being reinforced.

16. Assume that your classmate Eric generally laughs at your jokes. If you tell jokes only when Eric is around, what are you exhibiting?

   a. Observational learning
   b. Operant conditioning
   c. Stimulus generalization
   d. Stimulus discrimination

17. What might cause a 3-year-old girl to tell her doll, "You're making so much racket that you're giving me a migraine"?

   a. Classical conditioning
   b. Maturation
   c. Cognitive mapping
   d. Modeling

18. If you managed to stop biting your fingernails for several weeks but suddenly found yourself nibbling away again, what could explain this behavior?

   a. Instinctual drift
   b. Maturation
   c. Spontaneous recovery
   d. Habituation

19. If a father feels that it is necessary to punish his young son for patting strange dogs, when would be the most effective time?

   a. At the end of any day on which the boy has patted a strange dog
   b. At the beginning of any day on which the boy might pat a strange dog
   c. When the boy approaches a strange dog with his hand held out to pat it
   d. Just after the boy has finished patting a strange dog

20. Assume that when you were seriously ill as a child, your mother fed you chicken soup every day. If the thought of chicken soup makes you sick as an adult, what phenomenon might account for this?

   a. Operant conditioning
   b. Stimulus generalization
   c. Classical conditioning
   d. Extinction

21. Imagine that Brett's teacher calls on him whenever he raises his hand but ignores him when he calls out answers. If Brett raises his hand more often as a result, what type of learning has occurred?

   a. Classical conditioning
   b. Operant conditioning
   c. Latent learning
   d. Observational learning

22. Assume that Ms. C., a school counselor, is working with a child who rarely participates in class discussions. If she has the child watch a film which shows students eagerly entering into class discussions, what type of learning is she hoping will occur?

   a. Modeling
   b. Classical conditioning
   c. Operant conditioning
   d. Cognitive mapping

23. What type of learning is based on the imitation of models?

    a. Discrimination
    b. Observational learning
    c. Learned helplessness
    d. Cognitive mapping

24. What do people learn in a biofeedback clinic?

    a. How to avoid being overweight by sticking to a biologically sound diet
    b. How to avoid being underweight by sticking to a biologically sound diet
    c. How to control responses that are usually voluntary
    d. How to control responses that are usually involuntary

25. What circumstances lead to learned helplessness?

    a. Situations in which a person or animal experiences frequent negative reinforcement
    b. Situations in which a person or animal has little control over important aspects of the environment
    c. Situations in which instinctual drift is repressed
    d. Situations in which a person receives feedback about his or her physiological processes

Matching

Match each name in column A with one or more descriptive phrases in column B.

Column A	Column B
_____ 1. Ivan Pavlov	a. Used counterconditioning to eliminate a subject's fear of white rats, fur coats, and similar objects
_____ 2. John B. Watson	b. Used dogs in his famous studies of classical conditioning
_____ 3. Mary Cover Jones	c. Wrote a book that stressed the importance of purpose in learning
_____ 4. E. L. Thorndike	d. Created a special box equipped with a response lever and a food dispenser which is used in research on operant conditioning
_____ 5. B. F. Skinner	e. Known as the "father of behaviorism"
_____ 6. Keller and Marian Breland	f. Known as the foremost proponent of operant conditioning today
_____ 7. Edward C. Tolman	g. Demonstrated the conditioning of emotional responses in an experiment with little Albert
_____ 8. Albert Bandura	h. Formulated the law of effect

_____ 9. Martin Seligman

i. Prominent social-learning theorist
j. Has performed many experiments in vicarious learning
k. Has conducted studies in learned helplessness
l. Encountered the phenomenon of instinctive drift in training animals to do tricks
m. Developed the concept of cognitive maps

APPLICATION EXERCISES

These application exercises will test your understanding of and ability to apply the material you have read in your text. Suggested answers are provided at the end of the chapter so that you can check your responses.

1. In Pavlov's famous experiment, a dog was classically conditioned to salivate when it heard a tone. This was done by repeatedly sounding a tone just before giving the dog powdered meat. You can see from this experiment that classical conditioning involves four elements:

    a. *Unconditioned stimulus* (US) which naturally brings about a response (in Pavlov's experiment, the powdered meat)
    b. *Unconditioned response* (UR) which is inborn and does not have to be learned (in Pavlov's experiment, the dog's salivating when given the powdered meat)
    c. *Conditioned stimulus* (CS) which ordinarily wouldn't bring about a given response, but which becomes capable of eliciting the response after being paired with the unconditioned stimulus (in Pavlov's experiment, the tone)
    d. *Conditioned response* (CR) which

is very similar to the unconditioned response but brought about by the conditioned stimulus (in Pavlov's experiment, the dog's salivating to the tone without the powdered meat)

Now identify the elements in this example of classical conditioning.

You are watching your friend Kim learn to fire a pistol at a target. Each time the instructor shouts, "Ready. Aim. Fire!" Kim fires her pistol and you flinch at the loud noise. Once when the instructor shouts, "Ready. Aim. Fire!" Kim doesn't shoot, because she is out of ammunition. Nevertheless, you flinch at the word *fire*.

a. What is the US? _____
_____

b. What is the UR? _____
_____

c. What is the CS? _____
_____

d. What is the CR? _____
_____

2. B. F. Skinner's five-step procedure for studying operant conditioning was described in your text. If Ms. H., a high school teacher, is

interested in seeing whether this procedure will work to increase the number of times a shy boy raises his hand to answer a question in class, what should the teacher do?

Step 1 _____
_____
_____

Step 2 _____
_____
_____

Step 3 _____
_____
_____

Step 4 _____
_____
_____

Step 5 _____
_____
_____

3. Schedules, or patterns, of reinforcement play an important part in learning. In continuous reinforcement, an organism is reinforced for every correct response it makes. In partial, or intermittent, reinforcement, an organism is sometimes rewarded for correct responses and sometimes not. The four basic schedules of partial reinforcement are fixed-ratio, fixed-interval, variable-ratio, and variable-interval.

On a fixed-ratio schedule, an organism is rewarded after a set number of correct responses have been made. On a variable-ratio schedule, the number of correct responses that must be made before reinforcement occurs varies around some average. On a fixed-interval schedule, reinforcement is given following the first correct response made after a set period of time has passed. On a variable-interval schedule, reinforcement is given following the first correct response made after a period of time that varies around some average. Using these descriptions of the basic schedules of partial reinforcement, identify the type of schedule at work in each of the following situations.

a. You have been hired to type the manuscript of a novel. You are paid every time you submit 25 typed pages.

_____

b. Using your binoculars, you are observing some migrating hawks. You can scan the sky at regular intervals and are occasionally rewarded by spotting a hawk.

_____

c. Your mother visits you in your new apartment every Sunday afternoon and praises you if your apartment is neat when she arrives.

_____

d. You are at a shopping mall to gather signatures for a petition. The first person you approach refuses to sign, but the second and third persons agree. Then you have to ask four more people before getting another signature.

_____

4. Punishment is different from negative reinforcement. Punishment may involve presenting an unpleasant stimulus or withdrawing a pleasant stimulus. Whatever form punishment takes, it is designed to *reduce* the tendency to behave in a certain way. Negative reinforcement, on the other hand,

is designed to increase the probability of a response. In negative reinforcement, the removal of an unpleasant stimulus following a response increases the chances that the response will occur again. In the following situation, identify the behavior that is being punished, the behavior that is being negatively reinforced, the form of the punishment, and the form of the negative reinforcer.

Harold and Maude are taking a long car trip together on a cold winter day. Maude is a chain-smoker, and Harold detests the smell of smoke. Whenever Maude lights a cigarette, Harold rolls down his car window to get some fresh air. The cold air blows directly on Maude, making her extremely uncomfortable. Whenever Maude puts out a cigarette, Harold rolls the window back up.

a. What behavior of Maude's is being punished? _____
_____

b. What form is the punishment taking? _____
_____

c. What behavior of Maude's is being negatively reinforced?
_____
_____

d. What is the negative reinforcer?
_____
_____

5. Shaping is an operant conditioning technique which involves reinforcing responses that are increasingly similar to the final response that you are aiming for. Suppose a father wants to use shaping to teach his young daughter how to do a springing dive from the edge of a pool. What successive behaviors could he reinforce?

a. First behavior _____
_____
_____

b. Second behavior _____
_____
_____

c. Third behavior _____
_____
_____

d. Final behavior: Doing a springing dive from the edge of the pool

6. Modeling involves learning by observation. Your text describes four steps in this type of learning which were identified by Albert Bandura. How might the young girl described in question 5 learn to dive by watching her father instead of through shaping?

a. Step 1 _____
_____
_____

b. Step 2 _____
_____
_____

c. Step 3 _____
_____
_____

d. Step 4 _____
_____
_____

READING EXERCISE

The psychologist Martin E. P. Seligman has conducted extensive research on the phenomenon of learned helplessness. According to his theory, how people explain bad events to themselves can have an important effect on their lives. Seligman's research on explanatory style is described in the following article by Robert J. Trotter, which appeared in *Psychology Today*.

Stop Blaming Yourself

Martin E. P. Seligman is a gambler: bridge, volleyball, high-stakes poker--even his career. In 1966 he went against the odds and prevailing thought by arguing that animals could learn to be helpless. Now after 20 years of supporting research he is betting that the way we explain the things that happen to us may be more important than what actually happens. The way we explain bad things, he says, can affect our future behavior and can have serious implications for our mental and physical health.

Seligman got his first clue to this as a young graduate student at the University of Pennsylvania, when he saw a group of dogs that had failed a learning experiment. Usually, when an animal in such an experiment receives a shock, it runs around until it accidentally jumps over a barrier and escapes the shock. The next time, the dog knows just what to do. It has learned how to escape. But the animals in this experiment didn't try to escape. They sat there as if they were helpless. Seligman found out that these dogs had previously been exposed to a shock from which they could not escape and suggested that they had learned that efforts to escape were fruitless. It was not the shock that interfered with the animals' response, says Seligman, but the expectation that they would have no control over it.

Reprinted from *Psychology Today* magazine by permission of the publisher. Copyright (c) 1987 by the American Psychological Association.

Collaborating with fellow graduate students Steven F. Maier and Bruce Overmier (now at the University of Colorado and the University of Minnesota, respectively), Seligman worked for the next five years to document this learned helplessness phenomenon and link it to depression in humans. "When I first saw the helpless animals," he explains, "I thought it might be a model of human helplessness that would aid us in understanding the kind of helplessness seen in people suffering from depression." The idea of helping people was what made Seligman decide to become a psychologist in the first place, rather than a philosopher or a professional bridge player. He still likes to talk philosophy and is an excellent bridge player, but he says, "Psychology seemed just perfect for me. It combined enough serious intellectual challenge with a real opportunity to do something that might help people."

After earning his Ph.D. in 1967, Seligman taught for three years at Cornell University, exploring what he saw as obvious parallels between learned helplessness and the major symptoms of human depression. His students convinced him, however, that he just didn't know enough about depression. So he grew a beard and took a year of psychiatric residency at the University of Pennsylvania to learn about depression firsthand.

Seligman still sees a few clients as a licensed therapist but feels that he is more suited to research than therapy. "As a therapist," he says, "I might help 200 or 300 people during my life, but I think I can make a better contribution by trying to uncover general laws of psychology that might help many more people." That's why he stayed with the learned helplessness theory. "I want to follow it to the bitter end. I like low-probability/high-payoff science," he explains. "It is hard work, but it might make a difference." And that is what Seligman has been trying to do since he joined the psychology department at the University of Pennsylvania in 1971.

After getting his clinical training, Seligman wrote his first paper on depression and began experimenting with human helplessness. He says he was amazed to find that people reacted just like the animals when he exposed them to the same things, such as an inescapable loud noise. They acted as if they were helpless and didn't even try to turn off the noise. "This was counterintuitive," Seligman says. "Learning theory said that if you give inescapable events to humans or animals it would energize them, not make them passive."

Seligman continued to document the parallels between helplessness and depression for several years. Then, just as the bet was beginning to pay off, people (especially his students Lyn Abramson, Lauren Alloy and Judy Garber) began to have second thoughts. Seligman, just back from a year as a Guggenheim Fellow at the Institute of Psychiatry at Maudsley Hospital in London, was greeted with arguments that his theory of helplessness was wrong on several counts. For one thing, exposure to uncontrollable bad events does not always lead to helplessness and depression. Furthermore, the helplessness theory did not explain the loss of self-esteem often seen in depressed people. Why should people blame themselves for events over which they have no control?

Seligman and his colleagues worked for several years revising the theory to meet these objections. The revised

theory emphasizes what they call explanatory style. The reason uncontrollable bad events don't always lead to helplessness and depression is that people don't simply accept these events uncritically. They ask why. The answer, or explanation for the event, affects what they expect about the future and determines the extent to which they will be helpless or depressed.

Some bad events are truly uncontrollable--my house burned to the ground because it was struck by lightning--and a person's explanations for them are simple statements of fact. But in many instances, reality is ambiguous--my lover accepted a job in another city because it paid a lot more money or, possibly, to get out of our relationship. The revised helplessness theory says that people have a characteristic way of explaining bad events when reality is ambiguous. They explain the event as being caused by something stable or unstable, global or specific, internal or external. If your relationship breaks up, for example, you can come up with a variety of reasons. If you explain it as something that is stable over time (I always screw up my personal relationships), you will expect it to happen again and will show signs of helplessness in future relationships. If you explain it as global rather than specific (I'm incapable of doing anything right), you will expect bad things to happen in all areas of your life and feel even more helpless. If you explain it as internal rather than external (It was all my fault; my lover did everything possible to keep the relationship going), you are likely to show signs of lowered self-esteem.

According to Seligman's revised helplessness theory, a person who tends to explain the bad things in stable, global and internal terms (It's going to last forever, it's going to affect everything I do and it's all my fault) is most at risk for depression when bad events occur. To test this, Seligman and his colleagues first developed a method of measuring explanatory style. The Attributional Style Questionnaire (ASQ) consists of six bad and six good hypothetical events. People taking the test are asked to imagine themselves in each of these situations and to decide what they feel would be the major cause of the situation if it happened to them. Then they are asked to rate each cause on a scale of 1 to 7 for instability versus stability, specificity versus globality and internality versus externality.

In the first test of the revised theory, Seligman and his colleagues administered the ASQ to 143 college students and had them fill out a short form of the Beck Depression Inventory, a 13-item questionnaire that is highly reliable in detecting symptoms of depression. As expected, depression could be predicted by the kinds of explanations offered. Students who gave mainly stable, global and internal explanations for bad events were consistently more depressed than those who offered unstable, specific and external reasons. The researchers had similar findings with women on welfare, maximum-security prisoners, grade school children who showed signs of depression, college students who did poorly on a midterm exam and patients hospitalized for depression.

Since the first tests of Seligman's theory, there have been at least 104 experiments involving nearly 15,000 subjects, almost all showing that a pessimistic explanatory style is related to depression.

Seligman's most recent research goes beyond depression. He believes that explanatory style should be able to predict achievement as well as illness and death. It seems logical that people who habitually provide stable, global and internal explanations (such as stupidity) for their failures should be less likely to persist, take chances or rise above their potential than those who explain failure in unstable, specific and

external terms (such as luck). This link between learned helplessness and achievement has been demonstrated in work with children. Several researchers have found that the way children explain their performance strongly influences whether they give up following a failure (helpless children) or persist (mastery-oriented children).

When Leslie Kamen and Seligman gave the ASQ to 289 freshmen and 175 upperclassmen at the University of Pennsylvania they found that using explanatory style plus measures such as the Scholastic Aptitude Test and high school grades predicted a student's grade point average more accurately than using the more traditional measures alone. Students with the best explanatory style (unstable, specific, external) got better grades than the traditional methods predicted.

Explanatory style also predicts performance on the job. Seligman and Peter Schulman administered the ASQ to 101 insurance sales representatives right after they had been hired; a year later, those with a positive explanatory style were twice as likely as those with a negative style to be among the 42 agents still on the job. Furthermore the agents with the positive style had sold 25 percent more insurance, on average, than the others.

The insurance company executives were so impressed with these results that they agreed to a second experiment in which both the ASQ and the usual screening tests were given to thousands of applicants. One thousand were hired on the basis of the usual test. A special force of 100 who failed the industry test but had an optimistic explanatory style were also hired and compared with a group who passed the industry test but had a pessimistic explanatory style. The optimists are outselling the pessimists among the regularly hired agents, Seligman says, and the special force is outselling everybody. "I think we've got a test for who can face a stressful, challenging job and who can't," he says. "My guess is that this test could save the insurance company millions of dollars a year in training alone since it costs about $30,000 each to train new people, and half of them quit."

Seligman plans to take the test into other industries as well. "I think you can order jobs on this dimension--how a person deals with challenge and failure," he says. "It would be a much more humane way to hire people and place them in jobs, jobs that they are up to emotionally." Even defense departments, he says, could make use of such a test. "Some people are better able to cope with going out on the front line, while others are better off operating computers in the back room because they can't cope with failure and give up."

Explanatory style also plays an important role in physical health. Evidence is mounting that stressful life events, such as bereavement and school and family pressures, lead to increased vulnerability to infection and disease. But not everyone reacts in the same way. Some fight against stressors while others see them as uncontrollable and react with helplessness and passivity, characteristics that can be detected in their explanatory style. Seligman believes that people with a poor explanatory style are more likely to go on to have bad health than those with an optimistic outlook.

He cites a study that supports this prediction. Three months following a simple mastectomy for breast cancer, 69 women were asked how they viewed the nature and seriousness of the disease and how it had affected their lives. Five years later, 75 percent of the women who had reacted to the disease with a fighting spirit or who denied they had cancer were still alive and had no recurrence of the cancer. Only 35 percent of the women who had stoically or helplessly accepted the disease were still alive with no recurrence. A feeling of helplessness

appears to impair the body's ability to combat disease.

The immune system, the body's defense mechanism, is the obvious place to look for evidence that such psychological states can affect physical health. Kamen and Seligman, working with Judith Rodin of Yale University, have found that explanatory style does seem to be related to immune functioning. They took blood samples from a group of older people who had been interviewed regarding life changes, stress and health changes. The ones whose interviews indicated a pessimistic or depressive explanatory style had a larger percentage of suppressor cells. Since these cells are thought to undermine the body's ability to fight tumor growth, Seligman says, the findings suggest a link between explanatory style and susceptibility to diseases, including cancer.

Explanatory style can also predict actual illness. Seligman's colleague, Christopher Peterson of the University of Michigan, measured the explanatory style of 172 undergraduates and then questioned them one month later about how many days they had been sick and one year later about how often they had been to the doctor. He found a strong correlation between helpless explanatory styles and subsequent illness. To see if this relationship holds over the long term, Peterson and Seligman worked with psychiatrist George Vaillant, who has been keeping track of members of the Harvard classes of 1939 through 1944. In 1946, the men had responded to questionnaires about their experiences in World War II. Seligman analyzed their responses to see if their explanatory style for negative events was related to later physical health, which was assessed in 1980. The results are preliminary, he says, but they suggest that a person's explanatory style is a reliable predictor of physical health 20 to 35 years later.

He cautions, however, that psychology plays only a minor role in physical illness. "If a crane falls on you," he explains, "it doesn't matter what you think. If the magnitude of your cancer is overwhelming, your psychological outlook counts for zero. On the other hand, if your cancer is marginal or if an illness is just beginning, your psychological state may be critical."

"Some of the studies I'm involved in are long shots," Seligman admits, "but that's part of the intellectual adventure I enjoy. I'm not afraid to be wrong. It keeps me from getting bored and from being boring. My style is to follow an idea doggedly, to repeat each study until I am sure the results are reliable. This can be tedious, but if after all the work the long shot comes in and I am right, these are the studies that can really make a difference in terms of helping people."

If Seligman is right about the physical and psychological importance of explanatory style, then the way to help people is to find out how explanatory style originates and how it can be changed. Seligman, Joan Girgus and Susan Nolen-Hoeksema have identified several possible factors that might influence the development of explanatory style in children. The timing of a child's first trauma or serious loss, for instance, could have a major influence on later explanatory style.

One study, for example, found that middle- and working-class women in London were more likely to be depressed if before the age of 11 they had lost their mothers. In terms of Seligman's theory, the loss of a mother at an early age is a seriously negative event that has both stable and global implications: The mother will never return, and almost every aspect of the child's life will be affected. In addition, young children often blame themselves (internal) when bad events occur. Such a loss at an early age, Seligman says, could set a pattern for the interpretation of future losses or major difficulties.

He also thinks that children may adopt or imitate the explanatory style of their parents. One of his studies found a strong correlation between the way mothers, but not fathers, and children explain bad events.

Teachers are another model of explanatory style. There is considerable evidence that girls exhibit more helpless behavior than boys in school, and research suggests that this might be explained by the different way teachers treat children. When teachers criticize girls they tend to use stable and global terms commenting, for instance, on their intelligence. When they criticize boys they are likely to use more unstable and specific explanations accusing them of not concentrating. And the kids seem to get the message. In a study in which fourth-graders were presented with unsolvable problems, boys were less likely than girls to give helpless answers. They said things like "I wasn't trying hard," or "I don't care about your problem." Girls more often attributed their failure to incompetence or stupidity and said, "I just can't do it."

If children continually receive feedback indicating that they lack ability, they may begin to explain their failures in helpless terms. This could be prevented by teaching children to think differently about what happens to them, Seligman says. We might be able to immunize them against helplessness and depression. "I'd like to try that for 10 years and see if the rates of childhood disease, depression and suicide go down. The history of prevention has been much better than the history of cure," he says.

There is, however, a cure for bad explanatory style. "If you learned it," Seligman says, "you can unlearn it." This was shown rather dramatically when Seligman and Peterson asked psychiatrist Mardi Horowitz of the University of California, San Francisco, to send them excerpts from 12 therapy sessions with depressed patients who had recently suffered a severe loss. The idea was to read the excerpts as if they contained answers to the ASQ and make some conclusions about the patients based on their explanatory style. They did this and sent the 12 evaluations back to Horowitz.

"His response both surprised us and gratified us," say Seligman and Peterson, who thought the statements had come from 12 patients. Instead, Horowitz informed them, they had come from four patients at the beginning, middle and end of successful therapy. For each statement, the ranking of good versus bad explanatory style identified where the patient had been in the process of therapy. And the patient with the worst style at the beginning of therapy had been judged by Horowitz as suicidal.

Explanatory style, Seligman concludes, can change in response to important events in one's life, including psychotherapy. And he believes that cognitive therapy is the best approach, since it assumes that depression is a result of distorted thinking about the world (global), the future (stable) and oneself (internal). "Cognitive therapy works directly on explanations. You get people to look at what causes they are evoking when they feel depressed," he explains, "and then get them to think about new kinds of causes. It helps people. I'd bet on it."

QUESTIONS

Answer the following questions and then compare your responses with the suggested answers at the end of this chapter.

1. According to Seligman, people suffering from learned helplessness tend to explain unfortunate events in stable, global, and internal terms. People with more positive explanatory styles tend to explain bad events in unstable, specific, and external terms. Assume that a bank begins using automated teller machines and 5 out of 20 tellers subsequently lose their jobs.

   a. If one of the fired tellers, Mr. N., has a negative explanatory style, how might he explain this event?

   b. If another of the fired tellers, Ms. P., has a positive explanatory style, how might her explanation be different?

2. Seligman has used a test which measures explanatory style to predict job performance. According to Seligman, how does positive explanatory style affect job performance?

3. List three factors described in the article which might influence the development of a child's explanatory style.

ANSWERS

Correct Answers to Self-Test Exercises

Multiple-Choice			Matching
1. b	10. a	18. c	1. b
2. c	11. c	19. c	2. e, g
3. b	12. d	20. c	3. a
4. a	13. a	21. b	4. h
5. a	14. b	22. a	5. d, f
6. c	15. d	23. b	6. l
7. c	16. d	24. d	7. c, m
8. c	17. d	25. b	8. i, j
9. d			9. k

Suggested Answers to Application Exercises

1. a. Pistol shot
    b. Flinching at the sound of the shot
    c. The word *fire*
    d. Flinching at the word *fire*

2. Step 1. Ms. H. should identify the response or operant to be studied. In this case, the response is the student's raising his hand to answer a question.

    Step 2. She should determine the baseline rate of the response. For a 1-week period, the teacher could record the number of times the student raises his hand to answer a question.

    Step 3. She should decide how she will reinforce the desired behavior. She could plan to smile at the student when he raises his hand, call on him, and say something encouraging about his answer, even if it is wrong.

    Step 4. She should apply the reinforcer according to a schedule until the response increases. If she chooses a continuous-reinforcement schedule, whenever the student raises his hand to answer a question she should smile, call on the student, and say something pleasant about his answer. She should continue doing this until his question-answering behavior increases.

Step 5. If Ms. H. wants to make sure her reinforcement is responsible for the change in the student's behavior, she could stop reinforcing him to see if his hand-raising behavior drops back to the baseline rate. Under ordinary circumstances, a teacher's prime concern would be the welfare of the student, and this last step would not be carried out.

3. a. Fixed-ratio
    b. Variable-interval
    c. Fixed-interval
    d. Variable-ratio

4. a. Cigarette-lighting
    b. Having cold air blowing on her
    c. Putting out the cigarette
    d. Cold air. Negative reinforcement takes place when Harold stops the cold air by rolling up his window.

5. a. First, he could reward her for simply jumping feet first from the edge of the pool.
    b. Second, he could reward her for entering the water head first from a sitting position with her arms extended, bending forward from the waist.
    c. Third, he could reward her for diving from a standing position on the edge of the pool with her arms extended, bending forward from the waist.
    d. This should all lead to the final behavior of doing a springing dive from the edge of the pool.

6. Step 1. She would have to pay attention to her father's diving. She would also have to perceive the relevant aspects of his behavior. Noticing that he smiles and waves at her before he dives would not help her learn this skill. Relevant parts of the behavior would include the fact that he stands near the edge, extends his arms while keeping them close together, springs forward, and enters the water head first.

Step 2. She would have to remember (either through words or through mental images) how he dived.

Step 3. She would have to convert her memory of his diving into action. In other words, she would have to dive herself.

Step 4. She would have to be motivated to continue diving. If, on other days at the pool, children her own age were diving, she might be motivated to join in the fun.

Suggested Answers to Reading Questions

1. a. The teller with a negative explanatory style might explain the event as being stable (I'll never be able to hold a job), global (I fail at everything I try), and internal (If I had been a better teller, they would have picked someone else to fire).
    b. The teller with a positive explanatory style might explain the event as being unstable (I'm sure I'll be able to keep my next job), specific (My career

is not going so well right now, but I have a great marriage and I'm doing well in night school), and external (I was a victim of automation).

2. According to Seligman, people with positive explanatory styles are better able to cope with stress, challenges, and failures on the job.

3. Three factors which might influence a child's explanatory style are the timing of the child's first trauma, imitating the parents' explanatory styles, and accepting teachers' explanations of failure.

Chapter 6:

MEMORY

CHAPTER OUTLINE

I. Memory as a cognitive process
   A. How do we remember?
      1. A storage-and-transfer model of memory
         a. Sensory memory
           (1) The nature of sensory memory
           (2) Kinds of sensory memory
           (3) Pattern recognition in sensory memory
         b. Short-term memory
           (1) Short-term memory fades rapidly
           (2) Rehearsal helps to retain material in STM
           (3) Short-term memory is like your attention span
           (4) Capacity of short-term memory is small
           (5) We can expand the capacity of short-term memory
           (6) How we find information in short-term memory
           (7) How short-term memory and long-term memory work together
           (8) The importance of transfer from STM to LTM
         c. Long-term memory
           (1) Kinds of long-term memory
           (2) Encoding in long-term memory
              (a) Encoding by association
              (b) Encoding by organization
              (c) The "tip of the tongue"
              (d) The dual-coding hypothesis
      2. A levels-of-processing model of memory
   B. What do we remember?
      1. We tend to remember what is presented first and last: Serial-position curve
      2. We tend to remember the unusual: Von Restorff effect
      3. We tend to remember links to emotionally significant events: Flashbulb memory
      4. We reconstruct memory by filling in the gaps
   C. Why do we forget?
      1. Motivated forgetting: Repression
      2. Decay of the memory trace
         a. Poor perception
         b. Inability to rehearse
      3. Interference
      4. Failure of retrieval
      5. Are memories permanent?

II. The biological basis of memory
 A. How we study biological aspects of memory
  1. Laboratory experiments
  2. Studies of people with memory disorders
 B. How memories are stored in the brain
 C. Where memories are stored in the brain

III. Memory disorders
 A. Organic amnesia
 B. Psychogenic amnesia
 C. Theories of amnesia
  1. Encoding
  2. Consolidation
  3. Retrieval

IV. Exceptional memories

Boxes
 Psychology in your life: Testing memory--recognition, recall, and relearning
 In the forefront: Legal implications of memory research
 Psychology in your life: We don't learn what we don't need to remember
 Psychology in your life: How can you improve your memory?

LEARNING OBJECTIVES

After you study Chapter 6, you should be able to do the tasks outlined in the following objectives.

1. Describe the three basic steps in the memory process.

2. Describe the three types of memory proposed in the storage-and-transfer model of memory.

3. Explain what the tip-of-the-tongue phenomenon indicates about how information is coded in long-term memory.

4. Explain how recognition, recall, and relearning tasks can be used to study learning and memory.

5. Describe the primacy, recency, and von Restorff effects.

6. Define the levels-of-processing model of memory.

7. Cite the characteristics of flashbulb memories.

8. Explain what Ebbinghaus's curve of forgetting indicates about the rate at which we forget.

9. Summarize the following theories of forgetting: the theory of motivated forgetting, decay theory, and interference theory.

10. Contrast two points of view about the permanence of long-term memory.

11. Describe the difference between somatic and behavioral intervention.

12. Summarize Hebb's theory on how memories are stored in short-term and long-term memory.

13. Identify the brain structures that are believed to play an important role in memory.

14. Define anterograde and retrograde amnesia.

15. List some common conditions that can produce amnesia.

16. Describe some mnemonic devices and external memory aids.

KEY CONCEPTS

As you read Chapter 6 in your text, look for each of the following concepts. You should understand each concept.

1. Three Steps in Memory

Memory involves three basic steps: encoding, storage, and retrieval.

2. Storage-and-Transfer Model of Memory

According to this model of memory, we all have three different types of memory: sensory memory, short-term memory, and long-term memory.

3. Sensory Memory

We have sensory memories for all our senses. However, little research has been done for any but the iconic and echoic.

4. Short-Term Memory

Most people can keep about seven items in short-term memory. However, we can expand the capacity of short-term memory through chunking. Although retrieval from short-term memory is rapid, some research indicates that we examine items one at a time as we attempt to retrieve them from short-term memory.

5. Long-Term Memory

While simple rehearsal is an effective way to fix items in short-term memory, associational rehearsal is better for retaining information in long-term memory. Clustering is a useful technique for transferring material from short-term to long-term memory.

6. Tip-of-the-Tongue States

When we experience a tip-of-the-tongue state with regard to a word we are trying to recall, we may come up with words similar in meaning or sound.

7. Dual-Coding Hypothesis

Some research has indicated that we store, organize, and retrieve material in memory through two independent but interconnected systems. One system uses words and the other uses images.

8. Levels-of-Processing Model of Memory

According to this model of memory, the ability to remember is based on how deeply we have processed information. In deep processing, we consider the meaning of an item.

9. Three Measures of Retention

Memory researchers use three basic tests of retention: recall, recognition, and relearning tests. Relearning is used least because it is the most time-consuming.

10. Primacy, Recency, and von Restorff Effects

Studies of memory show that for many memory tasks, we remember best what we learned first, what we learned last, and what was unusual.

11. Flashbulb Memories

Many people have vivid and detailed memories of significant historical or personal events. The accuracy of such memories, however, is questionable.

12. Filling in Memory Gaps

Retrospective reports may be very inaccurate. In attempting to describe past events, we may unknowingly invent new information or incorporate information gained after the event.

13. How We Forget

Research indicates that people forget according to well-established principles. After material is learned, forgetting occurs rapidly at first and then slows down markedly. Overlearning can reduce the amount of material forgotten.

14. Motivated Forgetting

We may repress memories about some aspects of our lives because it is beneficial to do so. For example, we may forget certain embarrassing events.

15. Two Views on the Permanence of Memory

Some psychologists believe that information is permanently stored in long-term memory and that forgetting represents a retrieval problem. Other psychologists believe that some forgetting is due to the fact that material has been lost from long-term memory.

16. Theories of Unmotivated Forgetting

Decay theory suggests that learning creates memory traces, or engrams, which may decay if they are not used. Interference theorists maintain that new learning may cause us to forget something we have previously learned and that old learning may cause us to forget something we have learned more recently. Forgetting may also be due to retrieval failure caused by the absence of needed cues.

17. How Memory Is Studied

In order to examine the biological aspects of memory, researchers rely on laboratory experiments (usually with animals) and studies of people with memory disorders.

18. Storage of Memories in the Brain

Our knowledge of how and where memories are stored in the brain is limited. Some research indicates that different physiological processes are involved in short-term versus long-term memory storage. The transfer of material from short-term to long-term memory may involve actual physical changes in the brain. Certain brain structures, including parts of the limbic system, seem to play an important role in memory. Biochemical changes in the brain, including changes in the number of synaptic contacts, also appear to be associated with memory.

19. Memory Disorders

Amnesia is a general term for many types of memory loss. A person suffering from anterograde amnesia cannot create new permanent memories. Retrograde amnesia involves the inability to remember material learned before the onset of the amnesia. Memory disorders may result from organic causes such as neurologic illnesses, electroconvulsive shock, alcohol abuse, or damage to various parts of the brain. Psychogenic amnesia is caused by emotionally disturbing events. Memory disorders may involve problems with encoding, consolidation, or retrieval of information.

20. Exceptional Memories

A few people have such extraordinary memories that they rarely forget anything. These people are known as *memorists*. A specific type of exceptional memory, called *eidetic imagery,* involves the capacity to remember images in great detail. Eidetic imagery is found almost exclusively among children.

21. Improving Memory

Sensory memory can be improved by paying closer attention to information coming in through the senses. Rote rehearsal and chunking are techniques for improving short-term memory. Making new information personally meaningful is the best way to improve long-term memory.

22. Mnemonics

Mnemonic systems are designed to improve memory. Some common mnemonic systems are the method of loci, the peg-word method, and the narrative-chaining method. In the method of loci, you associate the items you want to remember with geographical points along a very familiar route. The peg-word method involves learning a jingle which contains peg words and then associating the items you want to

remember with the peg words. In the narrative-chaining method, you make up a story which incorporates the items you want to remember.

23. External Memory Aids

Common external memory aids include writing reminders to yourself, getting verbal reminders from others, setting an alarm to let you know when it is time to do something, putting an object in an unfamiliar place to jog your memory, and doing certain things at the same time each day.

TERMS TO KNOW

Define each of the terms listed. You can check your definitions in the text Glossary or on the text pages listed in parentheses.

Encoding   (p. 193)

Storage   (p. 193)

Retrieval   (p. 193)

Sensory memory (SM)   (p. 194)

Short-term memory (STM)   (p. 194)   Episodic memory   (p. 199)

Long-term memory (LTM)   (p. 194)   Semantic memory   (p. 199)

Storage-and-transfer model   Associational rehearsal   (p. 200)
of memory   (p. 194)

Iconic memory   (p. 195)   Clustering   (p. 201)

Echoic memory   (p. 195)   Tip-of-the-tongue
                                          states (TOTs)   (p. 202)

Rote rehearsal   (p. 196)   Levels-of-processing model
                                          of memory   (p. 202)

Chunking   (p. 196)   Recall   (p. 203)

Procedural memory   (p. 199)   Recognition   (p. 203)

Declarative memory   (p. 199)   Relearning   (p. 204)

Primacy effect   (p. 205)   Proactive interference (PI)   (p. 214)

Recency effect   (p. 205)   Retroactive interference (RI) (p. 214)

Serial-position curve   (p. 205)   Cue-dependent forgetting   (p. 214)

Von Restorff effect   (p. 206)   Somatic intervention   (p. 215)

Flashbulb memories   (p. 206)   Behavioral intervention   (p. 215)

Retrospective reports   (p. 208)   Amnesia   (p. 215)

Curve of forgetting   (p. 208)   Consolidation   (p. 216)

Repression   (p. 209)   Hippocampus   (p. 216)

Engram (memory trace)   (p. 209)   Protein synthesis   (p. 217)

Organic amnesia   (p. 219)

Anterograde amnesia   (p. 219)

Retrograde amnesia   (p. 219)

Korsakoff's syndrome   (p. 220)

Psychogenic amnesia   (p. 221)

Mnemonics   (p. 222)

Memorist   (p. 221)

Method of loci   (p. 222)

SELF-TEST

Multiple-Choice

Choose the one best response to each question. An answer key is provided at the end of this chapter.

1. In the past, how was most research on memory conducted?

   a. By asking people about their early memories
   b. By experiments in a laboratory
   c. By asking people about their memories of significant historical events
   d. By asking people about their memories of personally significant events

2. In what sequence do the three basic steps in memory occur?

   a. Storing, encoding, retrieving
   b. Encoding, storing, retrieving
   c. Storing, retrieving, encoding
   d. Encoding, retrieving, storing

3. According to what model is memory divided into three separate memory structures?

   a. Storage-and-transfer model
   b. Levels-of-processing model
   c. Triple-indexing model
   d. Structural-search model

4. According to the storage-and-transfer model, if you walk into a crowded party, where is the data that you take in initially recorded?

   a. Sensory memory
   b. Short-term memory
   c. Long-term memory
   d. Parallel memory

5. Approximately how long is information held in sensory memory?

a. 1 to 5 seconds
b. 40 to 50 seconds
c. 1 to 5 minutes
d. 40 to 50 minutes

6. If you remember the face of a clown you have seen on a circus poster, what type of memory is this?

a. Echoic memory
b. Iconic memory
c. Procedural memory
d. Semantic memory

7. If you remember how to ride a bicycle, what type of memory is this?

a. Echoic memory
b. Iconic memory
c. Procedural memory
d. Semantic memory

8. If you have asked for someone's zip code with the intention of writing it in your address book and you do not repeat the number to yourself, how quickly must you write it down to avoid having to ask again?

a. Within about 1 to 20 seconds
b. Within about 20 to 60 seconds
c. Within about 1 to 4 minutes
d. Within about 4 to 7 minutes

9. Approximately how many items can people keep in short-term memory?

a. 3 to 7
b. 5 to 9
c. 7 to 11
d. 9 to 13

10. Which of the following conclusions did Sternberg draw regarding how we find information in short-term memory?

a. Retrieval is parallel and exhaustive.
b. Retrieval is parallel and self-terminating.
c. Retrieval is serial and exhaustive.
d. Retrieval is serial and self-terminating.

11. What two basic signals are used by most people for encoding words into memory?

a. What a word means and where it was first encountered
b. How common a word is and when it was first encountered
c. How a word sounds and where it was first encountered
d. How a word sounds and what it means

12. According to the dual-coding hypothesis, one basic system for storing material in memory involves the use of words. What does the other system involve?

a. Associations
b. Cues
c. Images
d. Mnemonics

13. Which of the following would represent the deepest processing of the word *fleece* according to the levels-of-processing model of memory?

a. Noting that it is a one-syllable word
b. Noting that it rhymes with grease
c. Noting that it begins with the letter *f*
d. Noting that it would fit in the sentence, "The sheep's fleece was very thick."

14. Being asked to recite the presidents of the United States in chronological order is an example of what type of memory task?

a. Recognition
b. Free recall
c. Serial recall
d. Free recollection

15. Assume that you phone a travel agent, who quickly describes a whirlwind tour of Europe--10 countries in 12 days. What might account for the fact that when you hang up, you can remember the names of only the first two and last two countries?

    a. Effects of primacy and recency
    b. Von Restorff effect
    c. Dual-coding hypothesis
    d. Cue-dependent forgetting

16. Assume that the following items are listed on a menu: hamburger, club sandwich, beef stew, fillet of rattlesnake, and chili. According to the von Restorff effect which of the items will you probably remember best?

    a. Hamburger
    b. Club sandwich
    c. Fillet of rattlesnake
    d. Chili

17. According to Brown and Kulik, when do flashbulb memories occur?

    a. During moments of great relaxation
    b. During very significant events
    c. During states of mild depression
    d. During states of extreme boredom

18. What does Ebbinghaus's curve of forgetting indicate about the rate at which we forget?

    a. Forgetting occurs at a rapid and constant rate.
    b. Forgetting occurs at a slow and constant rate.
    c. Forgetting is rapid at first and then slows down markedly.
    d. Forgetting is slow at first and then speeds up markedly.

19. Assume that at a high school class reunion several of your former classmates recall the time you fell down the steps after being handed your diploma at graduation. What might account for your having no recollection of this event?

    a. Repression
    b. Poor perception
    c. Retroactive interference
    d. Proactive interference

20. If you find it difficult to remember your new zip code because it is so similar to your old zip code, what is probably taking place?

    a. Decay of a memory trace
    b. Cue-dependent forgetting
    c. Retroactive interference
    d. Proactive interference

21. If you first learn to count to 10 in Spanish, and then in French, and you later find that you have forgotten the Spanish, what has probably occurred?

    a. Repression
    b. Cue-dependent forgetting
    c. Retroactive interference
    d. Proactive interference

22. What might explain your seeing your mail carrier at a restaurant and not being able to remember who he or she is?

    a. Decay of a memory trace
    b. Cue-dependent forgetting
    c. Retroactive interference
    d. Proactive interference

23. Which of the following refers to the shift from a short-term memory trace to a permanent change in physical structure?

a. Somatic intervention
b. Synaptic transmission
c. Consolidation
d. Behavioral intervention

24. What were the results of Karl Lashley's research concerning the specific locations in the brain where memory traces exist?

   a. He was able to find only one specific location where memory traces exist.
   b. He was able to identify seven specific locations in the brain where memory traces exist.
   c. He was able to identify over 20 specific locations in the brain where memory traces exist.
   d. He was unable to find specific locations in the brain where memory traces exist.

25. Who is most likely to have the power of eidetic imagery?

   a. Children
   b. Young adults
   c. Middle-aged people
   d. Elderly people

Matching

Match each name in column A with the appropriate descriptive phrase from column B.

Column A

_____ 1. Wilder Penfield

_____ 2. Richard Atkinson and Richard Shiffrin

_____ 3. Endel Tulving

_____ 4. Hermann Ebbinghaus

_____ 5. Elizabeth F. and Geoffrey R. Loftus

_____ 6. Fergus I. M. Craik and Robert S. Lockhart

_____ 7. Gordon Bower

Column B

a. Works with simple organisms like the sea snail (aplysia) to explain complex learning and memory phenomena
b. Concluded from research that many memories cannot be recovered because they no longer exist
c. Proposed the levels-of-processing model of memory
d. Held that a physical change in the brain occurs when material goes from short-term to long-term memory
e. Proposed the storage-and-transfer model of memory
f. Coined the phrase *magical number plus or minus 2,* which refers to the largest number of items most people can keep in short-term memory
g. Conducted the partial-report experiment which showed that people could absorb more into sensory memory than was previously thought possible

_____ 8.   George Miller

h. Conducted research which showed that when presented with randomly arranged material, most people cluster the items into categories as they transfer the information from short-term to long-term memory

_____ 9.   George Sperling

i. Conducted the first systematic study of memory in 1885

APPLICATION EXERCISES

These application exercises will test your understanding of and ability to apply the material you have read in your text. Suggested answers are provided at the end of the chapter so that you can check your responses.

1.   Imagine that you have spent a memorable evening at a fine restaurant with an interesting conversationalist. A month later, as you are describing the evening to a friend, you find that you can vividly recall what you and your dinner companion talked about, the decor of the restaurant, and the food you ate.

    a. According to Atkinson and Shiffrin's storage-and-transfer model of memory, what processes took place that would account for your recollection of the evening? _____

    _____

    _____

    _____

    _____

    b. According to Craik, Lockhart, and Tulving's levels-of-processing model of memory, what processes took place that would account for your recollection of the evening? _____

    _____

    _____

    _____

    _____

2.   In each of the following examples, why would it be easier to keep in short-term memory the information on the right as opposed to the information on the left?

8043633341   804 363 3341
CIHRTSMPOUE   CHUTROSTEMP

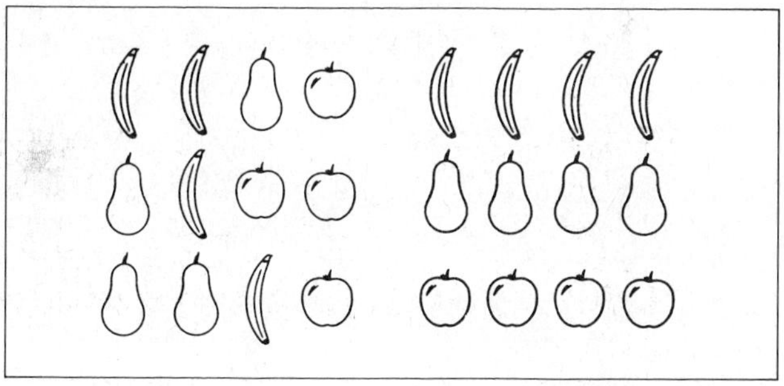

Fig. 6-1

_____

_____

_____

_____

_____

3. Assume that on a history test a student is asked to recall the last name of the inventor of wireless telegraphy. (Marconi is the inventor.) If the student experiences a tip-of-the-tongue state, which of the following names might he or she come up with in attempting to retrieve the correct answer?

___ Edison ___ Bryan
___ Bell ___ Mahoney ___ Calhoun

4. Recognition, recall, and relearning are three different types of memory tasks used by psychologists to study learning and memory. Assume that in your psychology class you are asked to design a simple experiment to determine whether nonsense syllables typed in capital letters are easier to remember than nonsense syllables typed in lowercase letters. This is the list of nonsense syllables: HEY, LUB, GAK, MOV, KAX, TOF, SID, DIT, BEP, FUM, CIL, JUC, POH, VEN, YIG, YAW, WOR, RET, NIM, and DEJ.

   a. How could you compare retention of nonsense syllables typed in capital versus lowercase letters using a recognition task? (Hint: You could use a list that looks like this: HEY, lub, GAK, mov, KAX, tof, SID, dit, BEP, fum, CIL, juc, POH, ven, YIG, yaw, WOR, ret, NIM, dej.)

      Recognition task _____
      _____
      _____
      _____
      _____

   b. How could you compare retention of the capitalized versus the lowercase syllables using a recall task? (Hint: Your list could look the same as the one in 4a.)

   Recall task _____
   _____
   _____
   _____
   _____

   c. How could you compare retention of the capitalized versus the lowercase syllables using a relearning task? (Hint: You could use two different lists, one typed in all capital letters, the other typed in all lowercase letters. You could also divide your subjects into two equal groups.)

      Relearning task _____
      _____
      _____
      _____
      _____
      _____

5. Your text describes a number of possible reasons for the decay of a memory. These include poor perception, inability to rehearse, proactive interference, retroactive interference, and cue-dependent forgetting. For each of the following situations, identify the probable reason for forgetting.

   a. Mike ordinarily keeps a bottle of vitamins next to some juice glasses in a kitchen cabinet. Every morning when he gets out a glass for his orange juice, he also gets out a vitamin, which he takes with the juice. While staying in a hotel during his vacation, Mike can't seem to remember to take his vitamins, although he has set them in plain view on a nightstand by his bed.

      Reason for forgetting _____

b. David is visiting his new wife's family for the first time. He is introduced to relatives from his mother-in-law's side of the family at lunch. At dinner, he meets relatives of his father-in-law. David finds that at dinner he keeps confusing Aunt Betty and Uncle Jim with Aunt Beatrice and Uncle John, whom he had met at lunch.

Reason for forgetting _____

c. Beth is washing dishes while she has a cake baking in the oven. Suddenly she smells something burning and realizes that it is the cake. Just as she rushes to the oven to rescue the cake, her young son darts through the kitchen and yells over his shoulder as he goes out the back door, "I'm going over to Greg's house." Moments later, as Beth disposes of the ruined cake, she cannot recall where her son said he was going.

Reason for forgetting _____

d. Diane reads a novel and subsequently sees a film based on the novel. The story ends on a happier note in the film than in the book. Several months later when Diane is recounting the plot of the novel to a friend, she incorrectly remembers the book as having a happy ending.

Reason for forgetting _____

e. Antoinette stops for a red light at a busy intersection. She calls to the driver of a car in the next lane, "Can you tell me how to get to Paradise Mall?" The driver hurriedly shouts back, "Go straight ahead three lights, not counting this light, and turn right on Parham. Stay in the left lane and take the second exit. Go south on Patterson past Circuit Breakers Audio and turn right at Furniture Universe into the mall. You can't miss it." Before Antoinette can repeat the directions, the light turns green. As she drives along she mutters to herself, "Now was that three lights and a left or two lights and a right?"

Reason for forgetting _____

6. The peg-word method is an effective mnemonic device for remembering objects, facts, tasks, and other types of items. As your text explains, this method involves making up mental images of the items you want to remember and "hanging" them on peg words taken from a familiar jingle.

Assume that you want to take the following items on an overnight back-packing trip: sunglasses, insect repellent, compass, trail map, sleeping bag, knife, toilet paper, matches, canteen, and flashlight. Using the number rhyme and what you have learned about the peg-word method, complete Table 6-1 by describing the mnemonic images you would use to remember these items. The first item has been done for you.

Table 6-1 Peg-Word Method of Recall

Peg Word	Camping Item	Mnemonic Image
One-bun	Sunglasses	Hamburger bun wearing sunglasses
Two-shoe	Insect repellent	_____
Three-tree	Compass	_____
Four-door	Trail map	_____
Five-hive	Sleeping bag	_____
Six-sticks	Knife	_____
Seven-heaven	Toilet paper	_____
Eight-gate	Matches	_____
Nine-wine	Canteen	_____
Ten-hen	Flashlight	_____

READING EXERCISE

Why might you find it difficult to remember how you got home on New Year's eve or what your crib looked like when you were an infant? The following article from *Newsweek* discusses new insights about questions such as these.

Memory

Before there is knowledge, there must be memory. Yet few subjects remain so unknown, so obscured in metaphor and myth. According to the ancient Greeks, life is the act of recollecting knowledge the soul forgot at the moment of its birth in a body. Shakespeare

Written by Sharon Begley, Karen Springen, Susan Katz, Mary Hager, and Elizabeth Jones. Reprinted from *Newsweek* magazine, September 29, 1986, by permission of the publisher. Copyright (c) by Newsweek Inc.

spoke of memory as "the warder of the brain." Later thinkers noted the perversity of memories--how nothing imprints them more strongly than the desire to forget. For millenniums, memory was the province of philosophers and poets. Now it is scientists' turn. They are achieving dazzling insights into this mother of the Muses, but the task is not easy. Memory, says psychobiologist Gary Lynch of the University of California, Irvine, is "the black hole at the center of neurobiology."

Mapping Out Memories

Today the scientific journey to the heart of the black hole proceeds along two paths. On one, neurobiologists are trying to chart the hardware of memory, the network of nerve cells--neurons-- within the brain whose activity and changes constitute the actual physical basis for memory. Ultimately, they believe, their approach will explain everything from how the mind can store an estimated 100 trillion bits of information--compared with which a computer's mere billions are virtually amnesiac--to why people forget where they put the car keys. On a parallel track, psychologists are probing the software of memory, describing what they call the puzzles of everyday memory. They are asking, and sometimes answering, whether there are different kinds of memory, how our recollections are organized and indexed and how emotions can strengthen memories to make them as vivid now as the day they were formed.

The psychologists' breakthrough came first: there is no single entity we can call "memory," a discovery illustrated with tragic clarity by amnesiacs. Take Clive Wearing, once an expert on Renaissance music and a producer for the British Broadcasting Corp. Eighteen months ago he came down with a rare form of encephalitis, which left him with a memory span that can only be measured in seconds. He doesn't remember a single event in his past--not the meal he just ate, not the song he just sang with friends around the organ. Yet he *can* sing and conduct a choir, for his musical ability remains eerily intact--a pinpoint of normality in a mind otherwise condemned to live in an eternal present. Wearing, his wife, Deborah, says, "is trapped forever in the groove of a scratched record." It seems, then, that some sections of the mind's archives store facts (names, images, events), while others store procedures (recollections of how to do things).

Memories are also distinguished by their duration. Short-term memory (STM) allows one to dial a number just found in the telephone directory and to forget it at the first "Hello." STM lasts moments--perhaps hours if one consciously pays attention to it. Its average capacity is five to nine bits of information (just right for phone numbers and ZIP codes). But long-term memory retains for decades something that is experienced in seconds. Once embedded in the mind, the memory stays forever, however much one may "forget" how to reach it. It is this type of memory that excites the most scientific curiosity.

Like books in a great library, long-term memories may be arranged by subject. Thus, a child's first Little League game might be recalled through thoughts of baseball in general, then through mental images of the hometown field. But the mind's cross-indexing puts the best librarian to shame. That same baseball memory may also be resurrected during a televised major-league game, or by the sight of children at bat--or even by the smell of a well-oiled glove.

Indeed, the sense of smell can evoke strong memories. One experiment in how scent reincarnates the past began with a jar of Vicks VapoRub: when nutritionist Cathy Folk of Vanderbilt University Medical Center was sick in bed, she found the aroma of the gel comforting; it led her to relive childhood scenes of her mother rubbing the medication on her. To see how smells unlock memories for other people, Folk exposed volunteers to such scents as mint, oranges, cinnamon and manure. Among her findings: oranges evoked Christmases past for older people, but not for younger (for the fruit now has no special holiday association). Oranges and VapoRub may seem homely next to the madeleine that inspired Proust's monumental "Remembrance of Things Past"; still, says Folk, they show that "some of the same [brain] structures handle odor reception, basic emotional responses and long-term memory."

Emotions may well underlie many long-term memories, serving either as index or fixative. In experiments with rats, for example, stress improved memory, apparently because it releases adrenaline. This flight-or-fight hormone, along with other emotionally tapped brain chemicals, seems to act as memory's indelible ink. Moreover, each emotion seems to have its own color ink. Psychologist Gordon Bower of Stanford University finds that when people learn material while happy, they recall it better when happy than when sad. Happy volunteers who read two stories--one of the Beatles' breakup and the other of a man's first love--recalled the latter much better, for it matched their mood at the time.

It is a commonplace of memory research that Americans of a certain age know what they were doing when they heard of John F. Kennedy's assassination. But their vivid recall of Nov. 22, 1963, is the product of more than simple emotion, believes cognitive psychologist Ulric Neisser of Emory University. He sees several forces at work. For one thing, he says, "You think about these special events a lot." This act of rehearsing may actually reproduce the neural events that formed the memory, making it event stronger. Also, we remember such "firsts" as a first kiss--an event for which the mind has to carve out a new category. But after the mind has processed the same kind of event many times, "the particulars are replaced by the general," says Neisser. "You can't remember what you had for breakfast two days ago because you've had so many breakfasts."

10,000 dots: What of those people who *can* recall that it was cornflakes Monday and muffins Sunday? Just as there are extraordinary musicians, there are people who have an innately superior memory--Neisser calls them "Mozarts of memory." Conductor Arturo Toscanini, for example, memorized every note for every instrument in 100 operas and 250 symphonies. To study such phenomenal memory, researchers asked a woman who seemed to have a photographic memory to look through a red lens like those used at 3-D movies. She saw 10,000 dots that the lens made visible on a page. Then, with the other eye, she looked through a green lens that made another 10,000 dots visible. When asked to describe what image would result from merging all 20,000 dots, she was able to do it. She had perfect recall of the dots. Says Michael Epstein of Rider College: "When you look at a scene and close your eyes quickly, you have an afterimage for a couple of seconds. People with photographic memory have that image for a much longer time." By one estimate, 10 out of 100 children have a photo-graphic memory, but somehow 9 of those 10 children eventually lose that ability: only 1 percent of adults have a photographic memory.

The other 99 percent are plagued with forgetting. Sometimes the failure is amazingly specific, as in people with a condition called prosopagnosia: they cannot recognize faces. When researchers at the University of Iowa recently showed a prosopagnosic pictures of family members, celebrities and strangers, she failed to recognize any. But the electrical activity of her skin--a measure of activity in the nervous system--grew more intense when she saw the celebrities and relatives. Iowa's Antonio Damasio thinks this finding supports the idea that the memory of a person includes a "template" of his face. Seeing the face activates the template which, like a fly moving along the silken threads of a spider's lair, sets up vibrations throughout the mental web that holds the memory of the person. But sometimes the vibrations stop short of triggering all the information needed to identify the face . . . or find the word, or remember the fact. That tip-of-the-tongue feeling is likely the failure to activate enough details for full recall.

The Labyrinthine Ways of the Brain

On the other track are neuroscientists, who aren't satisfied with explaining forgetfulness by analogies to spider webs. They want to know its neural basis. "Only by making memory concrete, in terms of connections and cells, can we really come to grips with what it is," says neuropsychologist Mortimer Mishkin of the National Institute of Mental Health. The grip may come soon: "A lot of people believe that a breakthrough in memory is coming in the next few years," says Lynch.

The advances are on three fronts. First, researchers are mapping the anatomy of memory, identifying where the brain forms and stores it. The structures involved include the hippocampus ("sea horse" in Latin), an S-shaped structure deep within both sides of the brain; the cortex, the brain's wrinkled covering and seat of higher thought; and the cerebellum, which resembles a cauliflower at the back of the skull. Wearing's amnesia for events probably arose from damage to his hippocampus. This structure is believed to process new facts and send them for storage elsewhere. In a forthcoming paper in The Journal of Neuroscience, researchers led by Stuart Zola-Morgan of UC, San Diego, claim to have located a layer of 4.6 million cells in the hippocampus where new fact memories are processed. Second, neuroscientists are tracing routes that memory takes in the brain. Finally, they are finding changes in the 100 billion or so neurons of the brain--more than there are stars in our galaxy--that accompany the formation of memories.

Discovering the role of the hippocampus explains a facet of memory crystallized by Proust's madeleine:

when he inhaled [its scent], seven volumes' worth of memories--which would become his "Remembrance of Things Past"--welled up in his mind. The reason is now clear: the olfactory nerve conveys scent information to the hippocampus. And since the hippocampus and neighboring brain structures have long been thought to control emotions, the importance of feelings in creating and maintaining memories finds a simple explanation. "It is not by accident that these structures are important for both memory and emotion," says Mishkin. Once past the hippocampus, fact memories probably travel to the cerebral cortex. Here, simple memories are apparently stored at sites that correspond to the senses. The aroma of a mowed lawn, for instance, is processed in one spot in the cortex, and the memory of it will settle in the same place. But memories not directly associated with a sense, like the plot of a novel, are so far impossible to locate.

Besides dissecting the anatomy of memory, neurobiologists are tracing its circuitry. One model resembles the story of Theseus trailing a string through the Minotaur's labyrinth: the labyrinth is the cortex and the string is the memory "trace." A memory-to-be enters the cortex through one of the senses and is analyzed--a striking still life is scanned, for example. The information then wends its way through the hippocampus area, where it is checked for emotional content, and finally into the depths of the brain. Here, chemical fountains begin spouting and somehow preserve a memory trace like bronze does baby shoes: neurons along the information's path into the brain may be forever altered so they store a representation of the painting. Seeing the painting again activates the trace and the memory.

Lost keys: This model explains such puzzles as why we forget where we put our keys. Because keys are left in many places, there is no one trace for their location: the mind must look for the most recent. Similarly, if a memory is not used for years, its trace may be usurped by a new one.

A trace is but a chain of nerve cells linked by "synapses" where a nerve impulse jumps from one cell to the next. These connections are vital to trace formation, so researchers led by William Greenough of the University of Illinois decided to see how synapses change when memories form. They raised some rats in cages filled with toys and others in nearly empty cages. Their finding: rats in the complex environment grew 20 percent more synapses in part of their cortex than the deprived rats did. Perhaps synapses, which form as the rats process information about the props in the cage, are the seeds of memories.

How do neurons form synapses that might constitute memories? Lynch has one theory, and although he modestly says "It's got the sex appeal of a worm," it is widely hailed as a breakthrough in the neurobiology of memory. He pictures neurons as something like surrealist trees that Dali might paint. Their branches are made of protein, draped with a gooey membrane and studded with an enzyme called calpain. When an electrical impulse throbs through the neuron, as it does when information comes in, calpain "eats" some of the neuron's branch and allows the membrane to flow. The membrane can then reach out and form synapses with neighboring neurons--synapses that might form the first link of a memory trace.

Membranes are the focus of another leading theory of memory. Daniel Alkon of the Marine Biological Laboratory in Woods Hole, Mass., has trained marine snails much as Pavlov did dogs: he exposed them to light (which attracts them) and then shook up the tube they lived in. Snails hate turbulence. Eventually they learned that light preceded a shake-up, and stopped moving toward light. Alkon has pinpointed how snails remember that light means turbulence ahead: channels that carry electrical signals through neurons close when the neuron "learns" the association. The closed channels eventually emit a "stop" signal that keeps the snail from moving toward light--and a memory is born. Such changes may constitute the basis for memory, and Alkon believes that "there is a very reasonable probability that these same changes occur in people."

Such theories of memory fail to explain why we don't remember everything. If neuron changes constitute memories, what makes some last for decades while others fade? Eric Kandel and colleagues at Columbia University think the answer lies in genes, the molecules of heredity. He suggests that if an incoming memory turns certain genes on and others off, these changes in activity might somehow make neuron changes--and hence memory--permanent. Genes contain the blueprints for our bodies; it would be fitting if they also contain specifications for our minds.

Stages of Life, Ages of the Mind

A man of 63 recalls his war years as a paratrooper in France as vividly as if a videotape were running in front of his mind's eye--the farm girls offering bread and wine, the lethally stupid pilot who let the boys jump out while the plane was still flying over the Atlantic Ocean at night--but he forgets his granddaughter's name. The granddaughter, 16 months, recognizes her toys and parents, and retains a precise mental map of her house; but as she grows up she will retain few, if any, conscious memories of the time before she was three.

Now that researchers have begun to crack the secrets of how the brain forms and stores remembrances of things past, they are tackling the puzzles of memory at the chronological extremes of life. "Infantile amnesia," for instance, in which people remember nothing of the time before they were three or so, has long bemused students of the mind. Freud attributed it to repression: he argued that children's thoughts are so incestuous and violent that the mature mind effectively silences them. But scientists today think otherwise. The most parsimonious theory notes simply that the brain structures necessary for declarative memory don't fully develop until age one and a half or two. "The hippocampus is one of the last structures in the brain to become fully functional," says Larry Squire of the UC, San Diego. Until it does, then, a child cannot permanently record fact memories.

Psychological explanations of infantile amnesia are more elaborate, but they capture better the nuances of what children remember. The mists that shroud our memory of childhood, says Emory's Neisser, arise because children view the world differently from adults. A little girl remembers a pet dog as a huge creature; seeing the same breed fifteen years later when she is three feet taller won't jog her memory. She is also unlikely to recall the birth of a sibling—neither her mother's departure for the hospital nor the squalling baby's debut at home—because she lacks a sense of what is usual and what is unusual. "Children are just as likely to remember routine [events] as distinctive ones," says psychologist Robyn Fivush of Emory. They have no more reason to note a sibling's birth than to remember a speeding train glimpsed during a car ride. Finally, the mature mind is built on words—words children have not learned. As a result, an adult who mentally flips through memories filed under "birthday" or "party" will almost certainly fail to retrieve the memory of a first birthday, for the preliterate child did not index the memory that way.

Gum-ball machine: One way to reach childhood memories is to try to see and think as a child does. One study found that 2 1/2-year-olds remember events of 9 to 12 months ago quite well,

suggesting that memories of babyhood stay in the mind and, for those who see with a child's eyes, remain within reach. Even adults can take a child's-eye view: when one of Neisser's students was kneeling down to install a gum-ball machine at his fraternity and thus viewing the world from a height of only a couple of feet, he felt an onrush of childhood memories.

Still, memories of youth are the exception more than the rule. Memory begins to deteriorate in the third decade of life, and by one estimate 85 percent of the *healthy* elderly—those over 65—suffer some memory impairment. What seems to happen is that as people grow older, the amount of information they store increases but the percentage they can recall without difficulty stays the same—so it seems as though they're forgetting more. In particular, the ability to remember the name of someone you've just been introduced to declines. Fifty-year-olds aren't as adept as 40-year-olds, who aren't as good as 30-year-olds. In general, what was difficult to remember in youth, like arbitrary lists or numbers, becomes harder to remember in maturity.

Now for the good news. The conventional wisdom of a continuous and serious loss of memory with age doesn't stand up to new scrutiny. Short-term memory doesn't become less complete or accurate, though it may get slower. But even the slowdown is modest; a 65-year-old who takes a minute longer to remember what he's supposed to order from the butcher may be annoyed, but, says James Fozard of the National Institute on Aging, "it is hardly a pathological problem."

More important, long-term memories endure. An immigrant may well recall her arrival on Ellis Island 60 years ago more clearly than yesterday's lunch, because dated memories have had more time to "consolidate," or link up with many locations in the cortex. The more connections, the likelier an elderly person is to hit on a neural pathway leading to the memory. Old memories also remain vivid because they are periodically revived. Neisser says that "most of our oldest memories are the product of repeated rehearsal and reconstruction." The more we relive a memory, the more permanent it becomes--even if the accuracy is distorted, says Thomas Crook of the Memory Assessment Clinic. In general, the elderly may remember the turning points in their lives better than they do, say, a zip code, because they reallocate their memory capacity to preserve and retain access to important things, not trivia. Old people "know what counts," says Neisser.

Now researchers are questioning whether memory deficits suggest that older adults are smarter at figuring out what can safely be forgotten. Last month, at the annual convention of the American Psychological Association, Cameron Camp of the University of New Orleans suggested that memory defects in the elderly may simply reflect a decision, not necessarily conscious, about what to sweep out of the mind. "Older adults may generate more 'forget' cues," he said, perhaps reflecting their greater store of knowledge. Older people are less likely than a youngster to encounter truly novel--that is, memorable--information, and may be more willing to forget what they learn because they are less likely to judge it important. "The ability to forget some previously learned information may allow older adults to focus on underlying principles," says Camp.

Blackouts Under the Influence

Movies like "The Lost Weekend" have made a cliche of the amnesia that follows too much ambrosia, but the syndrome is real: people do forget what they do, learn, see and say while intoxicated. That should not be surprising, since memory turns on the fine balance among the brain's natural chemicals and man-made compounds disrupt the balance.

Even moderate drinking can impair memory two ways. First, it is a depressant, and so makes people less alert and therefore less likely to remember what they did while under the influence. Alcohol also seems to act directly on brain regions that form memories. In a typical experiment, researchers led by Ben Jones, then at the University of Oklahoma, found that sober people usually recalled 40 of 72 words on 6 lists of 12 words each, while the inebriated remembered just 30. But the effects were subtle: people who had a few drinks had less trouble remembering words studied while sober than words seen *after* imbibing. "Alcohol appeared to interfere more with the consolidation of information into long-term memory than with the retrieval of it," says Jones. The reason is that alcohol seems to interfere with the hippocampus, and thus with the formation of new memory. But it doesn't seem to impair retrieval from long-term memory, as anyone who has suffered through a drunk's detailed account of his past can attest. Excessive drinking, though, can permanently impair memory.

Marijuana, too, interferes with memory formation, impeding the transfer from short- to long-term memory, but leaves existing long-term memory intact. "Once information gets into our memories, the retrieval of it seems to be less vulnerable to . . . marijuana," says psychiatrist Jared Tinklenberg of Stanford University. Rather, marijuana affects the encoding of new information--turning messages from the senses into the language of neurons--a step vital to filing it in long-term storage.

Stimulants, on the other hand, may sharpen memory, especially in fatigued people, simply by increasing alertness. Similarly, data showing that rats' memory is improved by drugs that provide more oxygen to the brain probably reflect the animals' heightened awareness, not intrinsically improved memory.

Secret compounds: Still, the search goes on for a memory drug. "Every drug house is interested in developing [one]," says UC's Lynch, who tests prospective memory drugs for industry by seeing which improve rats' memory for smells. "They have many compounds now, secret and otherwise, that they think might [work]."

One compound is modest indeed. Nutritionist Carol Leprohon-Greenwood of the University of Toronto has found that rats fed soybean oil performed 15 percent better in a memory experiment than rats fed lard. The fatty membranes of neurons involved in memory harden with age, but polyunsaturated fatty acids keep neurons pliable and more efficient at carrying nerve signals--and perhaps at preserving memories.

The latest candidate is Ayerst Laboratories' vinpocetine, a compound that seems to help rats retain memories longer and to restore "lost" memories. It works partially by making neurons use glucose more efficiently. The compound is undergoing clinical trials, and even if it proves effective would not be marketed before 1988. Moreover, vinpocetine is designed for victims whose memory has been hurt by a stroke, not people who are healthy but forgetful. Improving "normal" memory promises to be a harder task. "It's very hard to improve on what nature has provided us," says Tinklenberg. "We can make things worse, but it's hard to make them better."

Remembrance of Things Past

"The true art of memory," said Samuel Johnson, "is the art of attention." Nothing scientists have learned in the intervening 200 years has undercut Johnson's conclusion: we remember what we concentrate on. Mnemonics, then, although defined as methods that assist memory, are really exercises in concentration that force us to process information in the mind's deeper reaches. Researchers led by Rider's Epstein found that people who are instructed to find differences between related pairs of words (like shoe and boot) and similarities between unrelated pairs (like fence and helicopter) recall almost twice as many items as people who are told outright to memorize them. The psychologists think that "depth of processing" is related to retention; in some not-yet-understood sense, studying words for their meanings brings more of the mind into play than mere attempts at memorization. Moreover, the improved recall lasts. Information processed "at deeper semantic levels," Epstein says, is recalled better because it decays more slowly than information noted superficially. "If people paid attention they could improve their memories 50 percent," he says.

The myriad courses and books offering help in remembering anything, from the phone number for Chinese takeout to the names of a dozen strangers at a party, rely on just a few tricks. Among them:

*To remember a name, link it to an image with a similar sound, for visualization is one of the most powerful tools of memory. If a woman's name is Terry, imagine her picking berries. Or break the name into a silly idea: a man named Madison might be thought of as "mad at his son."

*Try rhymes. "I before E except after C" really does work. So do rhythms: Homer's hexameter undoubtedly helped preserve the "Iliad" in oral tradition.

*If you come up blank in your efforts to find a rhyme or a visual association for a name, rehearse it. Say it to yourself as soon as you're introduced, wait a few seconds and say it again. Wait twice as long and rehearse it a third time, then twice as long again and say it one final time.

The increasing "wait" periods make this technique more effective than simple repetitions, says psychologist Douglas Herrmann of Hamilton College, "because you have to sustain attention."

*To memorize unrelated things, like a shopping list, try the "loci" mnemonic, distributing items to be remembered along a familiar street. A Russian renowned for his memory could hear a list of 50 words and recite them back without error 15 years later. As he heard each item he mentally placed it along Moscow's Gorky Street, outside a shop he knew well. To remember the items, he took a mental walk down Gorky and picked them up one at a time.

*To recall a list of related words, make up a sentence of their initials. The planets can be recalled with the mnemonic "My very excellent mother just sells nuts until Passover." Often, the initial of a word (Mercury, Venus and so on) is enough to trigger the whole word. Making up your own mnemonic while studying the list works even better since it calls for extra concentration.

*Exploit "state-dependent memory." Just as happy moments are recalled better when happy than when sad, so duplicating other conditions surrounding an experience will bring it to mind. Students scheduled for an exam in one room, for instance, would do well to study for it in that room.

*To remember numbers, seek meaningful patterns in them. One student with an average memory learned to remember strings of numbers 80 digits long by relating them to running times (his favorite sport). Thus a string like 4, 2, 1, 9, 8, 5 became

4:21, a good time in the mile, and 9.85, a great time for the 100-meter dash. This mnemonic, like others, requires effort, but as Herrmann says, "There's lots of evidence that if you want to improve your memory, you can"--if you work at it.

The secret to good memory is in the storage. Sharp recall comes from storing information in "a rich, elaborate form," says psychologist Endel Tulving of Toronto. That is, relate it to something already known--lots of somethings, so there are many pathways leading to the fact. "Understanding the subject and relating it to something you know makes for powerful memory and storage," says Tulving.

Jorges Luis Borges tells of a boy who fell from a branch and, upon waking, had a photographic memory. He remembered the shape of every leaf on every tree in every forest he passed; every word on every page he read. His reality became that of a pointillist canvas seen too close: so many dots and details that all abstractions, all generalizations, melted away. He became an idiot savant. If there is a cautionary lesson in Borges's tale, nature learned it early. By one estimate, people typically can recall only 1 out of every 100 bits of information they receive in the course of daily life. How we do even that is mysterious enough, of course, but science is on the brink of understanding it. The next question belongs to a realm beyond science: how much better do we really want our memories to be?

QUESTIONS

Answer the following questions and then compare your responses with the suggested answers at the end of this chapter.

1. Neuroscientists are conducting research into the neural basis of memory. Cite three examples of such research discussed in the article.

3. How does alcohol affect memory?

2. What are some possible explanations for our inability to remember events which occurred during our first 3 years of childhood?

ANSWERS

Correct Answers to Self-Test Exercises

Multiple-Choice				Matching		
1. b	8. a	15. a	22. b	1. d	6. c
2. b	9. b	16. c	23. c	2. e	7. a
3. a	10. c	17. b	24. d	3. h	8. f
4. a	11. d	18. c	25. a	4. i	9. g
5. a	12. c	19. a		5. b	
6. b	13. d	20. d			
7. c	14. c	21. c			

Suggested Answers to Application Exercises

1. a. According to Atkinson and Shiffrin's storage-and-transfer model of memory, the material that you remember first came through your senses into sensory memory. For example, you may have temporarily recorded the sight of white linen tablecloths and the taste of lobster. Within a few seconds, the information either disappeared or was transferred to short-term memory for about 20 seconds. Some, but not all, of the material was then transferred to long-term memory. The memories you have of the dinner, however vivid, represent a condensation of what actually happened. For example, you probably can remember the most interesting stories that were told over the dinner, but you may have forgotten the waiter's or waitress's name.

    b. According to Craik, Lockhart, and Tulving's levels-of-processing model of memory, the deeper we process information, the longer it lasts. The deepest level of processing involves paying attention to the meaning of material. This theory would suggest that the information you can recall about the evening was processed at a deeper level than the information you have forgotten. For example, you may remember the lobster not only because of the sensory impression it made on you, but also because you thought of how expensive it is and how rarely you eat it.

2. In each example, the information on the right consists of less than the seven (plus or minus two) chunks of information, which most people can easily keep in short-term memory. The 10 single-digit numbers shown on the left are grouped on the right as three multidigit numbers. The 11 letters on the right would be much easier to keep in short-term memory than the 11 letters shown on the left because the letters on the right form three pronounceable syllables: CHU-TRO-STEMP. While the same number of apples, pears, and bananas are shown on the left as on the right, the three types of fruit are grouped together on the right, making it easier to keep this information in short-term memory.

3. A student who experiences a tip-of-the-tongue state while trying to recall the inventor Marconi might come up with names that are similar in sound, such as Manzoni and Mahoney. He or she also might come up with names that are associated in meaning, such as Edison and Bell, who were other inventors. The student would probably not come up with the names Bryan and Calhoun because they do not sound like Marconi nor are they associated in meaning.

4. a. To measure retention through a recognition task, you could ask your subjects to study the original list of nonsense syllables and then present them with a second list. The second list would contain some of the syllables from the original list and some new ones, with an equal number of old and new syllables typed in capital and lowercase letters. You would ask your subjects to indicate which words were on the original list. Finally, you could compare the

retention of the capitalized syllables versus the retention of the lowercase syllables.

b. To measure retention through a recall task, you could have your subjects study the list of nonsense syllables and then ask them to recall as many syllables from the list as possible. You could then compare the number of capitalized versus lowercase syllables recalled.

c. To measure retention through a relearning task, you could present the list typed in capital letters to one group and the same list typed in lowercase letters to the other group. You would then measure the time it takes for each member of the two groups to learn the lists perfectly. Next you would let enough time go by for each subject to forget the syllables. Later you would ask them to relearn the same lists. You could then determine how much more rapidly the lists were learned the second time and compare the time saved by the group which learned the capitalized syllables with the time saved by the group which learned the syllables in lowercase.

5. a. This is a case of cue-dependent forgetting. The juice glasses usually act as a cue for taking a vitamin. In Mike's hotel room, the cue is absent.

b. David's trouble is due to proactive interference. Learning the first set of names interferes with his ability to learn a new set of names on the same day.

c. This is a case of poor perception. Beth is so distracted by the burning cake that she doesn't pay attention when her son tells her where he is going.

d. Retroactive interference is at work in this situation. Seeing the film's happy ending causes Diane to forget the original ending of the novel.

e. Antoinette's confusion is due to inability to rehearse. She is given the lengthy set of directions in such a hurry that she forgets the information before she has the opportunity to rehearse it.

6.   Answer to Table 6-1 Peg-Word Method of Recall

Peg Word	Camping Item	Mnemonic Image
One-bun	Sunglasses	Hamburger bun wearing sunglasses
Two-shoe	Insect repellent	Giant insect wearing shoes
Three-tree	Compass	Compasses hanging from every branch of a tree
Four-door	Trail map	Trail map nailed on a door
Five-hive	Sleeping bag	Someone lying in a sleeping bag, staring up at a beehive hanging directly overhead
Six-sticks	Knife	Little old man whittling a stick with a knife
Seven-heaven	Toilet paper	Angels flying in twos, carrying toilet-paper banners between them
Eight-gate	Matches	Gate made of matchsticks
Nine-wine	Canteen	Red wine flowing from a canteen
Ten-hen	Flashlight	Hen picking at the *on* button of a flashlight

Suggested Answers to Reading Questions

1.   Neuroscientists are currently exploring the anatomy of memory, identifying locations in the brain where memories are formed and stored. A second focus of research is on the routes that memory takes in the brain. A third area of study deals with the billions of neurological changes that occur when memories are formed.

2.   One explanation for infantile amnesia holds that the necessary brain structures for declarative memory are not fully developed until age 1 1/2 or 2. Another maintains that a child's view of the world differs so greatly from an adult's that there are few correspondences to jog the memory. Yet a third explanation points to the differences between the ways children and adults index their memories. Adults, who rely on words as memory keys, find it difficult to retrieve childhood memories which were indexed in some other way.

3.   Moderate drinking can interfere with memory in two ways. First, because alcohol is a depressant,

people under the influence are less
alert than they normally are.
Consequently, they are less likely
to recall what they have done.
Also, alcohol seems to interfere
with areas of the brain that form
new memories. Finally, although
moderate drinking does not seem to
affect retrieval from long-term
memory, excessive drinking can
permanently impair memory.

Chapter 7:

INTELLIGENCE

CHAPTER OUTLINE

I. What is intelligence?
   A. Defining intelligence
   B. Theories of intelligence
      1. Psychometric approach
         a. Thurstone: Primary mental abilities
         b. Guilford: Structure-of-intellect theory
         c. Cattell and Horn: "Fluid" and "crystallized" intelligence
      2. Two new approaches
         a. Gardner's theory of multiple intelligences
         b. Sternberg's triarchic model
            (1) Componential element
            (2) Experiential element
            (3) Contextual element
      3. Piagetian approach

II. Intelligence testing
   A. A historical overview
      1. Early contributors
      2. Alfred Binet
      3. David Wechsler
      4. Subsequent tests
   B. Intelligence testing today
      1. Developing tests
         a. Test construction and standardization
         b. Reliability
         c. Validity
         d. Do intelligence tests measure aptitude or achievement?
      2. Tests in use today
         a. Stanford-Binet intelligence scale
         b. Wechsler scales
            (1) Wechsler adult intelligence scale (WAIS-R)
            (2) Wechsler intelligence scale for children (WISC-R)
            (3) Wechsler preschool and primary scale of intelligence (WPPSI)
         c. Group tests
      3. What's right--or wrong--with intelligence testing?
         a. The value of testing intelligence
         b. Some problems with intelligence tests

   c. Misuse of intelligence tests
    (1) "Rationalization" of racial discrimination
    (2) Overreliance on testing
    (3) Underestimation of IQ in the elderly
    (4) Underestimation of the intellectual abilities of handicapped children
   d. New directions in intelligence testing
    (1) Zelazo and Kearsley's information-processing approach
    (2) Considering the environment
    (3) Culture-free and culture-fair intelligence tests
    (4) Recognizing cultural differences
    (5) Testing for competence
     (*a*) Giving follow-up tests
     (*b*) Testing realistic behavior
    (6) Testing for practical intelligence
    (7) Assessing multiple intelligences

III. Influences on intelligence
 A. Heredity
  1. Twin studies
  2. Adoption studies
 B. Environment
  1. Social environment
  2. Family environment
  3. Nutrition
 C. Birth order
 D. Sex

IV. Extremes of intelligence
 A. The intellectually gifted
 B. The mentally retarded

Boxes
 Psychology in your life: How laypersons judge intelligence
 In the forefront: Developing children's abilities

LEARNING OBJECTIVES

After you study Chapter 7, you should be able to do the tasks outlined in the following objectives.

1. Define intelligence in four different ways.

2. Define the psychometric approach to intelligence.

3. Describe Charles Spearman's two-factor theory of intelligence.

4. Describe J. P. Guilford's structure-of-intellect model.

5. Describe the concepts of fluid and crystallized intelligence proposed by R. B. Cattell and J. L. Horn.

6. Describe Gardner's theory of multiple intelligences.

7. Explain the triarchic model of intelligence formulated by Robert Sternberg.

8. Describe the Piagetian approach to intelligence.

9. Explain how IQ scores are distributed in the general population.

10. Explain how IQ tests are standardized.

11. Describe three methods of establishing test reliability.

12. Define content validity, concurrent validity, and predictive validity.

13. Describe four intelligence tests in use today.

14. Discuss the uses and misuses of intelligence tests.

15. Discuss problems associated with developing culture-fair intelligence tests.

16. Describe the criterion-sampling approach to test development.

17. Discuss the relative roles of heredity and environment in determining intelligence.

18. Describe characteristics of the intellectually gifted.

19. Discuss the role of schooling in the development of exceptionally creative students.

20. Define mental retardation.

21. Describe the five levels of mental retardation.

KEY CONCEPTS

As you read Chapter 7 in your text, look for each of the following concepts. You should understand each concept.

1. Definition of Intelligence

There is no single agreed-upon definition of intelligence. It has been variously defined as the ability to think abstractly, the ability to adapt to one's surroundings, and the ability to "act purposely, to think rationally, and to deal effectively with the environment." The definition used in your text is a *constantly active interaction between inherited ability and environmental experience, which results in a person's being able to acquire, remember, and use knowledge; to understand both concrete and (eventually) abstract concepts; to understand relationships among objects, events, and ideas; and to apply and use all the above in a purposeful way to solve problems in everyday life.*

2. Psychometric Approach to Intelligence

This approach emphasizes the measurement of intelligence. Following this approach, a number of researchers have used factor analysis to detect the components, or factors, of intelligence. Spearman identified two types of factors, the *g* factor (general intelligence) and the *s* factors (specific abilities). Thurstone found seven factors: word fluency, verbal comprehension, space, perceptual speed, reasoning, number, and memory. Guilford has found 150 factors resulting from the interaction of operations, contents, and products. Cattell and Horn have proposed two types of intelligence, fluid and crystallized.

3. Theory of Multiple Intelligence

Although Gardner believes that intelligence is composed of different specific abilities, he attempts to broaden the concept beyond the traditional areas. He argues that human beings have at least seven separate, relatively independent intelligences. These are linguistic, logical-mathematic, spatial, musical, bodily-kinesthetic, interpersonal, and intrapersonal.

4. Sternberg's Triarchic Model

Sternberg's triarchic theory divides intelligence into three separate but interrelated parts. The first, componential, relates to one's analytic ability. The second, experiential, deals with the creative ability to utilize insight and generate new ideas. The third, contextual, relates to one's practical knowledge.

5. Piagetian Approach

This approach attempts to describe patterns of intellectual functioning from infancy through adolescence. These four stages occur in all normal people and follow the same sequence in everyone.

6. History of Intelligence Testing

Intelligence testing as we know it began in 1905, when Alfred Binet developed a test to identify children in the schools of Paris who lacked the mental ability to benefit from a regular academic education. On Binet's test, a child's score was expressed as mental level (later called *mental age*). A child who took the test was assigned a mental age which corresponded to the chronological age of normal children who had made a similar score on the test during its preparation. Scores were later reported in terms of IQ (intelligence quotient). On this test, IQ is the ratio of a person's mental age (MA) to chronological age (CA), multiplied by 100. A revised version of Binet's test, now called the *Stanford-Binet Intelligence Scale,* is still in use today.

7. Standardization of Tests

Standardization involves developing uniform procedures for giving and scoring tests. To standardize scoring, norms must be established.

8. Reliability of Tests

Reliability is a measure of a test's consistency. It can be assessed by giving the same person or group the same test more than once, by giving alternate or parallel forms of a test, or by comparing a person's performance on half the items on a test with his or her performance on the other half.

9. Validity of Tests

Validity is the extent to which a test measures what it is supposed to measure. Content validity is the degree to which a test appropriately covers a given area. Criterion-related validity is the degree to which a test correlates with some independent criterion.

10. IQ Tests in Use Today

Many different IQ tests are currently in use. Some are individual tests; others are group tests. There are also tests designed for different age groups.

11. Uses and Misuses of IQ Tests

IQ tests have many socially beneficial uses. They are the best available predictors of academic achievement and best available measures of retardation. On the other hand, IQ scores have been unfairly used as evidence of the inferiority of many racial groups. Traditional IQ tests may also underestimate the intelligence of handicapped children and the elderly.

12. New Approaches to Intelligence Testing

Psychologists are continually trying to improve methods of assessing intelligence. Recently several new approaches have been developed. In keeping with Piaget's theory of cognitive development, standardized scales have been constructed to measure the acquisition of adaptive concepts. An information-processing approach has been used to test children from 3 months to 3 years. A system for measuring learning potential has been formulated which takes into account environmental factors and level of social competence. Culture-fair tests that attempt to minimize cultural influences have been constructed. Finally, tests that sample real-life competencies have been developed.

13. Influence of Heredity and Environment on Intelligence

Because heredity and environment constantly interact, it is impossible to assess the degree to which each determines intelligence. Methods for determining the relative influence of heredity and environment include making IQ comparisons (1) between identical twins who grew up in different environments, (2) between adopted children and their biological and adoptive families, (3) between relatives and unrelated persons, and (4) before and after a known environmental change. Such studies indicate that both heredity and environment play significant roles in determining intelligence.

14. Influence of Birth Order on Intelligence

Recent studies have found that firstborn and only children are more likely to be high achievers than younger brothers and sisters. One explanation for this is that parents often spend more time with, and expect more from, firstborn and only children.

15. Influence of Sex on Intelligence

Sex is not a determinant of overall IQ. However, sex differences do exist with reference to some specific abilities. On the average, females are superior at performing tasks which require verbal ability, while males excel at tasks requiring spatial ability. Researchers are currently trying to determine whether biological or cultural influences account for these differences.

16. The Intellectually Gifted

Longitudinal studies of people with high IQs have shown that as children the intellectually gifted are superior in terms of physical health and social adjustment. As adults, they tend to be more successful than the average person. However, not all intellectually gifted adults are equally successful; this indicates that factors other than intelligence affect success.

17. The Mentally Retarded

In classifying the mentally retarded, psychologists consider level of adaptive behavior as well as IQ scores. The classifications of retardation are as follows: borderline, mild, moderate, severe, and profound. People in the borderline and mild categories (about 80 percent of all retarded people) can function fairly well in society, while those in the severe and profound categories must be closely cared for by others.

TERMS TO KNOW

Define each of the terms listed. You can check your definitions in the text Glossary or on the text pages listed in parentheses.

		Fluid intelligence	(p. 233)
		Crystallized intelligence	(p. 233)
Intelligence	(p. 229)	Multiple intelligences	(p. 234)
Factor analysis	(p. 229)	Triarchic theory of intelligence	(p. 235)
Psychometric approach	(p. 229)	Object permanence	(p. 236)
Two-factor theory	(p. 231)	Mental age	(p. 237)
Piagetian approach	(p. 231)	Intelligence quotient (IQ)	(p. 237)
Primary mental abilities	(p. 232)	Standard deviation	(p. 238)
Structure of intellect	(p. 232)	Standardization	(p. 238)

Norm	(p. 239)	Predictive validity	(p. 239)
Reliability	(p. 239)	Basal age	(p. 240)
Test-retest reliability	(p. 239)	Ceiling age	(p. 240)
Parallel forms	(p. 239)	Habituation	(p. 248)
Split-half reliability	(p. 239)	Culture-fair tests	(p. 249)
Validity	(p. 239)	Criterion sampling	(p. 251)
Content validity	(p. 239)	Heritability	(p. 254)
Criterion-related validity	(p. 239)	Organic retardation	(p. 262)
Concurrent validity	(p. 239)	Down's syndrome	(p. 262)

Hydrocephaly   (p. 262)

Familial retardation   (p. 263)

SELF-TEST

Multiple-Choice

Choose the one best response to each question. An answer key is provided at the end of this chapter.

1. How do psychologists define intelligence?

   a. As the ability to think abstractly
   b. As the ability to adapt to one's surroundings
   c. As whatever intelligence tests measure
   d. There is no universally agreed upon definition.

2. According to Charles Spearman, what two factors are involved in intelligence?

   a. General intelligence and specific abilities
   b. Verbal and mathematical abilities
   c. Logic and creativity
   d. Ability to solve problems and ability to get along with people

3. How many factors make up J. P. Guilford's model of intelligence?

   a. 2
   b. 7
   c. 20
   d. 150

4. Which of the following best describes a current trend in intelligence testing?

   a. Measuring one overall index of general intelligence
   b. Measuring intelligence as a collection of separate abilities
   c. Abandoning standardization procedures
   d. Abandoning the use of group testing

5. When is crystallized intelligence highest?

   a. In infancy
   b. In early adolescence
   c. In early adulthood
   d. Near the end of life

6. Which of the following originated the triarchic theory of intelligence?

   a. Cattell and Horn
   b. Gardner
   c. Sternberg
   d. Piaget

7. Without doing any calculations, what do you know about the IQ of a 7-year-old child with a mental age of 9?

   a. It is under 100.
   b. It is exactly 100.
   c. It is over 100.
   d. It cannot be determined without further information.

8. On an IQ test that has a mean of 100 and a standard deviation of 16, within what range will most people score?

   a. 68 to 100
   b. 84 to 116
   c. 100 to 132
   d. 116 to 148

9. If a test is being constructed to predict the ability of truck drivers to benefit from a safe-driving program, on which of the following groups would it be best to try out possible items?

   a. Group of teenagers who are taking a course in safe driving
   b. Group of truck drivers
   c. Group of adults who have lost their driver's licenses because of reckless driving
   d. Group of driving instructors

10. The fact that people tend to do better on a test the second time they take it presents a problem in which of the following situations?

    a. When split-half reliability is being calculated
    b. When concurrent validity is being measured
    c. When predictive validity is being measured
    d. When the test-retest method is being used to measure reliability

11. If a test is supposed to measure intelligence, but it actually measures reading ability, what is it lacking?

    a. Reliability
    b. Validity
    c. Standardization
    d. Norms

12. If a course in American history covers the years 1865 to 1987, but the items on the final examination cover only the nineteenth century, what does the exam lack?

    a. Content validity
    b. Concurrent validity
    c. Predictive validity
    d. Chronological validity

13. When does testing stop on the Stanford-Binet Intelligence Scale?

    a. When all the items on the test have been presented
    b. Exactly 30 minutes from the time the test begins
    c. When the person taking the test misses two of the items on a level
    d. When the person taking the test misses all of the items on a level

14. What is one way in which the Stanford-Binet differs from the Wechsler Adult Intelligence Scale (WAIS)?

    a. The Stanford-Binet has a heavier verbal emphasis than WAIS.
    b. The Stanford-Binet is given to individuals, whereas WAIS is given to groups.
    c. The Stanford-Binet is used primarily with adults, whereas WAIS is used primarily with children.
    d. The Stanford-Binet is not very reliable, whereas WAIS is highly reliable.

15. Among which of the following groups is the highest average IQ score found?

    a. White American children
    b. Black American children
    c. Japanese children
    d. Mexican children

16. Which of the following accurately describes most intelligence tests?

    a. They are good predictors of grades in school.
    b. They are good predictors of career success.
    c. They are good estimators of the intelligence of the elderly.
    d. They are good estimators of the intelligence of children with motor and speech handicaps.

17. If a test constructor wanted to use criterion sampling on a test for lifeguards, which of the following tasks would probably be part of the test?

   a. Defining words like *resuscitation*
   b. Treading water
   c. Explaining what the saying, "There's more than one fish in the sea," means
   d. Completing the analogy, "'Diving board' is to 'pool' as 'basket' is to _____."

18. Which of the following statements best describes culture-fair intelligence tests?

   a. Black children, on the average, score as well as white children on these tests.
   b. Black children, on the average, score higher on these tests than do white children.
   c. These tests emphasize nonverbal tasks.
   d. These tests are free of cultural influences.

19. Which of the following is probably the best explanation for the recent increase in IQ scores among Japanese children?

   a. Changes in the genetic structure of the population
   b. Easier intelligence tests
   c. Positive environmental changes
   d. Increased intermarriage with Americans

20. Which of the following statements best describes the influence of heredity and environment on intelligence?

   a. Intelligence is determined entirely by heredity.
   b. Intelligence is determined entirely by environment.

   c. Both heredity and environment determine intelligence, but heredity has the greater influence.
   d. Both heredity and environment determine intelligence, and their relative influence is a disputed point.

21. How does sex affect IQ?

   a. In general, males have higher IQ scores.
   b. In general, females have higher IQ scores.
   c. In general, females score higher on measures of verbal ability, and males score higher on measures of spatial ability.
   d. In general, females score higher on measures of spatial ability, and males score higher on measures of verbal ability.

22. Most people who are mentally retarded fall within which of the following categories (levels) of retardation?

   a. Borderline or mild
   b. Mild or moderate
   c. Moderate or severe
   d. Severe or profound

23. If retardation is accompanied by hydrocephaly, how would the retardation be classified?

   a. Borderline retardation
   b. Mild retardation
   c. Organic retardation
   d. Familial retardation

24. At which of the following levels of mental retardation would a person probably be capable of learning to read magazines and newspapers written at a sixth-grade level?

   a. Mild
   b. Moderate
   c. Severe
   d. Profound

25. Which of the following statements
is true of the group of
intellectually gifted people
studied by Terman and other
Stanford University researchers?

  a. As children, they were not as
  healthy as children of average
  intellect.

  b. As adults, they were especially
  creative.
  c. In college, they displayed
  scholastic superiority.
  d. As adults, they were equally
  distributed in all the
  occupational categories from
  highest to lowest.

Matching

Match each research psychologist in column A with the appropriate theory of
intelligence in column B.

Column A

_____ 1. Cattell and Horn
_____ 2. Robert Sternberg
_____ 3. Charles Spearman
_____ 4. Jean Piaget
_____ 5. J. P. Guilford
_____ 6. Howard Gardner
_____ 7. L. L. Thurstone

Column B

a. Structure-of-intellect theory
b. Theory of multiple intelligences
c. Primary mental abilities
d. Stages of intellectual development
e. Two-factor theory
f. Triarchic theory of intelligence
g. Fluid and crystallized
intelligence

APPLICATION EXERCISES

These application exercises will test
your understanding of and ability to
apply the material you have read in
your text. Suggested answers are
provided at the end of the chapter so
that you can check your responses.

1. Robert Sternberg's triarchic theory
of intelligence describes three
separate but interrelated
abilities: the componential, the
experiential, and the contextual.
In the following cases, identify
the intellectual ability that seems
most evident.

  a. Bonnie works for a fast-food
  restaurant and often wins the
  manager-of-the-year award
  because she consistently comes
  up with new ideas for preparing
  the food faster and for cutting
  expenses. Bonnie's dominant
  intellectual strength is _____

  _____ .

  b. Peter has just received tenure
  at a major university. While not
  noted for his teaching or his
  scholarship, he has been very
  successful in receiving large
  grants from the government. By
  keeping well informed on
  political tendencies and by

cultivating friendships among legislators, he has managed to submit timely grant proposals. Peter's dominant intellectual strength is

_____.

c. Kim works for H & R Block and handles tax returns more efficiently and more effectively than anyone else in the office. Everyone is impressed with her speed and accuracy. Kim's dominant intellectual strength is

_____.

2. On the Stanford-Binet Intelligence Scale, mental age is translated to IQ using the following formula:

$$IQ = \frac{mental\ age}{chronological\ age} \times 100$$

A 9-year-old child with a mental age of 10 would have an IQ of 110:

$$IQ = 10/9 \times 100$$
$$= 110$$

a. Why is the IQ a more useful score than mental age?

_____

_____

_____

b. What would be the IQ score of an 8-year-old child with a mental age of 6?

_____

3. Reliability is an important characteristic of intelligence tests as well as of other types of tests. Your text describes several ways of checking a test's reliability. These include determining the consistency of people's scores when they are given the same test twice, the consistency of people's scores on random parts of a test (split-half reliability), and the consistency of people's scores on alternate forms of a test. Study the graphs in Figures 7-1, 7-2, and 7-3 and then in each case indicate which test has the higher reliability.

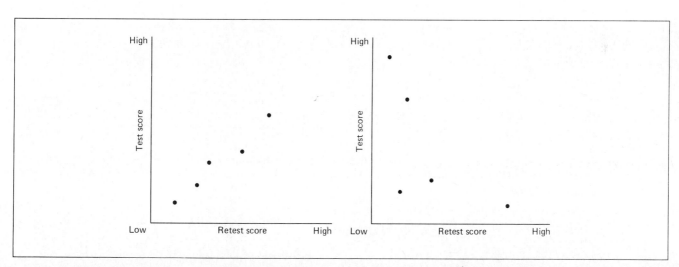

Figure 7-1

a. Which test has greater reliability? _____

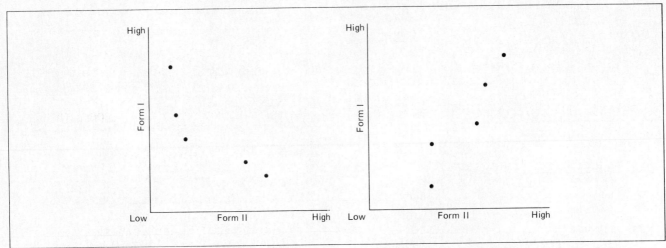

Figure 7-2

b. Which test has greater
reliability? _____

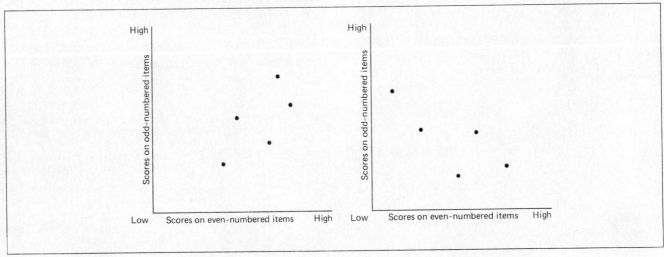

Figure 7-3

c. Which test has greater
reliability? _____

4. Test validity is the degree to
which a test measures what it is
supposed to measure. Your text
describes three types of validity:
content, concurrent, and
predictive. The tests described
below lack at least one of these

types of validity. In each case
describe the type of validity that
the test most obviously lacks.

a. A manufacturing company wants to
use a test to help select
employees who will come to work

regularly and on time. Before actually using the test results in making hiring decisions, the company wants to check its reliability. Job applicants are given the test but hired according to other criteria. Later, personnel records show that there is no relationship between the scores people made on the test and the number of days they have been absent from or late to work.

Type of validity lacking

_____

_____

b. Some school teachers are given a test which is supposed to measure their ability to handle discipline problems. Teachers who have been given high ratings on their ability to handle discipline problems by their supervisors do not score any higher on the test than teachers who have received low ratings. (Hint: In answering this question, assume that the supervisors' ratings were valid.)

Type of validity lacking

_____

_____

_____

c. At the beginning of the semester, Madame Menier tells her French class that learning to speak French and to understand it when it is spoken are just as important as learning to read and write the language. She places equal emphasis on the four skills throughout the semester. The final examination, however, contains no oral component; all the test items require only reading and writing.

Type of validity lacking

_____

_____

_____

5. Your text describes a number of intelligence tests in common use today. Complete the summary in Table 7-1, which highlights similarities and differences among these tests.

Table 7-1   Types of Intelligence Tests

Name of Test	Target Age Group	Characteristics
Stanford-Binet Intelligence Scale	Primarily for children	_____ _____ _____
_____	Adults	Yields separate scores for verbal and performance abilities as well as one overall IQ score
_____	6-16 years	Yields separate scores for verbal and performance abilities as well as one overall IQ score
Wechsler Preschool and Primary Scale of Intelligence	_____	Has good reliability; however, there is some relationship between scores earned and socioeconomic status

6. Your text describes five levels of retardation. The assignment of a person to one of these levels depends not only on intellectual functioning as measured by IQ tests but also on the person's adaptive behavior. Study the behaviors listed in the right-hand column of Table 7-2. Then decide whether a person classified at the level of retardation designated in the left-hand column would be capable of that behavior. Check the appropriate box.

Table 7-2   Behavior and Level of Retardation

Level of Retardation	Probably Capable	Probably not Capable	Behavior
Borderline	_____	_____	Hold a job
	_____	_____	Maintain own apartment
Mild	_____	_____	Make change
	_____	_____	Read a high school textbook
Moderate	_____	_____	Count objects
	_____	_____	Read a newspaper
Severe	_____	_____	Read simple directions
	_____	_____	Work under close supervision at putting shoes into boxes
Profound	_____	_____	Go for a walk alone
	_____	_____	Stay at home alone for an afternoon

READING EXERCISE

Robert J. Sternberg, professor of psychology and education at Yale University, has proposed a three-part theory of intelligence. According to Sternberg, the three aspects of intelligence which play an important part in all our lives are componential, experiential, and contextual. In the following article, which appeared in *Psychology Today,* each aspect of intelligence is described.

Three Heads Are Better Than One

I really stunk on IQ tests. I was just terrible," recalls Robert J. Sternberg.

Reprinted from *Psychology Today* magazine by permission of the publisher. Copyright (c) 1986 by the American Psychological Association.

"In elementary school I had severe test anxiety. I'd hear other people starting to turn the page, and I'd still be on the second item. I'd utterly freeze."

Poor performances on IQ tests piqued Sternberg's interest, and from rather inauspicious beginnings he proceeded to build a career on the study of intelligence and intelligence testing. Sternberg, IBM Professor of Psychology and Education at Yale University, did his undergraduate work at Yale and then got his Ph.D. from Stanford University in 1975. Since then he has written hundreds of articles and several books on intelligence, received numerous fellowships and awards for his research and proposed a three-part theory of intelligence. He is now developing an intelligence test based on that theory.

Running through Sternberg's work is a core of common-sense practicality not always seen in studies of subjects as intangible as intelligence. This practical bent, which stems from his early attempts to understand his own trouble with IQ tests, is also seen in his current efforts to devise ways of teaching people to better understand and increase their intellectual skills.

Sternberg got over his test anxiety in sixth grade after doing so poorly on an IQ test that he was sent to retake it with the fifth-graders. "When you are in elementary school," he explains, "one year makes a big difference. It's one thing to take a test with sixth-graders, but if you're taking it with a bunch of babies, you don't have to worry." He did well on the test, and by seventh grade he was designing and administering his own test of mental abilities as part of a science project. In 10th grade he studied how distractions affect people taking mental-ability tests.

After graduating from high school, he worked summers as a research assistant, first at the Psychological Corporation in New York, then at the Educational Testing Service in Princeton, New Jersey. These jobs gave him hands-on experience with testing organizations, but he began to suspect that the intelligence field was not going anywhere. Most of the tests being used were pretty old, he says, and there seemed to be little good research going on.

This idea was reinforced when Sternberg took a graduate course at Stanford from Lee J. Cronbach, a leader in the field of tests and measurements. Intelligence research is dead, Cronbach said; the psychometric approach--IQ testing--has run its course and people are waiting for something new. This left Sternberg at a loss. He knew he wanted to study intelligence, but he didn't know how to go about it.

About this time, an educational publishing firm (Barron's) asked Sternberg to write a book on how to prepare for the Miller Analogies Test. Since Sternberg had invented a scheme for classifying the items on the test when he worked for the Psychological Corporation, which publishes the test, he was an obvious choice to write the book. Being an impecunious graduate student, he jumped at the chance, but he had an ulterior motive. He wanted to study intelligence and thought that because analogies are a major part of most IQ tests, working on the book might help. This work eventually led to his dissertation and a book based on it.

At this stage, Sternberg was analyzing the cognitive, or mental, processes people use to solve IQ test items, such as analogies, syllogisms and series. His research gave a good account of what people did in their heads, he says, and also seemed to account for individual differences in IQ test performance. Sternberg extended this work in the 1970s and in 1980 published a paper setting forth what he called his "componential" theory of human intelligence.

"I really thought I had the whole bag here," he says. "I thought I knew what was going on, but that was just a delusion on my part." Psychology comes out of everyday experiences, Sternberg says. And his own experiences--teaching and working with graduate students at Yale--gave him the idea that there was much more to intelligence than what his componential theory was describing. He brings this idea to life with stories of three idealized graduate students--Alice, Barbara and Celia.

Alice, he says, is someone who looked very smart according to conventional theories of intelligence. She had almost a 4.0 average as an undergraduate, scored extremely high on the Graduate Record Exam (GRE) and was supported by excellent letters of recommendation. She had everything that smart graduate students are supposed to have and was admitted to Yale as a top pick.

"There was no doubt that this was Miss Real Smarto," Sternberg says, and she performed just the way the tests predicted she would. She did extremely well on multiple-choice tests and was great in class, especially at critiquing other people's work and analyzing arguments. "She was just fantastic," Sternberg says. "She was one of our top two students the first year, but it didn't stay that way. She wasn't even in the top half by the time she finished. It just didn't work out. So that made me suspicious, and I wanted to know what went wrong."

The GRE and other tests had accurately predicted Alice's performance for the first year or so but then got progressively less predictive. And what became clear, Sternberg says, is that although the tests did measure her critical thinking ability, they did not measure her ability to come up with good ideas. This is not unusual, he says. A lot of people are very good analytically, but they just don't have good ideas of their own.

Sternberg thinks he knows why people with high GRE scores don't always do well in graduate school. From elementary school to college, he explains, students are continuously reinforced for high test-smarts. The first year of graduate school is similar--lots of multiple-choice tests and papers that demand critical thinking. Then around the second year there is a transition, with more emphasis on creative, or synthetic,

thinking and having good ideas. "That's a different skill," Sternberg says. "It's not that test taking and critical thinking all of a sudden become unimportant, it's just that other things become more important."

When people who have always done well on tests get to this transition point, instead of being continually reinforced, they are only intermittently reinforced. And that is the kind of reinforcement most likely to sustain a particular type of behavior. "Instead of helping people try to improve their performance in other areas, intermittent reinforcement encourages them to overcapitalize on test smarts, and they try to use that kind of intelligence in situations in which it is not relevant.

"The irony is that people like Alice may have other abilities, but they never look for them," he says. "It's like psychologists who come up with a theory that's interesting and then try to expand it to everything under the sun. They just can't see its limitations. It's the same with mental abilities. Some are good in certain situations but not in others."

The second student, Barbara, had a very different kind of record. Her undergraduate grades were not great, and her GRE scores were really low by Yale standards. She did, however, have absolutely superlative letters of recommendation that said Barbara was extremely creative, had really good ideas and did exceptional research. Sternberg thought Barbara would continue to do creative work and wanted to accept her. When he was outvoted, he hired her as a research associate. "Academic smarts," Sternberg says, "are easy to find, but creativity is a rare and precious commodity."

Sternberg's prediction was correct. In addition to working full time as a research associate she took graduate classes, and her work and ideas proved to be just as good as the letters said they would be. When the transition came, she was ready to go. "Some of the most important work I've done was in collaboration with her," Sternberg says.

Barbaresque talent, Sternberg emphasizes, is not limited to psychology graduate school. "I think the same principle applies to everything. Take business. You can get an MBA based on your academic smarts because graduate programs consist mostly of taking tests and analyzing cases. But when you actually go into business, you have to have creative ideas for products and for marketing. Some MBA's don't make the transition and never do well because they overcapitalize on academic smarts. And it's the same no matter what you do. If you're in writing, you have to have good ideas for stories. If you're in art, you have to have good ideas for artwork. If you're in law. . . . That's where Barbaresque talent comes in."

The third student was Celia. Her grades, letters of recommendation and GRE scores were good but not great. She was accepted into the program and the first year, Sternberg says, she did all right but not great. Surprisingly, however, she turned out to be the easiest student to place in a good job. And this surprised him. Celia lacked Alice's super analytic ability and Barbara's super synthetic, or creative, ability, yet she could get a good job while others were having trouble.

Celia, it turns out, had learned how to play the game. She made sure she did the kind of work that is valued in psychology. She submitted her papers to the right journals. In other words, Sternberg says, "she was a street-smart psychologist, very street-smart. And that, again, is something that doesn't show up on IQ tests."

Sternberg points out that Alice, Barbara and Celia are not extreme cases. "Extremes are rare," he says, "but not good. You don't want someone who is incredibly analytically brilliant but never has a good idea or who is a total social boor." Like all of us, Alice, Barbara and Celia each

had all three of the intellectual abilities he described, but each was especially good in one aspect.

After considering the special qualities of people such as Alice, Barbara and Celia, Sternberg concluded that his componential theory explained only one aspect of intelligence. It could account for Alice, but it was too narrow to explain Barbara and Celia. In an attempt to find out why, Sternberg began to look at prior theories of intelligence and found that they tried to do one of three things:

Some looked at the relation of intelligence to the internal world of the individual, what goes on inside people's heads when they think intelligently. "That's what IQ tests measure, that's what information processing tasks measure, that's the componential theory. It's what I had been doing," Sternberg says. "I'd take an IQ test problem and analyze the mental processes involved in solving it, but it's still the same damned problem. It's sort of like we never got away from the IQ test as a standard. It's not that I thought the componential work was wrong. It told me a lot about what made Alice smart, but there had to be more."

Other theories looked at the relation of intelligence to experience, with experience mediating between what's inside—the internal, mental world—and what's outside—the external world. These theories say you have to look at how experience affects a person's intelligence and how intelligence affects a person's experiences. In other words, more-intelligent people create different experiences. "And that," says Sternberg, "is where Barbara fits in. She is someone who has a certain way of coping with novelty that goes beyond the ordinary. She can see old problems in new ways, or she'll take a new problem and see how some old thing she knows applies to it."

A third kind of theory looks at intelligence in relation to the individual's external world. In other words, what makes people smart in their everyday context? How does the environment interact with being smart? And what you see, as with Celia, is that there are a lot of people who don't do particularly well on tests but who are just extremely practically intelligent. "Take Lee Iacocca," Sternberg says. "Maybe he doesn't have an IQ of 160 (or maybe he does, I don't know), but he is extremely effective. And there are plenty of people who are that way. And there are plenty of people going around with high IQ's who don't do a damned thing. This Celiaesque kind of smartness--how you make it in the real world--is not reflected in IQ tests. So I decided to have a look at all three kinds of intelligence."

He did, and the result was the triarchic theory. A triarchy is government by three persons, and in his 1985 book, *Beyond IQ,* Sternberg suggests that we are all governed by three aspects of intelligence: componential, experiential and contextual. In the book, each aspect of intelligence is described in a subtheory. Though based in part on older theories, Sternberg's work differs from those theories in a number of ways. His componential subtheory, which describes Alice, for example, is closest to the views of cognitive psychologists and psychometricians. But Sternberg thinks that the other theories put too much emphasis on measuring speed and accuracy of performance components at the expense of what he calls "metacomponents," or executive processes.

"For example," he explains, "the really interesting part of solving analogies or syllogisms is deciding what to do in the first place. But that isn't isolated by looking at performance components, so I realized you need to look at metacomponents--how you plan it, how you monitor what you are doing, how you evaluate it after you are done.

"A big thing in psychometric theory," he continues, "is mental speed. Almost every group test is timed, so if you're not fast you're in trouble. But I came to the conclusion that we were really misguided on that. Almost everyone regrets some decision that was made too fast. Think of the guy who walks around with President Reagan carrying the black box. You don't want this guy to be real fast at pushing the button. So, instead of just testing speed, you want to measure a person's knowing when to be fast and when to be slow--time allocation--it's a metacomponent. And that's what the componential subtheory emphasizes."

The experiential subtheory, which describes Barbaresque talent, emphasizes insight. Sternberg and graduate student Janet E. Davidson, as part of a study of intellectual giftedness, concluded that what gifted people had in common was insight. "If you look at Hemingway in literature, Darwin in science or Rousseau in political theory, you see that they all seemed to be unusually insightful people," Sternberg explains. "But when we looked at the research, we found that nobody seemed to know what insight is."

Sternberg and Davidson analyzed how several major scientific insights came about and concluded that insight is really three things: selective encoding, selective combination and selective comparison. As an example of selective encoding they cite Sir Alexander Fleming's discovery of penicillin. One of Fleming's experiments was spoiled when mold contaminated and killed the bacteria he was studying. Sternberg says most people would have said, "I screwed up, I've got to throw this out and start over." But Fleming didn't. He realized that the mold that killed the bacteria was more important than the bacteria. This selective encoding insight--the ability to focus on the really critical information--led to the discovery of a substance in the mold that Fleming called "penicillin." "And this is not just something that famous scientists do," Sternberg explains. "Detectives have to decide what are the relevant clues, lawyers have to decide which facts have legal consequences and so on."

The second kind of insight is selective combination, which is putting the facts together to get the big picture, as in Charles Darwin's formulation of the theory of natural selection. The facts he needed to form the theory were already there; other people had them too. But Darwin saw how to put them together. Similarly, doctors have to put the symptoms together to figure out what the disease is. Lawyers have to put the facts together to figure out how to make the case. "My triarchic theory is another example of selective combination. It doesn't have that much in it that's different from what other people have said," Sternberg admits. "It's just putting it together that's a little different."

A third kind of insight is selective comparison. It's relating the old to the new analogically, says Sternberg. It involves being able to see an old thing in a new way or being able to see a new thing in an old way. An example is the discovery of the molecular structure of benzene by German chemist August Kekule, who had been struggling to find the structure for some time. Then one night he had a dream in which a snake was dancing around and biting its own tail. Kekule woke up and realized that he had solved the puzzle of benzene's structure. In essence, Sternberg explains, Kekule could see the relation between two very disparate elements--the circular image of the dancing snake and the hexagonal structure of the benzene molecule.

Sternberg and Davidson tested their theory of insight on fourth-, fifth- and sixth-graders who had been identified through IQ and creativity tests as either gifted or not so gifted. They used problems that require the three different kinds of insights. A selective-encoding problem, for example, is the old one about four brown socks and five blue socks in a drawer. How many do you have to pull out to make sure you'll have a matching pair? It's a selective-encoding problem because the solution depends on selecting and using the relevant information. (The information about the 4-to-5 ratio is irrelevant.) As expected, the gifted children were better able to solve all three types of problems. The less gifted children, for example, tended to get hung up on the irrelevant ratio information in the socks problem, while the gifted children ignored it. When the researchers gave the less gifted children the information needed to solve the problems (by underlining what was relevant, for example), their performance improved significantly. Giving the gifted children this information had no such effect, Sternberg explains, because they tended to have the insights spontaneously. Sternberg and Davidson also found that insight skills can be taught. In a five-week training program for both gifted and less gifted children, they greatly improved children's scores on insight problems, compared with children who had not received the training. Moreover, says Sternberg, the gains were durable and transferable. The skills were still there when the children were tested a year later and were being applied to kinds of insight problems that had never appeared in the training program.

Sternberg's contextual subtheory emphasizes adaptation. Almost everyone agrees that intelligence is the ability to adapt to the environment, but that doesn't seem to be what IQ tests measure, Sternberg says. So he and Richard K. Wagner, then a graduate student, now at Florida State University, tried to come up with a test of adaptive ability. They studied people in two occupations: academic psychologists, "because we think that's a really important job," and business executives, "because everyone else thinks that's an important job." They began by asking prominent, successful people what one needs to be practically intelligent in their fields. The psychologists and executives agreed on three things:

First, IQ isn't very important for success in these jobs. "And that makes sense because you already have a restricted range. You're talking about people with IQ's of 110 to 150. That's not to say that IQ doesn't count for anything," Sternberg says. "If you were talking about a range from 40 to 150, IQ might make a difference, but we're not. So IQ isn't that important with regard to practical intelligence."

They also agreed that graduate school isn't that important either. "This," says Sternberg, "was a little offensive. After all, here I was teaching and doing the study with one of my own graduate students, and these people were saying graduate training wasn't that helpful." But Sternberg remembered that graduate school had not fully prepared him for his first year on the job as an academic. "I really needed to know how to write a grant proposal; at Yale, if you can't get grants you're in trouble. You have to scrounge for paper clips, you can't get students to work with you, you can't get any research done. Five years later you get fired because you haven't done anything. Now, no one ever says you are being hired to write grants, but if you don't get them you're dead meat around here." Sternberg, who has had more than $5 million in grants in the past 10 years, says he'd be five years behind where he is now without great graduate students.

"What you need to know to be practically intelligent, to get on in an environment," Sternberg says, is tacit knowledge, the third area of agreement. "It's implied or indicated but not always expressed, or taught." Sternberg and Wagner constructed a test of such knowledge and gave it to senior and junior business executives and to senior and junior psychology professors. The results suggest that tacit knowledge is a result of learning from experience. It is not related to IQ but is related to success in the real world. Psychologists who scored high on the test, compared with those who had done poorly, had published more research, presented more papers at conventions and tended to be at the better universities. Business executives who scored high had better salaries, more merit raises and better performance ratings than those who scored low.

The tacit-knowledge test is a measure of how well people adapt to their environment, but practical knowledge also means knowing when not to adapt. "Suppose you join a computer software firm because you really want to work on educational software," Sternberg says, "but they put you in the firm's industrial espionage section and ask you to spy on Apple Computer. There are times when you have to select another environment, when you have to say 'It's time to quit. I don't want to adapt, I'm leaving.'"

There are, however, times when you can't quit and must stay put. In such situations, you can try to change the environment. That, says Sternberg, is the final aspect of contextual, or practical, intelligence--shaping the environment to suit your needs.

One way to do this is by capitalizing on your intellectual strengths and compensating for your weaknesses. "I don't think I'm at the top of the heap analytically," Sternberg explains. "I'm good, not the greatest, but I think I know what I'm good at and I try to make the most of it. And there are some things I stink at and I either try to make them unimportant or I find other people to do them. That's part of how I shape my environment. And that's what I think practical intelligence is about-- capitalizing on your strengths and minimizing your weaknesses. It's sort of mental self-management.

"So basically what I've said is there are different ways to be smart, but ultimately what you want to do is take the components (Alice intelligence), apply them to your experience (Barbara) and use them to adapt to, select and shape your environment (Celia). That is the triarchic theory of intelligence."

What can you do with a new theory of intelligence? Sternberg, who seems to have a three-part answer for every question (and whose triangular theory of love will be the subject of a future *Psyhology Today* article), says, "I view the situation as a triangle." The most important leg of the triangle, he says, is theory and research. "But it's not enough for me to spend my life coming up with theories," he says. "So I've gone in two further directions, the other two legs of the triangle--testing and training."

He is developing, with the Psychological Corporation, now in San Antonio, Texas, the Sternberg Multidimensional Abilities Test. It is based strictly on the triarchic theory and will measure intelligence in a much broader way than traditional IQ tests do. "Rather than giving you a number that's etched in stone," he says, "this test will be used as a basis for diagnosing your intellectual strengths and weaknesses."

Once you understand the kind of intelligence you have, the third leg of the triangle--the training of intellectual skills--comes into play. One of Sternberg's most recent books, *Intelligence Applied,* is a training program based on the theory. It is designed to help people capitalize on their strengths and improve where they are weak. "I'm very committed to all three aspects," Sternberg says. "It's really important to me that my work has an effect that goes beyond the psychology journals. I really think it's important to bring intelligence into the real world and the real world into intelligence."

QUESTIONS

Answer the following questions and then compare your responses with the suggested answers at the end of this chapter.

1. Why did Sternberg become dissatisfied with his early componential theory of human intelligence?

2. How does the discovery of penicillin illustrate the "Barbaresque" talent, or the experiential aspect of intelligence?

3. According to Sternberg, how can we best utilize all three aspects of intelligence?

ANSWERS

Correct Answers to Self-Test Exercises

Multiple-Choice

1. d	10. d	18. c
2. a	11. b	19. c
3. d	12. a	20. d
4. b	13. d	21. c
5. d	14. a	22. a
6. c	15. c	23. c
7. c	16. a	24. a
8. b	17. b	25. c
9. b		

Matching

1. g
2. f
3. e
4. d
5. a
6. b
7. c

Suggested Answers to Application Exercises

1. a. Experiential. Bonnie is creative enough to suggest procedural improvements in the fast-food-chain's system, a system that most employees accept as a given. By coming up with so many new ideas, she rightly deserves to be manager of the year.

    b. Contextual. Relative to his colleagues, Peter is not an outstanding professor, except for his ability to be at the right place at the right time with his grant proposals. He has political connections in crucial places and knows before everyone else what areas of research will receive large amounts of funding. He is a very practical professor.

    c. Componential. Kim is able to process large amounts of tax information quickly and accurately. Such analytic skill makes her a valuable tax preparer.

2. a. The IQ is a more useful score than mental age because it reflects the relationship between mental age and chronological age. Two children who have the same mental age differ in their intellectual ability if they are not actually the same age. Their IQ scores will reflect this difference.

    b. 75:
    $$IQ = 6/8 \times 100$$
    $$= 75$$

3. a. Test A
    b. Test B
    c. Test A

4. a. Predictive validity
    b. Concurrent validity
    c. Content validity

5.
Answers to Table 7-1 Types of
Intelligence Tests

Name of Test	Target Age Group	Characteristics
Stanford-Binet Intelligence Scale	Primarily for children	Consists of mainly verbal items on all age levels beyond infancy
Wechsler Adult Intelligence Scaleren	Adults	Yields separate scores for verbal and performance abilities as well as one overall IQ score
Wechsler Intelligence Scale for Children	6-16 years	Yields separate scores for verbal and performance abilities as well as one overall IQ score
Wechsler Preschool and Primary Scale of Intelligence	4-6-1/2 years	Has good reliability; however, there is some relationship between scores earned and socioeconomic status

6.

Answers to Table 7-2 Behavior and Level
of Retardation

Level of Retardation	Probably Capable	Probably not Capable	Behavior
Borderline	x	___	Hold a job
	x	___	Maintain own apartment
Mild	x	___	Make change
	___	x	Read a high school textbook
Moderate	x	___	Count objects
	___	x	Read a newspaper
Severe	___	x	Read simple directions
	x	___	Work under close supervision at putting shoes into boxes
Profound	___	x	Go for a walk alone
	___	x	Stay at home alone for an afternoon

Suggested Answers to Reading Questions

1. Sternberg became dissatisfied with his componential theory when his personal experiences as a teacher and a researcher led him to believe that there was more to intelligence than his theory was describing. He came to believe that intelligence encompasses not only critical thinking, but also the ability to come up with good ideas and the ability to get on well in a given environment.

2. Alexander Fleming's discovery is a good example of the experiential aspect of intelligence because it reflects a novel, creative response (selective encoding) to information that would probably have been viewed as useless by most people.

3. Sternberg suggests that we apply our analytical skills to our various experiences and use them to change or adapt to our environment.

Chapter 8:

LANGUAGE AND THOUGHT

CHAPTER OUTLINE

I. Language
   A. Studying language
      1. Some basic definitions
         a. Linguistics
         b. Language
         c. Grammar
            (1) Sound
            (2) Meaning
            (3) Structure
      2. How psychologists study language abilities
   B. Learning a language
      1. How children learn a language
         a. Prelinguistic speech
         b. Linguistic speech
            (1) First words
            (2) First sentences
               (a) Brown's stages of language
               (b) Characteristics of stages 1, 2, and 3
               (c) Characteristics of stages 4 and 5
      2. Theories about language aquisition
         a. Learning theories
         b. Nativism
         c. Motherese: How caretakers structure the child's language
            environment
            (1) Case study: A home without motherese
   C. Three controversies in linguistics
      1. Controversy 1: Is there a critical period for acquiring language?
      2. Controversy 2: Does thought structure language, or does language
         structure thought?
         a. Linguistic-relativity hypothesis
         b. Tests of the linguistic-relativity hypothesis
      3. Controversy 3: Can animals learn language?

II. Formation of concepts
   A. Well-defined concepts
   B. Ill-defined concepts
      1. What are ill-defined concepts?
      2. Aspects of ill-defined concepts
         a. Typicality
         b. Family resemblance
         c. Basic-level categories

III. Problem solving
    A. Theories about problem solving
        1. Learning theory
        2. Gestalt theory
        3. Information-processing theory
    B. Stages of problem solving
        1. Stage 1: Preparation
        2. Stage 2: Production
        3. Stage 3: Evaluation
    C. Insight and problem solving
        1. How insight works
        2. Insight and intelligence

IV. Creativity
    A. Measuring creativity
    B. Creativity and intelligence
    C. Influences on creativity
        1. What makes people creative?
        2. Implications for education and child rearing
        3. Implications for creativity in adults

Boxes
    In the forefront: Artificial intelligence
    Psychology in your life: How to be more creative

LEARNING OBJECTIVES

After you study Chapter 8, you should be able to do the tasks outlined in the following objectives.

1. Describe the stages of prelinguistic speech.

2. Describe the stages and characteristics of early linguistic speech.

3. Contrast the learning theorists' and the nativists' explanations of language acquisition.

4. Explain the function of motherese in helping a child to learn a language.

5. Cite evidence that supports the idea of a critical period for acquiring language.

6. Cite evidence for and against the linguistic-relativity hypothesis.

7. Explain how people form both well-defined and ill-defined concepts.

8. Compare and contrast the associationist, gestalt, and information-processing approaches to problem solving.

9. Explain what happens in the preparation, production, and evaluation stages of problem solving.

10. Describe three intellectual processes which are thought to be necessary for solving insight problems.

11. Describe the relationship between insight and intelligence.

12. Explain what is meant by *artificial intelligence*.

13. Explain why creativity is difficult to measure.

14. Describe the relationship between creativity and intelligence.

15. Identify five practices that will help young people be more creative.

16. Identify several conditions that will foster creativity in adults.

KEY CONCEPTS

As you read Chapter 8 in your text, look for each of the following concepts. You should understand each concept.

1. What Cognitive Psychologists Study

Cognitive psychologists study human thought. Language, problem solving, and creativity are aspects of thinking.

2. Definition and Basic Characteristics of Language

Language is a means of communicating through spoken sounds that express specific meanings and are arranged according to rules. Every language has a grammar which includes the rules of sound, meaning, and structure.

3. How Psychologists Study Language Abilities

To study language, psychologists observe and analyze the way people speak and the way they respond to the speech of others. Psychologists learn a great deal about human linguistic abilities by studying the language abilities of infants and children. The ability of infants to discriminate between sounds has been the focus of a number of research studies. The ability of older children to hear and reproduce speech sounds, comprehend speech, and apply linguistic rules has also been studied.

4. Prelinguistic Speech

Before babies say words, they produce sounds. Their sound production progresses through stages that are linked to chronological age. The sequence of sound production is crying, cooing, babbling, accidentally imitating sounds, and consciously imitating sounds.

5. Linguistic Speech

Babies usually say their first words at about 1 year. These first words are called *holophrases* because they express a complete thought in a single word. The acquisition of linguistic speech occurs in stages which are not closely tied to chronological age. Children's early speech is characterized by simplification, overregularization of rules, overextension of concepts and inability to express grammatical relations.

6. Theories of Language Acquisition

There are several theories about why and how children learn language. According to behaviorist theory, we learn language through reinforcement, discrimination, and generalization. From the point of view of social-learning theorists, we learn language primarily through observation and imitation. Nativists, like Noam Chomsky, believe that we have an inborn capacity for acquiring language. Chomsky calls this inborn capacity the *language acquisition device* (LAD). Many psychologists believe that we acquire language through the interaction of an inborn language capacity and environmental influences.

7. Motherese

When speaking motherese to young children, adults or older children heighten pitch, simplify, repeat, and use fewer pronouns and verbs. Motherese is essential in teaching young children their native language.

8. Critical Period for Acquiring Language

Some researchers believe that before puberty the brain is best organized to encourage the acquisition of language.

9. Linguistic-Relativity Hypothesis

According to this hypothesis, also known as the *Whorfian hypothesis,* language structures thought and shapes ideas. Researchers have found evidence that supports this hypothesis as well as evidence that tends to refute it.

10. Animals and Language

Although apes have been trained to communicate with symbols, the ability to formulate concepts seems to be an exclusively human trait. The extent to which animals can learn language, however, remains a controversial issue.

11. Concept Formation

The ability to classify nonidentical objects, events, and people enables us to generalize from previous experience and formulate rules for thought and action. Research on concept formation has shown that it is a thinking process which goes far beyond the strengthening or weakening of stimulus-response associations. In real life, concepts are usually ill-defined. We learn them through experience over time. Some items are more typical of a given concept than others. The more features an item has in common with other members of a category, the more typical it will be considered.

12. Learning-Theory Approach to Problem Solving

In this approach, problem solving is seen as a trial-and-error process. We learn correct problem-solving behaviors because of reinforcement.

13. Gestalt Approach to Problem Solving

According to this approach, sudden flashes of insight make it possible to solve certain problems. From this perspective, functional fixedness is viewed as a barrier to problem solving.

14. Information-Processing Approach to Problem Solving

In this approach, problem solving is seen as a complex activity involving such processes as registering information, retrieving related material from memory, and making purposeful use of both types of information.

15. Stages of Problem Solving

Most psychologists believe that problem solving occurs in stages. According to one theory, these stages are preparation, production, and evaluation. In the preparation stage, we gain an understanding of the nature of the problem. In the production stage, we generate possible solutions to the problem. We may use an algorithmic or heuristic strategy in generating solutions. In the evaluation stage, we judge our solutions. Before arriving at a final solution, we may go back and forth between the stages.

16. Insight Problems

Cognitive psychology (p. 269)

Solving insight problems involves encoding relevant information, combining seemingly unrelated pieces of information, and discovering relationships between old and new information which are not obvious. There is a high correlation between IQ and the ability to solve insight problems.

Linguistics (p. 270)

Language (p. 270)

17. Measuring Creativity

Tests have been devised to measure divergent thinking. While these tests are reliable, their validity (ability to predict creativity in real life) is highly questionable.

Grammar (p. 270)

18. Relationship between Creativity and Intelligence

Phoneme (p. 270)

Only modest correlations have been found between creativity and intelligence. While creative people tend to be relatively intelligent, high intelligence does not ensure creativity.

Semantics (p. 270)

19. Enhancing Creativity

Research suggests that creativity in both children and adults can be enhanced when the following conditions are present: intrinsic motivation, choice, stimulation, inspirational models, freedom from evaluation, and independence.

Morpheme (p. 270)

Syntax (p. 270)

TERMS TO KNOW

Define each of the terms listed. You can check your definitions in the text Glossary or on the text pages listed in parentheses.

Auditory evoked response (AER) (p. 271)

Holophrases	(p. 272)	Linguistic-relativity hypothesis	(p. 278)
Mean length of utterances (MLU)	(p. 272)	Well-defined concept	(p. 282)
Telegraphic speech	(p. 273)	Ill-defined concept	(p. 282)
Learning theorists	(p. 274)	Typicality	(p. 283)
Nativists	(p. 274)	Family resemblance	(p. 283)
Social-learning theory	(p. 274)	Insight	(p. 285)
Language acquisition device (LAD)	(p. 275)	Functional fixedness	(p. 286)
Motherese	(p. 275)	Algorithm	(p. 287)
Critical period	(p. 277)	Heuristic	(p. 287)

Selective encoding   (p. 288)

Selective combination   (p. 288)

Selective comparison   (p. 288)

Deductive reasoning   (p. 289)

Inductive reasoning   (p. 289)

Artificial intelligence (AI)   (p. 289)

Creativity   (p. 290)

Convergent thinking   (p. 291)

Divergent thinking   (p. 296)

SELF-TEST

Multiple-Choice

Choose the one best response to each question. An answer key is provided at the end of this chapter.

1. In which of the following approaches to psychology is the study of human thought processes--including language, concept formation, problem solving, and creativity--of most concern?

   a. Associationist
   b. Behavioral
   c. Gestalt
   d. Cognitive

2. How many phonemes are contained in the word *gate?*

   a. 1
   b. 2
   c. 3
   d. 4

3. How many morphemes are contained in the word *fate?*

   a. 1
   b. 2
   c. 3
   d. 4

4. Which of the following most accurately defines semantics?

   a. Set of rules for structuring a language
   b. Study of meaning in a language
   c. Study of rules for sound, meaning, and syntax
   d. Set of rules for ordering words into sentences

5. Which of the following sounds do infants make first?

   a. Crying sounds
   b. Cooing sounds
   c. Babbling sounds
   d. Imitative sounds

6. Which of the following would be a holophrase?

   a. "Give me truck."
   b. "Truck." (Meaning: "I want my truck.")
   c. "I want my truck."
   d. "Give truck."

7. Roger Brown, who has studied the phases of language acquisition, discusses syntactic skill in terms of mean length of utterance (MLU). What kind of utterance does he use in calculating average length?

   a. Syllables
   b. Morphemes
   c. Words
   d. Phonemes

8. Which of the following characteristics of early childhood speech would best explain a child's calling all four-wheeled objects *car?*

   a. Children overextend concepts.
   b. Children overregularize rules.
   c. Children understand grammatical relations that they cannot yet express.
   d. Children simplify.

9. The nativist theory of language acquisition is supported by which of the following phenomena?

   a. Babies reared at home babble more than babies reared in institutions.
   b. Children differ considerably in their language abilities.

   c. Newborns tend to move at the same tempo as the speech sounds they hear.
   d. Children in English-speaking nations speak English.

10. Which of the following aspects of language acquisition is not stressed by social-learning theorists?

    a. Observation of language production
    b. Imitation of language production
    c. Reinforcement for language production
    d. Production of novel speech

11. Which of the following statements accurately describes motherese?

    a. It is spoken only by mothers.
    b. It retards children's language development.
    c. It is essential in teaching children their native language.
    d. It neither promotes nor retards language development.

12. If a 16-year-old girl were to suffer injury to the left hemisphere of her brain in an automobile accident, which of the following predictions regarding her lost language skills would accurately reflect the critical-period hypothesis?

    a. The right hemisphere will take over and some of the language skills will return.
    b. The right hemisphere will take over, and most of the skills will return.
    c. The skills will gradually return, regardless of the role of the right hemisphere.
    d. The loss of the skills is likely to be permanent.

13. What are the implications of Genie's linguistic progress relative to the critical-period hypothesis?

a. Her progress confirms the hypothesis.
b. Her progress disconfirms the hypothesis.
c. Her progress both confirms and disconfirms the hypothesis.
d. Her progress does not have a significant bearing on the hypothesis.

14. Assume that a culture (the Buddians) has been discovered which uses 53 different words for *beer*. According to the linguistic-relativity (Whorfian) hypothesis, which of the following conclusions is appropriate?

a. The Buddians are born with mental "maps" containing such distinctions.
b. The Buddians think differently about beer because they have the vocabulary to do so.
c. The Buddian children have acquired all 53 words for beer from their environment in a stimulus-response fashion.
d. The Buddians have 53 words for beer because they think differently about beer.

15. If English-speaking people were not capable of making as many distinctions, or discriminations, between different kinds of beer as Buddian-speaking people, what would that suggest about the linguistic-relativity hypothesis?

a. It would tend to support the hypothesis.
b. It would cast considerable doubt upon the hypothesis.
c. Such a finding would neither support nor discredit the hypothesis.
d. Such a finding would suggest that the language we use is, at best, ambiguous.

16. Which of the following best describes a concept?

a. Particulars drawn from categories
b. Trial-and-error reasoning
c. Particulars organized into categories
d. A series of universals

17. What do studies of concept formation indicate about the processes people use in forming concepts?

a. Trial-and-error guessing
b. Systematic thought strategies
c. Imitation
d. Stimulus-response associations

18. Which of the following best exemplifies an ill-defined concept?

a. Cup
b. Bachelor
c. Banana
d. Program

19. Which of the following possesses the most typicality in its concept category?

a. Lyre
b. Dulcimer
c. Mandolin
d. Guitar

20. Which of the following theories can explain the phenomenon of typicality?

a. Associationism
b. Family resemblance
c. Reinforcement
d. Functional fixedness

21. Which of the following would be classified as a basic-level category?

a. Siamese cat
b. Cat
c. Mammal
d. Animal

22. The "aha!" experience (sudden insight) is an important concept within the framework of what problem-solving theory?

    a. Gestalt
    b. Associationism
    c. Learning theory
    d. Information processing

23. Which stage of problem solving contains algorithms and heuristics?

    a. Preparation
    b. Production
    c. Evaluation
    d. Motivation

24. With which stage of problem solving can functional fixedness interfere?

    a. Preparation
    b. Production
    c. Evaluation
    d. Motivation

25. Which of the following appears to be a necessary condition for creativity?

    a. High intelligence
    b. Deductive reasoning
    c. Divergent thinking
    d. Convergent thinking

Matching

Match the theorists in column A with one or more appropriate descriptive phrases in column B.

Column A	Column B
_____ 1. Nativists	a. Stress the role of observation in language acquisition
_____ 2. Social-learning theorists	b. Believe that children can extract grammatical rules from the language they hear
_____ 3. Cognitive psychologists	c. Stress the role of insight in solving problems
_____ 4. Behaviorists	d. Are concerned with language, concept formation, problem solving, and creativity
_____ 5. Gestalt theorists	e. Stress the role of imitation in language acquisition
	f. Believe that humans have an inborn capacity for language acquisition
	g. Stress the role of reinforcement, generalization, and discrimination in language acquisition

APPLICATION EXERCISES

These application exercises will test your understanding of and ability to apply the material you have read in your test. Suggested answers are provided at the end of the chapter so that you can check your responses.

1. Children go through a sequence of stages in acquiring language. Some utterances representative of these stages are listed below. Number them to indicate the order in which they typically would be made.

   _____ "Ha" (meaning "hi" or "hello").

   _____ "The dog bited me."

   _____ Cooing sounds

   _____ "Ba-ba-ba-ba."

   _____ "Doggie gone."

2. Learning theorists stress the role played by the environment in language acquisition. Nativists, on the other hand, emphasize the importance of an inborn capacity to learn language. Assume that a 2-year-old girl points to her teddy bear and says, "My teddy."

   a. How would a learning theorist account for the child's ability to use language in this way?

   _____
   _____
   _____
   _____
   _____

   b. How would a nativist explain the same phenomenon? _____
   _____
   _____
   _____
   _____

3. *Concepts* are categories of objects, events, or people. In forming categories, we group together items which have defining features in common. As we learn a concept, we learn what its defining features are, and we also learn to disregard irrelevant features. For example, one defining feature of automobiles is that they have four wheels. Color, on the other hand, is an irrelevant feature as far as cars are concerned.

   Study Figure 8-1. Then list the three defining features of a Mr. Bobo. Next, list three irrelevant features.

Figure 8-1

Defining features _____

Irrelevant features _____

4. Functional fixedness, an overreliance on old ways of seeing and doing things, can prevent us from coming up with creative solutions to problems. Read the following problematic situation to see if you can overcome functional fixedness and come up with a solution.

   David has recently moved to a farmhouse in the country. His job is delivering newspapers on a rural paper route. David currently has two problems. First, he doesn't know what to do with the extra newspapers he ends up with each day. His pile of old newspapers is rapidly turning into a small mountain. Second, he has a mattress but no bed. He would like to get his mattress off the floor and onto a bed before cold weather sets in. How could David solve both his problems at once?

   _____
   _____
   _____
   _____

5. According to one information-processing theory of problem solving, we go through three stages in solving problems: preparation, production, and evaluation. Figure 8-2 shows a word game. Assume that you have come across this game in a newspaper. Describe what you do during each of the stages as you solve the puzzle.

SCRAMBLES

Excalibur was a _____ .

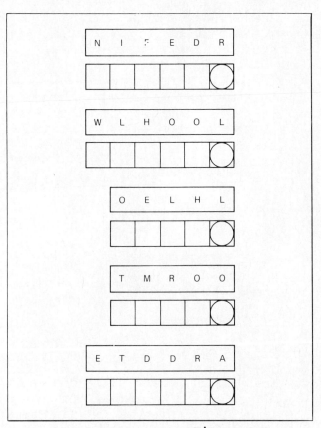

Figure 8-2

a. Preparation stage _____
   _____
   _____
   _____

b. Production stage _____
   _____
   _____
   _____

c. Evaluation stage _____
   _____
   _____
   _____

6. Although creativity seems to involve more than just divergent thinking, the ability to perceive the world in new and unusual ways

is a necessary condition of creative thought. Creating humor, for example, usually involves divergent thinking. Examine the cartoon in Figure 8-3 and describe three ways in which it reflects divergent thinking.

Inexplicibly, Bob's porcupine goes flat.

Figure 8-3

The Far Side by Gary Larson. Copyright (c) 1987 by Universal Press Syndicate. All rights reserved.

_____
_____
_____

READING EXERCISE

The sight of a person talking to himself or herself is likely to raise an eyebrow or two. A recent study by Laura E. Berk, however, suggests that such private speech in children is an important means by which they learn to

frequently told to keep still. If the development of private speech is facilitated by social speech, as Vygotsky believed, the early language environment of Appalachian children might account for the slow development we observed.

Finally, we discovered that talking to themselves increased dramatically when children were asked to solve difficult problems and teachers remained at a distance and did not inhibit such speech. This further supported Vygotsky's idea that children use private speech to facilitate their thinking and guide their behavior.

In the Appalachian study we worked with school-age children. In a second study, I searched for evidence that Piaget's theory of egocentric communication might explain the private speech of younger children. After collecting samples of the spontaneous speech of 93 3- to 5-year-old children in a variety of nursery school and day-care centers in lower- and middle-class areas of a small Midwestern city, I found practically no egocentric communication, even among the youngest.

I also confirmed what previous researchers had shown, that the most socially advanced preschool children talked to themselves the most, and that such speech was more frequent when children played together in large groups rather than alone, with one child or with an adult. Piaget expected that private speech would decline when children were with their peers, whom he thought would be unlikely to accept egocentric language. Instead, my findings supported Vygotsky's notion that even among very young children, private speech is stimulated and encouraged by social experience.

In a third study, I examined another basic aspect of Vygotsky's theory, the idea that private speech helps children control their actions and improves learning. Although private speech increases when children work on difficult tasks, the reason might be that their frustration produces stress,

anxiety and a consequent loss of verbal self-control. To rule out this explanation, I needed evidence that talking aloud helps children channel their behavior constructively and increases their success in solving problems.

I observed 75 first- and third-graders at a Midwestern school while they worked independently at their desks on math assignments. Such assignments maximize use of private speech, since children are likely to have difficulty solving at least some of the problems and must work matters out on their own without teacher guidance and assistance. We categorized the children's private speech using a system that reflected Kohlberg's developmental sequence described earlier.

The children's use of private speech was extremely high, occurring 60 percent of the time we observed them. Also, they followed Kohlberg's age-related pattern of moving from self-stimulating and externalized task-relevant private speech in the first grade to less audible private utterances by the third grade. Bright children developed faster, using more mature, inaudible forms of speech in the first grade than their average classmates did and moving toward complete internalization of speech earlier in the third grade.

We found that how well children did on their daily math assignments and on math achievement tests was related to private speech, but the relationship depended on their intellectual maturity. For example, among bright first-graders, those who used more internalized private speech (muttering) scored higher on tests than those who still talked aloud to themselves frequently. But among average first-graders, much of whose private speech was still audible, the amount of such audible task-relevant speech was the best predictor of success. By third grade, the average children had matured to the point that how much internalized private speech they used was strongly related to how well they did in math. But for bright third-graders, private speech was no longer a guide to performance, since their most effective approach was completely internal speech, which cannot be observed.

I also found that children who used less mature forms of private speech than would be expected, given their age and IQ, usually performed poorly on tests. For example, bright first-graders and average third-graders who talked to themselves a lot didn't do as well as those who used less audible private speech. Since children generally employ more audible private speech when tasks are harder for them, teachers might use such speech as a sign of trouble. When children who usually internalize their private speech in solving problems start speaking out loud, they may need special help with that particular task.

Finally, this third study supported Vygotsky's belief that private speech helps children learn to bring action under the control of thought. My observers and I found that children's private speech was related to how they sat at their desks while working on problems. First-graders who used a great deal of self-stimulating private speech that didn't relate to the task at hand often squirmed around in their seats, chewed and tapped their pencils and played with their arms and legs. They also had trouble paying attention to the task at hand.

On the other hand, first-graders who ordinarily used audible, task-relevant speech also relied on more task-related motor behavior, such as counting on fingers, using a pencil to follow a line or read a word and using objects to count in arithmetic problems. Finally, children whose private speech was largely internalized were highly attentive to the task and sat more quietly. The development of internalized private speech apparently goes hand in hand with the ability to inhibit extraneous motor behavior and focus attention.

Vygotsky believed that as children work on new tasks that push the limits of their current mental ability, they depend on instructions from adults or other, more skilled children to help them understand and master the activities. Then they take the language of the instructions, make it part of their own private speech and use this speech to organize their independent efforts in the same way.

My research shows that to help this process along, children need learning environments that permit them to be verbally active while solving problems and completing tasks. When they reach elementary school, children are expected to sustain attention for long periods of time, and the school day is devoted to mastering skills of increasing difficulty. One way children cope successfully with these demands is through greater use of self-guiding private speech. Talking aloud or muttering should not be interpreted as evidence of insufficient self-control or misbehavior.

Children who are less mature or have learning problems may need more adult guidance and may profit from special arrangements in their classrooms, such as study corners, where they can talk aloud more freely. Requiring such children to be quiet is likely to be counterproductive, because it suppresses forms of private speech that are crucial for learning.

Play experiences are also important in helping children develop their language and problem-solving abilities. Internalized verbal thinking is facilitated by the give-and-take that occurs as children cooperate to build a house with blocks, paint a mural or role-play a family activity.

Private speech is an important means through which children organize, understand and gain control over their behavior. Observations of private speech provide a rich source of information about how children's thinking develops, why some of them have learning problems and how to intervene to help children develop as far as possible.

VARIETIES OF PRIVATE SPEECH

Type	Child's Activity	Examples
Wordplay, repetition	Repeating words and sounds, often in playful, rhythmic recitation	Peter wanders around the room, repeating in a sing-song manner, "Put the mushroom on your head, put the mushroom in your pocket, put the mushroom on your nose."
Solitary fantasy play and speech addressed to nonhuman objects	Talking to objects, playing roles, producing sound effects for objects	John says, "Ka-powee ka-powee," aiming his finger like a gun. Nancy says in a high-pitched voice while playing in the doll corner, "I'll be better after the doctor gives me a shot. Ow!" she remarks as she pokes herself with her finger (a pretend needle).
Emotional release and expression	Expressing emotions or feelings directed inward rather than to a listener	Paula is given a new box of crayons and says to no one in particular, "Wow! Neat!" Rachel is sitting at her desk with an anxious expression on her face, repeating to herself, "My mom's sick, my mom's sick."
Egocentric communication	Communicating with another person, but expressing the information so incompletely or peculiarly that it can't be understood	David and Mark are seated next to one another on the rug. David says to Mark, "It broke," without explaining what or when. Susan says to Ann at the art table, "Where are the paste-ons?" Ann says, "What paste-ons?" Susan shrugs and walks off.
Describing or guiding one's own activity	Narrating one's actions, thinking out loud	Omar sits down at the art table and says to himself, "I want to draw something. Let's see. I need a big piece of paper. I want to draw my cat." Working in her arithmetic workbook, Cathy says to no one in particular, "Six." Then, counting on her fingers she continues, "Seven, eight, nine, ten. It's ten, it's ten. The answer's ten."

VARIETIES OF PRIVATE SPEECH (CONTINUED)

Type	Child's Activity	Examples
Reading aloud, sounding out words	Reading aloud or sounding out words while reading	While reading a book, Tom begins to sound out a difficult word. "Sher-lock Holm-lock," he says slowly and quietly. Then he tries again. "Sher-lock Holm-lock, Sherlock Holme," he says, leaving off the final "s" in his most successful attempt.
Inaudible muttering	Speaking so quietly that the words cannot be understood by an observer	Tony mumbles inaudibly to himself as he works a math problem.

QUESTIONS

Answer the following questions and then compare your responses with the suggested answers at the end of this chapter.

1. How does the author's Appalachian study of private speech compare and contrast with earlier studies by Kohlberg?

2. What seems to be the developmental relationship between private speech and intelligence?

3. What are the implications of Berk's research for the teaching-learning process?

ANSWERS

Correct Answers to Self-Test Exercises

Multiple-Choice

1. d	10. a	18. d
2. c	11. c	19. d
3. a	12. d	20. b
4. b	13. c	21. b
5. a	14. b	22. a
6. b	15. a	23. b
7. b	16. c	24. a
8. a	17. b	25. c
9. c		

Matching

1. b, f
2. a, e
3. d
4. g
5. c

Suggested Answers to Application Exercises

1. *3* "Ha" (meaning "hi" or "hello").

   5 "The dog bited me."

   1 Cooing sounds

   2 "Ba-ba-ba-ba."

   4 "Doggie gone."

2. a. Learning theorists would assert that the child learned to say, "My teddy," as a result of parental shaping. The child might have been reinforced by her parents for utterances which increasingly resembled the phrase "My teddy." Social-learning theorists would stress the importance of imitation and observation. For example, the child might have heard an older brother or sister say, "That's my teddy bear," and in attempting to imitate this statement have come up with a shorter version.

   b. Nativists would say that the child's inborn language capacity enabled her to extract grammatical rules from the language she has heard and to use those rules in her own speech. For example, the child may have heard her mother say, "My car keys," or, "My lipstick" and "Your teddy bear." The child's inborn language capacity would then have enabled her to say, "My teddy bear," even if she had never heard that phrase before.

3. The defining features of a Mr. Bobo are a hat, a smile, and a bow tie. Irrelevant features include the type of hat worn, whether he is thin or fat, and whether his bow tie is solid or has polka dots.

4. If David could overcome functional fixedness, he could solve both his problems by using the newspapers to make a bed. He could neatly stack the newspapers in a rectangular shape of bed-size dimensions and place his mattress on top. A newspaper bed would be firm but not hard and provide excellent insulation against the cold.

5. a. Preparation stage. During this stage you figure out what the problem is. You need to understand that your task is to unscramble the words and write them, one letter to a box, in the spaces provided. You also need to realize that the circled letters form the missing word in the statement, "Excalibur was a _____."

    b. Production stage. In this stage, you generate possible solutions. If you already know that Excalibur was a sword, you might fill in these letters first to help you unscramble the words. If you don't know this, you still probably will used heuristics to unscramble the words. Using your knowledge of English spelling, you will probably try likely combinations of letters rather than every possible combination of letters.

    c. Evaluation stage. During this stage, you evaluate your solution. If you are able to unscramble each word, and the circled letters form a reasonable word to go in the blank, you are reasonably certain your solution is correct. Did you come up with the solution in Figure 8-4?

Did you notice that for the last word you could have also had *traded?*

6. You could have listed any three of the following divergent aspects of the cartoon:
    a. Gathering of middle-class porcupine enthusiasts
    b. Deflated porcupine
    c. Fondling porcupines as if they were pets to be cuddled and held
    d. Matter-of-fact caption that treats the subject seriously
    e. Framed picture of a porcupine hanging on the wall
    f. Depiction of grotesque human beings

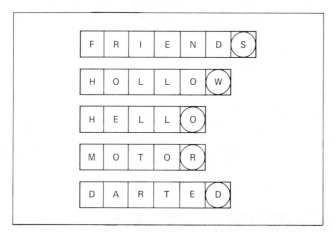

Figure 8-4

Suggested Answers to Reading Questions

1. The Appalachian study confirmed Kohlberg's observations that private speech is grounded in early social communication and that it follows a specific developmental pattern. The developmental rate among the Appalachian children, however, was much slower.

2. Brighter students' use of speech tends to peak earlier than that of other students.

3. Children need environments which permit them to be verbally active as they learn. Talking aloud or muttering should not be regarded as misbehavior and should not be surpressed.

Chapter 9:

EARLY DEVELOPMENT

CHAPTER OUTLINE

I. How we study development
   A. Research methods
      1. Cross-sectional method
      2. Longitudinal method
      3. Cross-sequential method
   B. Influences on development
      1. Normative and nonnormative influences
      2. Heredity and environment
         a. Relative effects of heredity and environment
         b. Heredity characteristics
         c. How genetic traits are transmitted
            (1) Creating a new life
            (2) Patterns of genetic transmission

II. Origins: Prenatal development
   A. Stages of prenatal development
   B. Hazards of prenatal development
      1. Maternal nutrition
      2. Maternal illness
      3. Maternal drug intake
      4. Risks associated with the father

III. The body: Early physical development
   A. At the beginning
   B. Growth
   C. Motor development
   D. How maturation and deprivation affect physical development

IV. The mind: Early cognitive development
   A. Piaget: A theory of cognitive development
      1. Sensorimotor stage (birth to 2 years)
      2. Preoperational stage (2 to 7 years)
      3. Concrete operations stage (7 to 11 years)
      4. Formal operations stage (12 years and older)
   B. Learning
      1. Learning in infancy
      2. Later learning
   C. Memory
      1. Memory in infancy
      2. Memory in childhood

V. The psyche: Early emotional and social development
   A. Erikson: A theory of psychosocial development
      1. Crisis 1: Trust versus mistrust (birth to 12-18 months)
      2. Crisis 2: Autonomy versus shame and doubt (18 months to 3 years)

      3. Crisis 3: Initiative versus guilt (3 to 6 years)
      4. Crisis 4: Industry versus inferiority (6 to 12 years)
   B. Emotional expression in early life
      1. Expressing emotions and feelings
         a. Smiling
         b. Laughing
         c. Crying
      2. The timing of emotional expression
   C. Temperament
   D. Attachment
      1. Mother-child attachment
         a. Patterns of mother-child attachment
         b. How mother-child attachment occurs
         c. Stranger anxiety
      2. Father-child attachment
      3. Sibling attachment
   E. Identification
   F. Getting along with peers

Boxes
   Psychology in your life: How parents' child-rearing styles affect
   their children
   In the forefront: Stress and resilience in childhood

LEARNING OBJECTIVES

After you study Chapter 9, you should be able to do the tasks outlined in the following objectives.

1. Identify the focus of developmental psychology.

2. Describe the approaches used in the study of development.

3. Explain the techniques used to study the relative effects of heredity and environment.

4. Describe the process of transmitting genetic traits.

5. Identify the causes of multiple births.

6. Specify the stages of prenatal development and describe the changes that occur during each stage.

7. Describe prenatal conditions that can adversely affect a fetus.

8. Describe the capabilities of neonates.

9. Explain the impact of nature and nurture on physical and motor development.

10. Specify the major changes in cognitive development according to Jean Piaget.

11. Explain how infants learn, and describe the development of learning during childhood.

12. Outline Erikson's theory of psychosocial development from birth to age 12.

13. Describe infants' emotional expression and patterns in temperament and attachment; explain possible outcomes.

14. Identify three child-rearing styles and explain their relationship to child development.

15. Describe factors that explain why some children are more resilient to stress.

KEY CONCEPTS

As you read Chapter 9 in your text, look for each of the following concepts. You should understand each concept.

1. Study of Development

Developmental psychologists are concerned with changes in people throughout their life span. They study physical, cognitive, and psychosocial changes. Some changes are slow and gradual; others occur in spurts.

2. Ways to Study Development

Psychologists use three major approaches to collect data on children: the cross-sectional method, the longitudinal method, and the cross-sequential method. The cross-sequential method combines the cross-sectional and longitudinal approaches, by testing a cross section of people more than once. When psychologists use the cross-sectional method, they compare several groups of people of different ages at the same point in time. When psychologists use the longitudinal method, they trace the development of one or more people over an extended time, comparing their development at various intervals.

3. Heredity and Environment

Development is influenced by both biological and environmental factors. Psychologists use a variety of specific techniques to determine the relative effects of heredity and environment. A number of characteristics have been found to have strong hereditary components.

4. Transmission of Genetic Traits

At conception 23 chromosomes from the father's sperm unite with 23 chromosomes in the mother's ovum. Only one chromosome determines sex; the mother's sex chromosome is always an X (female), while the father's chromosome may be a Y (male) or an X. Each of the 46 chromosomes contains genes composed of DNA. Inherited genes determine our genotype. Our genotype is not necessarily the same as our outward appearance (phenotype); often we are carrying recessive alleles.

5. Multiple Births

Fraternal twins result from the simultaneous release of two ova, which are subsequently fertilized by different sperm. Identical twins result from the splitting of a single ovum after it has been fertilized by one male sperm. Most multiple births are fraternal. Twin pregnancies have a higher rate of problems.

6. Stages of Prenatal Development

There are three stages of prenatal development: the germinal stage, the embryonic stage, and the fetal stage. The germinal stage (fertilization to 2 weeks) is a period of rapid cell division in the zygote. The embryonic stage (2 to 8 weeks) is the period when major body systems and organs develop and is the most vulnerable time during pregnancy. The fetal stage (8 weeks to birth) is characterized by the appearance of bone cells and changes in body form.

7. Prenatal Hazards

Conditions in the prenatal environment can affect the fetus. Maternal nutrition, maternal illness, and maternal drug intake, including hormones, tobacco, alcohol, marijuana, and cocaine, can each influence prenatal development. However, the combination of these factors in the maternal lifestyle is more significant than any single factor.

8. Neonatal Period

The neonatal period is a 28-day transition for babies, when they adjust to functioning independently. Researchers have found that neonates have sophisticated senses and show visual and auditory preferences.

9. Effect of Nature on Physical Development

Both physical development and the development of motor skills are largely based on maturation, but environmental influences can cause a temporary setback. Growth occurs most rapidly during the first 3 years of life and then slows down progressively until the pubertal growth spurt occurs at about age 12.

10. Motor Development

Motor development follows two principles, the cephalocaudal principle and the proximodistal principle. The cephalocaudal principle states that development progresses in a head-to-toe direction. The proximodistal principle states that development proceeds from the center of the body to the extremities. Age norms for motor development are averages; there are wide individual differences. Infants are born with several reflexes that disappear during their first year.

11. Piaget's Theory of Cognitive Development

On the basis of observation and a flexible method of questioning, Piaget proposed that all children progress through four stages of cognitive development: sensorimotor (birth to 2 years), preoperational (2 to 7 years), concrete operational (7 to 11 years), and formal operational (12 years and older).

12. How Infants Learn

There is evidence that infants are capable of learning from the first day of life. Whether classical conditioning occurs before birth is debatable. Operant conditioning is easier to establish than classical conditioning in infancy.

13. Development of Memory

Research based on habituation has found that memory develops rapidly during infancy. By the second grade children spontaneously use rehearsal techniques to improve memory. At about fifth grade clustering and chunking techniques are used.

14. Erikson's Theory of Psychosocial Development

Erik Erikson outlined eight stages of psychosocial development that occur through an entire life span. Each stage requires the resolution of a conflict or crisis. The four stages that occur during childhood are (1) basic trust versus basic mistrust (birth to 12-18 months), (2) autonomy versus shame and doubt (18 months to 3 years), (3) initiative versus guilt (3 to 6 years), and (4) industry versus inferiority (6 to 12 years).

15. Expression of Emotions

Babies communicate feelings by crying, smiling, and laughing. Longitudinal studies of babies have suggested that there are distinct differences in temperament which are consistent from birth. Children were identified as "easy," "difficult," or "slow to warm up."

16. Child-Rearing Styles

Three child-rearing styles have been identified: authoritative, authoritarian, and permissive. Children reared with authoritative discipline were found to be the most self-reliant, exploratory, and content.

17. Attachment

Most research on early attachment has studied the relationship between babies and their mothers. Three patterns of attachment have been identified: securely attached, avoidant, and ambivalent. These patterns persist until age 5. Between 8 and 12 months of age, all infants begin to fear strangers. Recent research has focused on the father-child bond and has found differences in mothers' and fathers' relationships with their children.

18. Resilient Children

Many factors influence children's reaction to stress. These factors include family, learning experiences, other stressors, and other positive experiences.

19. Identification

Psychologists believe that children develop a sense of who they are as an outgrowth of their Oedipus and Electra complexes when they finally identify with the same-sex parent. Social-learning theorists believe that identification results from imitating one or more models.

20. Siblings and Peers

Sibling relationships have been the focus of recent studies, with an emphasis on how the relationship is maintained throughout the life span. Peer relationships are evident in babies, but friendships are not apparent until age 3. Friendships become mutual after age 9.

TERMS TO KNOW

Define each of the terms listed. You can check your definitions in the text Glossary or on the text pages listed in parentheses.

Developmental psychologist   (p. 302)

Physical development   (p. 302)

Cognitive development   (p. 302)

Psychosocial development   (p. 302)

Quantitative changes	(p. 303)	Nature-nurture debate	(p. 304)
Qualitative changes	(p. 303)	Reaction range	(p. 305)
Cohort	(p. 303)	Study of twins	(p. 305)
Cross-sectional method	(p. 303)	Fraternal (dizygotic) twins	(p. 305)
Longitudinal method	(p. 303)	Identical (monozygotic) twins	(p. 305)
Cross-sequential method	(p. 303)	Concordant	(p. 305)
Normative age-graded events	(p. 304)	Adoption studies	(p. 305)
Normative history-graded events	(p. 304)	Consanguinity studies	(p. 306)
Nonnormative life events	(p. 304)	Selective breeding in animals	(p. 306)

Prenatal studies	(p. 306)	Genes	(p. 308)
Manipulating the environment	(p. 306)	DNA	(p. 308)
Comparisons of history	(p. 306)	Genotype	(p. 308)
Sperm	(p. 306)	Phenotype	(p. 308)
Ovum	(p. 306)	Alleles	(p. 308)
Zygote	(p. 306)	Homozygous	(p. 308)
Chromosomes	(p. 308)	Heterozygous	(p. 308)
Autosomes	(p. 308)	Dominant genes	(p. 308)
Sex chromosome	(p. 308)	Recessive genes	(p. 308)

Autosomal dominant inheritance	(p. 308)	Spina bifida	(p. 308)
Autosomal recessive inheritance	(p. 308)	Germinal stage	(p. 310)
Sex-linked inheritance	(p. 308)	Umbilical cord	(p. 310)
Multifactorial inheritance	(p. 308)	Placenta	(p. 310)
Congenital defects	(p. 308)	Amniotic sac	(p. 310)
Achondroplasia	(p. 308)	Embryonic stage	(p. 310)
Huntington's chorea	(p. 308)	Trimester	(p. 311)
Tay-Sachs disease	(p. 308)	Spontaneous abortion	(p.311)
Hemophilia	(p. 308)	Fetal stage	(p. 311)

Prenatal psychology	(p. 311)	Age norms	(p. 315)
Aquired immune deficiency syndrome (AIDS)	(p. 312)	Reflex	(p. 315)
Diethylstilbestrol	(p. 312)	Primitive reflex	(p. 315)
Fetal alcohol syndrome	(p. 312)	Rooting reflex	(p. 316)
Neonatal period	(p. 313)	Moro reflex	(p. 316)
Lanugo	(p. 313)	Darwinian reflex	(p. 316)
Habituation	(p. 314)	Swimming reflex	(p. 316)
Cephalocaudal principle	(p. 315)	Tonic neck reflex	(p. 316)
Proximodistal principle	(p. 315)	Babinski reflex	(p. 316)

Walking reflex   (p. 316)   Reversibility   (p. 320)

Placing reflex   (p. 316)   Identity   (p. 320)

Maturation   (p. 316)   Compensation   (p. 320)

Sensorimotor stage   (p. 317)   Formal operations stage   (p. 320)

Object permanence   (p. 318)   Classical conditioning   (p. 320)

Preoperational stage   (p. 319)   Operant conditioning   (p. 321)

Egocentric   (p. 319)   Visual-recognition memory   (p. 321)

Concrete operations stage   (p. 319)   Rehearsal   (p. 322)

Conservation   (p. 319)   Clustering   (p. 322)

Chunking	(p. 322)	Attachment	(p. 327)
Crisis	(p. 323)	Authoritative	(p. 328)
Basic trust versus basic mistrust	(p. 323)	Authoritarian	(p. 328)
Autonomy versus shame and doubt	(p. 323)	Permissive	(p. 328)
Initiative versus guilt	(p. 324)	Securely attached	(p. 329)
Industry versus inferiority	(p. 324)	Avoidant	(p. 329)
Facial Expression Scoring Manual (FESM)	(p. 324)	Ambivalent	(p. 329)
Temperament	(p. 327)	Resilient children	(p. 331)
Monoamine oxidase (MAO)	(p. 327)	Stranger anxiety	(p. 332)

Identification   (p. 335)

SELF-TEST

Multiple-Choice

Choose the one best response to each question. An answer key is provided at the end of this chapter.

1. What is the main concern of developmental psychologists?

   a. Genetic study of lower animals
   b. Birth process
   c. Behavior of infants and children
   d. Process of change throughout the life span

2. A developmental psychologist wishes to learn as much as possible about the development of a person. What should be studied?

   a. Genetic structure, physical development, and motor development
   b. Physical development, cognitive development, and psychosocial development
   c. Language abilities, motivation, and memory development
   d. Emotional and social changes

3. In the past 3 months, 5-year-old Lucretia has learned to read. How would a developmental psychologist label this change?

   a. Physical development
   b. Cognitive development
   c. Psychosocial development
   d. Genetic development

4. A psychologist, Ms. A., began testing the attention span of a group of 20 infants immediately after birth. She retested the same group at ages 3 months, 6 months, 1 year, and 2 years. What method is she using?

   a. Cross-sectional method
   b. Longitudinal method
   c. Biographical method
   d. Cohort method

5. What is the current view on the influences of nature versus nurture?

   a. Our development is largely controlled by nature, and nurture has very limited influence.
   b. Our development is largely controlled by nurture, and nature has very limited influence.
   c. Our development is influenced by both nature and nurture.
   d. Nature and nurture play little or no role in development.

6. Assume that a psychologist wishes to use a technique of behavior genetics to determine whether a family of highly intelligent mice can be developed. Which of the following techniques would be most appropriate?

   a. Selective breeding
   b. Twin studies
   c. Consanguinity studies
   d. Prenatal studies

7. How is the sex of a child determined?

   a. By the mother's sex chromosome
   b. By the father's sex chromosome
   c. By the mother's autosomes
   d. By the father's autosomes

8. What is the key composition of genes that determines our hereditary characteristics?

   a. DNA
   b. Alleles
   c. Thalidomide
   d. Karyotypes

9. Assume that you have brown eyes and are carrying alleles for only brown eyes. How would you describe your brown-eyed trait?

   a. Recessive
   b. Heterozygous
   c. Homozygous
   d. Multifactorial

10. During which stage of prenatal development do most developmental birth defects occur?

    a. Germinal stage
    b. Embryonic stage
    c. Fetal stage
    d. Just before birth

11. Which of the following statements best explains the effect of rubella on prenatal development?

    a. Rubella is most dangerous during the first 11 weeks of pregnancy and will cause heart defects and deafness.
    b. Rubella is most dangerous after the first 16 weeks of prenatal development and will cause heart defects and deafness.
    c. Rubella is dangerous throughout the entire course of pregnancy and can cause heart defects and deafness.
    d. Rubella is no longer believed to affect prenatal development.

12. Which type of picture would a newborn infant prefer?

    a. Landscape
    b. Charcoal sketch
    c. Portrait
    d. Straight lines on a plain paper

13. When does the greatest amount of physical growth occur?

    a. Between birth and age 3
    b. Between ages 3 and 6
    c. Between ages 6 and 9
    d. Between ages 9 and 12

14. A group of psychologists found that the normative age for a child to climb stairs is 18 months. What does this finding mean?

    a. Few children can climb stairs at 18 months.
    b. Children who cannot climb stairs at 18 months are retarded.
    c. The average child climbs stairs at 18 months.
    d. All children climb stairs at 18 months.

15. Piaget's theory suggests four stages of development. What kind of development is Piaget describing?

    a. Sexual
    b. Cognitive
    c. Motor
    d. Social

16. Why will 1-month-old infants not react to the removal of a teddy bear from their cribs?

    a. They do not understand reversibility.
    b. They notice only human faces.
    c. They are not capable of compensation.
    d. They have not achieved object permanence.

17. Sugar is poured from a long narrow bag into a large round bowl. A little girl says that the bowl contains less sugar than the bag because the sugar is "not as tall."

Her older brother explains that they both contain the same amount of sugar. What characteristic has the older brother developed that the little girl lacks?

a. Object permanence
b. Conservation
c. Egocentrism
d. Automatic responses

18. Which type of learning is easiest to establish in infants?

a. Cognitive skills
b. Memory abilities
c. Operant conditioning
d. Verbal recall

19. Which aspect of behavior in infancy appears to be a good predictor of future intelligence?

a. Early reflexes
b. Visual-recognition memory
c. Rate of motor development
d. Temperament

20. A 5-year-old boy is constantly asking, "Why?" His parents usually become annoyed and scold him. If this affects him, what might be the resolution of the child's conflict according to Erikson's scheme of psychosocial development?

a. Mistrust
b. Trust
c. Doubt
d. Initiative

21. According to Baumrind, which child-rearing style is most likely to produce self-reliant, exploratory, and content children?

a. Authoritative
b. Authoritarian
c. Permissive
d. Rigid

22. By age 2, what often happens to infants who are deprived of close, frequent contact with their mothers or other caregivers?

a. They show superior intelligence.
b. They are more curious than securely attached babies.
c. They are less socially involved than securely attached babies.
d. They are more comfortable with strangers than are securely attached babies.

23. According to social-learning theory, how does the process of identification occur?

a. As an outgrowth of the Oedipus and Electra complexes
b. By recognizing the same-sex parent as a potential aggressor
c. By progressing through cognitive stages
d. By imitating models

24. At what age do children's friendships become less selfish and begin to involve mutual feelings?

a. 3 years
b. 5 years
c. 9 years
d. 12 years

Matching

Match each name in column A with a descriptive phrase in column B.

Column A

_____ 1. Jean Piaget

_____ 2. Robert Fantz

_____ 3. Erik Erikson

_____ 4. Mary Salter Ainsworth

_____ 5. Harry and Margaret Harlow

_____ 6. Michael Lamb

_____ 7. Diana Baumrind

_____ 8. Alfred Adler

Column B

a. Identified three levels of attachment in babies: securely attached, avoidant, and ambivalent

b. Designed an apparatus for the study of infants' visual preferences

c. Linked parenting styles to children's behavior

d. Developed a theory of cognitive development based on observation of his three children

e. Outlined eight stages of development in the life span, each involving a crisis to be resolved

f. Emphasized the importance of sibling rivalry

g. Studied attachment in infants and found that early contact between mothers and neonates does not have lasting effects

h. Studied the attachment of monkeys to their mothers

APPLICATION EXERCISES

These application exercises will test your understanding of and ability to apply the material you have read in your text. Suggested answers are provided at the end of the chapter so that you can check your responses.

1. Your text describes seven methods useful for the study of the relative effects of heredity and environment. These are

Study of twins
Adoption studies
Consanguinity studies
Selective breeding in animals
Prenatal studies
Manipulating the environment
Comparison of actual histories

Read each of the following descriptions of research and indicate which of these seven methods is being used in each description.

a. A psychologist, Ms. A., wants to determine whether a tendency toward depression is hereditary. She is studying relatives of depressed patients to determine whether close relatives are also likely to have depressive symptoms.

Method _____

b. A researcher, Mr. B., is curious about whether sleep patterns are hereditary traits. He is studying identical twins reared in different homes and comparing their daily sleep behavior.

Method _____

c. A psychologist is interviewing parents to determine whether corporal punishment during a child's first 3 years is related to aggressive behavior in preschool.

Method _____

d. An educator wants to determine whether an enriched school program will influence the intelligence scores of students. Weekly field trips to museums, special library trips, and after-school programs are being planned for 2 years. IQ scores of students before and after the 2-year enrichment program will be compared.

Method _____

e. A researcher is studying a group of rats that have a similar genetic makeup and is recording their ability to run mazes.

Method _____

f. A group of psychologists are interested in whether diet and drug intake during the pregnancy will affect the primary teeth of the child. A number of mothers and their offspring are being followed.

Method _____

g. A research study is being conducted to determine the relative effects of heredity and environment on musical ability.

Fifty adopted children have been tested for musical aptitude. Their scores are being compared with the scores of their biological parents and their adoptive parents.

Method _____

2. Brown-eyed genes are dominant over blue-eyed genes. If a woman has alleles for both brown and blue eye color, her eyes will be brown. A woman carrying these two different alleles would be considered *heterozygous* for eye color. Imagine that this woman marries a man who was *homozygous* for blue eyes, carrying only alleles for blue eye color. They want to determine the probability of producing a blue-eyed child.

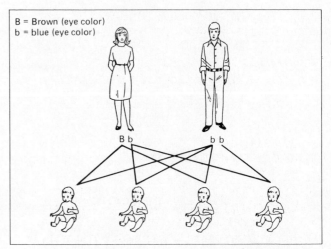

B = Brown (eye color)
b = blue (eye color)

Figure 9-1

a. Use Figure 9-1 to determine their chances of producing a blue-eyed child. _____

b. What are their chances for producing an offspring who is heterozygous for eye color?____

_____

3. Use Table 9-1 to summarize the characteristics of the three stages of prenatal development.

Table 9-1 Stages of Prenatal Development

Period	Time	Key Characteristics
Germinal		
Embryonic		
Fetal		

4. Your text describes factors that can create hazards in the prenatal environment. Based on these factors, list rules you could present as advice to pregnant women.

   a. Maternal nutrition

      Rule _____
      _____

   b. Weight gain

      Rule _____
      _____

   c. Maternal illness

      Rule _____
      _____

   d. Drug intake (medical)

      Rule _____
      _____

   e. Tobacco

      Rule _____
      _____

   f. Alcohol

      Rule _____
      _____

   g. Drug intake (marijuana and cocaine)

      Rule _____
      _____

5. Two psychologists are decorating a nursery for their infant. They have selected brightly printed wallpaper and large colored pictures of family members for the walls and are hanging circular mobiles from the ceiling. From what you have read about the visual preferences of infants, explain why each of these selections would be appealing to their baby.

   a. Wallpaper _____
      _____

   b. Family pictures _____
      _____

   c. Mobiles _____
      _____

6. Piaget described four stages of cognitive development based on his observation of children. During each of these stages, new skills or enhanced abilities are developed. In Table 9-2 indicate the cognitive changes that occur during each of these stages.

Table 9-2 Piagetian Stages of
Development
_____

Stage	Age	Development
Sensorimotor	Birth to 2 years	_____ _____
Preoperational	2 to 7 years	_____ _____
Concrete operational	7 to 11 years	_____ _____ _____ _____ _____ _____ _____
Formal operational	12 years and older	_____ _____

_____

7. Erikson believes we go through eight stages of psychosocial development during our lifetime. The first four stages are experienced during our first 12 years. At each stage we face a crisis which must be resolved. For each crisis there are two alternatives, one healthy and one unhealthy. These are basic trust versus basic mistrust, autonomy versus shame and doubt, initiative versus guilt, and industry versus inferiority. To complete this exercise, first determine which crisis the person is facing and then indicate the alternative that is being demonstrated.

   a. A 2-year-old girl enjoys dressing herself independently but knows she must not use a knife.

      Crisis _____

      Resolution _____

   b. An 8-year-old boy cries every morning and refuses to go to school. He says that the work is too hard and his peers ridicule him.

      Crisis _____

      Resolution _____

   c. Although her mother shows little affection and does not feed her regularly, a 1-year-old girl cries whenever her mother leaves the room.

      Crisis _____

      Resolution _____

   d. A 5-year-old boy is enjoying planning his birthday party. He has selected ice cream and cake flavors and is making up party games.

      Crisis _____

      Resolution _____

8. Assume that you are baby-sitting for the 1-year-old sons of three women. One boy, Huey, acts very upset before his mother leaves, throws objects around the room when she leaves, and kicks her when she finally returns. Another boy, Louie, cries for a few minutes when his mother leaves but then becomes absorbed in playing. However, when she returns he crawls over to her. The third boy, Dewey, barely notices that his mother leaves but acts angry and aloof toward her when she returns.

a. How would Ainsworth label each boy's pattern of behavior?

Huey _____

Louie _____

Dewey _____

b. Which boy is most likely to be sociable with strangers and why?

_____
_____
_____

9. Baumrind identified three styles of child rearing--*authoritative, authoritarian,* and *permissive*--and linked them to children's behavior. Read the following descriptions of parenting styles, identify the style being used, and state the behavior that is likely to result in the child.

a. Karen is permitted to throw toys all around the house. Although her parents often trip and have difficulty walking around the rooms, they believe that Karen should have her freedom. They also permit her to eat when and whatever she desires and to go to bed whenever she feels tired.

Parenting style _____

Probable resulting behavior

_____

b. Gary's parents have set rules that he must obey. Even though he felt sick to his stomach, his parents insisted that he eat his required breakfast before school. He is never permitted an exception to his 7 P.M. bedtime.

Parenting style _____

Probable resulting behavior

_____

c. David's parents have family rules but will make exceptions if David can present a good reason. For example, although his bedtime is usually 8 P.M., he was permitted to stay up an extra hour to watch a special movie, since he could sleep late the next morning.

Parenting style _____

Probable resulting behavior

_____

READING EXERCISE

In the following article from *The New York Times,* Daniel Goleman summarizes current research on the effects of terrorism and violence on children.

Terror's Children: Mending Mental Wounds

Recent efforts to treat and study young survivors of civil war and terrorism have yielded important new insights into the special emotional needs of violence-scarred children.

Scientists working with children caught in the civil strife of Cambodia and other countries as well as children who have suffered from family violence, have developed a new understanding of their long-term psychological wounds and how best to mend them.

The researchers are finding that, with time and the right care, most children show a great capacity for emotional renewal after even the most nightmarish experiences. But the psychological scars of terror and turbulence in childhood can impair emotional and intellectual growth. Symptoms, often disguised, can emerge years later.

The research has also found that children terrorized in radically different ways--from wartime atrocities to family violence--share certain remarkably similar symptoms of lasting emotional pain, some subtle, some blatant. The new evidence that trauma, even a single brush with it, can lead to serious, long-lasting problems has led to a plan to extend the psychiatric diagnosis of "post traumatic stress disorder" to children.

"The body and mind handle terror in the same way, whether you were beaten by your father or by Pol Pot's soldiers," said Bessel van der Kolk, a psychiatrist at Harvard Medical School who directs the Trauma Clinic at the Massachusetts Mental Health Center in Boston.

The new studies, most of them completed within the last five years, greatly extend older findings in a research area that has largely been dormant since World War II, when Anna Freud, John Bowlby, and a handful of others studied children who were evacuated during the London blitz, those who survived concentration camps as well as war orphans.

Although earlier work found that a child's reaction to trauma might be alleviated by the presence of a comforting adult, the new work has uncovered long-term effects regardless of how adults behaved in the crisis itself.

One of the major new studies described 40 Cambodian teen-agers held in Khmer Rouge camps between 1975 and 1979, when they were 12 or younger. Many suffered near-starvation and beatings and witnessed the torture and murder of family members. The children, who now live in Oregon, were examined in 1984 by a team of psychiatrists from the Oregon Health Sciences University in Portland. The research, led by Dr. David Kinzie, was reported in the Journal of the American Academy of Child Psychiatry last year.

The children, by then 14 to 20 years old, still suffered a range of psychological problems, including recurrent nightmares, difficulty in concentrating and in sleeping, and being easily startled. About half showed symptoms of depression: lack of energy or interest in life, brooding and feelings of self-pity, and a pessimistic outlook. "Despite their great inner distress, many said they

Copyright (c) 1987 by The New York Times Company. Reprinted by permission.

never told anyone about these feelings," said William Sack, one of the psychiatrists who studied the Cambodian teen-agers.

About two-thirds seemed to be suffering from remorse at having lived while other family members died. Many of these teen-agers said they "felt ashamed of being alive."

There was no direct relationship between the severity of the hardships the children endured and the severity of their symptoms years later. There was, however, a strong relationship between their current living situation and their psychological problems.

Role of the Family

While all the children had been separated from their families in the camps, those who were later able to reunite with family members fared better than the others. Of the 26 teen-agers living with relatives, only 12 had serious psychiatric problems, whereas of the 14 living in foster homes, 13 had such problems.

"If children feel there is someone they can cling to, someone to count on, they survive the brutality far better than those who have no one to turn to," said Dr. van der Kolk of Harvard.

Other aspects of the social environment, too, alter the effect of war on children. In Northern Ireland, Catholic children appear to show more signs of psychological damage than their Protestant counterparts do, according to Terry Tibbetts, a clinical psychologist at the State Diagnostic Center in Los Angeles, who has studied children in Belfast.

"The Protestant kids don't show as many signs of the stress: they perceive their world as well-protected, with the police and British troops on their side," said Dr. Tibbetts. "But the Catholic children grow up believing the police, the troops and the Protestant paramilitary are all out to get them.

They experience a more dangerous, threatening and unpredictable universe."

'Outlet for Anger'

Rona Fields, a psychologist who has studied children in Northern Ireland as well as in Beirut and other war-torn areas, has found that many who felt terrorized by war as children became easy recruits for the war itself as they approached adolescence. Similarly, said Dr. Tibbetts, when children in Northern Ireland who felt chronic fear and anxiety reach adolescence they translate those feelings into aggression; many join groups like the Irish Republican Army. "The IRA offers a Catholic kid a legitimate outlet for his anger," he said. "He can feel he's doing something to the people who caused him such pain."

Children as young as 8 or 9 are being recruited and trained as soldiers in Central America, Africa and the Middle East, according to a report in Cultural Survival Quarterly, published by a private anthropological group in Cambridge. The long-term effects for these children, some evidence suggests, may be more grim than for those who were passive victims of war.

"In the Cambodian refugee camps, some of the children who had the roughest time were those who had been soldiers for the Khmer Rouge," said Neil Boothby, a Duke University psychologist who has studied and treated Cambodian refugees both at camps in Thailand and after they were resettled in New England.

"They had done a lot of killing when they were as young as 8 years old and continued to assassinate people until they were around 14," he said. "They were psychologically intact as long as they stayed with the Khmer Rouge. But when they finally came to a refugee camp filled with Pol Pot's victims, they fell apart."

Tips for Relief Workers

On the basis of their experience with Cambodian and other children, Dr. Boothby and his colleagues have written "Unaccompanied Children: Care and Protection in Wars, Natural Disasters and Refugee Movements," to be published this spring by Oxford University Press. The book offers guidelines for those who run relief operations on how to minimize the psychological impact of such catastrophes. For instance, the book suggests that children be reunited with their parents as soon as possible because "the younger the child the more quickly separation will be experienced as a permanent loss."

A study of children who have come to Los Angeles as refugees from war in Central America shows that psychological problems vary with age, according to William Arroyo, a psychiatrist at the University of Southern California. His research was published in the book "Post-Traumatic Stress Disorders in Children" (American Psychiatric Press).

Adolescents generally react to violent trauma with misbehavior: truancy, promiscuity, drug abuse and delinquency, said Spencer Eth, a child psychiatrist at the U.C.L.A. Medical School who did the research with Dr. Arroyo. This was not the case with the Cambodian teen-agers, perhaps, the researchers suggest, because of cultural differences.

On the other hand, children under 5, who feel the most defenseless in the face of threat, often respond to trauma by regressing, showing such symptoms as a return to bed-wetting or loss of toilet training, extreme anxiety about strangers or a parent's leaving and the loss of recently mastered skills like speech.

School-age children often use play or daydreams to deny what actually happened by rewriting the past with a happier outcome. Or they may obsessively repeat joyless games that re-enact the event.

Paradoxically, re-enactment plays a part in a treatment technique being developed. In this "incident-specific" treatment, children with severe symptoms learn to master the trauma by reliving the event in great detail—but in the company of a specially trained therapist who seeks to help the child face what happened and then move beyond it.

"Merely talking about it will not suffice in undoing serious psychic trauma in children," said Calvin Frederick, a psychologist at U.C.L.A., who has used the method extensively with children including those at a Los Angeles elementary school where a sniper shot 15 students, killing 2, in February 1984.

However, there is, as yet, no single best treatment for trauma effects in children, according to Lenore Terr, a child psychiatrist at the University of California Medical School in San Francisco. At the same time, by learning as much as they can about the effects of trauma, the researchers are finding avenues of treatment.

For instance, one of the most frequent effects of extreme trauma on school-age children is problems in school. These problems, according to Dr. Eth, are caused by intrusive memories that distract the child from schoolwork. And the child's effort to forget the trauma can impair memory generally.

But not all school abilities suffer, "and many of these children do well in expressive arts, like painting and acting; these may be the best way to approach them in therapy," said Nina Murray, a clinical psychologist at Harvard who works with Dr. van der Kolk.

Although symptoms of trauma in children can persist for years—particularly in the absence of therapy—the long-term outlook is not all bleak. Dr. Murray cites a recent follow-up study of children who survived the Holocaust. Although they suffered greatly in childhood, "they are well-adjusted" as adults, said Dr. Murray. "They do have occasional symptoms, such as flashbacks and nightmares, but they are generally stable, productive, and compassionate people, who are not cynical or pessimistic, but optimistic, despite what they have lived through."

QUESTIONS

Answer the following questions and then compare your responses with the suggested answers at the end of this chapter.

1. Why are Catholic children in Northern Ireland more affected by the violence than Protestant children?

2. How do reactions to violence differ between children who are under 5, school-age children and adolescents?

3. What is the long-term outlook for children who have suffered from violent traumas?

ANSWERS

Correct Answers to Self-Test Exercises

Multiple-Choice

1. d
2. b
3. b
4. b
5. c
6. a
7. b
8. a
9. c
10. b
11. a
12. c
13. a
14. c
15. b
16. d
17. b
18. c
19. b
20. c
21. a
22. c
23. d
24. c

Matching

1. d
2. b
3. e
4. a
5. h
6. g
7. c
8. f

Suggested Answers to Application Exercises

1.
a. Consanguinity studies
b. Study of twins
c. Comparison of actual histories
d. Manipulating the environment
e. Selective breeding in animals
f. Prenatal studies
g. Adoption studies

2.
a. 50 percent, or 2 chances out of 4
b. 50 percent, or 2 chances out of 4 for producing a child with a dominant brown gene and a recessive blue gene

3.
Answers to Table 9-1 Stages of
Prenatal Development

Period	Time	Key Characteristics
Germinal	Fertilization to 2 weeks	Basic body organs, umbilical cord, placenta, and amniotic sac develop.
Embryonic	2 to 8 weeks	Major body systems and organs develop.
Fetal	8 weeks to birth	Bone cells develop, body changes form, and growth increases.

4. a. Be sure to eat a nourishing diet both before and during pregnancy.
    b. A woman should gain 26 to 35 pounds.
    c. Avoid exposure to rubella, particularly during the first 16 weeks of pregnancy.
    d. Consult your obstetrician about safety before taking any medication.
    e. Avoid smoking.
    f. Avoid alcoholic drinks.
    g. Avoid marijuana and cocaine.

5. a. The baby would like the bright colors and pattern.
    b. The baby would enjoy looking at faces.
    c. The baby would enjoy the three-dimensional nature of the mobiles, the circular motion, and the complex patterns of their movement.

6.
Answers to Table 9-3 Piagetian Stages
of Development

Stage	Age	Development
Sensorimotor	Birth to 2 years	Learning through action; object permanence
Preoperational	2 to 7 years	Language development; understanding relationships; egocentric approach
Concrete operational	7 to 11 years	Shed egocentrism; ability to categorize; numerical skills; reversibility; conservation; identity; compensation
Formal operational	12 years and older	Abstract thinking; hypothesis testing

7. a. Crisis: autonomy versus shame and doubt
       Resolution: autonomy
    b. Crisis: industry versus inferiority
       Resolution: inferiority
    c. Crisis: trust versus mistrust
       Resolution: mistrust
    d. Crisis: initiative versus guilt
       Resolution: initiative

8. a. Huey: ambivalent
        Louie: securely attached
        Dewey: avoidant
    b. Louie is likely to be more
       relaxed with strangers, since he
       is securely attached and has
       developed a sense of trust in
       his mother.

9. a. Permissive. Karen is likely to
       be immature, lack self-
       reliance and self-control, and
       avoid exploration.
    b. Authoritarian. Gary is likely to
       become discontented, withdrawn,
       and distrustful.
    c. Authoritative. David is likely
       to be self-reliant, self-
       controlled, assertive,
       exploratory, and content.

Suggested Answers to Reading Questions

1. The Protestant children feel
    protected by the police and British
    troops. The Catholic children feel
    threatened and in constant danger.

2. Children under 5 feel helpless and
    regress. School-age children use
    play and daydreams as forms of
    escape and denial and sometimes
    become obsessive. Adolescents
    usually misbehave (although this
    was not the case with the
    Cambodians).

3. Although they suffer in childhood,
    they are usually well-adjusted
    adults with only occasional
    symptoms.

Chapter 10:

DEVELOPMENT FROM ADOLESCENCE ON

CHAPTER OUTLINE

I. Adolescence
   A. Physical development: Physiological changes
   B. Cognitive development: Formal operations and moral reasoning
      1. Piaget's formal operations stage (11-12 years to adulthood)
      2. Moral development
         a. Kohlberg: Stages of moral reasoning
         b. Gilligan: Moral development in women
   C. Personality and social development: The search for identity
      1. Erikson's crisis 5: Identity versus role confusion (puberty to young adulthood)
      2. "Adolescent rebellion": Fact or myth?
      3. Work and careers

II. Early and middle adulthood
   A. Physical development: Continuity and change
      1. Health
      2. Midlife changes
         a. Menopause
         b. Male climacteric
         c. Psychological aspects of physical changes
   B. Cognitive development: Intellectual growth or stagnation?
   C. Personality and social development: Theories and issues
      1. Theoretical approaches
         a. Erikson: Crises during early and middle adulthood
            (1) Erikson's crisis 6: Intimacy versus isolation
            (2) Erikson's crisis 7: Generativity versus stagnation
         b. Levinson: Stages in adult development
         c. Clausen: Choices and commitments in adult development
         d. Evaluation of research on adult development
      2. Two psychosocial issues of early and middle adulthood
         a. Work and adult development
         b. How parenthood affects development

III. Late adulthood
   A. Physical development: Health and aging
      1. Theories of aging
         a. Programming theory
         b. "Wear and tear" theory
      2. Sensory functioning in old age
      3. Psychomotor abilities
      4. Health
         a. Health status in old age
         b. Dementia
            (1) Alzheimer's disease
            (2) Other kinds of dementia
   B. Cognitive development: Is decline inevitable?

    C. Personality and social development: Successful aging
        1. Psychosocial theories
           a. Erikson's crisis 8: Ego integrity versus despair
           b. Activity versus disengagement
               (1) Activity theory
               (2) Disengagement theory
        2. Retirement
  IV. Death and mourning: An important aspect of development
    A. Attitudes toward death and dying
    B. Dealing with death
        1. Accepting one's own death
        2. Facing the death of a loved one
        3. Widowhood

Boxes
    Psychology in your life: Cognition and behavior in adolescence
    In the forefront: Helping the elderly improve intellectual
    performance

LEARNING OBJECTIVES

After you study Chapter 10, you should be able to do the tasks outlined in the following objectives.

1. Describe the physiological changes in adolescents.

2. Describe the cognitive abilities of adolescents.

3. Contrast Kohlberg's and Gilligan's views of moral development.

4. Describe the development of personality in adolescents, including the role of the identity crisis.

5. Explain the role of physical, intellectual, and environmental factors in adjustment to adulthood.

6. Identify aspects of personality and social growth and change during adulthood.

7. Identify the stages of adult development.

8. Discuss how parenting affects adult development.

9. Describe physical changes in old age and recognize the possible causes of dementia.

10. Describe the intellectual abilities of the aged and describe the possible approaches to successful aging.

11. Explain the stages often involved in dying and mourning.

KEY CONCEPTS

As you read Chapter 10 in your text, look for each of the following concepts. You should understand each concept.

1. Physiological Changes in Adolescence

Adolescence, the period of transition from childhood to adulthood, begins with a process of body changes called *pubescence.* Sexual maturity is signaled by the menarche in girls and the presence of sperm in the urine for boys. The process of sexual changes takes about 2 years and ends in puberty.

2. Cognitive Development in Adolescence

According to Piaget, adolescents develop an ability to think abstractly and progress from the concrete operations level to a formal operations level. However, other studies have shown that formal operational thought may be dependent on environmental factors, and many adults remain at the concrete operations level.

3. Moral Development in Adolescence

Kohlberg identified six stages of moral development that are based on cognitive development. Kohlberg's research considered morality as the development of an individual sense of justice. Gilligan studied the development of morality in women and found that they consider morality as a responsibility to look out for others.

4. Personality Development in Adolescence

Erikson identified the adolescent crisis as identity versus role confusion. Adolescent rebellion has not been supported by recent research. Most adolescents don't feel alienated from their parents. Although work is not harmful to adolescents, it does not enhance their development either. There has been an enormous rise in unwanted teenage pregnancies in recent years, largely because young girls refuse to admit that they are sexually active and they do not use birth control. Most unmarried pregnant teenagers have abortions.

5. Physical and Health Status in Young and Middle Adulthood

Scientific study of development beyond childhood has only recently received emphasis. During young and middle adulthood, health, energy, strength, manual dexterity, and sexual capacity are generally good. Both men and women experience midlife biological changes (menopause for women and the male climacteric for men). Environmental factors play a larger role than hormone levels in influencing moods and attitudes of both males and females during midlife changes.

6. Intellectual Development in Adulthood

Crystallized intelligence (verbal ability) continues to develop throughout the life span. Fluid intelligence (ability to handle performance tasks) peaks in the late teens and then slowly declines.

7. Personality and Social Development during Adulthood

Although certain of our basic traits prevail throughout our life span, we do grow, change, and become more introspective during adulthood. Erikson identified intimacy versus isolation as the crisis faced in early adulthood, and generativity versus stagnation as the crisis faced in middle adulthood.

8. Stages in Adult Development

Recent research has studied the stages of adult development, but the samples used were either small or limited to white, middle-class men. Levinson theorized that the goal of adult development is the creation of a life structure that is reevaluated throughout life. Five stages of adult development were identified, and an additional three later-life stages were proposed. Clausen viewed the transition in adulthood as related to events rather than age.

9. Work and Adult Development

Americans value their family roles over their work roles, but work is still an area of concern, particularly for young single women.

10. How Parenthood Affects Development

Parenting provides an opportunity to relive early experiences and resolve conflicts, along with a chance to build a new emotional relationship. Although expectant mothers and fathers generally have mixed feelings about pregnancies, they usually find parenting a major source of satisfaction.

11. Physical and Health Status in Old Age

Old age (senescence) begins at different ages for different people and is characterized by a dulling of sensory abilities and a decrease in psychomotor speed. Two theories have attempted to explain the aging process: the programming theory and the wear-and-tear theory. Programming theory holds that every organism has cells that can endure and divide for only a limited time. For humans the life span is limited to about 110 years. The wear-and-tear theory proposes that internal and external stresses wear down parts of our body. Most elderly people are reasonably healthy.

12. Dementia

Only a small percentage of old people experience dementia (senility). Most cases of dementia are caused by Alzheimer's disease, a brain disorder without an effective cure. Other possible causes of dementia include overmedication, depression, underlying disease, and difficulty adjusting to social change. These can be treated.

13. Intellectual Status in Old Age

Intellectual abilities appear to hold up very well with age, and older people can continue to improve their intellectual skills. However, the performance of older people does not always demonstrate their true intellectual competence, since they tend to work more slowly, become anxious about testing situations, have seeing and hearing difficulties, and may lack sufficient motivation for working on a test.

14. Successful Aging

Erikson proposed the final life crisis as integrity versus despair. Integrity is based on a sense of accepting the life you have lived. Two opposing views of successful aging have been proposed: activity theory and disengagement theory. According to activity theory, the key to successful aging is keeping active and busy. Disengagement theory holds that successful aging involves cutting down on activities and involvements. Research suggests that there is no single approach to successful aging, but health and income are important factors in adjusting to retirement in old age.

15. Death

Elisabeth Kübler-Ross suggests that most people go through five stages in dealing with their own death: denial, anger, bargaining, depression, and acceptance. Although some people go through all stages, others skip stages or vary the order of stages. There are individual "death styles."

16. Mourning

Normal grief usually involves four stages, beginning with a sense of shock, disbelief, and numbness. The second stage is characterized by overwhelming sadness. During the third stage the bereaved person becomes obsessed with a search for meaning in the death. The final stage occurs about a year later, when the survivor becomes more active socially. Adjustment to the death of a spouse appears to be based on economic conditions, personality styles, and the nature of the marital relationship.

TERMS TO KNOW

Define each of the terms listed. You can check your definitions in the text Glossary or on the text pages listed in parentheses.

Adolescence   (p. 343)

Pubescence   (p. 343)

Puberty   (p. 343)

Menarche   (p. 344)

Formal operations   (p. 345)

Concrete operations   (p. 345)

Imaginary audience   (p. 345)

Personal fable   (p. 345)

Moral development   (p. 345)

Moral dilema   (p. 345)

Preconventional   (p. 348)

Identity versus role confusion (p. 347)   Fluid intelligence   (p. 356)

Young adulthood   (p. 347)   Crystallized intelligence   (p. 356)

Conventional role conformity   (p. 348)   Intimacy versus isolation   (p. 358)

Autonomous moral principles   (p. 348)   Generativity versus
                                          stagnation   (p. 358)

Middle adulthood   (p. 350)   Life structure   (p. 359)

Old age   (p. 350)   Early adult transition   (p. 360)

Menopause   (p. 355)   Entering the adult world   (p. 360)

Male climacteric   (p. 355)   Age 30 transition   (p. 360)

Estrogen   (p. 355)   Settling down   (p. 360)

Midlife transition (p. 360) Dementia (p. 366)

Age 50 transition (p. 360) Senility (p. 366)

Culminating life structure
for adulthood (p. 360) Alzheimer's disease (p. 366)

Empty nest (p. 363) Acetylcholine (p. 367)

Young-old (p. 363) Exercised abilities (p. 368)

Old-old (p. 363) Unexercised abilities (p. 368)

Senescence (p. 364) Terminal drop (p. 368)

Programming theory (p. 364) Ego integrity versus despair (p. 368)

Wear-and-tear theory (p. 364) Life review (p. 369)

Activity theory (p. 370)

Disengagement theory (p. 370)

Thanatology (p. 372)

SELF-TEST

Multiple-Choice

Choose the one best response to each question. An answer key is provided at the end of this chapter.

1. Which of the following marks the onset of adolescence?

   a. Puberty
   b. Pubescence
   c. Sexual maturity
   d. Menarche

2. Which of the following is a characteristic of formal operational thought?

   a. Strict adherence to concrete ideas
   b. Ability to imagine a variety of possibilities in hypothetical situations
   c. Ability to understand the basic rules of morality and apply them
   d. Ability to use sensory abilities in picturing situations

3. A woman donates money to the March of Dimes because she is afraid her neighbors will disapprove of her if she doesn't. According to Kohlberg, what level of moral development is she exhibiting?

   a. Preconventional
   b. Conventional role conformity
   c. Autonomous moral principles
   d. Goodness as self-sacrifice

4. Although told that people will pay up to $6 for one of her pecan pies, Ms. B., a baker, refuses to charge more than $2. She feels that her conscience will not allow her to overcharge people. She also believes that she is making a fair profit. According to Gilligan, what stage of moral development is she demonstrating?

   a. Preconventional
   b. Orientation of individual survival
   c. Morality of nonviolence
   d. Conventional role conformity

5. According to Erikson, what crisis occurs during adolescence?

   a. Basic trust versus basic mistrust
   b. Identity versus role confusion
   c. Generativity versus stagnation
   d. Intimacy versus isolation

6. Which of the following statements applies to stages of adult development?

   a. They are not universal.
   b. They are genetically controlled.
   c. They occur in a given sequence.
   d. They are related to the release of sex hormones.

7. When are we at the peak of our strength and manual dexterity?

   a. Between 15 and 20
   b. Between 20 and 25
   c. Between 25 and 30
   d. Between 30 and 40

8. Which of the following increases during adulthood and old age?

   a. Fluid intelligence
   b. Crystallized intelligence
   c. Spatial abilities
   d. Visual acuity

9. A woman is described as a "loner." She has difficulty maintaining lasting personal friendships. Which conflict is not being resolved in proper balance?

   a. Initiative versus guilt
   b. Generativity versus stagnation
   c. Integrity versus despair
   d. Intimacy versus isolation

10. A man feels that the first part of his life is over, and he wants to be sure to fulfill his goals in the coming years. What is the probable stage of his development?

    a. Early adult transition
    b. Age 30 transition
    c. Settling down
    d. Midlife transition

11. Which of the following adults are most likely to value their work roles?

    a. Young fathers
    b. Young mothers
    c. Young single women
    d. Older fathers

12. What type(s) of attitude do most women have toward their pregnancies?

    a. Positive
    b. Negative
    c. Ambivalent
    d. Positive, negative, and ambivalent

13. According to programming theory, what is the cause of aging?

    a. Physical wear and tear on our bodies
    b. Psychological stress
    c. Inability of cells to continue to divide
    d. Accumulation of chemical medications

14. What is the most common cause of dementia in old age?

    a. Depression
    b. Lack of adjustment
    c. Overmedication
    d. Alzheimer's disease

15. Which of the following statements best describes intellectual activity in old age?

    a. Old age is a period of deterioration of intellectual ability.
    b. Old age is a period of rapid growth in intellectual ability.
    c. Many intellectual abilities are maintained in old age.
    d. Memory deteriorates but motor skills improve in old age.

16. According to Erikson, what is the final crisis in life?

    a. Intimacy versus isolation
    b. Integrity versus despair
    c. Generativity versus stagnation
    d. Basic trust versus basic mistrust

17. Which of the following is the best rule for aging successfully?

    a. Remain as active as possible.
    b. Cut down on activities and involvements.
    c. Alternate between activity and disengagement.
    d. Indulge in activities of leisure as you see fit.

18. Which two factors seem to be critical for satisfaction in retirement?

    a. Health and money
    b. Health and religion
    c. Religion and money
    d. Religion and sex life

19. A woman has been told she is dying. She responds, "You must be mistaken!" According to Elisabeth Kübler-Ross, what stage is she experiencing?

    a. Denial
    b. Anger
    c. Bargaining
    d. Acceptance

20. Which of the following is the most difficult adjustment for both widows and widowers?

    a. Economic adjustment to the loss of a partner
    b. Physical adjustment to facing illnesses
    c. Physical adjustment to a change in sexual behavior
    d. Emotional adjustment to the loss of a partner

Matching

Match each name in column A with a descriptive phrase in column B.

Column A

_____ 1. Jean Piaget

_____ 2. Lawrence Kohlberg

_____ 3. Carol Gilligan

_____ 4. Erik Erikson
_____ 5. G. Stanley Hall

_____ 6. Albert Bandura

_____ 7. Daniel Levinson

_____ 8. Bernice Neugarten

_____ 9. Leonard Hayflick

_____ 10. Elisabeth Kübler-Ross

Column B

a. Described adolescence as a period of identity crisis

b. Suggested that the myth of adolescent turmoil persists as a self-fulfilling prophecy

c. Proposed that adolescents progress from a concrete operations level to a formal operations level of thought

d. Identified five stages of dying

e. Proposed that women define morality as a willingness for self-sacrifice for the welfare of others

f. Differentiated between the young-old and the old-old

g. Formulated the first psychological theory of adolescence, describing it as a period of storm and stress

h. Proposed the programming theory of aging

i. Defined moral development as the development of a sense of justice and identified six stages of moral development

j. Proposed that the goal of adult development is the creation of a life structure

APPLICATION EXERCISES

These application exercises will test your understanding of and ability to apply the material you have read in your text. Suggested answers are provided at the end of the chapter so that you can check your responses.

1. Lawrence Kohlberg studied how people think about morality and described three broad levels of moral development. Carol Gilligan also studied moral development but described three stages using a different definition of morality from Kohlberg's. In Table 10-1, contrast Kohlberg's and Gilligan's views of morality.

Table 10-1 Morality: Two Views

	Kohlberg	Gilligan
Definition		
Level I		
Level II		
Level III		
Sexual Bias		

2. There is an enduring myth that the physiological changes in women during menopause (the climacteric) cause psychological problems, particularly depression. From what you have read in your text, cite four types of evidence that indicate that any psychological problems are more likely to be caused by environmental factors.

a. _____

b. _____

c. _____

d. _____

3. A typical scenario of development through the adult years was outlined in your text and included the following stages:

Early adult transition

Entry life structure for early adulthood

Age 30 transition

Culminating life structure for early adulthood

Age 50 transition

Read each of the following descriptions of behavior and indicate which stage the person is experiencing.

a. Adele is 33 and has a successful career. She and her husband had agreed that they did not want children. In the past few months she has been reevaluating her life and thinking about having a baby.

_____

b. Jonathan is 43 and is beginning to realize that his life is half over. He has decided to enjoy life more fully by spending additional time with his family and singing with a local group.

_____

c. Stanley is 25, has just completed law school, and has accepted a job with a large New York law firm. He will have his own apartment and for the first time will be financially independent.

_____

d. Isabelle is 18 and is working during the summer. She plans to enter college in the fall. She would like to have her own apartment but realizes she would not be able to save enough money for college if she did not live with her parents.

_____

e. Edna is 37 and has served as a junior partner to an established medical doctor for the past 8 years. She is now convinced that she wants her own medical practice by the time she is 40.

_____

4. The conflicts that Erikson describes for childhood are primarily based on the development of personal competence and achievement. However, Erikson changes his focus when describing adolescent and adult development. List the four conflicts that Erikson ascribes to adolescent and adult development, indicate the focus of these four stages, and specify the area of development that Erikson downplays.

a. Adolescent and adult conflicts

_____
_____
_____
_____

b. Focus _____

c. Area downplayed _____

5. About 10 percent of the population over age 65 show some symptoms of dementia, including forgetfulness, a limited attention span, a decline in intellectual ability, and difficulty responding to people. List five conditions that cause dementia and indicate whether or not each condition is treatable.

a. _____

b. _____

c. _____

d. _____

e. _____

6. Psychologists have identified a four-stage pattern of normal grief after the death of a loved one. Assume that a woman has just heard about the sudden death of her husband and will follow a normal pattern of grief. Indicate how she will probably behave at the following time:

a. Today _____
_____

b. In 10 days _____
_____

c. Next month _____
_____

d. Next year _____
_____

READING EXERCISE

The following article by Jeff Meer from *Psychology Today* presents evidence that older people have many abilities that compensate for any loss of speed.

The Reason of Age

The golden years are making a comeback. As researchers spend less time looking at what we lose as we get older and more at what we keep or gain, aging is looking better.

Consider Andrés Segovia, still giving acclaimed concerts on the classical guitar at age 92 . . . Claude Pepper, who came in with the 20th century and has served in Congress for most of the past 50 years . . . Bob Hope, entertaining and golfing his way around the world 82 years after his birth in Eltham, England.

But aren't these people exceptions? Of course they are. Men and women with unusual abilities are always exceptions, whatever their age. Ability and activity vary among people in their 70s, 80s and 90s just as they do earlier in life.

Evidence is piling up that most of our mental skills remain intact as long as our health does, if we keep mentally and physically active. Much of our fate is in our own hands, with "use it or lose it" as the guiding principle. We are likely to slow down in some ways, but there is evidence that healthy older people do a number of things better than young people.

Psychologist James Birren, dean of the Andrus Gerontological Center at the University of Southern California, is one of many researchers to show that older people perform tasks more slowly, from cutting with a knife and dialing a telephone to remembering lists. There are numerous theories about what body changes are responsible but no conclusive answers.

Reprinted with permission from *Psychology Today* Magazine. Copyright (c) 1986 (APA).

More important, slowing down doesn't make much difference in most of what we do. Slower reflexes are certainly a disadvantage in driving an automobile, but for many activities speed is not important. And when it is, there are often ways to compensate that maintain performance at essentially the same level. "An awful lot of what we can measure slows down," says psychologist Timothy Salthouse of the University of Missouri at Columbia, "but it isn't clear that this actually affects the lives of the people we study in any significant way."

As an example, Salthouse cites an experiment in which he tested the reaction time and typing skills of typists of all ages. He found that while the reactions of the older typists were generally slower than those of younger ones, they typed just as fast. It could be that the older typists were even faster at one time and had slowed down. But the results of a second test lead Salthouse to believe that another factor was at work.

When he limited the number of characters that the typists could look ahead, the older typists slowed greatly, while the younger ones were affected much less. "There may be limits, but I'm convinced that the older typists have learned to look farther ahead in order to type as quickly as the younger typists," Salthouse says.

A similar substitution of experience for speed may explain how older people maintain their skills in many types of problem-solving and other mental activity. Because of this, many researchers have come to realize that measuring one area of performance in the laboratory can give only a rough idea of a person's ability in the real world.

As an example, psychologist Neil Charness of the University of Waterloo in Ontario gave bridge and chess problems to players of all ages and ability levels. When he asked the bridge players to bid and the chess players to choose a move or remember board positions, the older players took longer and could remember fewer of the chess positions. But the bids and the moves they chose were every bit as good as those of younger players. "I'm not sure exactly what the compensatory mechanisms are," Charness says, "but at least until the age of 60, the special processes that the older players use enable them to make up for what they have lost in terms of speed and memory ability."

Many researchers now believe that one reason we associate decline with age is that we have asked the wrong questions. "I suspect that the lower performance of older people on many of the tasks we have been testing stems from the fact that they have found that these things are unimportant, whereas young people might enjoy this kind of test because it is novel," says psychologist Warner K. Schaie of Pennsylvania State University. Relying on their experience and perspective, he says, older people "can selectively ignore a good many things."

Memory is probably the most thoroughly studied area in the relationship between age and mental abilities. Elderly men and women do complain more that they can't remember their friends' names, and they seem to lose things more readily than young people. In his book *Enjoy Old Age,* B.F. Skinner mentions trying to do something that one learned to do as a child--folding a piece of paper to make a hat, for example--and not remembering how. Such a failure can be especially poignant for an older person.

But the fact is that much of memory ability doesn't decline at all. "As we get older, old age gets blamed for problems that may have existed all along," says psychologist Ilene Siegler of the Duke University Medical Center. "A 35-year-old who forgets his hat is forgetful," she says, "but if the same thing happens to grandpa we start wondering if his mind is going." If an older person starts forgetting things, it's not a sure sign of senility or of Alzheimer's disease. The cause might be incorrect medication, simple depression or other physical or mental problems that can be helped with proper therapy.

Psychologists divide memory into three areas, primary, secondary and tertiary. Primary or immediate memory is the kind we use to remember a telephone number between the time we look it up and when we dial it. "There is really little or no noticeable decline in immediate memory," according to David Arenberg, chief of the cognition section at the Gerontology Research Center at the National Institute on Aging. Older people may remember this type of material more slowly, but they remember it as completely as do younger people.

Secondary memory, which, for example, is involved in learning and remembering lists, is usually less reliable as we get older, especially if there is a delay between the learning and the recall. In experiments Arenberg has done, for example, older people have a difficult time remembering a list of items if they are given another task to do in between.

Even with secondary memory, however, where decline with age is common, the precise results depend on exactly how memory is tested. Psychologist Gisela Labouvie-Vief of Wayne State University in Detroit has found that older people excel at recalling the metaphoric meaning of a passage. She asked people in their early 20s and those in their 70s to remember phrases such as "the seasons are the costumes of nature." College students try to remember the text as precisely as they can. Older people seem to remember the meaning through metaphor. As a result, she says, "they are more likely to preserve the actual meaning, even if their reproduced sentence doesn't exactly match the original." In most situations, understanding the real meaning of what you hear or read is more important than remembering the exact words.

Part of the problem with tests of memory is that most match older people against students. "As long as we accept students as the ideal, older people will look bad," Labouvie-Vief says. Students need to memorize every day, whereas most older people haven't had to cram for an exam in years. As an example of this, psychologist Patricia Siple and colleagues at Wayne State University found that older people don't memorize as well as young students do. But when they are matched against young people who are not students, they memorize nearly as well.

The third kind of memory, long-term remembrance of familiar things, normally decreases little or not at all with age. Older people do particularly well if quickness isn't a criterion. Given time and the right circumstances, they may do even better than younger men and women. When psychologist Roy Lachman of the University of Houston and attorney Janet Lachman tested the ability to remember movies, sports information and current events, older people did much better, probably because of their greater store of information. Since they have more tertiary memory to scan, the Lachmans conclude, older people scan that kind of memory more efficiently.

Psychologist John Horn of the University of Denver and other researchers believe that crystallized knowledge such as vocabulary increases throughout life. Horn, who has studied the mental abilities of hundreds of people for more than 20 years, says, "If I were to put together a research team, I'd certainly want some young people who might recall material more quickly, but I'd also want some older crystallized thinkers for balance."

Researchers often echo the "use it or lose it" idea. When psychologist Nancy Denney of the University of Wisconsin-Madison uses the game "20 questions" in experiments, she finds that the needed skills are not lost. "The older people start off by asking inefficient questions," she says, "but we know that the abilities are still there because once they see the efficient strategy being used by others, they learn it very quickly."

Psychologist Liz Zelinski of the University of Southern California makes a similar point when she tests the ability to read and understand brief passages. People in their 70s and 80s show no significant decline in comprehension. "Our tests don't involve the kind of questions that require older people to store information temporarily in memory," she cautions. "Tests like that might show declines." Zelinski has also found that older men and women read her tests just as fast as younger people do. "It is a good guess that they maintain the ability to read quickly because they do it all the time," she says.

Even when skills atrophy through disuse, many people can be trained to regain them. Schaie and psychologist Sherry Willis of Pennsylvania State University recently reported on a long-term study with 4,000 people, most of whom were older. Using individualized training, the researchers improved spatial orientation and deductive reasoning for two-thirds of those they studied. Nearly 40 percent of those whose abilities had declined returned to a level they had attained 14 years earlier.

Mnemonics is another strategy that can help people memorize something as simple as a shopping list. Arenberg has found that older people are much better at remembering a 16-item list if they first think of 16 locations in their home or apartment and then link each item with a location. With practice, they master this technique very easily, Arenberg says, "and become very effective memorizers."

When it comes to aging's effect on general intelligence, as measured by standard IQ tests, the same questions of appropriateness, accuracy and motivation complicate the findings. Psychologist Paul Costa, chief of the laboratory of personality and cognition of the Gerontology Research Center at the National Institute on Aging in Baltimore, points out that many early studies on aging tested older people and younger people at the same time, instead of testing the same people over a period of years. These studies were, in effect, measuring the abilities of older people, largely lower-income immigrants, against the generations of their children and grandchildren. "The younger people enjoyed a more comfortable life-style, were better educated and didn't face the same kind of life stresses," he says, "so comparisons were mostly inappropriate."

Most researchers today are uncomfortable with the idea of using standard intelligence tests for older people. "How appropriate is it to measure the 'scholastic aptitude' of a 70-year-old?" asks University of Michigan psychologist Marion Perlmutter.

She and others, including Robert Sternberg at Yale, believe that aspects of adult functioning, such as social or professional competence and the ability to deal with one's environment, ought to be measured along with traditional measures of intelligence. "We are really in the beginning stages of developing adequate measures of adult intelligence and in revising what we think of as adult intelligence,"

Perlmutter says. "If we had more comprehensive tests including these and other factors, I suspect that older people would score at least as well and probably better than younger people."

Erroneous ideas about automatic mental deterioration with age hit particularly hard in the workplace. Although most jobs require skills unaffected by age, many employers simply assume that older workers should be phased out. Psychologists David Waldman and Bruce Alvolio of the State University of New York at Binghamton recently reviewed 13 studies of job performance and found little support for deterioration of job performance with increasing age. Job performance, measured objectively, increased as employees, especially professionals, grew older. The researchers also discovered, however, that if supervisors' ratings were used as the standard, performance seemed to decline slightly with age. Expectation became reality.

Despite all the experiments and all the talk about gains and losses with age, we should remember that many older people don't want to be compared, analyzed or retrained, and they don't care about being as fast or as nimble at problem solving as they once were. "Perhaps we need to redefine our understanding of what older people can and cannot do," Perlmutter says. Just as children need to lose some of their spontaneity to become more mature, perhaps "some of what we see as decline in older people may be necessary for their growth." While this does not mean that all age-related declines lead to growth or can be ignored, it does highlight a bias in our youth-oriented culture. Why do we so often think of speed as an asset and completely ignore the importance of patient consideration?

QUESTIONS

Answer the following questions and then compare your responses with the suggested answers at the end of this chapter.

1. According to the article, what weaknesses do older people experience?

2. How do older people compensate for their weaknesses?

3. Why are researchers uncomfortable about using standardized tests on older people?

ANSWERS

Correct Answers to Self-Test Exercises

	Multiple-Choice					Matching	
1. b	6. a	11. c	16. b		1. c	6. b	
2. b	7. c	12. d	17. d		2. i	7. j	
3. b	8. b	13. c	18. a		3. e	8. f	
4. c	9. d	14. d	19. a		4. a	9. h	
5. b	10. d	15. c	20. d		5. g	10. d	

Suggested Answers to Application Exercises

1. Answers to Table 10-1
   Morality: Two Views

	Kohlberg	Gilligan
Definition	Development of sense of justice	Ability to take another person's view and to sacrifice oneself for another
Level I	Preconventional	Orientation of individual survival
Level II	Morality of conventional role conformity	Goodness as self-sacrifice
Level III	Morality of autonomous moral principles	Morality of nonviolence
Sexual Bias	Males	Females

2. a. Reduction in hormone production causes only hot flashes, thinning of the vaginal lining, and urinary dysfunction, all physiological problems.
   b. Recent research shows no evidence to attribute psychiatric illness to physical changes in women's bodies.
   c. Women in cultures that value older women experience fewer problems with menopause.
   d. Men are just as subject to psychological problems from environmental pressures in middle age.

3. a. Age 30 transition
   b. Age 50 transition
   c. Entry life structure for early adulthood
   d. Early adult transition
   e. Culminating life structure for early adulthood

4. a. Identity versus role confusion; intimacy versus isolation; generativity versus stagnation; integrity versus despair
   b. Social and family interaction
   c. Role of work

5. a. Alzheimer's disease; not treatable
   b. Overmedication; treatable
   c. Depression; treatable
   d. Underlying disease; treatable
   e. Difficulty adjusting; treatable

6. a. She will be in a state of shock and disbelief.
   b. She will feel overwhelming sadness, cry, and possibly suffer from a loss of appetite, insomnia, and other physical problems.
   c. She will be reliving the death in her mind and searching for reasons.
   d. She will become more socially active and feel an added strength, knowing she has survived an emotional trauma and ordeal.

Suggested Answers to Reading Questions

1. They perform tasks more slowly and show some decline in secondary memory.

2. A study by Salthouse found that older people look farther ahead when typing to maintain their typing speed. They often substitute experience for speed, preserve meanings rather than exact words, and use mnemonics effectively.

3. Standardized IQ tests measure scholastic aptitude, not a major concern of older people. Many older people are not motivated during tests, since they prefer not to be compared, analyzed, and retrained.

Chapter 11:

MOTIVATION AND EMOTION

CHAPTER OUTLINE

I. Determinants of Motivation

II. Motivation
   A. Theories of motivation and emotion
      1. Instinct theories
      2. Drive theories
         a. Sigmund Freud: Unconscious motivators
         b. Clark Hull: Drive-reduction theory
      3. Opponent-process theory: Sensory stimulation
      4. Abraham Maslow's theory: Hierarchy of needs
      5. Cognitive theories
   B. Hunger and eating
      1. How the body regulates hunger
         a. Short-term regulation
         b. Long-term regulation: Set-point theory
      2. Why we eat the way we do
         a. Preparation for famine
         b. Enjoyment of the sensory qualities of food
         c. Learned cues for eating
   C. Aggression
      1. Do we inherit a tendency toward aggression?
      2. Is there a biological basis for aggression?
      3. What triggers aggression?
         a. We are frustrated
         b. We are insulted or receive a negative evaluation
         c. We are depressed
      4. How do we learn to be aggressive?
         a. We learn from people around us
         b. We learn from societal attitudes
         c. Do we learn from television?
   D. Achievement
   E. Arousal, curiosity, and boredom
      1. How we become aroused
      2. How we feel about arousal
      3. How arousal affects performance
      4. Effects of sensory deprivation
      5. Boredom

III. Emotion
   A. Classifying emotions
   B. Theories of emotion
      1. James-Lange theory: Feelings are physical
      2. Cannon-Bard theory: Feelings are cognitive

3. Schacter-Singer theory: Emotions depend on double cognitive labeling
4. Facial-feedback theory: Facial expressions lead to emotions

C. Questions about emotions
   1. Are emotions inborn?
   2. Which comes first--thinking or feeling?
      a. "Emotion is primary"
      b. "Thought is primary"

D. Cognitive-chemical interactions in emotion

Boxes
   In the forefront: Family violence
   Psychology in your life: Lie detectors--foolproof or fraudulent?

LEARNING OBJECTIVES

After you study Chapter 11, you should be able to do the tasks outlined in the following objectives.

1. Define *motivation* and identify three factors involved in motivation.

2. Explain instinct, drive, and opponent-process theories, Maslow's hierarchy of needs, and cognitive approaches to motivation.

3. Describe the physiological components involved in feelings of hunger.

4. Explain three theories of the causes of overeating.

5. Describe the biological and learning explanations for the causes of aggression.

6. Identify five factors that contribute to family violence.

7. Identify factors that influence the need for achievement.

8. Explain the relationship between arousal level and complexity of task, and describe the effects of sensory deprivation and boredom.

9. Describe how emotions have been categorized.

10. Explain three theories of emotion and facial-feedback theory.

11. Discuss the controversy over whether emotions are inborn or require cognitive appraisal.

12. Describe the cognitive chemical interactions that occur in emotional states.

13. State the limitations of the polygraph test.

KEY CONCEPTS

As you read Chapter 11 in your text, look for each of the following concepts. You should understand each concept.

1. Overview of Motivation and Emotion

Motivation is the force that gives direction to our behavior. The study of motivation is concerned with why people behave as they do. Research on motivation has examined three kinds of factors: biological, learned, and cognitive. Emotions are an important element in our motivation. It is often difficult to distinguish between motivation and emotion.

2. Biological Theories of Motivation

The earliest biological theories were based on the inheritance of human instincts. Researchers were unable to prove the existence of these instincts, and the theories could not account for individual differences. More recent biological theories are based on drives, both physiological and psychological. Drive theories fail to account for thinking and learning. Opponent-process theory explores reactions to sensory stimulation. Learning theorists emphasize the importance of rewards and other environmental influences on motivation. Maslow developed a pyramid showing the hierarchy of our needs.

3. Cognitive Approaches

Cognitive approaches emphasize our methods of interpreting events, as well as our incentives and expectations based on the locus of control.

4. Regulation of Hunger

Feelings of hunger result from stomach contractions. Stomach contractions are caused by an increase in the levels of insulin in the blood. Insulin is a hormone that converts the blood glucose and carbohydrates into energy. Sugar raises insulin levels higher than any other food; thus eating sweet foods leads to greater feelings of hunger. According to set-point theory, each person has an ideal weight and is equipped with a set point. In some people weight and set point are higher.

5. Causes of Overeating

Three theories have contributed to explanations of overeating:

a. Preparation for famine. Through evolutionary adaptation people stored food in the form of fat in order to be sustained during food shortages.
b. Enjoyment of sensory qualities of food. People overeat to extend their enjoyment of the taste and texture of food.
c. Learned cues for eating. Obese people are more likely to respond to external cues like time of day, food ads, and aromas than to internal cues caused by low blood glucose.

6. Causes of Aggression

Biological approaches to aggression suggest that we are born with a predisposition toward aggression that is influenced by hormones and chemicals. Other theories cite frustration, insults, negative evaluations, depression, observation, societal attitudes, and television as influences on aggressive behavior.

7. Family Violence

The home is the most violent place in the United States. Abusers were often mistreated in childhood and feel powerless to control themselves. Victims are often demanding and show negative behavior. There are usually disputes within abusive families, along with social isolation from the community. Cultural attitudes toward violence affect family behavior.

8. Achievement

Differences in achievement needs have been measured using the Thematic Apperception Test (TAT). People with high achievement needs enjoy realistic challenges, take personal responsibility for their success, and are optimistic. Although achievement needs may be partly inherited, they can also be influenced by child-rearing techniques and training programs.

9. Arousal and Curiosity

Arousal is a physiological state moderated by the reticular activation system. Curiosity requires a relatively high level of arousal. Easy tasks are performed best at low levels of arousal; difficult tasks are performed best at lower levels of arousal. Studies of sensory deprivation have demonstrated that lack of stimulation for an extended time is intolerable but may have some benefits. Boredom is a state of low arousal that can cause problems or can lead us to explore new activities.

10. Classification of Emotions

Psychologists have categorized emotions in different ways, but most classifications are based on fundamental or primary emotions. Emotions within a given classification can be radically different, since there can be wide differences in intensity.

11. Theories of Emotion

There are three possible explanations of emotions:

a. Emotions are caused by physical factors (James-Lange theory).
b. Emotions are cognitive, since the same physical changes accompany different emotions (Cannon-Bard theory).
c. Emotions result from the interaction of physical changes and cognitive appraisals (Schacter-Singer theory).

Facial-feedback theory supports the James-Lange theory.

12. Nature of Emotions

Zajonc argued that emotions are innate and independent of thought. His view is supported by research on the universal nature of facial expressions. Lazarus has countered that thought is a necessary condition of emotion. He notes that people in different cultures experience different emotions in similar situations.

13. Cognitive-Chemical Interactions in Emotion

The neurotransmitters serotonin and norepinephrine are related to emotion. Males in a position of dominance secrete more serotonin, and animals in positions of control secrete more norepinephrine.

14. Polygraph Tests

A polygraph test, commonly known as a *lie detector test,* is based on the notion that lying causes physiological arousal. Breathing rate, blood pressure, and electrodermal response are monitored during questioning and compared with baseline scores. Many factors can affect the test results, and polygraphs are not very reliable.

TERMS TO KNOW

Define each of the terms listed. You can check your definitions in the text Glossary or on the text pages listed in parentheses.

Motivation	(p. 383)	Secondary (acquired) drives	(p. 385)
Emotions	(p. 383)	Opponent-process theory	(p. 386)
Instincts	(p. 384)	Self-actualization	(p. 386)
Ethologists	(p. 384)	Cognitive approaches	(p. 387)
Drive theory	(p. 385)	Incentives	(p. 387)
Eros	(p. 385)	Locus of control	(p. 387)
Thanatos	(p. 385)	Glucose	(p. 388)
Homeostasis	(p. 385)	Diabetes	(p. 388)
Primary drives	(p. 385)	Insulin	(p. 388)

Fructose (p. 389)

Set point (p. 389)

Ventromedial nuclei of the hypothalamus (p. 389)

Lateral hypothalamus (p. 389)

Basal metabolism rate (BMR) (p. 389)

Yo-yo syndrome (p. 390)

Beta-endorphin level (p. 390)

Internal cues for eating (p. 391)

External cues for eating (p. 391)

Behavior-modification approaches to dieting (p. 391)

Chance-learning theory (p. 391)

Aggression (p. 392)

Violence (p. 392)

Premenstrual syndrome (PMS) (p. 393)

Hypoglycemia (p. 393)

Frustration (p. 393)

Machismo (p. 395)

Need to achieve (*n*Ach) (p. 397)

Thematic Apperception
Test (TAT)   (p. 397)   Autonomic arousal   (p. 401)

Achievement imagery   (p. 397)   Reticular formation   (p. 401)

Internal causes   (p. 397)   Reticular activation system   (p. 401)

External causes   (p. 397)   Sensation-seeker   (p. 402)

Stable causes   (p. 397)   Type T personality   (p. 402)

Unstable causes   (p. 397)   Type t personality   (p. 402)

Arousal   (p. 400)   Yerkes-Dodson law   (p. 402)

Curiosity   (p. 400)   Sensory deprivation   (p. 403)

Electroencephalogram   (p. 401)   Boredom   (p. 404)

Ten fundamental emotions   (p. 405)   Serotonin   (p. 412)

Eight primary emotions   (p. 405)   Norepinephrine   (p. 412)

James-Lange theory   (p. 406)   Learned helplessness   (p. 412)

Cannon-Bard theory   (p. 407)   Polygraph test   (p. 412)

Cortex   (p. 407)   Electrodermal response (EDR)   (p. 413)

Thalamus   (p. 408)   Baseline score   (p. 413)

SELF-TEST

Schacter-Singer theory   (p. 408)

Multiple-Choice

Choose the one best response to each question. An answer key is provided at the end of this chapter.

Epinephrine   (p. 408)

1. Which of the following questions is asked in the study of motivation?

   a. What physiological changes occur with age?
   b. Which types of behavior are most important?
   c. Why do people behave as they do?
   d. Who should control behavior?

Facial-feedback theory   (p. 410)

2. According to the current definition, which of the following examples best defines instinctive behavior?

   a. Child scratching an itch
   b. Wrestler pinning an opponent
   c. Bird building a nest
   d. Student learning psychology

3. Jenny, a college student, tried hang gliding during her spring break and was at first frightened almost to the point of panic. As she continued the activity, she experienced a sense of exhilaration. Now she plans to enjoy hang gliding on all her future vacations. Which of the following theories of motivation could explain the reversal of her initial feelings?

   a. Instinct theory
   b. Primary-drive theory
   c. Opponent-process theory
   d. Theory of unconscious motivators

4. According to Maslow, what is self-actualization?

   a. Need for arousal and curiosity
   b. Need for safety and security
   c. Need for self-fulfillment
   d. Need for social approval

5. According to Maslow's hierarchy, which of the following needs would you try to satisfy last?

   a. Need for friends
   b. Need for food
   c. Need to develop musical talent
   d. Need to live in a safe neighborhood

6. Which aspect of human behavior is emphasized in cognitive theories of motivation?

   a. Imitation
   b. Thought processes
   c. Innate behavior
   d. Biological processes

7. You have not eaten for 14 hours, and your stomach muscles are contracting. What is causing these contractions?

   a. High level of glucose
   b. High level of insulin
   c. High level of fructose
   d. Low level of insulin

8. According to set-point theory, what is the cause of obesity?

   a. Obese people have higher set points and eat more.
   b. Obese people have not developed set eating habits and indulge in binges.
   c. Obese people have set eating habits that cannot be changed.
   d. Obesity is caused by diabetes.

9. According to Rodin's research on people who react to internal and external cues, how do "externals" react to the sight of appealing food?

   a. They become aggressive.
   b. They produce beta-endorphin.
   c. They produce more fat cells.
   d. They produce more insulin.

10. Which of the following substances is least likely to affect aggression?

    a. Testosterone
    b. Norepinephrine
    c. Alcohol
    d. Insulin

11. When you feel angry and frustrated, how are you likely to behave?

a. You will probably show aggression.
b. You will be motivated to achieve.
c. You will have a slower sexual response.
d. You will experience sensory deprivation.

12. Assume that you want to predict whether children will behave aggressively as adults. On the basis of research, at which age should their television-viewing habits be checked?

a. 4
b. 8
c. 10
d. 12

13. How is the Thematic Apperception Test used in determining motivation?

a. The test measures sexual arousal to pornography.
b. The test is used to measure achievement needs.
c. The test is used to determine aggressive tendencies.
d. The test is used to diagnose obesity.

14. Imagine that you are working on an extremely difficult and complex task. According to the Yerkes-Dodson law, what would be your best level of arousal?

a. Extremely high
b. Moderately high
c. Relatively low
d. Fluctuating between extremely high and extremely low

15. Which of the following changes is likely to occur when you are working on a boring task?

a. You secrete more insulin.
b. You secrete less insulin.
c. Your reticular activation system speeds up.
d. Your reticular activation system slows down.

16. If you encountered a man with a live boa constrictor draped around his neck, according to James-Lange theory what sequence of events would follow?

a. You would experience fear and physiological changes at exactly the same time.
b. You would experience fear and then aggression.
c. You would experience fear first and then physiological changes.
d. You would experience physiological changes first and then fear.

17. In a study of facial expression, psychologists found that our bodies respond slightly differently to different emotions. What was the other finding?

a. Thoughts produce more significant physiological changes than do facial expressions.
b. Facial expressions produce more significant physiological changes than do thoughts.
c. Facial expressions and thoughts produce identical physiological responses.
d. Facial expressions cannot be separated from thoughts.

18. What is the current view on whether emotions are innate or learned?

a. Emotions are innate.
b. Emotions are learned.
c. Emotions are innate but are influenced by learning.
d. Emotions are neither innate nor learned.

19. Which of the following persons would be most likely to have the highest level of serotonin?

    a. President of a college fraternity
    b. Optimistic, placid woman
    c. Man who is suffering from learned helplessness
    d. Woman who is lying

20. Which of the following statements best describes the accuracy of polygraph tests?

    a. Polygraph tests are foolproof.
    b. Polygraph tests are highly reliable.
    c. Polygraph tests do not measure physiological changes.
    d. Polygraph tests are not always reliable.

Matching

Match the names in column A with a descriptive phrase in column B.

Column A

_____ 1. William McDougall

_____ 2. Sigmund Freud

_____ 3. Clark Hull

_____ 4. Richard Solomon

_____ 5. Abraham Maslow

_____ 6. Judith Rodin

_____ 7. Konrad Lorenz
_____ 8. Henry Murray

_____ 9. David McClelland

_____ 10. Donald Hebb

_____ 11. Robert Plutchik

_____ 12. William James and Carl Lange

Column B

a. Organized needs in the form of a pyramid

b. Suggested that increases in physiological arousal can lead to more intense emotional reactions

c. Noted that people who eat in response to external cues have a larger insulin reaction to food

d. Devised a method for analyzing achievement motivation based on responses to the Thematic Apperception Test

e. Believed that all behaviors are instinctive

f. Introduced the drive theory of motivation, stressing the importance of primary and secondary drives

g. Defined the need to achieve (*n*Ach)

h. Stated that emotional experiences and psychological changes occur simultaneously

i. Proposed that people are driven by eros and thanatos forces

j. Proposed a model relating arousal level to performance

k. Proposed that aggression is inherited genetically

l. Classified eight primary emotions that can interact to produce complex feelings

____ 13. Walter Cannon and Philip Bard

____ 14. Stanley Schacter and
          Jerome Singer

____ 15. Robert Zajonc

____ 16. Richard Lazarus

m. Maintains that thought is required
   for emotion
n. Claimed that emotions are based
   on the perception of psychological
   changes
o. Maintains that emotions are
   primary and do not require thought
p. Proposed the opponent-process
   theory

APPLICATION EXERCISES

These application exercises will test your understanding of and ability to apply the material you have read in your text. Suggested answers are provided at the end of the chapter so that you can check your responses.

1. Abraham Maslow suggested that there are individual differences in human psychological and physiological needs. He organized human needs in the form of a pyramid and placed basic physiological needs at the base. According to Maslow, this pyramid is like a ladder; needs at lower rungs must be met before we can progress upward. Higher-level needs appear only when those at lower levels are satisfied. Although there are some individual exceptions, Maslow's theory has been generally accepted.

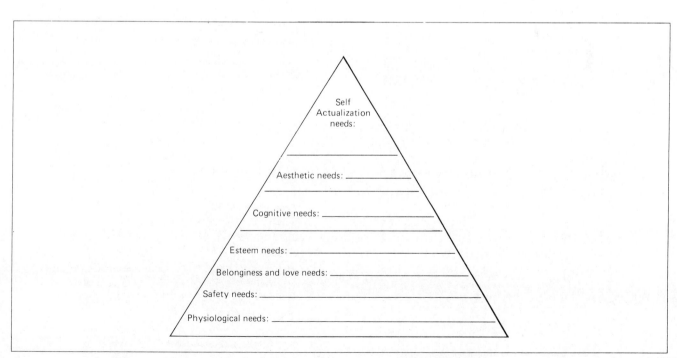

Self Actualization needs: _____

Aesthetic needs: _____

Cognitive needs: _____

Esteem needs: _____

Belonginess and love needs: _____

Safety needs: _____

Physiological needs: _____

Figure 11-1

Read the following examples of needs and place each need on the appropriate rung of Maslow's pyramid (Figure 11-1).

a. Need to achieve an A on a test
b. Need to be accepted by your friends
c. Need for food
d. Need to straighten a crooked picture
e. Need to fulfill your complete potential
f. Need to understand what you are reading
g. Need to escape from a burning building

2. In studies involving laboratory rats, surgical lesions in two parts of the hypothalamus had profound effects on their eating as well as their weight level. What did these studies show about the relation between eating and weight level that supports the role of the hypothalamus as a set-point mechanism? _____
_____
_____
_____
_____

3. Read the following scenario and identify three events that could trigger an aggressive reaction.

Carolyn raced to the airport, but when she arrived she found that her flight to Houston had been canceled. This meant that she would miss an important national meeting of her organization. She telephoned her boss to explain her problem. He called her a "scatterbrain" and told her that missing the meeting might cause her to lose her job.

a. _____
_____

b. _____
_____

c. _____
_____

HERMAN JAMES UNGER

© 1986 Universal Press Syndicate

"My wife doesn't like me working late at the office."

Figure 11-2

Herman
Copyright 1986 Universal Press Syndicate. Reprinted with permission. All rights reserved.

4. The man carrying his file cabinet (Figure 11-2) appears to have a strong *n*Ach. On the basis of this assumption and his portrayal in the cartoon, respond to the following:

How would Weiner describe his locus of control? _____
_____
_____

Given a choice of very difficult, moderately difficult, and easy tasks, which would the man probably prefer? _____

_____

Name two probable unattractive personality characteristics of this man. _____

_____

What child-rearing practices did his mother probably use? _____

_____

5. There are three principal theories concerning the sequence of events in experiencing emotions. The James-Lange theory indicates that you experience physiological changes before you feel an emotion. The Cannon-Bard theory proposes that physiological arousal and emotions occur simultaneously, with the cortex and thalamus playing key roles. The Schacter-Singer theory suggests that emotions are based upon the appraisal of both physiological arousal and the probable events that are causing the arousal.

Now imagine that you are sitting studying in your room; you suddenly hear the screeching alarm of a smoke detector. Describe your reaction according to each of these three theories.

a. James-Lange theory _____

_____

_____

_____

_____

b. Cannon-Bard theory _____

_____

_____

_____

_____

c. Schacter-Singer theory _____

_____

_____

_____

_____

READING EXERCISE

Your text describes the characteristics of type T and type t personalities. Connie Zweig's article from *OMNI* explains some of Frank Farley's research on these two personality types.

The Big Thrill

During the past year, Milwaukee journalist Roger Salick has skydived from 12,500 feet, flown into the eye of a hurricane aboard a weather reconnaissance plane, raced a hydroplane at 60 miles per hour with his face 18 inches above water, and saddled up a bucking buffalo.

Salick embodies what University of Wisconsin psychologist Frank Farley calls a Type T personality--a perpetual risk taker and avid adventurer whose life is molded by the "thrill factor." Farley believes the same mechanism that motivates people like Salick to perform reckless and death-defying feats also

Copyright (c) 1987 by Connie Zweig and reprinted with the permission of Omni Publications International Ltd.

may explain other risk-taking behavior, both good and bad: why people win the Nobel prize; become wealthy entrepreneurs or juvenile delinquents; or drive under the influence of alcohol.

Salick, who writes a biweekly column called "Thrillseeker" for *The Milwaukee Journal's* Sunday magazine, asks readers to pose daring challenges for him to attempt. At the world championships for off-road racing, for instance, someone proposed that Salick accompany a driver in a race. "This is the most violent mechanized sport I've tried," he says. "We were in giant trucks with sixteen shocks, going one hundred miles per hour on a dirt track. We collided with another truck at ninety miles per hour. He lost control and we hit him broadside. He rolled over, and my driver just kept going, didn't even hit the breaks. It's when I'm pushed beyond the familiar parameters, when I don't know the outcome, that I get a visceral rush, a real kick," Salick says. But Farley has another explanation: "Type T's are predisposed to pursue adventure because they actually *need* more stimulation than the rest of us to get revved up."

According to the bearded investigator, who also conducts a monthly seminar on psychology trends for members of the U.S. Congress, it seems that the human brain seeks to maintain an optimal level of activity, called arousal. "If arousal is too high or too low," Farley says, "we try to adjust it to a middle ground. We do this unconsciously, of course, by choosing environments or experiences that are either soothing or stimulating. Type T's may be born with a low ability to become aroused. They are typically not too responsive to stimuli."

Besides genetic makeup, Farley speculates that there are a number of variables that help form the Type T personality: birth and early-infancy experiences--exposing a child to, say, early swimming lessons or a lot of visual or tactile stimulation; the type of food in the home--feeding a child too much sugar or protein; and the effects of hormones such as testosterone.

Farley, who immigrated to the United States from Canada in 1966, is now in his late forties and stands over six feet tall. He has been fascinated with stimulation "and all its variety and intensity" since he first began studying human motivation three decades ago. "I'm a moderate Type T," he says. "The study of thrill seekers is my thrill." Today, Farley sees "risk taking as a central core of both creativity and violence." Many great scientists, he believes, "live life on the edge of uncertainty, just like criminals."

At the opposite end of the spectrum is the Type t (little *t*) personality. These people try to keep stimulation to a minimum, clinging to certainty and dreaming of a pension after retirement. Based on his studies, Farley estimates that Type T's make up about 25 percent of the population. "There are more big T's than little t's," he says. "And the big T's exert an inordinate amount of creative influence in our society."

Critics of his theory argue that typing people merely pigeonholes them. The nuances and complexity of human behavior can't be explained this simply. "But this is not a typology," Farly is quick to point out. "It's a continuum, and Type T is toward one end."

Farley and his colleagues have studied hundreds of people, using both physiological measures of arousal--skin-resistance tests, perception tests--and psychological measures of arousal. Farley uses standard maze tests and personality questionnaires ("I would rather be a cowboy/cowgirl than a shepherd"/"I have a strong need for excitement"). When a Type T person is given a booklet of maze tests, for instance, he usually varies his route through each maze. The Type t personality, however, usually follows the same course through each maze.

Farley has also developed an index of the arousal value of mental and physical stimuli--works of art, natural and man-made environments, crimes, and sexual activities. He can tell if the Type T person is more of a physical thrill seeker or a mental risk taker.

Journalist Salick and daredevil Evel Knievel are examples of the physical thrill seeker. Mental Type T's--artists, scientists, and entertainers--pursue novel ideas and move easily from one thinking mode to another, such as from the abstract to the concrete. He calls this skill "transmutative thinking"--a characteristic of many Nobel prize-winners, who derive intense stimulation from their investigations. "What distinguishes anyone engaged in intellectual pursuits from real mental T's," Farley says, "is the amount of mental risk involved, the degree to which they pursue novelty and the unknown."

Nobel winner Francis Crick, codiscoverer of DNA structure, has moved from one unknown area of interest to another. "He moved from molecular biology to the study of the origins of life and then to dreams," Farley says. "He doesn't get bogged down in details but loves the uncertainty of the big problems."

Mental T's and physical T's share a common cluster of traits. They have more experimental tastes, prefer novelty to routine, thrive on conflict, and perform extremely well in unstructured work situations. They enjoy more variety in their sex lives and report that they are happier than Type t's.

Most recently, Farley tested financial risk takers and compared them with those averse to taking financial risk. He found a link between entrepreneurial behavior and thrill seeking. "The financial risk takers," he says, "listed success and competence as their first goals, while the risk

avoiders listed happiness. The risk takers were less lonely, more self-motivated, had fewer emotional problems at home, and, curiously, tended to believe more in God."

But the big T has a dark side, which Farley calls T-. Many criminals and juvenile delinquents fit into this category. According to Farley, juvenile delinquents possess more Type T traits than nondelinquents of the same age, gender, race, and social class. In a study of imprisoned male delinquents, Farley and colleague Maria Astorga found that escape rates were seven times higher among T's than t's. "The escape rate is interesting because of the risk and excitement of escape," Farley says. "The hunt seems tailor-made for people with big-T motivation."

Farley's findings also may help to explain why some Vietnam veterans have not been able to readjust to life after their return: These vets found the high-stress life of combat more suitable to their temperaments than everyday life.

Some Type T people can switch from being very creative (T+) to being very destructive (T-). Farley thinks that the late *Saturday Night Live* star John Belushi seems to have slipped from a T+ pattern as a creative, improvisational comedian into a T- pattern of lethal drug abuse.

A change in the other direction, from T- to T+, may have even greater social implications. If a Type T child is identified early enough, his or her potential can be channeled into positive creativity. "Many people in education are aware of individual differences among students," Farley says. "But they focus on differences in abilities, not personalities. If we could tailor experiences to their stimulation needs, then kids could maintain a motivation for learning and not need to turn to delinquent or criminal acts."

Farley points to Outward Bound as an organization that deals successfully with delinquent adolescents. And VisionQuest, a Tucson-based program for hard-core delinquents, teaches them to break wild horses, go ocean sailing, and survive on wagon trains traveling the West Coast. "Preparing these youngsters in routinized trades--to become carpenters, plumbers, or electricians--fails to satisfy their T tendencies, which spiral into unemployment or criminal behavior."

Farley also has conducted studies of drunk drivers and has found a link between driving speed and the need for stimulation. In the United States 25,000 people a year are killed in alcohol-related car accidents. Farley and his colleagues found that driving accidents were twice as high among big T's as among little t's. "Most of this debate centers on creating stricter laws or technological improvements, but no one asks, 'Who is causing this mayhem?' My hunch is that personality is at the core," Farley says.

Almost every state has a mandate for counseling groups for people convicted of driving under the influence of alcohol. "But the counseling typically has no focus," Farley says. "It needs to address the needs of Type T's by providing healthy forms of risk taking as a prevention." In his home county Farley is putting this idea into effect.

The Type T personality may be an American archetype. "America was

explored by dreamers and adventurers--strong-willed individualists. They took enormous risks, were excited by the unknown, and left their homes to create environments ideal for Type T's, such as freedom from excessive government." Farley believes these traits have been bred into generations of American risk takers, who either reject social conventions as avant-garde artists and scientists, or defy legal conventions, such as the ban on drinking and driving.

"Immigrants tend to be Type T people," Farley says. "In a recent study of Indians who applied for immigration to Canada and the United States, there were more Type T people among the immigrants than in the control group that stayed at home." Wave upon wave of American immigrants have kept the Type T force alive in this country. "The implications of this are enormous," Farley says. "There's going to be another great age of exploration in the next century: the exploration of outer space and inner space, the stars and the brain. If the creative force of the Type T can be mobilized, the United States will remain a strong leader. Compared with cultures such as Japan and China, which revere tradition and order, the United States certainly fits the profile of a Type T nation."

QUESTIONS

Answer the following questions and then compare your responses with the suggested answers at the end of this chapter.

1. According to Farley, why do type T's pursue adventure?

2. List four factors that Farley believes are involved in forming type T personalities.

3. What are the characteristics of mental type T's?

4. According to Farley, why are the Outward Bound and VisionQuest programs successful?

ANSWERS

Correct Answers to Self-Test Exercises

Multiple-Choice

1. c
2. c
3. c
4. c
5. c
6. b
7. b
8. a
9. d
10. d
11. a
12. b
13. b
14. c
15. d
16. d
17. b
18. c
19. a
20. d

Matching

1. e
2. i
3. f
4. p
5. a
6. c
7. k
8. g
9. d
10. j
11. l
12. n
13. h
14. b
15. o
16. m

Suggested Answers to Application Exercises

1. a. Self-actualization needs: need to fulfill your complete potential

b. Aesthetic needs: need to straighten a crooked picture
c. Cognitive needs: need to understand what you are reading
d. Esteem needs: need to achieve an A on a test
e. Belongingness and love needs: need to be accepted by your friends

f. Safety needs: need to escape from a burning building
g. Physiological needs: need for food

2. Damage to the ventromedial nuclei in the hypothalamus resulted in overeating and a high set point for maintenance of obesity. Damage to the lateral hypothalamus resulted in minimal food intake and a low set point for maintenance of low body weight. The research suggested that these two mechanisms in the hypothalamus interact in determining a normal set point.

3. a. Missing her plane and the important meeting would lead to *frustration*.
b. Being called a "scatterbrain" is an *insult*.
c. Her boss gave her a *negative evaluation* when he suggested that she might lose her job.

4. Weiner would describe his locus of control as internal since the man seems to rely on his own efforts rather than on luck.

He would probably prefer tasks of moderate difficulty that would present a challenge and give him a sense of accomplishment.

If he is similar to others with a high *n*Ach, he may have a tendency to cheat and show an insensitivity to other people.

It is likely that his mother encouraged independence and accomplishments.

5. a. James-Lange theory. You would experience an increase in heart rate, breathing, and muscle tension as you jumped from your seat, before you experienced fear.
b. Cannon-Bard theory. As you heard the screeching of the alarm, nerve impulses would be sent simultaneously to the cerebral cortex to interpret the sound as an indication of fire and to the thalamus. Your thalamus would produce physiological changes that would give you added energy to flee from the building if necessary.
c. Schacter-Singer theory. As you heard the screeching sound you would quickly appraise both the intensity of the physiological changes in your body and the possibility of a fire in the building. On the basis of your appraisal of these two factors, you would sense an appropriate amount of fear.

Suggested Answers to Reading Questions

1. According to Farley, type T people need more stimulation than other people; they have a low ability to become aroused.

2. Genetic makeup, experiences at birth and during early infancy, food, and hormones

3. They have novel ideas, change thinking modes quickly, and enjoy mental risks.

4. They appeal to the T tendencies with activities such as breaking wild horses, ocean sailing, and survival outings.

Chapter 12:

SEXUALITY AND GENDER ROLES

CHAPTER OUTLINE

I. Gender and gender identity
  A. Sex and gender differences
    1. How do males and females differ?
      a. Physical differences
      b. Psychological differences
        (1) Cognitive differences
        (2) Personality differences
        (3) Other psychological differences
    2. Why do males and females differ?
      a. Hormones and their effects
      b. Environmental influences
        (1) Parents
        (2) The media
        (3) Cultural attitudes
    3. How do ideas about gender affect our lives?
  B. Theories of gender identity
    1. Social-learning theory
    2. Cognitive-developmental theory
  C. Gender identity disorders
    1. Gender identity disorder of childhood
    2. Transsexualism
II. Sexuality
  A. Physiology of human sexual response
    1. Sexual response cycle
      a. Excitement
      b. Plateau
      c. Orgasm
      d. Resolution
    2. Arousal of sexual desire
      a. Hormones
      b. Stimulation
      c. Learning
      d. Cognitive factors
      e. Emotional factors
  B. A life-span perspective on human sexuality
    1. Childhood
    2. Adolescence
    3. Young adulthood
    4. Middle adulthood
    5. Late adulthood
  C. Sexual orientation: Heterosexuality and homosexuality

D. Psychosexual problems and their treatment
   1. Psychosexual dysfunction
      a. Inhibited sexual desire (ISD)
      b. Inhibited sexual excitement
      c. Inhibited female orgasm
      d. Inhibited male orgasm
      e. Premature ejaculation
      f. Vaginismus
      g. Dyspareunia
      h. Sexual burnout
      i. Causes of sexual dysfunctioning
   2. Paraphilias
   3. Sex therapy
      a. Masters and Johnson's program
      b. Sex therapy today

Boxes
   In the forefront: Gender differences in communication
   Psychology in your life: Sexual turning points throughout life
   In the forefront: Is there a link between pornography and sexual
   violence against women?

LEARNING OBJECTIVES

After you study Chapter 12, you should be able to do the tasks outlined in the following objectives.

1. Describe physical differences between the sexes, including chromosomal differences and differences in vulnerability to pathological conditions.

2. Cite three cognitive differences between males and females.

3. Discuss research findings concerning other possible psychological differences, including aggressive and empathic behavior.

4. Describe gender differences in communication.

5. Discuss research findings concerning differences in hormonal balance as a cause of behavioral differences between males and females.

6. Discuss environmental influences on behavioral differences between the sexes, including the influence of parents, the media, and cultural role expectations.

7. Describe two major contemporary theories concerning the acquisition of gender identity.

8. Describe two gender identity disorders.

9. Identify and describe four stages of human sexual response.

10. Identify and discuss five factors which affect arousal of sexual desire.

11. Describe sexual development in childhood, adolescence, young adulthood, middle adulthood, and late adulthood.

12. Cite six hypotheses which have been advanced to account for the existence of homosexuality.

13. Describe eight psychosexual dysfunctions.

14. Describe the group of psychosexual disorders known as *paraphilias*.

15. Discuss current research findings concerning the possible relation between violent pornography and sex crimes.

16. Discuss the sex-therapy approach of Masters and Johnson and some contemporary modifications of their approach.

KEY CONCEPTS

As you read Chapter 12 in your text, look for each of the following concepts. You should understand each concept.

1. Sex and Gender

In your text, the term *sex differences* refers to physical differences between males and females. The term *gender* refers to aspects of behavior that may or may not be tied to biology. Gender is the awareness that one is male or female. *Gender roles* are the behaviors, attitudes, and interests regarded as "appropriate" for males and females in a given culture. *Gender stereotypes* are exaggerated generalizations about masculine and feminine attitudes and behavior.

2. Similarities between the Sexes

In most ways, males and females are more alike than they are different. While there are both physical and psychological differences between the sexes, the psychological differences tend to be quite small.

3. Physical Differences

Females are born with two X sex chromosomes (XX); males are born with one X and one Y (XY). This difference seems to give females a lifelong health advantage which begins at conception. At all ages, males die at higher rates than females.

4. Cognitive Differences

In most cognitive areas studied, including general intelligence, learning, memory, the formation of concepts, reasoning tasks, problem solving, and creativity, research has shown no consistent differences between males and females. However, three consistent cognitive differences have been found. After about the age of 10 or 11, girls do better on many tasks involving word skills, while boys excel in math and in spatial relations. Most studies have shown these differences to be very small.

5. Personality Differences

A recent analysis of the literature on gender and aggressive behavior found that men are more aggressive than women and that this difference is greater for physical aggression. Another body of research suggests that females are more empathic than males. However, the research concerning gender differences with reference to aggression and empathy is not conclusive, indicating that these differences are, at most, modest.

6. Differences in Thinking about Moral Issues

Some studies have found that in considering moral issues, men are more concerned about justice and fairness, while women are more concerned about looking out for a specific person or persons. However, most research on moral development has shown little evidence of gender differences.

7. Differences in Verbal Communication

Research has shown that, contrary to the popular stereotype, men talk considerably more than women do. The amount of gossip among women is only slightly higher than among men, and the kind of gossip, in terms of positive and negative statements about a third party, is identical. Women's speech often suggests uncertainty because of their tendency to speak with a raised inflection at the end of a sentence and to add tag questions to declarative statements, as in, "It was a great party, wasn't it?" Finally, women are more likely to talk about feelings and personal topics such as family matters and to listen to each other, showing understanding. Men are more apt to talk about objects, events, and impersonal topics and to give logical advice for solving everyday problems.

8. Differences in Nonverbal Communication

Men take up more personal space than women, who hold their bodies more tightly contained and sit and stand closer to other people. While men and women do the same amount of touching, women smile more, laugh more, and maintain more eye contact in conversation than men do. Finally, women tend to be better at reading other people's facial expressions.

9. Causes of Gender Differences in Communication

The reasons for gender differences in communication are not clear. One theory holds that women communicate differently because of their subordinate social position. Another compatible explanation emphasizes the socialization in "ladylike" behaviors that females experience throughout their lives.

10. Nature and Nurture as Causes for Differences between Males and Females

The available evidence suggests that females and males have some different biological tendencies, but that learning modifies these tendencies, either accentuating them or discouraging them. The evidence also suggests that no inborn tendencies are unchangeable.

11. Effects of Hormones

The effects on behavior of the different hormonal balances found in men and women are unclear. Evidence from research with animals indicates that, in general, low levels of androgens (male sex hormones) before or at about the time of birth result in an animal's showing female characteristics; higher levels result in typically male behaviors. Most human research has been limited to persons born with certain hormonal disorders and to persons with unusual prenatal exposure to hormones. While some researchers do explain behavioral differences along hormonal lines, their conclusions are questionable.

12. Influence of Parents

In some respects, parents treat their sons and daughters differently from infancy. They seem to be more actively involved with their male infants and to treat them more roughly. Middle-class and better-educated mothers talk to their daughters more than to their sons. Such differences in treatment may help to explain males' aggressiveness and females' fluency with words.

Fathers tend to pay more attention to sons and to emphasize competence and achievement. With their daughters, fathers tend to stress relationships and encourage dependency. In many other respects, parents treat their sons and daughters about the same.

13. Influence of the Media

Until very recently, television was one of the most effective media for spreading highly gender-stereotyped attitudes. Males were seen more often than females and were portrayed as more aggressive, more active, and more competent than females. Content analyses of children's books have shown that they also present gender-stereotyped behaviors and attitudes. Today both television producers and publishers of children's books are attempting to portray both sexes in a more realistic and less stereotyped fashion.

14. Influence of Cultural Attitudes

Cultural attitudes about gender roles exert a powerful influence on behavior. Recently in our own society there has been a shift toward more egalitarian attitudes and away from belief in traditional roles.

15. Adverse Effects of Gender Stereotypes

In our culture males are expected to be dominant, aggressive, active, independent, and competitive, while females are expected to be nurturant, compliant, and dependent. Acceptance of these gender stereotypes leads people to deny natural inclinations and abilities that do not match stereotyped expectations. Most contemporary psychologists view the healthiest person as one who possesses a balanced combination of the most positive characteristics normally associated with maleness and femaleness.

16. Two Theories of Gender Identity

Social-learning theorists maintain that children acquire gender identity as they imitate the parent of the same sex and are rewarded by parents and other adults for "appropriate" behavior and punished for "inappropriate" behavior. One problem with this theory is that children do not necessarily imitate the parent of the same sex, nor even necessarily a parent at all. A second problem is that there are more similarities than differences in the way parents treat their sons and daughters. Cognitive-developmental theorists believe that gender identity is a natural corollary of cognitive development. Children actively categorize themselves as "male" or "female," learn the societal prescriptions for each gender's role, and try to live up to these roles.

17. Two Gender Identity Disorders

In a gender identity disorder of childhood, a young child fails to develop a normal sense of maleness or femaleness. Such a child is often the offspring of parents who have encouraged extreme forms of cross-gender behavior. In transsexualism, a person feels "trapped" in the body of the wrong sex and wants to live as a member of the other sex. Transsexuals may receive hormones to make them look like the other sex and have sex-change surgery to alter their genitals so that they can be sexually active as members of the other sex.

18. Physiology of Human Sexual Response

A pioneering research team, William H. Masters, M.D., and Virginia E. Johnson, conducted a 12-year research program in which they studied the physiology of human sexual response. They identified four stages of sexual response: excitement, plateau, orgasm, and resolution.

19. Role of Hormones in Arousing Sexual Desire

The connection between sex hormones and arousability or sexual activity in human beings has not been well established. However, studies have shown that in the male life cycle, when testosterone levels are high, the male is more inclined to engage in sexual behavior. There is also evidence that women with high levels of testosterone have sex more often and enjoy it more.

20. Effects of Drugs on Sexuality

Drugs can impair sexual functioning in both men and women. Drug-related effects on sexuality usually disappear when a person stops taking the drug.

21. Role of Learning in Sexual Behavior

Research indicates that learning plays an important part in the sexual behavior of animals, and therefore it is assumed that learning plays an even greater role in human sexual response. Learning seems to play a considerable role in a person's choice of and behavior with sexual partners. In addition, there seems to be a preponderance of repressive upbringing among people with sexual dysfunctions.

22. Role of Cognitive and Emotional Factors in Sexual Behavior

The way we think affects our sexual behavior. For example, extroverts and introverts seem to think differently, and one study has found that their

sexual behavior differs as well. Our feelings also affect our sexual behavior. Our culture stresses the tie between affectionate and sexual feelings.

23. Sexual Development in Childhood

Many lasting sexual beliefs and values are developed during the early childhood years. Adults' reactions to children's sex play, masturbation, and sexual questions have a great impact on the attitudes formed in childhood.

24. Sexual Development in Adolescence

During early adolescence, the reproductive functions and sex organs mature. The average age of puberty (when a person is sexually mature and able to reproduce) is 12 for girls and 14 for boys. By the age of 16, 25 percent of white boys and girls, 50 percent of black girls, and 90 percent of black boys have had sexual intercourse. Boys and girls are more like each other today than in the past in terms of both actual behavior and standards for appropriate behavior.

25. Teenage Pregnancy

The teenage birth rate in the United States is among the highest in the western world: 1 out of 10 American teenagers become pregnant every year, and almost half of these pregnancies result in births. Failure to use birth control may stem from ignorance, fear of parents' finding out, or reluctance to plan ahead for sex. Many communities are instituting programs aimed at preventing teenage pregnancy.

26. Sexual Development in Young Adulthood

This is typically an age of experimentation and an age when sexuality merges with emotional commitment to another person. Over the past 30 years, sexual attitudes and behaviors have changed, with more people engaging in premarital sex, with more of them having a succession of partners, and with more egalitarian attitudes toward sexual standards. However, over the past few years, there seems to have been a decrease in casual sexual activity, a fact attributed to the desire to avoid contracting genital herpes or acquired immune deficiency syndrome (AIDS). Married people are having sexual intercourse more often, engaging in more varied sexual activities, and having extramarital sex more frequently than in the past.

27. Sexual Development in Middle and Late Adulthood

Middle-aged people are engaging in sexual activity more often and in more varied ways than in the past. However, physiological changes, especially in men, make sexual activity different during the middle years. While these physical changes become more intense in old age, elderly men and women are still able to enjoy a fulfilling and satisfying sexuality.

28. Hypotheses Concerning Homosexuality

Many hypotheses have been advanced to account for the existence of homosexuality. The oldest, that it represents a kind of mental illness, has been rejected by the American Psychiatric Association, which now classifies homosexuality as a mental disorder only in people who want to be heterosexual. Two other theories, for which no scientific support has been found, are (1) that male homosexuality is caused by a family constellation with a dominating mother and a weak father and (2) that homosexuality results from a chance-learning situation involving seduction by someone of the same sex. Theories that homosexuality is related to a genetic factor or a hormonal imbalance are supported only by very tentative evidence. The hypothesis which has garnered the most support is that there are probably several reasons why a person becomes homosexual, and those reasons involve interaction among various hormonal and environmental events.

29. Psychosexual Dysfunctions

A psychosexual dysfunction is a recurrent and persistent disturbance in the sexual response cycle that is not caused by a physical condition. The following psychosexual dysfunctions tend to begin early in adulthood, to have variable courses, and to be caused by or result in troubled marital and love relationships: inhibited sexual desire (ISD), inhibited sexual excitement, inhibited female orgasm, inhibited male orgasm, premature ejaculation, vaginismus, dyspareunia, and sexual burnout. Most of these conditions can be successfully treated.

30. Causes of Sexual Dysfunctioning

Problems with sex may be traced to medical conditions; an upbringing marked by severely antisexual attitudes; anxiety; guilt; depression; poor self-esteem; ignorance about one's own or one's partner's body; acceptance of cultural myths; and problems in a relationship. In most cases, sexual problems do not stem from deep-seated personality problems.

31. Paraphilias

Paraphilias are psychosexual disorders characterized by sexual arousal only in response to unusually bizarre imagery, objects, or acts. The implication of the paraphilias can be major, ranging from interference with a normal sexual relationship to a person's becoming a public danger. The cause of such tendencies is unknown. Treatment usually involves some form of behavior therapy.

32. Pornography and Sexual Violence

Some people have concluded that violent pornography contributes to sexually violent crimes against women and children and are pressing for laws against sexually explicit materials that "subordinate, objectify, or degrade" women. Other people believe that such laws would endanger our right to freedom of speech under the First Amendment. Research concerning a causal link between violent sexual imagery and violent sexual crime is limited and, thus far, provides no strong evidence for a link between the two.

33. Sex Therapy

Sex therapy is treatment designed to remove specific obstacles to sexual functioning. The pioneering team of Masters and Johnson virtually created sex therapy as we know it today. In their program, couples rather than individuals are treated by a female and a male therapist working together. After the therapists have interpreted the sexual difficulty, the couple participates in daily sessions with the therapists, and in private they engage in sexual activities as recommended. This program lasts approximately 2 weeks. Sex therapists today have built on and modified Masters and Johnson's approach. The effectiveness of sex therapy varies, depending on the

particular dysfunction and client, and the success rate ranges from about 30 to 95 percent for the various dysfunctions.

TERMS TO KNOW

Define each of the terms listed. You can check your definitions in the text Glossary or on the text pages listed in parentheses.

Sex differences   (p. 419)

Gender identity   (p. 419)

Gender roles   (p. 419)

Gender stereotypes   (p. 419)

Chromosomes   (p. 419)

Genes   (p. 419)

Androgens	(p. 424)	Pubescence	(p. 435)
Androgynous	(p. 427)	Primary sex characteristics	(p. 435)
Gender identity disorder	(p. 429)	Secondary sex characteristics	(p. 435)
Gender identity disorder of childhood	(p. 429)	Puberty	(p. 435)
Transsexual	(p. 429)	Heterosexuals	(p. 440)
Erogenous zones	(p. 430)	Homosexuals	(p. 440)
Testosterone	(p. 433)	Psychosexual dysfunction	(p. 441)
Estrogen	(p. 433)	Inhibited sexual desire (ISD)	(p. 441)
Progesterone	(p. 433)	Inhibited sexual excitement	(p. 442)

Inhibited female orgasm   (p. 442)   Pornography   (p. 443)

Inhibited male orgasm   (p. 442)   Obscenity   (p. 443)

Premature ejaculation   (p. 442)   **SELF-TEST**

Multiple-Choice

Vaginismus   (p. 442)   Choose the one best response to each question. An answer key is provided at the end of this chapter.

1. According to your text, which of the following would represent a sex difference?

Dyspareunia   (p. 442)

   a. The fact that women are born with two X sex chromosomes and men are born with one X and one Y

   b. The fact that girls do better than boys on a wide range of tasks involving word skills

Sexual burnout   (p. 442)

   c. The idea that boys are more aggressive than girls

   d. The idea that girls are more empathic than boys

Paraphilia   (p. 443)

2. Which of the following statements best describes the health of females versus the health of males?

Sex therapy   (p. 443)

   a. Males seem to enjoy a lifelong health advantage.

   b. Females seem to enjoy a lifelong health advantage.

   c. Males are healthier than females until middle age, when both sexes seem to experience equally good health.

Erotica   (p. 443)

d. Males are healthier than females until middle age, when females seem to experience better health than males.

3. In which of the following cognitive areas are there well-established differences between boys and girls?

   a. General intelligence
   b. Learning
   c. Memory
   d. Spatial relations

4. Over the past 20 years, what has happened to the gap between males and females in verbal and mathematical ability?

   a. It has narrowed slightly.
   b. It has narrowed significantly.
   c. It has widened slightly.
   d. It has widened significantly.

5. What types of studies show males to be the more aggressive?

   a. Studies involving self-reports
   b. Studies involving parent reports
   c. Studies involving teacher reports
   d. Studies involving direct observation

6. Which of the following best describes the amount of talking done by men and women?

   a. Women talk considerably more than men do.
   b. Women talk slightly more than men do.
   c. Men talk more than women do.
   d. Men and women do an equal amount of talking.

7. Research on animals shows that low levels of androgens before or at about the time of birth generally result in which of the following?

a. The animal shows typically female behaviors.
b. The animal shows typically male behaviors.
c. The animal shifts back and forth between typically male and female behaviors.
d. The animal's behavior seems not to be affected.

8. In which of the following ways have parents been shown to treat their sons and daughters differently?

   a. They expect more independence from boys with regard to bathing and dressing themselves.
   b. They are more actively involved with their male infants.
   c. They allow young boys to go further away from home.
   d. They allow boys to be more aggressive.

9. Which of the following is a father *least* likely to emphasize for his son?

   a. Competence
   b. Achievement
   c. Relationships
   d. Career

10. What group of theorists maintains that gender identity is developed as children imitate the parent of the same sex and are rewarded for appropriate behavior?

    a. Social-learning theorists
    b. Psychoanalytic theorists
    c. Cognitive-developmental theorists
    d. Gestalt theorists

11. According to cognitive-developmental theory, which of the following children would adapt most quickly to the gender-role stereotypes of a given culture?

a. Child whose intelligence is far below average
b. Child whose intelligence is slightly below average
c. Child of average intelligence
d. Child whose intelligence is above average

12. What happens to men in the resolution stage of the sexual response cycle?
    a. Pulse rate and blood pressure increase.
    b. The penis becomes completely erect.
    c. Rhythmic muscular contractions of the pelvic organs occur.
    d. A refractory period is experienced.

13. Your text describes a recent study of 188 men who were impotent. What was the single largest cause of their dysfunction?

    a. Sexually repressive upbringing
    b. Use of medications
    c. Poor relationship with the sexual partner
    d. Fear of sexual failure

14. Freud called the years from 6 to puberty the *latency stage,* believing that children are relatively uninterested in sex during this period of their development. How do contemporary psychologists view the latency stage?

    a. They agree with Freud.
    b. They agree with Freud in part; they believe that children do not engage in sexual activities but are curious about sex during this period.
    c. They disagree with Freud; they believe that the latency stage begins later than age 6.
    d. They disagree with Freud; they believe that the latency stage does not exist.

15. Approximately how long does pubescence usually last?

    a. 6 months
    b. 1 year
    c. 2 years
    d. 4 years

16. What is the average age of puberty?

    a. Age 12 for girls and age 14 for boys
    b. Age 14 for girls and age 12 for boys
    c. Age 14 for girls and age 16 for boys
    d. Age 16 for girls and age 14 for boys

17. Which of the following statements about teenage sexual activity by the age of 16 is correct?

    a. White boys are more likely to have had sexual intercourse than white girls.
    b. White girls are more likely to have had sexual intercourse than white boys.
    c. Black boys are more likely to have had sexual intercourse than black girls.
    d. Black girls are more likely to have had sexual intercourse than black boys.

18. A boy is most likely to have his first sexual intercourse with which of the following partners?

    a. Younger girl who is a steady girlfriend
    b. Girl of the same age who is a steady girlfriend
    c. Older girl whom he knows casually
    d. Adult woman whom he knows casually

19. Approximately how many teenage girls become pregnant each year?

a. 1 in 10
b. 1 in 50
c. 1 in 100
d. 1 in 200

20. Which of the following approaches to prevention of teenage pregnancy seems to be most effective?

    a. Encouraging the postponement of dating
    b. Encouraging the postponement of sexual relations
    c. Decreasing the opportunities available for teenagers to have sex
    d. Improving self-esteem in adolescents

21. Which of the following hypotheses advanced to account for the existence of homosexuality has garnered the most support?

    a. It represents a kind of mental illness.
    b. In the case of male homosexuality, it springs from a family constellation with a dominating mother and a weak father.
    c. It is a result of a chance-learning situation.
    d. It results from the interaction of various hormonal and environmental events.

22. Which of the following individuals seems to be suffering from a psychosexual disorder?

    a. Young man who occasionally is not "in the mood" for sex
    b. Young woman who has been unable to experience orgasm for several years
    c. Man who has been impotent since he began taking a certain medication
    d. Young man who occasionally experiences premature ejaculation

23. Which of the following statements correctly describes research concerning a possible link between pornography and sexual violence?

    a. Violent pornography has been shown to cause sex crimes.
    b. Nonviolent pornography has been shown to cause sex crimes.
    c. Watching violent films and videos of any kind has been shown to cause sex crimes.
    d. Research has produced no strong evidence linking pornography to sex crimes.

24. For which of the following sexual dysfunctions has treatment proved least successful?

    a. Inhibited sexual desire
    b. Premature ejaculation
    c. Vaginismus
    d. Inhibited female orgasm

25. Which of the following practices characterizes Masters and Johnson's approach to sex therapy?

    a. Exclusive use of female therapists
    b. Extensive analysis of events in the past to uncover reasons for the present problem
    c. Focused, short-term period of treatment
    d. Emphasis on treating the individual with the problem

Matching

Match each psychosexual disorder listed in column A with an appropriate descriptive phrase in column B.

Column A

_____ 1.   Inhibited sexual desire

_____ 2.   Inhibited sexual excitement

_____ 3.   Inhibited female orgasm

_____ 4.   Inhibited male orgasm

_____ 5.   Premature ejaculation

_____ 6.   Vaginismus

_____ 7.   Dyspareunia

_____ 8.   Sexual burnout

Column B

a. Therapy for this disorder has a success rate of 90 to 95 percent.

b. Of the disorders listed, this one is the most resistant to treatment.

c. Most people recover spontaneously from this disorder, but about 10 percent of those affected become celibate for life.

d. Learning how to become orgasmic, possibly through masturbation, may help a woman overcome this problem.

e. Individuals suffering from this disorder find intercourse painful.

f. This disorder might result from trying to delay ejaculation too long.

g. In males this disorder is also known as *impotence*.

APPLICATION EXERCISES

These application exercises will test your understanding of and ability to apply the material you have read in your text. Suggested answers are provided at the end of the chapter so that you can check your responses.

1. Parents, without realizing it, sometimes treat their sons and daughters differently. This may account, in part, for differences in adult behavior between females and males. Fathers consistently show more gender-stereotyping behavior than mothers do. After reading the following description of a father spending a Saturday with his son and daughter, describe the gender-stereotyping behavior of the father.

Saturday begins with Mr. Copolla having breakfast with his 13-year-old daughter Angelica and his son Curt, who is 12. During the meal, Mr. Copolla asks Curt what grades he expects to make on his next report card and stresses the importance of Curt's doing well in school. He talks with Angelica about a recent argument she has had with her best friend and encourages her to patch things up.

After breakfast, Angelica tells her father that her bike has a flat. Mr. Copolla quickly finds the leak and repairs the tire in a matter of minutes. Next, Mr. Copolla asks Curt to lend a hand with a deck he is adding to the rear of the house. Although Curt is clumsy with hammer and nails, Mr. Copolla is patient and tells Curt just what to do and how to do it right. As they work on the deck, Mr. Copolla explains to Curt what an architectural engineer does and tells him that there are good opportunities for most types of engineers. While they are working, Angelica comes out on the deck to watch. Curt jokingly tells her that she should be inside practicing her clarinet for next week's solo recital. Mr. Copolla defends her, saying that Curt should know what all work and no play will do to Angelica. After working on the deck all morning, Mr. Copolla and Curt spend the afternoon watching a baseball game.

In what ways did Mr. Copolla exhibit gender-stereotyping behavior? _____
_____
_____
_____
_____

2. Theorists have different views concerning the development of gender identity. Read the following description of two children playing and then describe how a social-learning theorist and a cognitive-developmental theorist might account for their behavior.

    Natalee and Eric are two bright 5-year-olds who have slipped away from a family picnic in a park and have found some mud to play in. Without hesitation, Eric sits right down in the mud and starts to build a "fort." Natalee squats at the edge of the mud and makes "cupcakes." Soon Eric is completely covered with mud, while only Natalee's hands are dirty.

    a. How might a social-learning theorist explain the difference in their behavior?
    _____
    _____
    _____

    b. How might a cognitive-developmental theorist explain the difference in their behavior? _____
    _____
    _____
    _____
    _____

3. Masters and Johnson identified four stages of sexual response which occur in the same pattern regardless of the kind of stimulation. The four stages are described below, but they are not listed in the correct order. Label each stage and indicate the correct order of occurrence.

    a. Both sexes experience a series of rhythmic muscular contractions of the pelvic organs at about 0.8-second intervals.

    Stage: _____

    Order of Occurrence: _____

    b. The woman's vaginal walls thicken, the opening becomes smaller, the clitoris draws up into the body, the uterus enlarges, and the color of the inner labia deepens. The man's penis is completely erect, the testes are enlarged, and a few drops of fluid appear at the tip of the penis.

    Stage: _____

    Order of occurrence: _____

    c. The female experiences lubrication of the vagina, enlargement of the breasts, erection of the nipples, swelling of the glans of the clitoris, and an expansion of the upper two-thirds of the vagina. The male's penis becomes erect, the skin of the scrotal sac smoothes out, and the testes are drawn closer to the body.

Stage: _____

Order of occurrence: _____

d. The male enters a refractory period, but the female does not.

Stage: _____

Order of occurrence _____

Doonesbury   By Garry Trudeau

Figure 12-1

Doonesbury by Garry Trudeau. Copyright (c) 1987 by G. B. Trudeau. Reprinted with permission of Universal Press Syndicate. All rights reserved.

4. Are the people who responded to the survey on extramarital sex in Figure 12-1 really as "average" as the cartoon suggests?

_____

_____

_____

5. Controversy surrounds the issue of a possible link between pornography and sexual violence. Researchers have conducted experiments, studies of criminals, and cross-cultural studies in an effort to discover whether pornography is, in fact, linked to sexual violence. Cite findings derived from each type of study.

a. Experiments: _____

_____

_____

_____

_____

b. Studies of criminals: _____

_____

_____

_____

c. Cross-cultural studies: _____

_____

_____

_____

_____

READING EXERCISE

Although 60 to 75 percent of students in this country receive some type of sex education in school, 1 out of 10 teenage girls becomes pregnant every year. The following article, which was written by Elizabeth Stark and appeared in *Psychology Today,* discusses reasons for the high rate of teenage pregnancy in the United States and characteristics of effective sex-education programs.

Young, Innocent and Pregnant

One out of ten teenage girls in the United States becomes pregnant every year and almost half of these pregnancies result in births--30,000 of them to girls under the age of 15.

Part of the reason for the high rate of teenage pregnancy is obvious: Teenagers are becoming sexually active at younger ages. During the 1970s, the number of sexually active teenagers increased by two-thirds. Today, among 15- to 17-year-olds in this country, almost half of the boys and a third of the girls are sexually active.

Unfortunately, teenagers' sense of responsibility and ability to plan for the future have not kept pace with their sexual sophistication. Only 14 percent of teenage girls use contraceptives the first time they have intercourse. Most wait until they have been sexually active for nine months or more before they visit a birth-control clinic. And a major reason for a visit to a clinic is for a pregnancy test.

Among teenagers who do use contraceptives, many depend on such unreliable methods as withdrawal or rhythm. All in all, nearly two-thirds of unwed sexually active teenage girls either never or inconsistently practice birth control. Why are teenagers so lax about using contraception?

"The first time, it was like totally out of the blue. . . . I mean, you don't know it's coming, so how are you to be prepared?" a 16-year-old girl

Reprinted from *Psychology Today* magazine by permission of the publisher. Copyright (c) 1986 by the American Psychological Association.

told Ellen Kisker, a demographer at the Office of Population Research at Princeton University.

"If I did [use a contraceptive] then I'd have sex more. Then it would be too easy. . . . I don't feel it's right. I haven't been raised that way," said another teenager, reflecting a major reason for the delay in obtaining contraceptives--ambivalence. As Karen Pittman, a sociologist at the Children's Defense Fund in Washington, D.C., explains it, "Many teenagers can reconcile their sexual activity if it's spontaneous or unplanned."

Studies that support this idea have been conducted by psychologists Donn Byrne, at the State University of New York in Albany, and William Fisher, at the University of Western Ontario in London, Ontario. In many cases, they find, a teenager's desire for completely spontaneous sex is tied to the belief that being "swept off your feet" or "carried away" is forgivable, but having premeditated sex is not. According to Fisher, "many adolescents are comfortable enough to have intercourse, especially with the aid of lust, love or liquor, but they are not comfortable enough to plan for it in advance."

Byrne and Fisher found that college students with negative attitudes toward sex were less likely to use birth control than those with more positive attitudes. The reason those who have negative attitudes are more likely to risk unwanted pregnancy, Byrne and Fisher believe, is that their negative feelings, while not strong enough to inhibit them from having sex, prevent them from going through the steps necessary to use contraception. They deny the possibility that sex may occur, are too embarrassed to get birth control or to discuss it with their partners and are inhibited about using birth-control devices. "The more guilt and anxiety you have about sex, the less likely you are to use contraception," Byrne says.

Young teenagers are simply not capable of internalizing contraceptive information, according to Irma Hilton, a psychologist at the Ferkauf Graduate School of Psychology. She believes that "young people just don't have the psychological strength to recognize the consequences of their actions." Teenagers tend to be impulsive and have trouble deferring gratification and making long-range plans, Hilton says. She points out that the older teenagers are when they initiate sexual activity, the more likely they will be to use contraceptives.

Another reason, according to Hilton, is that "maybe deep down they want to get pregnant." For those who feel isolated, the prospect of a baby offers the possibility of someone to love. Pregnancy also brings attention to a girl who may be feeling neglected. The ploy of entrapping a reluctant suitor may motivate some teenagers. Others may see pregnancy as a way to assert their independence from their parents or to become their mothers' equal. Some may want to keep up with their pregnant girlfriends. Unfortunately, says Hilton, most teenage girls who see someone else's cute, cuddly baby are in for a rude awakening when their own baby cries through the night and interferes with their social life.

Gerard Kitzi, director of the Adolescent Resources Corporation in Kansas City, Missouri, which runs three school-based health clinics, agrees that many teenage pregnancies are on some level deliberate. He says that they have teenagers who come in for a

pregnancy test and "are disappointed when the test is negative."

And it is not only teenage girls who may desire a child. In one study Hilton found that teenage fathers were generally happy about their girlfriend's pregnancy, whether or not they had any intention of caring for the child. They felt that the pregnancy affirmed their manhood.

Many of the motivations for a teenage pregnancy are born of hopelessness, the feeling that opportunities in life are few and limited and one might as well have a baby as do anything else, according to Fisher. These feelings, many experts believe, are most common among lower-income teenagers who see success in school or work as impossibilities for themselves. "They're people who've fallen out of the system," Fisher says. Studies have shown that teenagers who are behind academically in school are three times more likely to become unwed parents.

"The bottom line is kids don't feel good about themselves, especially those in lower-socioeconomic groups, who have no feeling of the future," says Kitzi. "So they do something that for them seems 'temporary': go out and start a family."

In addition, Hilton believes that lower-income teenagers are more likely to become pregnant because of attitudes within the family. According to her studies, a tolerant family attitude toward early sexual activity and pregnancy predicts high rates of teenage pregnancy. But if a teenage girl has a good relationship with her mother and if her mother is opposed to teenage pregnancy, it is less likely.

The first step in combatting teenage pregnancy, many experts agree, is teaching children about sex and sexuality from an early age. Although some school administrators claim that parents are opposed to sex education, 85 percent of the people polled by Louis Harris in the summer of 1985 said they wanted sex education taught in the schools. In addition, 78 percent said that television should air messages about birth control, and 67 percent thought that schools should establish links with family-planning clinics so that teenagers can obtain and learn about contraceptives.

Between 60 and 75 percent of students in this country receive some type of sex education before they graduate from high school, but the effectiveness and quality of these classes are questionable, according to Douglas Kirby, director of the Center for Population Options. Many schools that claim to offer sex education just provide one biology or health class on basic reproduction and do not address the real questions teenagers have about sex. Not all programs discuss birth control, and even when they do, they are unlikely to affect teenagers' use of contraception.

The most effective sex-education classes don't just teach basic reproduction and contraception; they discuss dating and relationships, as well as beliefs and life goals, according to Kirby, who did an evaluation of 13 sex-education programs in the United States. The attempt in the past to teach sex education free of values may have been a mistake, Kirby says. He believes it is important to discuss basic values such as "all people should be treated with respect and dignity" and "no one should use subtle pressure or physical force to get someone else to engage in unwanted sexual activity."

Although these sorts of sex-education classes appear to help, they are most effective in reducing teenage pregnancies and births when combined with the resources of a clinic, according to Kirby's report.

There are about 50 school-based clinics in the country, and many of them show promise in reducing pregnancy rates and keeping teenage mothers from dropping out of school or becoming pregnant again. The prototype of such clinics, the St. Paul Maternal and Infant Care Program in St. Paul, Minnesota, began its school-based clinic more than a decade ago. It was originally set up to offer prenatal and postpartum care to pregnant teenagers at an inner-city high school. The focus soon shifted to preventing pregnancies by offering contraceptive counseling, but students were reluctant to attend since "there was no question why someone was going in there," says Ann Ricketts, program administrator. So the clinic quickly expanded to include more health services, such as athletic and college physicals, immunizations and weight-control programs, to broaden its appeal and to encourage more teenagers to visit.

There are now four school-based clinics in St. Paul. Each has a core group made up of a nurse practitioner, social worker and technician. A nutritionist, pediatric nurse, pediatrician and obstetrician visit once a week. The clinics offer sex-education courses in the school, and participation in the clinics is completely voluntary, confidential and free for all students.

The clinics have helped reduce pregnancies among their students by more than 50 percent, have kept pregnant teenagers from dropping out of school (80 percent return to school and graduate after their delivery) and have increased teenagers' use of contraceptives. Most impressive, the percentage of repeat pregnancies among students is less than 2 percent.

Laurie Schwab Zabin, director of the Social Science Fertility Research Unit at the Johns Hopkins School of Medicine, and her colleagues recently completed an evaluation of an adolescent pregnancy prevention program that ran for three years in Baltimore's inner city. The health program was based in two schools--a junior and senior high. A social worker and a nurse practitioner taught sex-education classes in the schools and provided birth-control information and devices at the nearby clinics. In addition, seven "peer resources" students publicized the centers and acted as counselors. The program was extremely successful. Among high school students involved with the program for at least two years, the pregnancy rate decreased by 30 percent, while the rates rose 58 percent at similar schools in the area, according to Zabin.

Another encouraging finding was the high attendance at the clinic of boys, especially at the junior high school level. Various researchers have pointed out the importance of getting teenage boys motivated to use contraception since two of the most popular methods among teenagers, condoms and withdrawal, depend on male cooperation. Many have claimed that it's impossible to get young men interested in practicing contraception, but Zabin says that this isn't true "if you get them interested at young ages."

One result of the program, which surprised some, was that those who participated in it became sexually active on average seven months later than did teenagers attending schools with no such programs. According to Zabin this "once and for all refutes the notion that these sorts of programs encourage sex."

She explains that "the staff was willing to tell kids that they thought sex was inappropriate at young ages. It was discussed in the context of future goals. We tried to develop values in these kids. The focus was 'make a life for yourself before you make another life.'"

Various programs around the country encourage teenagers to "say no" to sex. One called "Will Power/Won't Power" helps 12- to 14-year-olds deal with the pressures of becoming sexually active and increases their assertiveness and skills in saying "no." In other programs teenagers learn responses to come-ons and pressures to have sex by role-playing and following scripts. But a few researchers question the effectiveness of such programs.

"I'm not saying it's a bad idea," says Byrne. "Society might be a better place for it. But in our present society with movies, TV and magazines glamorizing sex, the idea of just telling kids to say no is not realistic."

Pittman believes simply telling teenagers to say no is "naive as a single strategy, but can be important as one of many strategies, especially among younger teenagers. There are teens who didn't want to do it but were pushed into it. We should support those teens who don't want to be sexually active."

Fisher suggests that teenagers who aren't ready for sexual activity should be encouraged to pursue "virginity with affection," in which they achieve orgasm without intercourse. Various other programs have promoted the same sort of idea, which is sometimes referred to as "outercourse."

Fisher also believes that society needs to develop fantasies that involve birth control. Most of our fantasies don't include contraception, he says, and if they do they're often "bad" fantasies, as in the awkwardness of buying condoms in *Summer of '42* or the horror of having a parent discover a diaphragm, as in *Good-bye Columbus.* "It's possible to replace those bad fantasies with good ones," he says. But he admits that this is not the total solution, especially among lower-income teenagers. "They need the possibility of jobs and a future. No amount of pro-contraception fantasy can change that," he says.

Almost everyone who has looked at the problem agrees that poverty-stricken teenagers need to know that opportunities await them before they can be motivated to avoid pregnancy. As Pittman puts it, "all kids don't have equally compelling reasons to delay parenthood." She believes that programs that help increase teenagers' self-esteem and their abilities to succeed in the working world will lower teen pregnancy rates. If they feel valued as human beings they will be less likely to get pregnant to fill a void in their lives.

According to Pittman, the movement to help these teenagers find positive alternatives to pregnancy must go beyond the schools into churches, youth groups, summer camps, recreation centers, after-school centers and of course the home--any place where a teenager's self-esteem can be bolstered and where he or she can be offered possibilities for the future.

"The more teens, male or female, think they have to lose with a pregnancy," says Pittman, "the more likely they will try to avoid parenthood."

QUESTIONS

Answer the following questions and then compare your responses with the suggested answers at the end of this chapter.

1. According to this article, what is the relationship between feelings of ambivalence about sex and the use of contraceptives?

2. This article maintains that some girls get pregnant because, at some level, this is what they want. What are some of the motivations cited for teenage pregnancy?

3. Douglas Kirby, director of the Center for Population Options, has studied sex-education programs around the country. What characterizes effective programs according to Kirby?

ANSWERS

Correct Answers to Self-Test Exercises

	Multiple-Choice							Matching	
1.	a		10.	a		18.	c		1.	b
2.	b		11.	d		19.	a		2.	g
3.	d		12.	d		20.	d		3.	d
4.	b		13.	b		21.	d		4.	f
5.	d		14.	d		22.	b		5.	a
6.	c		15.	c		23.	d		6.	a
7.	a		16.	a		24.	a		7.	e
8.	b		17.	c		25.	c		8.	c
9.	c								

Suggested Answers to Application Exercises

1. In talking with Curt about his report card, Mr. Copolla stressed achievement. He also encouraged Curt to be both independent and competent in building the deck. He discussed career possibilities and, in general, paid more attention to Curt. With Angelica, Mr. Copolla stressed getting along with a friend. He fostered dependence by repairing her tire for her. Finally, he deemphasized achievement by failing to encourage her to practice for her recital.

2. a. A social-learning theorist might say that Natalee chose to make cupcakes because she has seen her mother make them and that Eric decided to build something because he has observed his father building various things. Natalee may have avoided getting muddy because she has been praised in the past for staying clean and punished for getting dirty. Eric, on the other hand, may have been unconcerned about the mud because he has never been punished for getting dirty and may even have received some positive attention for this type of behavior.

   b. A cognitive-developmental theorist might explain that both Natalee and Eric are actively categorizing themselves as "female" and "male," respectively, and are behaving according to gender-role concepts that they have internalized. Natalee knows that she is a girl, and she believes that girls cook and generally stay clean. Eric builds things and gets dirty because he believes that is what boys are supposed to do.

3. a. Orgasm; 3

   b. Plateau; 2

   c. Excitement; 1

   d. Resolution; 4

4. Yes, the results of Redfern's survey are similar to results from recent studies which have found that 50 to 75 percent of married

men and 34 to 43 percent of married women have had extramarital sex by age 40 or 50.

5. a. Experiments: One experiment has shown that seeing a violent, erotic or a violent, nonerotic film as opposed to a nonviolent, erotic or a nonviolent, nonerotic film makes male college students more willing to administer electric shock to a female who has angered them. Another experiment has shown that men who see films showing a woman becoming aroused by rape see the victim as more responsible for her own rape than they do when the woman seems to suffer.

b. Studies of criminals: One study found that jailed sex offenders had had less exposure to sexually explicit materials than had prisoners convicted of other offenses. Other studies have found that jailed sex offenders and non-sex offenders both in and out of prison had experienced similar exposure to erotica.

c. Cross-cultural studies: While bondage and rape are often featured in Japan's sexually oriented media, Japan has one of the lowest rates of rape of any industrialized country. After relaxation of laws against erotica in Denmark, no increase in rape or other sex offenses occurred.

Suggested Answers to Reading Questions

1. Teenagers may feel guilty about having sex and, therefore, prefer to think of their sexual activity as spontaneous rather than premeditated. The use of contraceptives would require a degree of planning that would make them uncomfortable.

2. Lonely girls may want someone to love. A neglected girl may feel that pregnancy will bring her attention. Pregnancy may be viewed as a means of entrapping a boyfriend, asserting independence from parents, or becoming the equal of a mother. Finally, to a hopeless teenager who sees few opportunities for the future, pregnancy may be regarded as something meaningful to do.

3. Effective programs discuss not only basic reproduction processes and birth-control methods, but also concerns related to dating, relationships, and basic values. The most effective programs include sex-education classes combined with the resources of a health clinic.

Chapter 13:

**THEORIES AND
ASSESSMENT OF
PERSONALITY**

CHAPTER OUTLINE

I. Theories of personality development
  A. Psychoanalytic approaches
    1. Classic psychoanalytic theory: Sigmund Freud
      a. A brief history of Freudian theory
      b. The structure of personality
        (1) Id
        (2) Ego
        (3) Superego
      c. Defense mechanisms of the ego
        (1) Displacement
        (2) Sublimation
        (3) Repression
        (4) Regression
        (5) Projection
        (6) Reaction formation
        (7) Rationalization
      d. Psychosexual development
        (1) Oral stage
        (2) Anal stage
        (3) Phallic stage
        (4) Latency stage
        (5) Genital stage
      e. Evaluation of Freudian theory
    2. Analytic psychology: Carl Jung
    3. Individual psychology: Alfred Adler
    4. Cultural psychology
    5. Psychosocial theory: Erik Erikson
  B. Humanistic approaches
    1. Self-actualization theory: Abraham H. Maslow
    2. Person-centered theory: Carl Rogers
  C. Environmental (or learning) approaches
    1. Radical behaviorism: B. F. Skinner
    2. Social-learning theory: Albert Bandura
  D. Trait approaches
    1. Psychology of the individual: Gordon W. Allport
    2. Factor theory: Raymond B. Cattell

II. Testing personality
   A. Types of personality tests
      1. Objective tests
         a. Minnesota Multiphasic Personality Inventory (MMPI)
         b. Cattell's Sixteen Personality Factor Questionnaire (16PF)
      2. Projective tests
         a. Rorschach test
         b. Thematic Apperception Test
      3. Interview techniques
   B. Ethics of personality testing

Boxes
   Psychology in your life: Your temperament and personality
   In the forefront: The person-situation controversy

LEARNING OBJECTIVES

After you study Chapter 13, you should be able to do the tasks outlined in the following objectives.

1. Define personality.

2. Describe the structure of personality according to the psychoanalytic view.

3. Identify and provide examples of seven defense mechanisms.

4. Explain psychosexual development according to Freud's theory.

5. Criticize Freud's theory.

6. Identify the modifications in psychoanalytic theory proposed by neo-Freudians (Jung, Adler, Horney, and Erikson).

7. Explain the humanistic approaches proposed by Abraham Maslow and Carl Rogers.

8. Describe and provide examples of two environmental approaches to personality.

9. Describe Gordon Allport's trait theory and specify three types of traits.

10. Explain Raymond Cattell's method for determining source traits.

11. Describe the person-situation controversy.

12. Identify three general approaches to evaluating personality.

13. Recognize the ethical concerns in personality testing and interpretation.

KEY CONCEPTS

As you read Chapter 13 in your text, look for each of the following concepts. You should understand each concept.

1. Definition of Personality

Personality makes each person a unique human being. It is a complex constellation of relatively consistent behaviors a person uses in handling other people and situations.

2. Psychoanalytic View of the Structure of Personality

Freud identified three different parts to the personality: the id, the superego, and the ego. The id is composed of basic instincts and operates on a pleasure principle, constantly seeking immediate satisfaction. The superego is composed of internalized values of right and wrong based on the values of parents and society. The ego operates on the reality principle, constantly seeking compromises between the demanding id and the restricting superego.

3. Defense Mechanisms

Defense mechanisms are unconscious distortions of reality that help us cope with anxiety. Defense mechanisms include displacement, sublimation, repression, regression, projection, reaction formation, and rationalization.

4. Psychosexual Development

Freud outlined five stages of personality development: the oral stage (birth to 12-18 months), the anal stage (12-18 months to 3 years), the phallic stage (3 to 6 years), the latency stage (6 years to puberty), and the genital stage (from puberty on). Freud believed that sexuality begins at birth and progresses through each of the five stages. Problems during the first three stages can affect a person's personality for life.

5. Evaluation of Freud's Theory

Freud's major contributions were the concepts of the unconscious and his emphasis on the importance of early experience on later development. Freud has been criticized for his emphasis on the sexual drive and his view of women as inferior persons. Humanists have argued that Freud did not allow for any element of self-control because he worked primarily with troubled people. Research on Freud's theories is difficult because his terms and

concepts are vague and difficult to define. It has also been proposed that Freud's theories may have been influenced by his own defense mechanisms.

6. Neo-Freudians

Neo-Freudians were followers of Freud who felt that sex and aggression had been overemphasized by Freud and who were more concerned with social influences on development. Carl Jung stressed the importance of racial and historical influences on personality and introduced the constructs of introvert and extrovert. Alfred Adler focused on the uniqueness of personality and was concerned with human needs to overcome feelings of inferiority. Karen Horney strongly opposed Freud's views on women and attributed neurosis to a child's difficulty in dealing with a potentially hostile world. Erik Erikson emphasized the conflict between internal instincts and the demands of society.

7. Humanistic Approaches

Humanistic approaches take a positive view of people, stress the unique experiences of each individual, and focus on the importance of self-fulfillment and personal growth.

8. Maslow's Self-Actualization Theory

Maslow, a humanist, developed a hierarchy of human needs. Basic needs must be met before a person can self-actualize and develop full potential. Maslow has been criticized for lack of objectivity and scientific rigor. His hierarchy has been criticized because the sequence it establishes is not always followed in real life.

9. Rogers' Person-Centered Theory

Rogers, a humanist, stressed the concept of self. Self-acceptance is of prime importance. Congruence occurs when there is close agreement between how we see ourselves and how we would like to be. According to Rogers, a congruent person can grow to self-actualization.

10. Environmental Approaches

Skinner, in his theory of radical behaviorism, proposes that our behavior is learned on the basis of rewards and punishments (operant conditioning). Bandura, in his social-learning theory, stresses that we learn behavior by imitating models. We are more likely to imitate models who are rewarded.

11. Allport's Trait Theory

Allport was interested in the unique makeup of traits in each individual. He described three types of traits: cardinal (dominant and prevailing in every situation), central (the handful of basic traits that generally hold true in a personality), and secondary (traits that only appear occasionally or in specific situations). Allport was more concerned with describing personality than with explaining it.

12. Cattell's Factor Theory

Cattell identified two types of traits: surface traits that are observable and source traits that are the underlying causes. He used the statistical technique of factor analysis to determine source traits.

13. Person-Situation Controversy

There is some debate over whether personality is relatively stable over time or whether behavior varies according to specific situations. It seems impossible to isolate the person from the situation, and psychologists are concluding that behavior results from an interaction between dominant personality features and the characteristics of a specific situation.

14. Purpose of Personality Testing

Personality tests have been used to provide proper counseling and to identify people with specific problems. They have also been used by researchers who are studying various aspects of personality. Reliability and validity are important considerations in judging the usefulness of personality tests.

15. Types of Personality Tests

The most common methods for assessing personality are objective tests (as the MMPI and Cattell 16PF), projective tests (as the Rorschach and TAT), and interviews (structured or unstructured).

16. Ethics of Personality Testing

Results of personality tests should be considered confidential. Further, the actual validity of tests has been questioned.

TERMS TO KNOW

Define each of the terms listed. You can check your definitions in the text Glossary or on the text pages listed in parentheses.

Personality	(p. 452)	Ego	(p. 455)
Psychoanalytic theory	(p. 454)	Reality principle	(p. 455)
Psychoanalysis	(p. 454)	Reality testing	(p. 455)
Id	(p. 454)	Superego	(p. 455)
Life instinct (eros)	(p. 454)	Perfection principle	(p. 455)
Libido	(p. 454)	Ego-ideal	(p. 455)
Death instinct (thanatos)	(p. 454)	Conscience	(p. 455)
Pleasure principle	(p. 454)	Defense mechanism	(p. 455)
Displacement	(p. 455)	Sublimation	(p. 456)

Repression   (p. 456)   Oral stage   (p. 458)

Regression   (p. 456)   Anal stage   (p. 458)

Projection   (p. 456)   Phallic stage   (p. 458)

Reaction formation   (p. 457)   Oedipus complex   (p. 458)

Rationalization   (p. 457)   Castration complex   (p. 458)

Psychosexual development   (p. 458)   Electra complex   (p. 459)

Erogenous zones   (p. 458)   Penis envy   (p. 459)

Fixation   (p. 458)   Latency stage   (p. 459)

Infantile sexuality   (p. 458)   Genital stage   (p. 459)

Unconscious	(p. 459)	Creative self	(p. 462)
Personal unconscious	(p. 461)	Inferiority complex	(p. 462)
Collective unconscious	(p. 461)	Superiority complex	(p. 462)
Archetypes	(p. 461)	Humanistic psychology	(p. 464)
Persona	(p. 461)	Phenomenological view	(p. 464)
Anima	(p. 461)	Self-actualization theory	(p. 464)
Animus	(p. 461)	Hierarchy of needs	(p. 464)
Introvert	(p. 461)	D needs	(p. 464)
Extrovert	(p. 461)	B needs	(p. 464)

Person-centered theory   (p. 465)   Secondary trait   (p. 468)

Congruence   (p. 465)   Character   (p. 468)

Behaviorism   (p. 466)   Temperament   (p. 468)

Tabula rasa   (p. 466)   Nomothetic (dimensional)
                                            approach   (p. 468)

Radical behaviorism   (p. 466)   Idiographic (morphogenic)
                                            approach   (p. 468)

Social-learning theory   (p. 467)   Surface traits   (p. 468)

Modeling   (p. 467)   Source traits   (p. 468)

Cardinal trait   (p. 468)   Factor analysis   (p. 468)

Central trait   (p. 468)   Cattell's Sixteen Personality
                                            Factor Questionnaire (16PF) (p. 469)

Person-situation controversy   (p. 469)   Content   (p. 475)

Reliability   (p. 473)   Popularity   (p. 475)

Validity   (p. 473)   Thematic Apperception
                                           Test (TAT)   (p. 476)

Objective tests   (p. 473)   Structured interview   (p. 477)

Minnesota Multiphasic   Unstructured interview   (p. 477)
Personality Inventory (MMPI)   (p. 473)

Projective tests   (p. 475)   **SELF-TEST**

                                           Multiple-Choice

                                           Choose the one best response to each
Rorschach test   (p. 475)   question. An answer key is provided at
                                           the end of this chapter.

                                           1. According to your text, what is
                                              personality?

Location   (p. 475)   a. Set of traits that occur in all
                                                 situations
                                              b. Unconscious urges that control
                                                 behavior
                                              c. Complex network of relatively
Determinants   (p. 475)   consistent behaviors
                                              d. Pattern of learned responses to
                                                 specific stimuli

2. According to Freud, which part of the personality has the greatest sense of reality?

   a. Ego
   b. Id
   c. Superego
   d. Thanatos

3. According to Freud, which component of your personality constantly seeks pleasure?

   a. Id
   b. Ego
   c. Superego
   d. Conscience

4. Which of the following help us deal with anxiety?

   a. Source traits
   b. Cardinal traits
   c. Defense mechanisms
   d. Archetypes

5. A careless driver's car was "totaled" in an accident. He remarked, "It was getting old anyway and I'm ready for a new car." Which defense mechanism was the driver using?

   a. Sublimation
   b. Regression
   c. Rationalization
   d. Projection

6. Assume that a young woman is angry at her boyfriend and decides to write a blues song. Which defense mechanism would she be using?

   a. Regression
   b. Fixation
   c. Reaction formation
   d. Sublimation

7. According to Freud, when do girls develop an incestuous love for their fathers?

   a. During the oral stage
   b. During the anal stage
   c. During the phallic stage
   d. During the genital stage

8. According to Freud, a 17-year-old would probably be in what stage of psychosexual development?

   a. Oral
   b. Anal
   c. Phallic
   d. Genital

9. Which of the following is a valid criticism of psychodynamic theory?

   a. Freudian theory ignores the unconscious.
   b. Freudian theory overlooks pathological problems.
   c. Freudian concepts are abstractions that are difficult to measure and prove.
   d. Freudian theory puts too much stress on rewards and imitation of behavior.

10. How do neo-Freudians differ from Freud in their emphasis?

    a. They emphasize social environment.
    b. They emphasize cognitive abilities.
    c. They emphasize sexuality and instincts.
    d. They emphasize innate behavior.

11. According to Jung, what does the collective unconscious contain?

    a. Archetypes
    b. Libido
    c. Eros
    d. D needs

12. According to Adler, what are we striving for?

a. Self-actualization
b. Congruence
c. Superiority
d. Love

13. Which approach to personality stresses positive qualities and the need for personal growth and fulfillment?

    a. Humanism
    b. Psychoanalysis
    c. Social-learning theory
    d. Radical behaviorism

14. Maslow stressed the importance of developing our full potential. What is this attainment called?

    a. Reality testing
    b. Self-actualization
    c. Congruence
    d. Popularity

15. Assume that a young man enjoys bird-watching but his friends disapprove. How would Carl Rogers have defined his problem?

    a. As congruence
    b. As incongruence
    c. As a D need
    d. As a fixation

16. If you are a kind, generous person, how would a social-learning theorist view your characteristics?

    a. As innate
    b. As based on unconscious urges
    c. As ones you have seen rewarded
    d. As proof that your superego overpowers your id

17. Which theory of personality uses adjectives such as *generous, dependent, honest,* etc., to describe individual differences in personality?

a. Allport's psychology of the individual
b. Rogers' person-centered theory
c. Bandura's social-learning theory
d. Skinner's radical behaviorism

18. Assume that a man is fastidious about his car but otherwise relaxed and even somewhat sloppy. How would Allport have described his fastidiousness?

    a. As a cardinal trait
    b. As a secondary trait
    c. As a central trait
    d. As part of his character

19. Which of the following is a procedure used to reduce and classify data about traits and personality characteristics?

    a. Modeling
    b. Psychoanalysis
    c. Factor analysis
    d. Fixation

20. What does Cattell's 16PF test measure?

    a. Relative strength of source traits
    b. Strength of defense mechanisms
    c. Relative strength of reinforcements that shape personality
    d. Degree of congruence in the self-concept

21. What is the currently accepted view on the person-situation controversy of personality?

    a. Personality is relatively stable in situations.
    b. Specific situations cause severe personality changes.
    c. Behavior results from an interaction of personality features and situation characteristics.
    d. Behavior tends to be haphazard and cannot be analyzed.

22. Which of the following criteria
should be used to determine whether
a personality test is "good"?

a. Reliability and validity
b. Objectivity and projective
nature
c. Content and popularity
d. Structure and determinants

Matching

Match each name in column A with a descriptive phrase in column B.

Column A

_____ 1. Sigmund Freud

_____ 2. Carl Jung

_____ 3. Alfred Adler

_____ 4. Karen Horney

_____ 5. Erik Erikson

_____ 6. Abraham Maslow

_____ 7. Carl Rogers

_____ 8. John B. Watson

_____ 9. B. F. Skinner

_____ 10. Albert Bandura

_____ 11. Gordon Allport

_____ 12. Raymond Cattell

Column B

a. Proposed that the mind consists of an ego, a personal unconscious, and a collective unconscious
b. Maintained that human behavior is lawful and results from a number of stimulus-response sequences
c. Used factor analysis to develop a list of 16 basic source traits
d. Stressed the importance of congruence in a healthy personality
e. Developed the technique of psychoanalysis
f. Considered personality a dynamic organization of traits
g. Described eight stages of development, each with a crisis to be resolved
h. Proposed that much of personality results from modeling
i. Coined the term *inferiority complex*
j. Identified characteristics that distinguish self-actualizers from the average person
k. Believed that a healthy person is flexible in moving toward people, against people, and away from people
l. Considered the "father of behaviorism"

APPLICATION EXERCISES

These application exercises will test your understanding of and ability to apply the material you have read in your text. Suggested answers are provided at the end of the chapter so that you can check your responses.

1. Freud identified three components of personality: the id, the ego, and the superego. The id, filled with libido, operates on the pleasure principle; the superego operates on the perfection principle, and the ego operates on the reality principle.

   Imagine that you are at a party. You see an exciting and attractive person you want to date. Your id wants you to impulsively rush over and hug this person. How might your superego and ego react?

   a. Superego _____
   _____
   _____

   b. Ego _____
   _____
   _____

2. From a Freudian perspective, we feel anxiety when the id, superego, and ego are out of balance. The ego uses a number of defense mechanisms, or unconscious tactics, to help us cope with threatening or anxiety-ridden situations. Seven common defense mechanisms are displacement, sublimation, repression, regression, projection, reaction formation, and rationalization.

   Read each of the following descriptions of behavior and identify which defense mechanism is being used.

   a. Janet had stopped sucking her thumb when she was 3. At age 6, she was told that her parents were divorcing and she would be living with her father and a "new mother." Janet began sucking her thumb again.

   _____

   b. Bob has bickered constantly with his mother. They never seem to agree on issues and avoid seeing each other. In choosing a tattoo, he selected a large heart with "MOM" in the center.

   _____

   c. Whenever Susan is angry, she works off her anger in the garden, raking, digging, and transplanting bushes. She has one of the most attractive gardens in the neighborhood.

   _____

   d. About a month ago, Dick left his wallet containing $50 on a bus and it has not been returned. He told a friend, "Probably some poor person found it. I'm glad I was able to help."

   _____

   e. In checking his calendar, Jeremy noticed that he had neglected to keep his appointment with his literature professor that morning. They were supposed to discuss a term paper he had done poorly on.

   _____

   f. Beth's boss told her she would not receive a merit raise this year. She worked quietly all day but when she arrived home, she was extremely crabby with her family.

   _____

g. Cindy is known to flirt with almost every man she meets at parties. She complains that the men she dates are fickle.

_____

3. There are many variations of Freud's psychoanalytic theories. Among the neo-Freudians who made changes in Freud's theory are Carl Jung, Alfred Adler, Karen Horney, and Erik Erikson. Jung emphasized growth and change throughout life. Adler rejected Freud's sexual-instinct theory and showed concern for the individual's striving for superiority. Horney proposed that we develop strategies for coping with anxiety based on childhood fears. Erikson suggested that we face conflicts between instincts and social demands through eight stages in life. Describe what these four modifications of Freud's theory have in common.

_____
_____
_____
_____
_____
_____
_____
_____

4. Carl Rogers stressed the importance of congruence in a healthy personality. He believed that congruence occurs when our ideal self is close to our real self and when we feel accepted by others. On the basis of Rogers' concept of congruence, identify two possible causes of anxiety and possible pathology.

a. _____
_____

b. _____
_____

5. Environmental approaches to personality view behavior as the essential component of personality. Suppose you are a competitive person who must have the highest grades on tests and win at sports. According to the two environmental approaches, how did you develop these personality behaviors?

Radical behaviorism _____
_____
_____

Social learning _____
_____
_____

6. Gordon Allport's psychology of the individual is based on the concept of traits. Allport categorized traits according to how generally they influence our behavior. A cardinal trait is extremely general and influences a wide range of behaviors. Allport believed that few of us have cardinal traits. A central trait does not determine as many behaviors as a cardinal trait, but is considered highly characteristic of our personality and occurs regularly and consistently. A secondary trait occurs only in some situations or under specific circumstances.

"Martha hates clutter."

Figure 13-1   Drawing by Cheney; (c) The
New Yorker Magazine, Inc.

Figure 13-1 describes a trait of
Martha's. Specify how Allport would
have classified Martha's trait in
each of the following situations.

a. Martha hates clutter only in her
   living room.

   _____

b. Martha hates clutter anywhere.

   _____

c. Martha hates clutter but
   sometimes enjoys shopping in
   cluttered flea markets.

   _____

d. Martha hates clutter so much
   that she must leave a cluttered
   area if she cannot tidy it.

   _____

7. In this chapter, you have read four
   different views of personality:
   psychoanalytic, environmental,
   humanistic, and type-trait. Read
   each of the following sentences and
   indicate which type of personality
   theorist would be most likely to
   make the statement. Then criticize
   the statement according to the view
   indicated.

   a. People strive for congruence so
      that they can grow to
      self-actualize.
   Statement by _____

   Criticism by trait theorist

   _____
   _____
   _____
   _____

b. Human behavior is influenced
   more by personality traits than
   by environmental situations.
   Statement by _____

Criticism by environmentalist

_____

_____

_____

_____

c. People are at the mercy of their
   unconscious urges and have
   little control in their lives.
   Statement by _____

Criticism by humanist

_____

_____

_____

_____

d. The human infant is like a blank
   slate and can be molded and
   shaped.
   Statement by _____

Criticism by psychoanalytic
theorist

_____

_____

_____

_____

READING EXERCISE

The following article by Daniel Goleman from *The New York Times* reports the results of a 7-year study of twins to determine whether personality characteristics are largely inherited or acquired.

Major Personality Study Finds That Traits Are Mostly Inherited

The genetic makeup of a child is a stronger influence on personality than child rearing, according to the first study to examine identical twins reared in different families. The findings shatter a widespread belief among experts and laymen alike in the primacy of family influence and are sure to engender fierce debate.

The findings are the first major results to emerge from a long-term project at the University of Minnesota. Since 1979, more than 350 pairs of twins in the project have gone through six days of extensive testing that has included analysis of blood, brain waves, intelligence and allergies.

The results on personality are being reviewed for publication by the Journal of Personality and Social Psychology. Although there has been

Copyright (c) 1986 by The New York Times Company. Reprinted by permission.

wide press coverage of pairs of twins reared apart who met for the first time in the course of the study, the personality results are the first significant scientific data to be announced.

For most of the traits measured, more than half the variation was found to be due to heredity, leaving less than half determined by the influence of parents, home environment and other experiences in life.

The Minnesota findings stand in sharp contradiction to standard wisdom on nature versus nurture in forming adult personality. Virtually all major theories since Freud have given far more importance to environment, or nurture, than to genes, or nature.

Even though the findings point to the strong influence of heredity, the family still shapes the broad suggestion of personality offered by heredity; for example, a family might tend to make an innately timid child either more timid or less so. But the inference from this study is that the family would be unlikely to make the child brave.

The 350 pairs of twins studied included some who were raised apart. Among these separately reared twins were 44 pairs of identical twins and 21 pairs of fraternal twins. Comparing twins raised separately with those raised in the same home allows researchers to determine the relative importance of heredity and of environment in their development. Although some twins go out of their way to emphasize differences between them, in general identical twins are very much alike in personality.

But what accounts for that similarity? If environment were the major influence in personality, then identical twins raised in the same home would be expected to show more similarity than would the twins reared apart. But the study of 11 personality traits found differences between the kinds of twins were far smaller than had been assumed.

"If in fact twins reared apart are that similar, this study is extremely important for understanding how personality is shaped," commented Jerome Kagan, a developmental psychologist at Harvard University. "It implies that some aspects of personality are under a great degree of genetic control."

The traits were measured using a personality questionnaire developed by Auke Tellegen, a psychologist at the University of Minnesota who was one of the principal researchers. The questionnaire assesses many major aspects of personality, including aggressiveness, striving for achievement, and the need for personal intimacy.

For example, agreement with the statement "When I work with others, I like to take charge" is an indication of the trait called social potency, or leadership, while agreement with the

sentence "I often keep working on a problem, even if I am very tired" indicates the need for achievement.

Among traits found most strongly determined by heredity were leadership and, surprisingly, traditionalism or obedience to authority. "One would not expect the tendency to believe in traditional values and the strict enforcement of rules to be more an inherited than learned trait," said David Lykken, a psychologist in the Minnesota project. "But we found that, in some mysterious way, it is one of traits with the strongest genetic influence."

Other traits that the study concludes were more than 50 percent determined by heredity included a sense of well-being and zest for life; alienation; vulnerability or resistance to stress, and fearfulness or risk-seeking. Another highly inherited trait, though one not commonly thought of as part of personality, was the capacity for becoming rapt in an aesthetic experience, such as a concert.

Vulnerability to stress, as measured on the Tellegen test, reflects what is commonly thought of as "neuroticism," according to Dr. Lykken. "People high in this trait are nervous and jumpy, easily irritated, highly sensitive to stimuli, and generally dissatisfied with themselves, while those low on the trait are resilient and see themselves in a positive light," he said. "Therapy may help vulnerable people to some extent, but they seem to have a built-in susceptibility that may mean, in general, they would be more content with a life low in stress."

The need to achieve, including ambition and an inclination to work hard toward goals, also was found to be genetically influenced, but more than half of this trait seemed determined by life experience. The same lower degree of hereditary influence was found for impulsiveness and its opposite, caution.

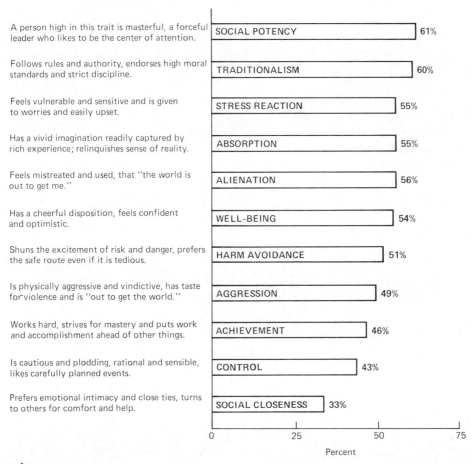

The Roots of Personality

The degree to which eleven key traits of personality are estimated to be inherited, as gauged by tests with twins. Traits were measured by the Multidimensional Personality Questionnaire, developed by Auke Tellegen at the University of Minnesota.

Description	Trait	Percent
A person high in this trait is masterful, a forceful leader who likes to be the center of attention.	SOCIAL POTENCY	61%
Follows rules and authority, endorses high moral standards and strict discipline.	TRADITIONALISM	60%
Feels vulnerable and sensitive and is given to worries and easily upset.	STRESS REACTION	55%
Has a vivid imagination readily captured by rich experience; relinquishes sense of reality.	ABSORPTION	55%
Feels mistreated and used, that "the world is out to get me."	ALIENATION	56%
Has a cheerful disposition, feels confident and optimistic.	WELL-BEING	54%
Shuns the excitement of risk and danger, prefers the safe route even if it is tedious.	HARM AVOIDANCE	51%
Is physically aggressive and vindictive, has taste for violence and is "out to get the world."	AGGRESSION	49%
Works hard, strives for mastery and puts work and accomplishment ahead of other things.	ACHIEVEMENT	46%
Is cautious and plodding, rational and sensible, likes carefully planned events.	CONTROL	43%
Prefers emotional intimacy and close ties, turns to others for comfort and help.	SOCIAL CLOSENESS	33%

Percent (0, 25, 50, 75)

Figure 13-2

The need for personal intimacy appeared the least determined by heredity among the traits tested; about two-thirds of that tendency was found to depend on experience. People high in this trait have a strong desire for emotionally intense relationships; those low in the trait tend to be loners who keep their troubles to themselves.

"This is one trait that can be greatly strengthened by the quality of interactions in a family," Dr. Lykken said. "The more physical and emotional intimacy, the more likely this trait will be developed in children, and those children with the strongest inherited tendency will have the greatest need for social closeness as adults."

No single gene is believed responsible for any one of these traits. Instead, each trait, the Minnesota researchers propose, is determined by a great number of genes in combination, so that the pattern of inheritance is complex and indirect.

No one believes, for instance, that there is a single gene for timidity but rather a host of genetic influences. That may explain, they say, why previous studies have found little connection between the personality traits of parents and their children. Whereas identical twins would share with each other the whole constellation of genes that might be responsible for a particular trait, children might share only some part of that constellation with each parent.

That is why, just as a short parent may have a tall child, an achievement-oriented parent might have a child with little ambition.

The Minnesota findings are sure to stir debate. Though most social scientists accept the careful study of twins, particularly when it includes identical twins reared apart, as the best method of assessing the degree to which a trait is inherited, some object to using these methods for assessing the genetic component of complex behavior patterns or question the conclusions that are drawn from it.

Further, some researchers consider paper-and-pencil tests of personality less reliable than observations of how people act, since people's own reports of their behavior can be biased. "The level of heritability they found is surprisingly high, considering that questionnaires are not the most sensitive index of personality," said Dr. Kagan. "There is often a poor relationship between how people respond on a questionnaire and what they actually do."

"Years ago, when the field was dominated by a psychodynamic view, you could not publish a study like this," Dr. Kagan added. "Now the field is shifting to a greater acceptance of genetic determinants, and there is the danger of being too uncritical of such results."

Seymour Epstein, a personality psychologist at the University of Massachusetts, said he was skeptical of precise estimates of heritability. "The study compared people from a relatively narrow range of cultures and environments," he said. "If the range had been much greater—say Pygmies and Eskimos as well as middle-class Americans—then environment would certainly contribute more to personality. The results might have shown environment to be a far more

powerful influence than heredity," he said.

Dr. Tellegen himself said: "Even though the differences between families do not account for much of the unique attributes of their children, a family still exercises important influence. In cases of extreme deprivation or abuse, for instance, the family would have a much larger impact—though a negative one—than any found in the study. Although the twins studied came from widely different environments, there were no extremely deprived families."

Gardner Lindzey, director of the Center for Advanced Studies in the Behavioral Sciences in Palo Alto, Calif., said the Minnesota findings would "no doubt produce empassioned rejoinders."

"They do not in and of themselves say what makes a given character trait emerge," he said, "and they can be disputed and argued about, as have similar studies of intelligence."

For parents, the study points to the importance of treating each child in accord with his innate temperament.

"The message for parents is not that it does not matter how they treat their children, but that it is a big mistake to treat all kids the same," said Dr. Lykken. "To guide and shape a child you have to respect his individuality, adapt to it and cultivate those qualities that will help him in life.

"If there are two brothers in the same family, one fearless and the other timid, a good parent will help the timid one become less so by giving him experiences of doing well at risk-taking, and let the other develop his fearlessness tempered with some intelligent caution. But if the parent shelters the one who is naturally timid, he will likely become more so."

The Minnesota results lend weight and precision to earlier work that pointed to the importance of a child's temperament in development. For instance, the New York Longitudinal Study, conducted by Alexander Thomas and Stella Chess, psychiatrists at New York University Medical Center, identified three basic temperaments in children, each of which could lead to behavioral problems if not handled well.

"Good parenting now must be seen in terms of meeting the special needs of a child's temperament, including dealing with whatever conflicts it creates," said Stanley Grossman, a staff member of the medical center's Psychoanalytic Institute.

QUESTIONS

Answer the following questions and then compare your responses with the suggested answers at the end of this chapter.

1. According to this study, what is the role of the environment in shaping personality?

2. According to the researchers, how are personality genes transmitted?

3. What is Seymour Epstein's criticism of this study?

ANSWERS

Correct Answers to Self-Test Exercises

Multiple-Choice			Matching	
1. c	9. c	17. a	1. e	8. l
2. a	10. a	18. b	2. a	9. b
3. a	11. a	19. c	3. i	10. h
4. c	12. c	20. a	4. k	11. f
5. c	13. a	21. c	5. g	12. c
6. d	14. b	22. a	6. j	
7. c	15. b		7. d	
8. d	16. c			

Suggested Answers to Application Exercises

1. a. Your superego would remind you that such behavior is wrong. Your ego-ideal might remind you that good people maintain their composure and self-control. Your conscience might remind you that you will feel guilty if you hug a person you do not know.
   b. Your ego might do some reality testing. A plan might be developed to satisfy both your id and your superego. You might, for example, plan to approach this person, make some casual remarks, and then perhaps introduce yourself.

2. a. Regression
   b. Reaction formation
   c. Sublimation
   d. Rationalization
   e. Repression
   f. Displacement
   g. Projection

3. All four neo-Freudians emphasize the importance of social factors in the development of personality. They also downplay Freud's emphasis on sex.

4. a. Wide differences between our real self and our ideal self; expectations that cannot be achieved
   b. Discrepencies between our own personal acceptance and the acceptance of others

5. a. You have been rewarded for your academic and sports achievements. Perhaps you have won the approval of others.
   b. You have seen others receive rewards for academic and athletic accomplishments.

6. a. Secondary
   b. Cardinal
   c. Central
   d. Cardinal

7. a. Humanist
      These terms are vague and cannot be observed or measured accurately.
   b. Type-trait theorist
      Behavior can be shaped and changed by rewards and punishments and by copying other behavior that is rewarded.
   c. Psychoanalytic theorist
      Your theories are based on experiences with troubled people and you do not appreciate the strength of a healthy mind. You cannot generalize about normal people from observations of people with emotional problems.
   d. Environmentalist
      An infant has inborn drives and unconscious urges that are beyond environmental control.

Suggested Answers to Reading Questions

1. The environment has a more limited role than had been anticipated. Family influences can shape or modify personality but cannot cause major changes.

2. Apparently a great number of combined genes compose personality characteristics, and the pattern of transmission is complex and not directly related to a particular gene.

3. The environmental influences used in the study are too narrow and limited. A greater range of cultural exposures should be studied.

Chapter 14:

ABNORMAL PSYCHOLOGY

CHAPTER OUTLINE

I. Approaches to abnormal psychology
   A. What is abnormal?
   B. Ways of looking at abnormal behavior: Models
      1. Moral model
      2. Medical model
      3. Psychoanalytic model
      4. Behavioral model
      5. Other models
         a. Social-consequence model
         b. Family, or systems, model
         c. Sociocultural model
         d. Humanistic model
   C. How common is abnormality?

II. Measuring and diagnosing abnormality
   A. Problems and issues
   B. DSM III

III. Types of abnormality
   A. Anxiety disorders
      1. Forms of anxiety disorders
         a. Phobic disorders
         b. Obsessive-compulsive disorders
         c. Post-traumatic stress disorder
         d. Other anxiety states
         e. Generalized anxiety disorder
      2. Causes of anxiety disorders
         a. Medical model of anxiety
         b. Psychoanalytic model of anxiety
         c. Behavioral model of anxiety
   B. Somatoform disorders
      1. What are somatoform disorders?
      2. Causes of somatoform disorders
   C. Dissociative disorders
      1. Forms of dissociative disorders
      2. Causes of dissociative disorders
   D. Affective disorders: Depression and mania
      1. Depression
      2. Mania (bipolar disorder)

3. Causes of affective disorders
   a. Genetic explanations
   b. Biological explanations
   c. Psychoanalytic explanations
   d. Cognitive explanations
      (1) Cognitive theory: Aaron Beck
      (2) Learned-helplessness theory: Martin E. P. Seligman
   e. Seasonal explanations
E. Suicide
  1. Who are the people most likely to take their own lives?
  2. What makes people resort to suicide?
   a. Biological predisposition
   b. Influence of heredity
   c. Life stresses
   d. Hearing about other suicides
F. Personality disorders
  1. What is a personality disorder?
  2. The antisocial personality
G. Schizophrenic disorders
  1. Symptoms of schizophrenia
  2. Course of schizophrenia
  3. Causes of schizophrenic disorders: Current perspectives
   a. Genetic factors
      (1) Evidence for genetic transmission
      (2) How genetic transmission may be manifested: Brain dysfunctions
   b. Environmental factors
      (1) Family pathology
      (2) Life stress as a trigger

Boxes
  Psychology in your life: Helping to prevent suicide
  In the forefront: The borderline personality

LEARNING OBJECTIVES

After you study Chapter 14, you should be able to do the tasks outlined in the following objectives.

1. Define the concept of abnormality.

2. Describe eight models for explaining abnormal behavior.

3. Describe the prevalence and measurement of abnormality.

4. Identify the axes used in DSM III and explain the purpose of the manual.

5. Criticize DSM III.

6. Describe anxiety disorders and identify five types of anxiety disorder.

7. State the causes of anxiety disorders from the psychoanalytic, learning, and medical views.

8. Identify the characteristics of somatoform disorders and dissociative disorders.

9. Define affective disorders and describe the characteristics and causes of depression.

10. Identify the characteristics of mania.

11. Identify the possible causes and warning signs of suicide.

12. Specify the general characteristics of personality disorders and identify the symptoms of two types of personality disorders.

13. Describe the characteristics and possible causes of schizophrenia.

KEY CONCEPTS

As you read Chapter 14 in your text, look for each of the following concepts. You should understand each concept.

1. Concept of Abnormality

Abnormality is characterized by an inability to recognize reality, by statistical rarity, and by undesirable behavior. Further, persons with psychological disturbances cannot perform productive work, do not have close relationships with others, are unable to perform tasks of daily living independently, and are unhappy much of the time.

2. Models for Explaining Abnormal Behavior

Abnormal behavior can be interpreted from a number of different perspectives, or models. The moral model, prevalent during the Middle Ages, views mental disturbances as the result of sin, devil possession, or personal inadequacies. The medical model considers a mental disorder as a mental illness or sickness. According to the psychoanalytic model, mental disorders result from overwhelming conflicts between the superego and id.

The behavioral model holds that abnormal behaviors are learned. The social-consequence model holds that mental disorders result from difficulties in coping with society and from lack of a sense of responsibility. The family, or systems, model holds that difficulties arise because of an entire family or group rather than from one person. The sociocultural model blames society for abnormal behavior. The humanistic model sees abnormal behavior as a failure to achieve self-actualization. No single model provides a comprehensive explanation of all types of mental disturbances.

3. Prevalence of Abnormality

About one out of every five Americans suffers from a form of psychological disturbance. Only one-fifth of the people thought to need treatment for disturbances are receiving help. Age and education are factors that are related to mental disturbances.

4. Measuring Abnormality

Measuring abnormality is extremely difficult, as evidenced in the controversy over the study by David Rosenhan. Even professionals have difficulty distinguishing a truly disturbed person from someone who is pretending to be disturbed. Further, the label *abnormal* tends to stay with a person, even after he or she is seen behaving normally.

5. Diagnostic and Statistical Manual of Mental Disorders (DSM III)

The goal of DSM III, a guidebook of the American Psychiatric Association, is to help clinicians treat and manage persons and to bring some consistency to diagnostic terms. The document has been subject to controversy for dropping homosexuality as a mental disorder, for sex bias, for eliminating the term *neurosis,* and for using medical explanations of abnormal behavior. Nonetheless, DSM III is the most comprehensive guide for defining mental disturbances. DSM III uses a total of five axes, three for summarizing data and two for supplementary information.

6. "Neurotic" Disorders

The term *neurosis* was excluded from DMS III. "Neurotic" disorders are now classified as anxiety disorders, affective disorders, somatoform disorders, and dissociative disorders.

7. Anxiety Disorders

Anxiety disorders include phobic, obsessive-compulsive, panic, generalized anxiety, and post-traumatic stress disorders. Phobic disorders are characterized by persistent, intense, unrealistic fears. Obsessions and compulsions are often paired together. Obsessions are persistent thoughts and impulses that cannot be consciously controlled. Compulsions are repetitive, irrational behaviors that a person feels obligated to act out. Panic disorders have physical symptoms, including dizziness, choking, breathing difficulties, sweating, and chest pains. Generalized anxiety disorders involve a general state of uneasiness and discomfort that cannot be attributed to anything specific. Post-traumatic stress disorder is characterized by the reexperiencing of a traumatic event and the associated anxieties months and even years after the traumatic event.

8. Causes of Anxiety Disorders

Each of the models offers an individual explanation for the causes of anxiety disorders. The psychoanalytic model proposes a four-stage explanation involving id-superego-ego conflicts and the repression of drives. Learning theorists view anxiety as a result of learning inappropriate behaviors. The medical model offers biochemical explanations.

9. Somatoform Disorders

Somatoform disorders are characterized by physical symptoms with no physical cause. Conversion disorder is an example of a somatoform disorder.

10. Dissociative Disorders

Dissociative disorders are quite rare and are characterized by a sudden temporary change in either consciousness, identity, or motor activity. Dissociative disorders include multiple personality, psychogenic amnesia, psychogenic fugue, and depersonalization disorder.

11. Affective Disorders

Affective disorders are mood disorders involving either mania or depression or an alternation between the two extreme moods.

12. Characteristics of Depression (Unipolar Disorder)

Symptoms of depression include sadness, loss of energy, and sleeping, eating, concentration, and sexual difficulties. Psychotic depression involves additional symptoms, possibly delusions, hallucinations, and confused thinking. Depression may result from an upsetting event (reactive or exogenous type) or occur for no apparent reason (process or endogenous type).

13. Characteristics of Mania (Bipolar Disorder)

Manic episodes are much rarer than depression. The onset of manic episodes is usually rapid, and episodes can last from a few days to a few months. Mania is characterized by euphoria, talkativeness, and exuberance. Most people who experience a manic episode will also have a depressive episode.

14. Causes of Affective Disorders

Research results have suggested that depression may be inherited and may be linked to a malfunction of specific neurotransmitters. Psychoanalytic explanations claim depression may result from early mother-infant relationships. Both cognitive theory and learned-helplessness theory view depression as a result of distortions in thinking.

15. Suicide

About half the suicides in the United States are attempted by people suffering from depression. Possible causes include a biological predisposition, heredity, life stresses, and hearing about other suicides. It is important to recognize the warning signs of suicide and provide assistance.

16. Personality Disorders

Personality disorders encompass a wide range of behaviors and are characterized by a rigid pattern of maladaptive behavior. The affected person usually does not see the behavior as maladaptive. Examples of personality disorders include borderline personality and antisocial personality.

17. Characteristics of Schizophrenia

Schizophrenia is a psychosis with four major subtypes: disorganized, catatonic, paranoid, and undifferentiated. Symptoms may be positive (delusions, disturbances of thought, hallucinations, bizarre and disorganized behavior, and inappropriate emotional responses) or negative (vague and impoverished speech, blunt or flat emotional response, inability to experience pleasure or intimacy, and difficulty paying attention). Patients with more positive symptoms have a better prognosis than patients with more negative symptoms.

18. Causes of Schizophrenia

Most research suggests that schizophrenia is caused by a combination of an inherited biochemical predisposition and environmental stresses. Physiological explanations consider dopamine a critical factor. Differences in the sugar glucose level and physical appearance of brain capillaries have also been noted in schizophrenics. Adoption studies, twin studies, and risk studies have suggested an inherited predisposition toward schizophrenia. Environmental theories emphasize the effect of confusion and stress in triggering schizophrenic attacks.

TERMS TO KNOW

Define each of the terms listed. You can check your definitions in the text Glossary or on the text pages listed in parentheses.

Abnormal psychology   (p. 482)   *Diagnostic and Statistical*
                                           Manual of Mental Disorders
                                           (DSM III)   (p. 491)

Moral model   (p. 485)   Neurotic disorder (neurosis) (p. 494)

Medical model   (p. 486)   Psychosis   (p. 494)

Psychoanalytic model   (p. 486)   Anxiety   (p. 495)

Behavioral model   (p. 486)   Anxiety disorders   (p. 495)

Social-consequence model   (p. 487)   Phobic disorders   (p. 495)

Family, or systems, model   (p. 487)   Simple phobia   (p. 495)

Sociocultural model   (p. 488)   Agoraphobia   (p. 496)

Humanistic model   (p. 488)   Social phobia   (p. 496)

Obsessions   (p. 496)   Dissociative disorders   (p. 500)

Compulsions   (p. 496)   Multiple personality   (p. 500)

Obsessive-compulsive   Amnesia   (p. 500)
disorders   (p. 496)

Post-traumatic stress   Psychogenic amnesia   (p. 500)
disorder   (p. 497)

Panic disorders   (p. 497)   Psychogenic fugue   (p. 500)

Generalized anxiety disorder   (p. 498)   Depersonalization disorder   (p. 501)

Concordant   (p. 498)   Affective disorders   (p. 501)

Somatoform disorders   (p. 499)   Mania (bipolar disorder)   (p. 502)

Conversion disorder   (p. 499)   Depression (unipolar
                                                   disorder)   (p. 502)

Dysthymic disorder (depressive personality)	(p. 502)	Antisocial personality	(p. 511)
Libidinal approach	(p. 505)	Borderline personality disorder	(p. 511)
Ego-psychological theory	(p. 505)	Schizophrenic syndrome	(p. 513)
Object-relations theory	(p. 505)	Disorganized schizophrenia	(p. 514)
Cognitive theory	(p. 505)	Catatonic schizophrenia	(p. 514)
Learned-helplessness theory	(p. 506)	Paranoid schizophrenia	(p. 514)
Seasonal affective disorder (SAD)	(p. 507)	Undifferentiated schizophrenia	(p. 514)
Personality disorder	(p. 511)	Positive symptoms	(p. 514)
Paranoid personality	(p. 511)	Negative symptoms	(p. 514)

Mixed schizophrenia   (p. 514)

Hallucinations   (p. 514)

Prodromal phase   (p. 515)

Active phase   (p. 515)

Residual phase   (p. 515)

Dopamine   (p. 517)

SELF-TEST

Multiple-Choice

Choose the one best response to each question. An answer key is provided at the end of this chapter.

1. Which of the following are general characteristics of abnormality?

   a. Stress, hysteria, and hallucinations
   b. Departure from reality, statistical rarity, and undesirable behavior

c. Antisocial and compulsive behavior
d. Amnesia, unpopularity, and unique personality characteristics

2. A woman visited a therapist who referred to her as a "patient" and suggested she had a "mental illness." What view does the therapist probably hold?

   a. Behavioral
   b. Medical
   c. Humanist
   d. Sociocultural

3. Which model assumes that abnormal behavior results from faulty learning?

   a. Medical
   b. Psychoanalytic
   c. Behavioral
   d. Humanistic

4. What percentage of American people suffer from some form of psychological disturbance?

   a. 1 percent
   b. 10 percent
   c. 20 percent
   d. 50 percent

5. On the basis of David Rosenhan's study, what would you expect to happen to a normal man who was labeled *abnormal?*

   a. The label *abnormal* would stay with him.
   b. He would be considered cured and relabeled *completely normal.*
   c. He would be labeled *normal,* and the original mistake would be acknowledged.
   d. He would probably remain in an institution for the rest of his life.

6. What is the main advantage of a classification system for abnormal behavior?

   a. It permits the labeling of individuals.
   b. It allows open disagreements between psychologists and psychiatrists.
   c. It permits consistency in communication among therapists.
   d. It allows a complete and definitive diagnosis.

7. Which of the following diagnostic categories is characterized by excessive unfounded anxiety?

   a. Neurosis
   b. Affective disorders
   c. Personality disorders
   d. Psychosis

8. A person who was in an automobile accident now refuses ever to ride in a motor vehicle again. How would this reaction be classified?

   a. Normal fear
   b. Phobia
   c. Conversion hysteria
   d. Obsessive-compulsive behavior

9. According to Freud, what is the cause of neurosis?

   a. Improper conditioning
   b. Unconscious conflicts
   c. A chaotic world
   d. Chemical imbalance

10. A man is constantly concerned about the cleanliness of his hands. Regardless of where he is, he washes his hands twice every 5 minutes. Which of the following best describes his condition?

    a. Multiple personality
    b. Obsessive-compulsive behavior
    c. Schizophrenia
    d. Unipolar disorder

11. Ms. A., an artist, is under pressure to produce 11 paintings for an art show. She suddenly suffers from blindness, but physicians cannot find any physical cause. Which of the following conditions might be the cause of her blindness?

    a. Conversion disorder
    b. Unipolar disorder
    c. Dysthymic disorder
    d. Bipolar disorder

12. One form of dissociative reaction is multiple personality. What occurs in multiple personality?

    a. A person has two or more complete but alternating personalities.
    b. A person becomes schizophrenic.
    c. A person has severe mood swings between euphoria and depression.
    d. A person becomes antisocial.

13. Which of the following is an affective disorder?

    a. Hysteria
    b. Depression
    c. Multiple personality
    d. Schizophrenia

14. What is one difference between neurotic and psychotic depression?

    a. The neurotic depressive is anti-social and the psychotic depressive is not.
    b. The psychotic depressive is anti-social and the neurotic depressive is not.
    c. The neurotic depressive loses contact with reality and the psychotic depressive does not.
    d. The psychotic depressive loses contact with reality and the neurotic depressive does not.

15. Which of the following is usually also experienced by people who experience mania?

    a. Multiple personality
    b. Depression
    c. Antisocial behavior
    d. Passive-aggressive behavior

16. According to both cognitive theory and learned-helplessness theory, what is the cause of depression?

    a. Distortions of thinking
    b. Depressing experiences
    c. Unconscious conflicts
    d. Abnormal capillaries in the brain

17. Which of the following persons is demonstrating antisocial behavior?

    a. Homosexual man
    b. Woman who hallucinates
    c. Woman who steals without feeling guilt
    d. Man who is certain that he is constantly being followed

18. If a woman has completely lost contact with reality, what would she be considered?

    a. Antisocial
    b. Manic
    c. Psychotic
    d. Obsessive-compulsive

19. Which of the following symptoms are common in schizophrenia?

    a. Severe mood swings with deep depressions
    b. At least two distinct personalities
    c. Disturbances in thought and distortions of reality
    d. Sleep and eating difficulties and feelings of persecution

20. Which factors are probably involved in causing schizophrenia?

    a. Only genetic factors
    b. Only biochemical factors
    c. Only environmental factors
    d. Genetic, biochemical, and environmental factors

Matching

Match each name in column A with a descriptive phrase in column B.

Column A	Column B
_____ 1. Sigmund Freud	a. Proponent of the humanistic model
_____ 2. Thomas Szasz	b. Learning theorist who emphasizes the importance of thought in producing behavioral changes
_____ 3. Carl Rogers	c. Performed a study with pseudo patients and concluded that psychiatrists cannot detect mental health when they see it
_____ 4. David Rosenhan	d. Geneticist who supports a genetic link in schizophrenia
_____ 5. Albert Bandura	e. Held that abnormal behavior results from conflicts between the id and superego

_____ 6.   Aaron Beck

f. Proponent of cognitive theory who believes that depressed persons suffer from cognitive as well as emotional dysfunction

_____ 7.   Martin Seligman

g. Proponent of learned-helplessness theory who believes that depression results from feeling unable to solve problems

_____ 8.   Irving Gottesman

h. Proponent of the social-consequence model

APPLICATION EXERCISES

These application exercises will test your understanding of and ability to apply the material you have read in your text. Suggested answers are provided at the end of the chapter so that you can check your responses.

1. Your text identifies seven elements of abnormal behavior. Read the following scenario and indicate the behaviors that demonstrate each of seven characteristics of abnormal behavior.

    Most people stare at Harry and are puzzled by his behavior. As he walks along the street, he argues in a loud voice. He insists that strange creatures talk to him and are trying to capture him. He hears their voices as they plot against him. He rarely smiles and is sometimes prone to tears. He often loses his sense of direction and has to be forced into a bus or taxi to be brought back to his home. He is supported by his parents but has never had a close relationship with them, or with anyone else for that matter.

Reported Behavior	Characteristic of Abnormal Behavior
a. _____	_____
_____	_____
b. _____	_____
_____	_____
c. _____	_____
_____	_____
d. _____	_____
_____	_____
e. _____	_____
_____	_____
f. _____	_____
_____	_____
g. _____	_____
_____	_____

2. Each of the eight models of abnormal behavior mentioned in your text approaches the causes of abnormality differently. Read the following hypothetical case and complete Table 14-1 by indicating how each model of abnormality would explain the cause of maladaptive behavior in general and in this case specifically. The first model is done for you.

    Bob, a 47-year-old man, has had difficulty controlling his tears for the past 3 weeks. He feels despondent and worthless and finds himself crying several times a day. He has remained at home during the past week, since he fears the embarrassment of crying in front of his friends and coworkers. He has strong guilt feelings about missing work, and his crying is becoming more frequent and more intense.

Table 14-1
Eight Models of Abnormal Behavior

Model	General Cause	Case-Specific Cause
Moral model	Moral lapse	Inability to gain self-control, perhaps a punishment for evil he has done
Medical model		
Psychoanalytic model		
Behavioral model		
Social-consequence model		
Family, or systems, model		
Sociocultural model		
Humanistic model		

3. Your text outlines the major categories in axis I of DSM III, which classifies disorders according to symptom clusters. Four of the major diagnostic categories are anxiety disorders, somatoform disorders, dissociative disorders, and affective disorders. Identify the disorder suggested by each of the following descriptions.

a. Denise is 23 years old and has been treated by many different doctors for a number of vague physical complaints for the last 2 years. No physical causes can be found for her complaints.

Diagnostic category _____

b. When Barbara's close friend died, she began to feel that she was a hopeless failure. She is tired most of the time and has difficulty sleeping and eating.

Diagnostic category _____

c. Ted insists on brushing his teeth every 15 minutes. If he is unable to get to a sink, he becomes frightened and feels that his teeth will begin to decay.

Diagnostic category _____

d. For the past month Willy has had the jitters. He feels on edge, sweats profusely, and has trouble sleeping. He cannot find any reason for his shakiness and discomfort.

Diagnostic category _____

e. Nanette has two separate personalities. She is usually a quiet, kind person. However, she sometimes lapses into a different role, calling herself Babette. She becomes boisterous, mischievous, and highly aggressive. The psychiatrist who is treating her claims that she may have even more than these two personalities.

Diagnostic category _____

f. Emily almost drowned when she fell out of a canoe at age 5. For the 10 years since the accident, she has had an intense fear of water. She will not go near the shore, nor will she even take a shower or a bath.

Diagnostic category _____

4. The use of a classification system such as established in DSM III assists communication among professionals and therapists. However, an important difficulty with such classification involves self-fulfilling prophecy. Both the therapist and the person diagnosed may believe so strongly in the diagnosis that they fail to notice behaviors that may contradict it. The diagnosis becomes self-fulfilling.

    Suppose a therapist diagnosed a man as "depressed." How could this diagnosis become self-fulfilling?

    _____
    _____
    _____
    _____

5. As indicated in your text, personality disorders encompass a broad range of behaviors. Two prominent personality disorders are the antisocial personality and the borderline personality.
    Identify the personality disorders suggested by each of the following descriptions.

a. This person is almost entirely indifferent to the concerns of others and breaks laws freely.

_____

b. This person has a constant feeling of emptiness and boredom and cannot tolerate being alone.

_____

c. This person is unstable and unpredictable and usually has strong feelings for others that last only a short time.

_____

d. This person has been called a *sociopath* and does not respond to rewards and punishments.

_____

6. Symptoms of schizophrenia have been classified into two categories: positive symptoms and negative symptoms. Positive symptoms are behaviors that are unique to schizophrenics. Negative symptoms are behaviors that are characteristic of normal people but are defective in schizophrenics. People with positive characteristics are more likely to respond to treatment and improve.

    Read each of the following descriptions of behavior and indicate whether the symptom is positive or negative.

a. A woman shows no emotion.

_____

b. A man hears voices giving him ideas about new inventions.

_____

c. A man thinks that he is constantly being followed by the IRS.

_____

d. A woman will bring up irrelevant subjects and shift ideas several times during a conversation.

_____

e. A woman speaks very few words and rarely puts together sentences or even phrases.

_____

READING EXERCISE

The following article by Sally Squires, reprinted from the *Washington Post*, reports that scientists now suspect that a virus may cause schizophrenia; Squires describes the present evidence.

In Schizophrenia, a Virus Is Suspected

Could schizophrenia, the debilitating mental disorder, be caused by a virus that triggers the body's immune system to attack the brain?

Possibly, according to an old theory that is gaining new momentum as a result of recent research into autoimmune diseases.

In these disorders, the body's immune system seems to go awry and destroy the very cells that it is supposed to protect. Scientists suspect a virus may be the culprit, triggering these abnormalities of the immune system.

Based on these new findings, plans are under way to see if schizophrenic patients respond to steroid drugs, which suppress the body's immune system, said Dr. Steven Paul, chief of clinical neuroscience at the National Institute of Mental Health. If the drugs work, researchers would gain important evidence that schizophrenia is indeed an autoimmune disease.

At a conference last week at the National Institutes of Health,

Reprinted with permission of *The Washington Post,* copyright (c) 1987.

scientists presented a case for the viral-immune theory of schizophrenia.

Immunologist John Knight, a guest researcher from New Zealand's University of Orago Medical School, said many aspects of schizophrenia are similar to aspects of known autoimmune diseases.

For one, schizophrenia is not present at birth, Knight said, but develops during adolescence or young adulthood--much the way Grave's disease (which affects the thyroid) or myasthenia gravis (which affects the muscles) begin.

Schizophrenia also "appears to go through cycles of remission and relapse," Knight said--a pattern seen in autoimmune diseases.

Like other known and suspected autoimmune diseases, schizophrenia seems to have a genetic component. For instance, studies show that children with one schizophrenic parent have about a 13-fold increased risk of developing the disease.

The notion that schizophrenia may be caused by a virus-induced autoimmune disorder was first proposed in 1912 by Russian researcher V. K. Khoroshko. The theory resurfaced in the 1930s and '60s prior to its current resurgence.

To many scientists, the most compelling evidence today for an autoimmune basis to schizophrenia is the discovery of brain autoantibodies in the blood of schizophrenics. These antibodies are proteins produced by the immune system to attack the brain.

In a study at the National Institute of Neurological and Communicative Disorders and Stroke, scientists compared the blood of 20 schizophrenic patients with 20 patients with depression and 30 control individuals. Drs. Craig Venter, Claire Fraser and George McNeil found that both the schizophrenics and the depressed patients had types of autoantibodies that were specific for the human brain. In addition, the autoantibodies found in the blood of schizophrenics were very different from those found in the depressed patients.

"We want to be very cautious, but the autoimmune basis of this disease is certainly one of the interpretations of the data," Venter said. Another explanation for the findings could be that certain drugs used to treat schizophrenics may produce changes in the immune system.

Scientists have also discovered an increase in levels of certain HLA antigens among schizophrenic patients. HLA stands for human leukocyte antigen. These substances are produced by white blood cells and help regulate the body's immune response. Many diseases known or suspected to have an autoimmune or infectious cause produce similar elevations in HLA levels.

There seems to be a link, too, between schizophrenia and herpes. In one study, researchers found abnormal proteins in the cerebrospinal fluid of some schizophrenics. These unusual proteins "were not present in 100 normal people," said Dr. Michael Harrington, a visiting associate in NIMH's Clinical Neurogenetics Branch, who conducted the study with Dr. Carl

R. Merril. But they were found in 30 percent of schizophrenics in this study and in 90 percent of people with herpes simplex encephalitis. In addition, the proteins were discovered in multiple sclerosis patients, Parkinson's disease patients, and in more than two thirds of patients with Creutzfeldt-Jakob's disease--a debilitating mental disorder.

"I think that it is interesting that there is either a viral--or alleged viral--cause for all of these diseases," Harrington said.

Exactly what might trigger the sequence of events that leads to schizophrenia is still not known, but one likely suspect is a viral infection during pregnancy.

According to this scenario, a slow virus infects the fetus and gradually produces pathological changes over a long period of time. Possible viruses are cytomegalovirus (CMV) and herpes. Swedish researchers have shown that herpes virus infections in mice produce changes in levels of the brain chemical dopamine similar to changes seen in the dopamine levels of schizophrenics.

Part of the support for the theory of in-utero infections also comes from the fact that some 20 studies have shown that a disproportionately high number of schizophrenics are born in the winter and spring months. Since the mothers of babies born during these months are likely to have had influenza or colds during their pregnancy, it may be that these common infections lay the foundation for schizophrenia.

Medical scientists speculate that if such an infection were coupled with a genetic predisposition to schizophrenia, the disease could be triggered.

In Japan, researchers have already linked this kind of seasonal birth pattern in schizophrenics with a viral infection called Japanese encephalitis. Babies born during certain times of the year are most susceptible to the disease later in life. But this effect is seen only in children born during severe Japanese encephalitis epidemic years.

The idea is that the unborn baby's developing immune system may not be able to recognize the virus as a foreign invader. Later in life, when the immune system sees the virus again, it may allow the virus to enter the brain.

In some patients, it may be that a viral infection later in childhood or adolescence begins the damaging process. Psychiatrist Karl Menninger studied the influenza epidemics of 1889-92 and 1918-19 and showed that certain strains of influenza could trigger schizophrenic symptoms weeks, months or years after infection. More recently, English researchers showed evidence that some schizophrenic patients have impaired immunity to the mumps virus, suggesting that mumps or a related virus may trigger schizophrenic episodes in certain people.

Schizophrenia afflicts an estimated 1.6 million Americans--or slightly less than 1 percent of the population. The disease often begins in adolescence or during the early adult years, and because of its long-term, chronic symptoms costs at least $7 billion annually to treat.

About 200,000 schizophrenics have such severe symptoms that they must be cared for in nursing homes or mental hospitals. Another 500,000 schizophrenics are treated during short-term hospitalizations or on an outpatient basis. The rest receive unknown care, according to Dr. Darrel Regier, director of the division of clinical research at NIMH.

Scientists believe that they will probably discover a number of different causes of schizophrenia just as there are multiple causes of heart disease and of cancer.

The autoimmune idea fits well with other theories about schizophrenia, said Dr. Fuller Torrey, a psychiatrist with NIMH's neuropsychiatry branch at St. Elizabeths Hospital, and a leading proponent of a viral theory.

If researchers can find enough evidence that schizophrenia is caused by some specific agent such as a virus, it would open the door to new approaches to therapy. "If you determine part of the cause, you can design a specific cure," said Venter, who is chief of NINCD's section of receptor biochemistry and molecular biology. "It could lead the way to a very major advance in treatment."

QUESTIONS

Answer the following questions and then compare your responses with the suggested answers at the end of this chapter.

1. The immunologist John Knight noted that schizophrenia is similar to known autoimmune diseases. What three similarities did he report?

2. What is the significance of the finding that schizophrenic patients have an increase in certain levels of HLA antigens?

3. Why are scientists excited about finding a virus or a specific agent that causes schizophrenia?

ANSWERS

Correct Answers to SELF-TEST Exercises

Multiple-Choice

1.	b	8.	b	15.	b
2.	b	9.	b	16.	a
3.	c	10.	b	17.	c
4.	c	11.	a	18.	c
5.	a	12.	a	19.	c
6.	c	13.	b	20.	d
7.	a	14.	d		

Matching

1.	e	7.	g
2.	h	8.	d
3.	a		
4.	c		
5.	b		
6.	f		

Suggested Answers to Application Exercises

1.

	Reported Behavior	Characteristic of Abnormal Behavior
a.	People stare and are puzzled by his behavior.	Statistical rarity
b.	He argues in a loud voice.	Undesirable behavior
c.	He hears voices of strange creatures	Inability to recognize reality
d.	He rarely smiles and is prone to tears.	Unhappy much of the time
e.	He loses his sense of direction and has to be brought home	Unable to perform tasks of daily living
f.	He is supported by his parents	Cannot perform productive work
g.	He never had a close relationship with parents or others	Does not have close relationships with others

2.

Answers to Table 14-2 Eight Models of Abnormal Behavior

Model	General Cause	Case-Specific Cause
Moral model	Moral lapse	Inability to gain self-control, perhaps a punishment for evil he has done
Medical model	Physical illness	May be over-tired or have a chemical imbalance
Psychoanalytic model	Conflict between superego and ego	Probably has an oral fixation caused by problems in his relationship with his mother in infancy, and now has lowered self-esteem because he cannot succeed in love relationships

(Continued)

Answers to Table 14-2 (Continued)

Behavioral model	Maladaptive learning	May have been rewarded for crying as a child, which behavior is no longer adaptive
Social-consequence model	Not taking the responsibility to cope with society	Is using his depression to avoid facing his problems
Family, or systems, model	Problems within the family	Perhaps his entire family has difficulty communicating or is supporting his depression in some way.
Sociocultural model	Harsh environment	He may have been discriminated against or feel pressures from his environment.
Humanistic model	Inability to achieve self-actualization	He may have made more choices in the past --perhaps his job or spouse is unsuitable.

3. a. Somatoform disorder
   b. Affective disorder
   c. Anxiety disorder (obsessive-compulsive disorder)
   d. Anxiety disorder (generalized anxiety disorder)
   e. Dissociative disorder (multiple personality)
   f. Anxiety disorder (phobia)

4. Once a diagnosis of depression is made, the therapist might focus on symptom behaviors. The man may feel helpless about his depression and feel inadequate. These attitudes may contribute to a further decline into depression.

5. a. Antisocial personality
   b. Borderline personality
   c. Borderline personality
   d. Antisocial personality

6. a. Negative
   b. Positive
   c. Positive
   d. Positive
   e. Negative

Suggested Answers to Reading Questions

1. Schizophrenia is not present at birth; it appears to go through cycles of remission and relapse; and it seems to have a genetic component.

2. These antigens regulate the immune response and are elevated in patients with diseases that have known autoimmune or infectious causes.

3. If the cause is determined, it will be easier to find a specific cure.

Chapter 15:

THERAPY

CHAPTER OUTLINE

I. Who undergoes therapy?

II. Who provides therapy?
   A. Psychotherapy
      1. Dynamic therapies
         a. Psychoanalysis
         b. Psychoanalytically inspired therapy
      2. Humanistic therapy
         a. Person-centered approach
            (1) Acceptance
            (2) Empathic understanding
            (3) Congruence
         b. Gestalt therapy
      3. Behavior therapies
         a. Systematic desensitization
         b. Aversive therapy
         c. Modeling therapy
         d. Positive reinforcement (operant therapy)
         e. Cognitive (behavioral) therapies
            (1) Rational-emotive therapy: Albert Ellis
            (2) Cognitive therapy: Aaron T. Beck
      4. Group and family approaches
         a. Group therapy
         b. Family therapy
         c. Couples therapy
      5. Brief therapies
   B. Medical therapies
      1. Psychosurgery
      2. Electroconvulsive therapy
      3. Drug treatments
         a. What disorders can be helped by drugs?
            (1) Schizophrenia
            (2) Depression
            (3) Bipolar disorder (manic depression)
            (4) Anxiety disorders
         b. How do drugs work?
         c. How well do drugs work?
   C. Environmental therapy
      1. Institutionalization
      2. Deinstitutionalization

329

III. Evaluation of the various therapies
    A. Is therapy better than no therapy?
    B. Is any one therapy "best"?
        1. Psychotherapy versus drug therapy
            a. Evidence on psychotherapy
            b. Evidence on drug therapy
        2. Psychoanalytically oriented therapy versus behavior therapy
    C. Is a particular therapy best for a particular problem?
    D. Is a combination of therapies better than a single therapy?
    E. Is there a common denominator for all therapies?

Boxes
    Psychology in your life: Some typical therapeutic dialogues
    In the forefront: Light therapy for seasonal affective disorder
    Psychology in your life: Choosing therapy and a therapist

LEARNING OBJECTIVES

After you study Chapter 15, you should be able to do the tasks outlined in the following objectives.

1. Recognize the extent of psychiatric care and identify the reasons for receiving therapy.

2. Specify the types of professionals who offer therapy and state three major forms of therapy.

3. Define psychotherapy and identify three major approaches and three newer orientations.

4. Describe the techniques used in dynamic therapies and critique classical psychoanalysis.

5. Identify the goals in humanistic therapies and describe the methods used in a person-centered approach and in gestalt therapy.

6. Identify the focus of behavior therapies and provide examples of four techniques used in behavior therapy.

7. Identify the focus of cognitive-behavioral therapies and explain the methods used in rational-emotive therapy and Beck's cognitive therapy.

8. State the advantages of group and family approaches to therapy.

9. Specify the purpose and techniques of brief therapies.

10. Describe three forms of medical therapy.

11. Explain the positive and negative features of drug treatments.

12. Identify the purpose of environmental therapy.

13. Evaluate the various therapies.

KEY CONCEPTS

As you read Chapter 15 in your text, look for each of the following concepts. You should understand each concept.

1. Who Undergoes Therapy?

People receive therapy for a number of reasons, including psychosis, anxiety disorders, feelings of distress or discontent, unruly behavior, and as a preparation to practice therapy.

2. Types of Therapists

Therapists are trained to offer a specific type of treatment. Therapists include clinical psychologists, psychiatrists, social workers, psychoanalysts, psychiatric nurses, and counselors. The three major forms of therapy used are psychotherapy, somatic therapy, and environmental therapy.

3. Psychotherapy

Psychotherapy refers to nonmedical forms of treatment that involve changing behavior. The three major approaches to psychotherapy are dynamic, humanistic, and behavioral. Newer orientations include cognitive, brief, and interpersonal approaches.

4. Dynamic Therapies

Dynamic therapies help people develop insight into the forces in their unconscious. In classical psychoanalysis, as developed by Freud, techniques of free association and analysis of dreams are used. The analyst asks questions as the person (analysand) speaks. Transference and countertransference (the feelings of the patient and therapist toward each other) play an important role in psychoanalysis. Newer dynamic therapies (psychoanalytically inspired psychotherapy) are more directive and require less time. Ego-analytic therapy draws on techniques from psychoanalysis but stresses present behavior, strengthening the ego, and personal control.

5. Humanistic Therapies

Humanistic therapies aim to rebuild personalities and help people realize their full potential. The patient receiving therapy is respected and plays a large role in the success of the therapy.

6. Person-Centered Approach

In a person-centered approach (a humanistic therapy), the therapist attempts to view the world as the client does and shows acceptance and understanding of the client. The goal in person-centered therapy is congruence and complete self-acceptance.

7. Gestalt Therapy

Gestalt therapy, a humanistic therapy, stresses the integration of various parts of the personality into an organized whole. Therapists use techniques such as role-playing, games, and visual imaging to help clients develop a unified self. Therapists often point out contradictions between clients' nonverbal and verbal behaviors.

8. Behavior Therapies

Behavior therapies are based on learning principles and help individuals overcome maladaptive habits. According to behaviorists, abnormal behaviors are the result of faulty learning. Therapy focuses on the here and now and on changing the maladaptive behavior.

9. Techniques Used in Behavior Therapy

Behavior therapists vary their techniques according to the problem being treated, the personality of the client, and their own orientation. These techniques include systematic desensitization, aversive therapy, modeling therapy, and positive reinforcement (operant therapy).

10. Cognitive-Behavioral Therapies

Cognitive-behavioral therapies emphasize the identification of distortions in thinking. Rational-emotive therapy (RET) helps clients find flaws in the logic of their thinking. Beck's cognitive therapy uses active approaches to help clients organize their thinking and behavior.

11. Group, Family, and Couple Approaches

Group therapy sessions usually have between five and eight members and meet once a week. People learn from each other, role-play, express their feelings in a safe setting, and become aware of other people's problems. The goal in family therapy is to strengthen the family group. The family system is examined and the entire family is the patient. Couples therapy aims to improve the relationship between two people.

12. Brief Therapies

Most conventional therapy is open-ended. The client doesn't know how long it will last. During the past 20 years brief therapies have been developed, requiring fewer than 20 sessions. Brief therapies come from all schools and usually focus on only one or a few symptoms. The therapist is active and gives advice freely.

13. Medical Therapies

Medical therapies include psychosurgery, electroconvulsive (shock) therapy, and drug treatments. Prefrontal lobotomies—performed during the 1940s and 1950s on patients with schizophrenia, obsessions, and pain—are rarely performed today. Electroconvulsive therapy is used to alleviate despair in severely depressed and suicidal patients as a last resort when drug therapy is not effective.

14. Drug Treatments

Drug treatments are a form of medical therapy that have become more common. Chlorpromazine and phenothiazines are used to control schizophrenic symptoms but do not cure the condition. These antipsychotic drugs can also produce problematic side effects. Tricyclics and monoamine oxidase (MAO) are anti-depressants that have been useful in treating persons suffering from depression that has no apparent cause. Lithium carbonate is used to control extreme manic states. Benzodiazepines (misleadingly called *minor tranquilizers*) have dropped in popularity in treating general anxiety because they are habit-forming and can cause drowsiness and unsteadiness. However, they have been successful when combined with tricyclics in treating phobias.

15. Environmental Therapy

Environmental therapy includes institutionalization, or sending a person to a hospital, small group home, foster home, or day care center. Although drug therapies have decreased the need for institutionalization, more than half the patients released from institutions return within 1 year.

16. Evaluation of the Various Therapies

Recent studies using objective standards have found that therapy is effective for most people. There is no one "best" therapy, but particular therapies are best suited for certain types of problems. A combination of drug treatment and family therapy was found effective in the treatment of schizophrenia. Electroconvulsive (shock) therapy is quite effective in the treatment of severely depressed and suicidal patients. Behavior therapies are well adapted for the treatment of phobias, obsessions and compulsions, and some types of sexual dysfunction. A combination of medical therapy and psychotherapy is most effective. In general, the therapist–client relationship is more significant than the type of therapy being used.

Psychologically shaken   (p. 525)

Unruly   (p. 525)

Discontented   (p. 525)

Therapist   (p. 525)

Clinical psychologist   (p. 525)

TERMS TO KNOW

Define each of the terms listed. You can check your definitions in the text Glossary or on the text pages listed in parentheses.

Psychiatrist   (p. 526)

Therapy   (p. 525)   Social worker   (p. 526)

Psychotic   (p. 525)   Psychoanalyst   (p. 526)

Anxiety disorders   (p. 525)   Psychiatric nurse   (p. 526)

Counselor   (p. 526)   Free association   (p. 528)

Psychotherapy   (p. 526)   Resistance   (p. 529)

Medical therapy   (p. 527)   Transference   (p. 529)

Environmental therapy   (p. 527)   Countertransference   (p. 529)

Dynamic therapies   (p. 527)   Ego-analytic therapy   (p. 529)

Humanistic therapies   (p. 527)   Person-centered approach   (p. 531)

Behavior therapies   (p. 527)   Self-actualization   (p. 532)

Classical psychoanalysis   (p. 528)   Acceptance   (p. 532)

Analysand   (p. 528)   Empathic understanding   (p. 532)

Advanced empathy	(p. 532)	Operant therapy (positive reinforcement)	(p. 535)
Congruence	(p. 532)	Cognitive-behavioral therapies	(p. 536)
Gestalt therapy	(p. 532)	Rational-emotive therapy (RET)	(p. 536)
Antimentalistic approach	(p. 533)	Beck's cognitive therapy	(p. 536)
Systematic desensitization	(p. 534)	Group therapy	(p. 537)
In imagination phase	(p. 534)	Closed groups	(p. 538)
In vivo phase	(p. 534)	Open groups	(p. 538)
Aversive therapy	(p. 535)	Family therapy	(p. 538)
Modeling therapy	(p. 535)	Presenting problem	(p. 538)

Couples therapy	(p. 539)	Antipsychotic drugs	(p. 544)
Divorce therapists	(p. 539)	Neuroleptics	(p. 544)
Brief therapies	(p. 540)	Major tranquilizer	(p. 544)
Psychosurgery	(p. 541)	Tardive dyskinesia	(p. 544)
Prefrontal lobotomy	(p. 541)	Tricyclics	(p. 544)
Electroconvulsive therapy	(p. 542)	Lithium	(p. 544)
Psychoactive drugs	(p. 543)	Monoamine oxidase (MAO)	(p. 544)
Chlorpromazine	(p. 544)	Light therapy	(p. 545)
Phenothiazines	(p. 544)	Seasonal affective disorder (SAD)	(p. 545)

Amoxapine   (p. 545)

Diazepam (Valium)   (p. 545)

Benzodiazepines   (p. 545)

Dopamine   (p. 547)

Deinstitutionalization   (p. 548)

Placebo effect   (p. 551)

Therapeutic alliance   (p. 554)

SELF-TEST

Multiple-Choice

Choose the one best response to each question. An answer key is provided at the end of this chapter.

1. What are the three major forms of therapy?

   a. Dynamic, drug, and behavioral
   b. Rational, cognitive, and psychosurgical
   c. Psychotherapeutic, medical, and environmental
   d. Person-centered, group, and family

2. What is psychotherapy?

   a. Form of medical therapy that requires the use of drugs
   b. Medical procedure that follows psychosurgery
   c. Newer form of psychoanalysis
   d. Nonmedical treatments that involve changing behavior

3. What is the role of the therapist in classical psychoanalysis?

   a. To create an atmosphere of acceptance
   b. To interpret and communicate the person's unconscious conflicts
   c. To give specific direction to the person
   d. To help the person develop congruence

4. According to Freud, the patient attributes characteristics of significant persons in his or her life to the therapist during the course of the treatment. What is this called?

   a. Free association
   b. Transference
   c. Countertransference
   d. Resistance

5. In psychoanalysis the therapist sometimes asks a person to express thoughts openly, saying everything and holding back nothing. What is this technique called?

   a. Free association
   b. Transference
   c. Countertransference
   d. Resistance

6. Which of the following is a disadvantage of psychoanalysis?

   a. Psychoanalysts are not well trained.
   b. There is minimal individual attention, since it usually involves groups.
   c. The past is ignored in therapy.
   d. It is costly and time-consuming.

7. Which of the following is true of both dynamic and humanistic therapies?

   a. Both therapies use free association and dream analysis.
   b. The goal of both therapies is self-knowledge.
   c. Both therapies stress repressed feelings from the past.
   d. Behavioral techniques are used in both therapies.

8. Which of the following therapists would be most likely to attempt to establish an atmosphere of total acceptance so that the client can deal with personal feelings?

   a. Behavior therapist
   b. Rational-emotive therapist
   c. Person-centered therapist
   d. Cognitive-behavioral therapist

9. Which of the following is an important element in a person-centered approach to therapy?

   a. Acceptance of present feelings
   b. Exploration of the unconscious
   c. Feedback from other people
   d. Recollection of past experiences

10. What is the focus of gestalt therapy?

    a. Who the significant persons are in the client's life
    b. What the client is feeling and how the client is behaving

    c. When the client learned current behaviors
    d. Why the client is behaving in a certain way

11. What is emphasized in the various forms of behavior therapy?

    a. Repressed past experiences
    b. Errors in thought processes
    c. Overt changes in behavior
    d. Self-actualization

12. Assume that a man is being treated for fear of heights. While he is in a very relaxed state, his therapist asks him to imagine climbing a short ladder. What technique is the therapist using?

    a. Modeling
    b. Aversive therapy
    c. Systematic desensitization
    d. Rational-emotive therapy

13. What is the client's goal in systematic desensitization?

    a. To relax in situations that usually provoke anxiety
    b. To resolve unconscious conflicts
    c. To receive feedback from other people
    d. To become sensitive to the feelings of others

14. What is one premise of rational-emotive therapy?

    a. Mistaken beliefs lead to maladaptive behavior.
    b. Denial of feelings leads to maladaptive behavior.
    c. Thoughts have little to do with maladaptive behavior.
    d. The family rather than the individual is responsible for maladaptive behavior.

15. Which form of therapy is most likely to help a person realize that other people have similar problems?

a. Behavior therapy
b. Person-centered therapy
c. Psychoanalysis
d. Group therapy

16. What is one typical goal in family therapy?

   a. To set family rules
   b. To identify the family troublemaker
   c. To facilitate conflict resolution in the family
   d. To focus on problems outside the family

17. What is the role of therapists in brief therapies?

   a. To be active and provide advice
   b. To listen and allow the clients to resolve their own problems
   c. To provide clients with techniques to analyze their dreams
   d. To convince clients that they require longer therapy

18. Which of the following persons would benefit most from electroconvulsive therapy?

   a. Schizophrenic
   b. Person with bipolar disorder
   c. Severely depressed suicidal person
   d. Person with mild phobias

19. For which of the following disorders might chlorpromazine be prescribed?

   a. Schizophrenia
   b. Mild depression
   c. Anxiety
   d. Bipolar disorder

20. What is a major drawback of drugs in treating psychopathology?

   a. They cannot relieve depression.
   b. They cannot be paired with other forms of therapy.
   c. If they are not taken, the pathology usually returns.
   d. They usually produce additional anxiety and tension.

21. Which of the following factors has decreased the need for institutionalization?

   a. Increase in electroconvulsive therapy
   b. Increase in psychosurgery
   c. Decrease in psychosurgery
   d. Increase in drug therapies

22. What appears to be the most significant factor in determining the success of therapy?

   a. Therapist-client relationship
   b. Type of therapy
   c. Type of problem
   d. Amount of time spent in therapy

Matching

Match each name in column A with a descriptive phrase in column B.

Column A

_____ 1. Sigmund Freud
_____ 2. Karen Horney

_____ 3. Carl Rogers
_____ 4. Frederick Perls
_____ 5. Albert Ellis

_____ 6. Aaron T. Beck
_____ 7. Alfred Adler

_____ 8. Hans J. Eysenck

Column B

a. Early critic of psychotherapy
b. Incorporated an active approach in cognitive therapy
c. Invented psychoanalytic therapy
d. Developed person-centered therapy
e. One of the earliest advocates of group therapy
f. Developed rational-emotive therapy
g. Used the gestalt view in psychotherapy
h. Ego-analytic therapist

APPLICATION EXERCISES

These application exercises will test your understanding of and ability to apply the material you have read in your text. Suggested answers are provided at the end of the chapter so that you can check your responses.

1. Classical psychoanalysis has lost popularity in recent years and given way to a modification called *psychoanalytically inspired psychotherapy.*

    a. List three reasons why classical psychoanalysis has had limited popularity.

    _____
    _____
    _____

    b. How does psychoanalytically inspired psychotherapy differ from classical psychotherapy?

    _____
    _____
    _____

2. Both the person-centered approach of Carl Rogers and the gestalt therapy of Frederick Perls are forms of humanistic therapy. What are the "humanistic" similarities in the two therapies?

    _____
    _____
    _____
    _____
    _____

3. Behavior therapists believe that maladaptive behavior has been learned and that clients need to learn new, acceptable behaviors. To achieve their goal, behavior therapists use a number of different techniques, including systematic desensitization, aversive therapy, modeling therapy, and positive reinforcement. For each of the following examples, indicate which technique or combination of techniques is being used.

    a. A snake-phobic adolescent uses relaxation exercises while viewing a film showing people engaging in progressively more fear-provoking activities with a large snake.

_____

b. A therapist gives a depressed woman a small piece of chocolate candy each time she mentions something positive about herself or her environment.

_____

c. An alcoholic woman has taken Antabuse so that she will become nauseated and violently ill if she drinks alcohol.

_____

4. Rational-emotive therapy assumes a critical interaction between thoughts and emotions. Ellis used alphabet letters to analyze irrational thought processes. Read the following scenario and identify the components that belong with each letter of the alphabet in Table 15-1.

   Joanne is frightened to speak out in front of her peers. When she is called upon in a college class, her face flushes and she mumbles inaudibly in total embarrassment. She is certain that she will make a complete fool of herself, that no one will ever speak to her again, and that she will lose her friends. Her therapist points out that people often give incorrect or inappropriate responses in class and still remain worthwhile and desirable. Joanne is told to volunteer in her next class, and if her response is imperfect, it will be inconvenient but will not make her worthless.

Table 15-1 Components of Ellis's Alphabet-Letter Technique

A (activating experiences)

B (belief system)

C (upsetting emotional consequences)

D (dispute)

E (better-functioning effects)

5. Your text identifies several advantages of group therapy. Consider a woman who has just been deserted by her husband and is participating in group therapy to cope with her trauma and anxiety. What advantages might group therapy have over individual therapy for this woman?

_____
_____
_____
_____
_____

6. Although psychoactive drugs have permitted millions of people to lead better lives, there are some problems associated with these drugs. Explain why drug therapy is not the sole solution to psychological disorders.

_____
_____
_____
_____
_____

READING EXERCISE

The following article by Roger Kramer and Ira Weiner, reprinted from *Psychology Today*, addresses the problems therapists face in dealing with patients who suffer from borderline personality problems and are difficult to treat.

Psychiatry on the Borderline

More than 25 years ago, psychiatrist T. F. Main described what he called "The Ailment"--signs of strain among hospital staff working with a group of patients who proved unusually difficult to treat. The patients were often suicidal, insatiably demanding, sad, and filled with rage. Doctors who had treated the patients before admission offered various diagnoses and stressed the patients' "special" qualities. "Some seemed to feel that nobody but themselves could really get the hang of the subtleties of feeling in the patient, and that they would be in danger of being judged insensitively as unmanageable rather than special."

Main found the same pattern among staff doctors and nurses who treated those "special" patients. Believing that they alone understood the patient, they used more and more drastic therapies, from occasional sedation to sleep induction and electroconvulsive therapy, with little success. One nurse went so far as to recommend brain surgery. The staff members resentfully blamed one another for the failure. Only when they began to discuss these patients among themselves did they realize how they were being split into two contending factions.

Today, many clinicians would say that the patients Main described were suffering from borderline personality disorders. The psychiatrist's latest Diagnostic and Statistical Manual of Mental Disorders (DSM III) has given that label official sanction: Borderline patients are impulsive and

Reprinted with permission from Psychology Today Magazine. Copyright (c) 1983 (APA).

unpredictable, intolerant of being alone, often self-destructive. They display inappropriate or intense anger, chronic feelings of emptiness or boredom, unstable relationships, mood swings, and confusion about their identity.

But is the confusion entirely theirs? The history of what we now call the borderline syndrome recalls the story of the blind men and the elephant. The condition has at one time or another been labeled pre-schizophrenia, psychotic character, ambulatory schizophrenia, hysteroid dysphoria, or oral hysteria. Have we yet seen the whole elephant? Or does one really exist?

Not everyone is convinced that there is an elephant to be described. One study suggests that the definition of borderline syndrome represents so much of the range of psychopathology as to be meaningless. Another study concludes that borderline personality disorder cannot be distinguished from histrionic or antisocial disorders. And a third complicates matters further by subdividing the diagnosis into four types.

Those who accept the reality of the condition have developed a variety of theories on its origin. Some view it as a special type of mood imbalance and hypothesize a biochemical deficit to account for the abrupt shifts in feeling states. At the other end of the spectrum are social critics who see the borderline patient as a reflection of our culture's alienation and estrangement, the result of delegating traditional family functions to the state or the corporation. In between are the psychodynamic theories, which emphasize the problem of separation from the mother: An infant who cannot overcome feelings of abandonment and emerge from a dependent and symbiotic state with a coherent and stable sense of identity, according to the theories, is at risk for the borderline syndrome.

Given the confusing range of possible causes, the range of proposed treatments is predictably wide: in-patient or out-patient treatment, short-term or long-term therapy, confrontive or supportive approaches, major tranquilizers, antidepressants, lithium, stimulants, and narcotics.

Psychiatrist Paul Russell, a professor at Harvard Medical School, said at a symposium on the disorder: "At times, when our hold upon the world is slippery, naming can be more a problem than a solution. There is a risk of pseudo-reality, of confirming what may be at best a premature objectivity--and worse, the possibility of naming nothing more than a projection of ourselves, a piece of paranoia." The same possibility was raised by psychiatrist Wilfred R. Bion in his introduction to a collection of articles on the problem. He suggested that mental-health professionals, like borderline patients, have an intolerance for unfilled space. They fill the theoretical vacuum with elaborate theories to soothe their own frustration. The very insistence on cataloguing the disorder may be a symptom of its effects on those trying to cure it.

The profession itself is being stretched to its limits. It is being confronted with an apparently increasing number of "difficult" patients who create chaos in therapy, wreak havoc in emergency rooms, and get worse on the analyst's couch. The insights of Russell and Bion suggest that it may be time to reconsider Main's perception: Possibly the strongest unifying thread is not the specific traits of the patients but what they do to us.

In their day-to-day work with borderline patients, therapists are exposed to the patients' fantasies and unconscious manipulations. Two of the most common are known as "splitting," seeing the world and other people in strongly polarized, good-or-bad terms, and "projective identification," dissociating an intolerable aspect of the self by projecting it onto another. Both can be seen as defense mechanisms that help the patient ward off anxiety, but they also have powerful effects on the therapist.

Some accounts in the clinical literature read like scenes from *The Invasion of the Body Snatchers*. Therapists find themselves fulfilling patients' expectations, as if they were compelled to behave according to a distorted perception. Main and others have said that borderline patients intuitively choose the therapist most likely to respond this way. Psychiatrist Leon Grinberg suggests that the relationship between such a patient and a therapist is like that between hypnotist and subject. The patient projects a "parasitic superego" that can cause the therapist to act just as the patient knows or fears that all authority figures will act.

One seasoned clinician experienced with borderline patients and their families tells of a nightmare in which she sees herself standing in front of her childhood dresser. Peering into the mirror, she sees the reflection of her own face and body, but her hair is that of one of her borderline patients. Another therapist says she had an argument with her husband one day and found herself sulking on her front step, thinking, "I'll get him by getting a kitchen knife and scratching my wrists." Startled, she realized that she might be "catching" her patients' habitual responses.

The phenomenon is common enough that some therapists use it as a diagnostic criterion. They talk of a characteristic borderline "feel," a pull toward fusion. "If you schedule a 45-minute session and end up spending twice that long with the patient," one says, "the fact that you've gotten sucked in should be a warning."

As Main noticed, borderline patients cause dissension within a hospital. One group, drawn to the borderline patients, is seen by other doctors and nurses as "collusive, unrealistic, and overindulgent." In turn, they consider the others "suppressive, insensitive to the strains on an immature ego, and lacking in proper feeling."

Such a division can grow until it disrupts an entire institution. Borderline patients have a tendency to split clinicians from administrators: They write letters of complaint to the hospital director, complain to their therapists' supervisors, and sometimes threaten the hospital with ruin in the form of a malpractice suit.

Faced with a bureaucracy they can't comprehend, rules they don't understand, and staff who "never seem to care enough," borderline patients use every means at their command to call attention to themselves and create the illusion of being in control. Their tactics are like those Harvey Schlossberg, a policeman turned psychologist, describes in an article on terrorists:

"We must assume that individuals who turn to terrorism are experiencing total and overwhelming feelings of inadequacy. They are incapable of obtaining what they want; they deal with intense frustration by resorting to the most drastic course of action. The display of unchecked aggressiveness and violence gives the actor the psychological feeling of power, although he accomplishes no satisfaction of his needs."

One staff nurse we know summed up the effect these patients can have in these words: "I think I'm losing my mind. I used to know right from wrong, now I'm not sure. I'm losing my perspective, my patience. I think I'm

beginning to hate myself, but worse, I'm beginning to resent the people I'm supposed to be helping. I've never felt this way before."

Hospital staff members should be aware of borderline patients' potential as psychic terrorists. They threaten, issue ultimatums, and force those dealing with them into more and more extreme countermeasures. They toy with the profession's most cherished assumptions: legal and ethical responsibility for patient care, prediction and control of behavior, even the basic ability to help. They push the profession to the borders of its ability to respond.

However much psychological theorists disagree about the definition and appropriate treatment of borderline patients, most agree that there is a real increase in their number, a fact attested to not only by the new listing in DSM III, but by a plethora of articles and symposiums on what some feel is becoming today's predominant form of severe mental illness.

Is there something in our culture that fosters this pattern, with its desperate need for attention, its projection of inner conflicts onto all those within reach? British author Colin Wilson believes that today many of us function predominantly on an automatic level, with little need to think or concentrate. This can lead to boredom, depression, even panic, in susceptible individuals. To regain control, we place ourselves in dangerous situations, identify with the excitement surrounding celebrities, or try through mystical, religious, or pharmacological means to alter our consciousness. Some of us become terrorists, others are terrorized; some act as cult leaders, others as followers; some become borderline patients, others therapists.

Psychiatrist Richard Restak, author of *The Self Seekers,* offers a related view. He traces the increase in borderline pathology to "the decrease in 'structure' within contemporary society, narcissism, moral relativism, and the impact of video with its strident emphasis on violence and sex. Each of these factors contributes in its own way toward replacing inner standards of self-definition and self-worth with a structureless, 'free-form' approach to life. . . . As a result of these changes, we are encountering more and more . . . Mark David Chapmans and John Hinckleys, who, in varying degrees, have turned the life instinct on its head: Meaning for them can only come from acts of destruction aimed at self and others."

It is striking how often borderline patients follow the same sequence: starting with private therapy, through clinical treatment regimes of increasing gravity and risk, and ending in state mental hospitals, the ultimate catchall for unmanageable patients. Main's description still holds true: "Finally, with the cover of staff goodwill cracking, the patient was transfered to other care, or treatment was abandoned, with everyone concerned feeling guilty but continuing to believe in the validity of their own viewpoint and openly or silently blaming the others."

The reflexive, complementary pattern in the borderline personality syndrome makes us wonder whether therapists themselves are playing a part in the syndrome's increasing incidence. There are more mental-health professionals than ever, more schools of therapy offering relief from every routine discomfort of life. The expectation of a cure for all psychic ills has never been greater.

Are we creating the increase in borderline pathology by pulling more people into the mental-health system? Is the patient-therapist relationship, with its unlimited demands on the therapist's tolerance and understanding, the ideal arena for psychic terrorism? We have made great progress in successfully treating many neurotic and psychotic disorders in the last 25 years, but we find the vacuum being filled by a seemingly new kind of patient. Do we perhaps need them as much as they need us?

QUESTIONS

Answer the following questions and then compare your responses with the suggested answers at the end of this chapter.

1. What seems to be the strongest unifying thread in patients with borderline personality disorders?

2. What pattern of therapy do most borderline patients follow?

3. According to the article, how might patient-therapist relationships contribute to the increasing incidence of borderline personality syndrome?

ANSWERS

Correct Answers to Self-Test Exercises

<table>
<tr><td colspan="3" align="center">Multiple-Choice</td><td colspan="2" align="center">Matching</td></tr>
<tr><td>1. c</td><td>9. a</td><td>17. a</td><td>1. c</td><td>5. f</td></tr>
<tr><td>2. d</td><td>10. b</td><td>18. c</td><td>2. h</td><td>6. b</td></tr>
<tr><td>3. b</td><td>11. c</td><td>19. a</td><td>3. d</td><td>7. e</td></tr>
<tr><td>4. b</td><td>12. c</td><td>20. c</td><td>4. g</td><td>8. a</td></tr>
<tr><td>5. a</td><td>13. a</td><td>21. d</td><td></td><td></td></tr>
<tr><td>6. d</td><td>14. a</td><td>22. a</td><td></td><td></td></tr>
<tr><td>7. b</td><td>15. d</td><td></td><td></td><td></td></tr>
<tr><td>8. c</td><td>16. c</td><td></td><td></td><td></td></tr>
</table>

Suggested Answers to Application Exercises

1. a. It is extremely expensive. It is very time-consuming. It is not suitable for everyone.
   b. Psychoanalytically inspired therapy is more directive and has a goal-directed approach. Sessions are less frequent and the duration is short-term. Therapists raise questions rather than waiting for patients to bring them up.

2. Both therapies try to free people from their own personally imposed constraints. Both take an optimistic view that people should live life to the fullest and become self-actualizing.

3. a. Systematic desensitization and modeling (symbolic)
   b. Positive reinforcement
   c. Aversive therapy

4. Answers to Table 15-1 Components of Ellis's Alphabet-Letter Technique

A (activating experience)	Giving an incorrect response in class
B (belief system)	Incorrect responses make a person worthless and cause a loss of friends.
C (upsetting emotional consequences)	Embarrassment, concern about losing her friends and about being worthless
D (dispute)	People give imperfect responses and remain worthwhile.
E (better-functioning effects)	Joanne will speak out in class without indulging in irrational thought.

5. You should have identified some of the following advantages:
Realization that other people have similar problems
Feedback from other members of the group
Learning from others in the group
A safe environment in which to try new behaviors

6. Psychoactive drugs are not effective for some conditions. Even drugs with high success rates for specific disorders are not effective for everyone with the disorder. Further, many drugs have intolerable side effects.

Suggested Answers to Reading Questions

1. Borderline patients split the world and people into "good" and "bad." They also project their intolerable characteristics onto others. Both of these mechanisms have a powerful effect on their therapists.

2. Borderline patients usually begin with private therapy, receive increasing amounts of clinical treatment, and end in state mental hospitals.

3. Therapists are expected to be tolerant and understanding and become perfect targets for people with this disorder.

Chapter 16:

HEALTH PSYCHOLOGY

CHAPTER OUTLINE

I. What is health psychology?

II. Stress
  A. What is stress?
  B. Reacting to stress
    1. Physiological and cognitive aspects of stress
      a. A physiological perspective
      b. A cognitive perspective
    2. Stress and development
    3. Stress and life events
      a. Major life events
      b. Minor life events: Hassles and uplifts
      c. Control and predictability of life events
  C. Coping with stress
    1. Personality
    2. Social support
    3. Specific coping techniques
      a. "Commonsense" techniques
      b. Stress-inoculation training
  D. Living with stress

III. Wellness and health practices
  A. Influences on health practices
    1. Social factors
    2. Sociological factors
    3. Environmental factors
    4. Emotional factors
    5. Cognitive factors
    6. Physical factors
  B. How health habits affect wellness
    1. Diet
      a. Diet and heart disease
      b. Diet and cancer
      c. Diet and weight
      d. Eating disorders
        (1) Obesity
        (2) Anorexia nervosa
        (3) Bulimia
    2. Exercise
    3. Use of tobacco
    4. Use of alcohol
    5. Other practices

   C. Intervention: Promoting good health practices
      1. Public health programs
      2. Changing social norms
      3. School programs
      4. Individual approaches
      5. Self-help groups

IV. Illness
   A. Two major health problems
      1. Heart disease
      2. Cancer
   B. Health care and the patient-practitioner relationship

Boxes
   Psychology in your life: Losing weight by applying psychological principles
   Psychology in your life: Do you have a drinking problem?
   In the forefront: The mind and the immune system

LEARNING OBJECTIVES

After you study Chapter 16, you should be able to do the tasks outlined in the following objectives.

1. Define health psychology and identify four themes.

2. Define stress in physiological terms.

3. Explain what happens at each stage of the general adaptation syndrome.

4. Describe the cognitive perspective on stress and anxiety.

5. Summarize the findings of Holmes and Rahe concerning the relationship between major life changes and illness.

6. Summarize the findings of Lazarus concerning the relationship between minor hassles and illness.

7. Compare the effects of predictable and controllable stressors with the effects of unpredictable and uncontrollable stressors.

8. Cite the two major functions of coping responses according to Lazarus.

9. Explain how personality, expectations, and personal resources affect our ability to cope with stress.

10. Describe what is involved in stress-inoculation training.

11. Describe the concept of wellness and identify six factors that influence the practice of health behaviors.

12. Identify the relationship between diet and wellness and apply psychological principles to a weight-loss program.

13. Describe the symptoms of anorexia nervosa and bulimia.

14. Explain the importance of exercise and the dangers of tobacco and alcohol.

15. Describe programs and methods that have been used to promote good health habits.

16. Contrast the type A and type B behavior patterns and describe the relationship between these patterns and the likelihood of having coronary heart disease.

17. Identify the risk factors associated with cancer.

18. Explain the importance of active participation in health care.

KEY CONCEPTS

As you read Chapter 16 in your text, look for each of the following concepts. You should understand each concept.

1. Themes in Health Psychology

Health psychology, one of the newest fields in psychology, studies factors that promote health, influence illness, and affect recovery from illness. Four themes in health psychology are (1) we cannot separate mind and body in discussing health, (2) social and psychological factors influence health, (3) a sense of control is essential for health, and (4) we need to play an active role to become and stay healthy.

2. Stress as Part of Life

From our prenatal existence to our death we experience stress. Stress is involved in both positive and negative life events.

3. Physiological Perspective on Stress

Hans Selye defined stress as the *nonspecific response of the body to any demand.* The body's increased energy output is a nonspecific response to stressful events.

4. General Adaptation Syndrome (GAS)

Selye believed we have a three-stage reaction to stressful events: alarm, resistance, and exhaustion. The alarm stage has two phases. First the shock of the stressful event temporarily diminishes the body's ability to resist, and then the body's defenses are mobilized. In the resistance stage the body demonstrates above-normal resistance. In the exhaustion stage the body's ability to resist is eventually depleted. It is not an event itself which creates stress; it is the individual's perception of an event. What is stressful to one person may not be stressful to another.

5. Cognitive Perspective on Stress

From this point of view, stress results in part from the way we think about events. Stress results from a transaction between person and environment.

6. Stress and Development

Some degree of stress is necessary for development. Most of us actively place ourselves in stress-inducing situations.

7. Major Life Changes as Correlates of Stress and Illness

Two researchers, Holmes and Rahe, found that the more changes take place in a person's life, the greater the likelihood of illness within 1 or 2 years. A number of researchers, however, have questioned the conclusions drawn by Holmes and Rahe.

8. Everyday Hassles as Correlates of Stress and Illness

Richard C. Lazarus found that the small irritations of everyday life were better predictors of physical and psychological health than were major life events. Furthermore, he reasoned that the effects of major events may be related to the small hassles which are associated with these events. According to Lazarus, we may be more affected by small hassles than major events because we feel we should be able to control minor aspects of our lives. We feel out of control when these small matters aren't going well.

9. Unpredictability and Lack of Control of Stressors

The stressors that affect people most negatively are those which they cannot control or predict. Studies have shown that uncontrollable and unpredictable stress interferes with our ability to perform tasks and makes us less likely to treat others in a humanitarian fashion. The learned-helplessness theory offers one explanation of these effects.

10. Coping with Stress

According to Lazarus, coping with stress involves responding to stress in two major ways. First, coping involves solving the problem that is creating the stress, either by changing the environment or by changing our own actions or attitudes. Second, coping involves managing stress-related emotional and physical responses so that we keep up our morale and continue to function.

11. Personality and Coping with Stress

Our personality style affects the way we handle stress. Three characteristics are conducive to effective coping: commitment, control, and challenge. Commitment allows us to maintain a sense of purpose in life. Control is the belief that we have the power to do something about our life circumstances. Challenge is based on the belief that change is a normal and positive part of life.

12. Stress-Inoculation Training

This type of training teaches people to cope with stressful situations. Stress-inoculation-training programs combine cognitive therapy, which makes people aware of their feelings and what they are doing and saying to themselves to bring about those feelings, and behavior modification, which shows them how to change their negative behavior. This form of training has been used to help people overcome test anxiety and phobias, cope with pain, and control anger.

13. Wellness

Wellness is an ideal state of enriched health and enriched life. Most people are inconsistent in their health practices; their behaviors are influenced by social, sociological, environmental, emotional, cognitive, and physical factors.

14. Diet and Weight

Diet has been linked to many diseases, including gout, diabetes, heart disease, and cancer. Obesity (the state of being 20 percent over desirable weight) is a factor in high blood pressure, heart disease, certain cancers, allergies, and sinus attacks. Obesity can also create severe psychological problems. Although maintaining a weight loss is difficult, the most effective weight-loss programs begin with a reduction of food intake followed by behavior modification methods and increased exercise.

15. Eating Disorders

Both anorexia nervosa and bulimia have become more common in recent years. Anorexia nervosa is a form of self-starvation and can cause death. Bulimics eat large quantities of food and then force themselves to vomit.

16. Exercise

Exercise improves cardiovascular health, appetite, digestion, resistance to colds, athletic abilities, and attitudes. Exercise is more likely to become a habit if a person chooses an appropriate, enjoyable activity and takes time to warm up and cool down before and after engaging in the activity.

17. Use of Tobacco

Tobacco is the single most important cause of preventable illness. Although cigarette smoking is on the decline, health psychologists are challenged to keep young people from starting to use tobacco and to find ways to help people give it up.

18. Use of Alcohol

Alcohol is the most abused drug in this country. Use of alcohol during pregnancy can produce fetal alcohol syndrome in the baby. Alcohol impairs judgment, reaction time, and motor ability and is the cause of a high number of traffic accidents. Although there has been some controversy over whether teaching controlled drinking is superior to advising total abstinence from alcohol as a method of therapy, controlled-drinking techniques are currently considered a realistic

treatment for problem drinkers who are not alcholics.

19. Promotion of Good Health Habits

Individual success in promoting improvement in health habits has been better than the success rate of formal intervention programs. Community and school programs have used educational methods, mass media, and face-to-face instruction. Social norms for smoking have changed, and it is likely that the standard of a suntanned look for beauty will also change.

20. Type A and Type B Behavior Patterns

People exhibiting the type A behavior pattern are impatient, harried, and often frustrated at delays. They are so involved in their work that they have little time for family, friends, or leisure activities. Type B people are patient, relaxed, and take time off from work to be with other people and pursue personal interests. Type A people are twice as likely to develop heart trouble as type B people. Type A persons secrete more noradrenaline (a substance that may trigger blood clots) than do type B persons.

21. Cancer

Cancer is a term used to describe more than 100 different diseases caused by abnormal cell growth. Smoking, sunlight, drinking, depression, and family history of cancer have been described as risk factors in some studies.

22. Individual Health Care

Good health care requires that each patient keep informed, ask questions, and be an active participant.

TERMS TO KNOW

Define each of the terms listed. You can check your definitions in the text Glossary or on the text pages listed in parentheses.

		Nonnormative stress	(p. 563)
Health psychology	(p. 562)	General adaptation syndrome (GAS)	(p. 563)
Health psychologists	(p. 562)	Alarm reaction	(p. 564)
Biopsychosocial model	(p. 562)	Shock	(p. 564)
Biomedical model	(p. 562)	Countershock	(p. 564)
Stressor	(p. 563)	Stage of resistance	(p. 564)
Stress	(p. 563)	Stage of exhaustion	(p. 564)
Normative stress	(p. 563)	Primary appraisal	(p. 566)

Secondary appraisal   (p. 566)   Cognitive therapy   (p. 574)

Life change units (LCU)   (p. 567)   Behavior modification   (p. 574)

Learned-helplessness theory   (p. 567)   Wellness   (p. 575)

Social Readjustment   Cholesterol   (p. 577)
Rating Scale (SRRS)   (p. 567)

Coping   (p. 571)   Overweight   (p. 578)

Hardiness   (p. 572)   Obesity   (p. 578)

Commitment   (p. 572)   Anorexia nervosa   (p. 579)

Challenge   (p. 572)   Bulimia   (p. 580)

Stress-inoculation training   (p. 574)   Osteoporosis   (p. 581)

Fetal alcohol syndrome (p. 583)   IgA (p. 590)

Detoxification (p. 587)   Psychoneuroimmunology (p. 589)

Alcoholics Anonymous (p. 587)   Lymphocytes (p. 590)

Coronary heart disease (CHD) (p. 588)   **SELF-TEST**

Multiple-Choice

Choose the one best response to each question. An answer key is provided at the end of this chapter.

Type A behavior pattern (p. 588)

1. At what stage of your life is it likely that you first encountered stress?

   a. In the womb
   b. As an infant
   c. During early childhood
   d. During puberty

Type B behavior pattern (p. 588)

Testosterone (p. 588)

2. Someone breaks into your room and steals your wallet, which contains a month's pay. Which of the following terms would best describe this sudden loss of cash?

Noradrenaline (p. 588)

   a. Nonstress
   b. Normative stress
   c. Secondary stress
   d. Nonnormative stress

Cancer (p. 589)

3. You have just finished eating a large anchovy pizza and have washed it down with a quart of orange juice. What kind of body response best describes the wrenching you now feel in your stomach?

   a. Shock
   b. Specific response
   c. Resistance
   d. Nonspecific response

4. Which of the following stages of the general adaptation syndrome would best describe your fumbling attempt to apply a makeshift tourniquet to your own leg after you have been bitten by a snake with red, black, and yellow banded markings?

   a. Shock
   b. Countershock
   c. Resistance
   d. Exhaustion

5. Which of the following statements best represents the cognitive perspective on stress?

   a. Our reactions to stress are determined by the nature of the stressors which confront us.
   b. Most of us react to the same stressors in the same way.
   c. Our reactions to stress are determined by the way we think and feel about the stressors which confront us.
   d. Our reactions to stress are genetically determined.

6. On which of the following grounds may the conclusions of Holmes and Rahe regarding the relationship between life stress and illness be questioned?

   a. No statistical correlations exist between life events and subsequent illness.

   b. Subsequent research has supported the contention that positive life events contribute to poor health.
   c. In some cases an illness may trigger one or more life changes, but it may seem as if the life changes led to the illness.
   d. The scale takes into account individual differences in response to stress.

7. You are a construction carpenter who was laid off indefinitely because of a recession. You decided to take design classes in your free time and have now turned to designing and making tables and cabinets, which are selling well in a neighborhood shop. Which of the following best describes your response to the layoff?

   a. Family stress
   b. Stress inoculation
   c. Positive coping
   d. Expectation

8. Problem solving and the successful management of stress-related emotional and physical responses are two major functions of which of the following?

   a. Expectation
   b. Coping
   c. Interpretation
   d. Preparing for a stressor

9. Commitment, control, and challenge are three components of which of the following factors that affect our capacity to cope with stress?

   a. Personality
   b. Expectation
   c. Interpretation
   d. Personal resources

10. Which of the following characteristics allows us to believe in the truth, importance, and interest of who we are and what we are doing?

    a. Control
    b. Challenge
    c. Commitment
    d. Expectation

11. Which of the following techniques is used in stress-inoculation training?

    a. Dream therapy
    b. Reality therapy
    c. Drug therapy
    d. Behavior modification

12. You are on your first date with a highly desirable partner who has talked you into riding the Thunderbolt, a roller coaster noted for its terrifying loops. You have always been afraid of heights. While standing in line, you keep telling yourself, "Don't worry. This could be rough, but I know how to deal with it. I can work out a plan to handle this." What category of coping self-statements used in stress-inoculation training would your statements fall into?

    a. Confronting and handling a stressor
    b. Coping with arousal
    c. Preparing for a stressor
    d. Reinforcing self-statements

13. After successfully coping with your hair-raising ride, you congratulate yourself on how well you handled the situation. What would these self-statements be called?

    a. Coping with arousal
    b. Reinforcing successes
    c. Confronting and handling a stressor
    d. Preparing for a stressor

14. Which of the following factors are likely to influence the practice of health behaviors?

    a. Social and sociological
    b. Environmental and emotional
    c. Cognitive and physical
    d. All the above

15. A young woman is pathetically skinny and is suffering from anorexia nervosa. How is she likely to view herself?

    a. Obese
    b. Attractive and normal
    c. Somewhat thin
    d. Pathetically skinny

16. Assume that you have a friend who drinks, smokes, overeats, and is inactive. He is willing to give up one bad habit to improve his health. To maximize his health, which bad habit should he eliminate?

    a. Drinking
    b. Smoking
    c. Overeating
    d. Inactivity

17. On the basis of research, which of the following persons is least likely to return to smoking?

    a. Bob, who gave up smoking on his own
    b. Rob, who gave up smoking after joining a self-help group
    c. Ned, who made a $500 bet with his colleagues that he wouldn't smoke for a month
    d. Ted, who gave up smoking after participating in a community health seminar

18. Which of the following statements relates to type A behavior?

a. It is more common in underdeveloped countries.
b. It does not correlate with coronary heart disease before age 70.
c. It is more commonly found in men than in women.
d. It is more commonly found in women than men.

19. A research study of U.S. Army officers found that training helped reduce type A behavior. What else was reduced in the trained group?

a. Serum cholesterol level
b. IgA
c. Lymphocytes
d. All the above

20. What is the best advice to give a patient?

a. Be a "good" patient and follow your doctor's advice.
b. Ignore your doctor and manage your own health.
c. Be an active patient; ask questions and seek second and third opinions.
d. Argue with doctors, to "keep them on their toes."

Matching

Match each name in column A with the appropriate descriptive phrase from column B.

Column A

_____ 1. Selye

_____ 2. Holmes and Rahe

_____ 3. Lazarus

_____ 4. Seligman

_____ 5. Kobasa

Column B

a. Proposed learned-helplessness theory
b. Emphasized the role of cognition and everyday hassles in stress
c. Developed the Social Readjustment Rating Scale
d. Identified commitment, challenge, and control as three dimensions of hardiness
e. Did pioneer work on stress and identified the model for GAS

APPLICATION EXERCISES

These application exercises will test your understanding of and ability to apply the material you have read in your text. Suggested answers are provided at the end of the chapter so that you can check your responses.

1. Your text describes the general adaptation syndrome (GAS) as a three-stage reaction to stress,

consisting of alarm, resistance, and exhaustion. Read the following scenario and then describe what probably took place in each of these stages.

Mr. Selby, a top executive for an oil company, is driving to work one morning on a lonely road when he sees a black van blocking his way. He pulls up to the van and impatiently honks his horn. At that moment, three men wearing masks jump out of the van and rush up to Selby's car. They drag him from his car and, with great difficulty, manage to force him into the van. Selby puts up a good fight. As the van pulls off with a squeal, Selby continues to struggle with his captors. As the van races along, the commotion in the back eventually subsides as Selby gives up his efforts to resist his abductors.

a. Alarm stage _____
   _____
   _____
   _____
   _____

b. Resistance stage _____
   _____
   _____
   _____
   _____

c. Exhaustion stage _____
   _____
   _____
   _____
   _____

2. After reading the following descriptions of two events which might occur in the life of a woman, indicate which event would be more likely to correlate with subsequent illness, according to Richard C. Lazarus, and explain your answer.

   Laura Hendley and her husband are the parents of two small children and are also partners in a busy law firm in Boston.

   Event A: Laura receives a letter from her brother in San Francisco explaining that their mother, who also lives in that city, has been placed in a nursing home.

   Event B: Laura's trustworthy, reliable housekeeper and baby-sitter, whom she has employed for the past 5 years, quits without notice to get married.

   Explanation _____
   _____
   _____
   _____
   _____

3. Two pairs of stress-inducing situations are described below. For each pair, indicate which situation would be more stressful and explain why.

   a. Ian is the editor of a monthly magazine. She experiences a great deal of pressure each month during the final week before the magazine goes to press.

   Dawn is a nurse who works the night shift in a hospital emergency room. She is sporadically under intense pressure when a large number of emergency cases come in at the same time.

   Explanation _____
   _____
   _____

   b. Keith lives in a small apartment with two teenagers. He continually has to tell them to turn down the stereo.

   Jose lives near a busy airport. The roar of the airplanes

bombards him from morning until night.

Explanation _____

_____

_____

4. What we say to ourselves when we face stress-inducing situations can affect our feelings and our behavior. In one facet of stress-inoculation training, individuals are taught to replace negative self-statements with positive ones. Assume that a college student is very anxious about making his first speech in Oral Communication 101. Substitute a positive self-statement for the negative self-statements which follow.

   a. Preparing for a stressor: "I can't possibly get through the speech tomorrow. I'll make a fool of myself."

      Positive self-statement _____

      _____

   b. Confronting and handling a stressor: "I can't begin. What if I open my mouth and no sound comes out?"

      Positive self-statement _____

      _____

   c. Coping with the feeling of being overwhelmed: "I'm only halfway through my speech, and all those people are staring at me. I can't remember what I'm supposed to say next."

      Positive self-statement _____

      _____

   d. Reinforcing or nonreinforcing self-statements: "I'll bet that's the worst speech the

instructor ever heard. I'll probably flunk this course."

      Positive self-statement _____

      _____

5. Assume that you want to lose weight by applying motivational principles and are confronted with some choices. On the basis of the guidelines presented in your text, circle the choice that is more likely to help you achieve your goal of losing weight.

   Which would you choose?

   a. Eating in one place   or   Eating in a variety of locations

   b. Using a large plate   or   Using a small plate

   c. Eating slowly   or   Eating quickly

   d. Eating rich-tasting "dietetic" foods"   or   Avoiding rich-tasting "dietetic" foods

   e. Distracting yourself with another activity while eating   or   Concentrating on your food without distraction

   f. Keeping some variety in your diet   or   Eating only one or two types of food

   g. Eating alone   or   Eating with others

   h. Doing aerobic exercise at least three times a week   or   Avoiding exercise as much as possible

"Ah, yes—Benson, party of two, nonsmoking, high-fiber, low-sodium section."

Figure 16-1 Reprinted with permission of The Saturday Evening Post Society, Div. of B.F.L. & M.S., Inc. Copyright (c) 1987.

6. In Figure 16-1 the Bensons are demonstrating some concerns about smoking and diet. If the Bensons truly want to achieve wellness, what else should they do?

_____
_____
_____
_____

7. Your text describes the type A and type B behavior patterns. People with type A behavior patterns are twice as likely to develop coronary heart disease as people with type B patterns are. Read the following statements, which describe several people in business. Indicate which would be characteristic of type A behavior and which would typify type B behavior.

a. Mr. A. never has a purely social luncheon engagement on a workday.

b. Mr. B. is extremely trustful of other people.

c. Mr. C. refuses to rush his work and frequently takes breaks.

d. Ms. D. accepts only last-minute social invitations because she wants to make sure that she is free to work if necessary.

e. When Mr. E.'s secretary is sick, he takes the inconvenience in stride.

READING EXERCISE

Your text identifies stress as a factor that affects the immune system. The following brief article by Ruth Borgman that appeared in *Omni* presents research suggesting that loneliness may also lower resistance to disease.

Lone Dangers

"All the available data point to chronic loneliness, social isolation, and the sudden loss of a loved one as being among the leading causes of premature death in the United States," says James Lynch, psychologist and codirector of the Psychophysiological Clinic and Laboratories at the University of Maryland School of Medicine.

Lynch's assertion is backed up by the results of recent studies in epidemiology and immunology: Loneliness lowers your resistance to disease, weakening both the immune and cardiovascular systems. And lonely women are at a higher risk for breast cancer than women who have lots of social contacts.

Last year Peggy Reynolds and George A. Kaplan, epidemiologists at the California Department of Health Services, published a study on the relationship between cancer and social isolation. Drawing on an earlier survey of nearly 7,000 healthy adults in Alameda County, California, they found that socially isolated women had an appreciably greater chance of getting cancer and dying from it. (The same was not true of isolated men.)

"It wasn't only social isolation based on lack of social contacts," Reynolds emphasizes. "The important factor is perceived isolation, or the feeling of loneliness." Women who felt isolated even though they had many social contacts had 2.4 times the risk of dying from hormone-related cancers; women who had few social contacts *and* felt isolated were five times as likely to die. Reynolds hesitates to interpret the data any further than to say, "There is a clear correlation between emotions and high risk in specific types of cancer, such as breast,

uterine, and ovarian cancer." Because emotions affect hormonal regulation, perceived social isolation may have a direct impact on the development of these cancers.

Janice Kiecolt-Glaser and Ronald Glaser, a psychologist and immunologist, respectively, at Ohio State University College of Medicine in Columbus, are conducting studies on the relationship between loneliness and the immune system. Like Reynolds and Kaplan, the Glasers have focused on the individual's perception of being lonely. In a study of 33 psychiatric patients, the Glasers looked at the activity of natural killer (NK) cells, which monitor and destroy cancer cells and cells infected by viruses. The patients who reported feeling lonely had significantly lower levels of NK cells. And in five separate studies of medical students who were preparing for final examinations, they found the same phenomenon: Those who felt lonely showed lower levels of NK cells than their peers.

"When you're lonely, you're disconnected," says Lynch. "And the feeling of isolation affects the body." At his Maryland clinic, James Lynch conducts tests on hypertensive individuals to show the link between speech and the cardiovascular system. He hooks up clients to computers that monitor blood pressure and pulse rate. The point: to convince the person that his thoughts are his body, that his speech *is* his blood pressure.

"Speech is a uniquely human bodily function," Lynch says. "The baby's first cry probably is a substitute for the umbilical cord. That cry keeps us connected to our bodies, to one another, and so, in tune with our health." The lonely don't know they have a social membrane, a second skin—phrases Lynch uses to describe our interaction with others. "In human communication we literally project our hearts into what we say," Lynch says.

Copyright 1987 by Elizabeth Borgman and reprinted with the permission of Omni Publications International Ltd.

"We want, physically, to be understood." Love, Lynch adds, is anchored in our bodies.

"We all experience times when we are lonely," says Paul Pearsall, psychologist and director of the Problems of Daily Living Clinic at Sinai Hospital in Detroit. "Only the lonely person can judge whether the experience is positive or negative." Pearsall objects to defining loneliness simply as a negative state. While a certain amount of stress benefits some people, the same stressful situation harms others. "What we can't predict is who will react to what," says Pearsall.

In a recently published book, *Super Immunity* (McGraw-Hill), Pearsall identifies different reactions to loneliness as "hot" (hostile) or "cold" (depressive). He believes that cardiovascular problems are more likely to occur when a person is in a hot phase; cancers are associated with the cold phase.

One of Pearsall's patients at the Detroit clinic was suffering from the recent loss of his wife and talked about how much time he was spending alone. Although everyone encouraged him to get out and keep busy, he said he preferred to be alone, reminiscing and feeling sad. One day, after therapy, the man brightened: "So what I have to do is learn to be alone better!" Pearsall is happy with that insight. "Loneliness is, after all, a beautiful adaptive response to the situation of being alone," he says. Pearsall believes that the state of being lonely is neurologically based in the oldest part of the brain, a physical response similar to the fight-or-flight response. "Loneliness is a constructive rescue phenomenon," Pearsall continues. "We act or look lonely instinctively, which elicits a response from others that will alleviate our feelings of isolation. And the more we accept it and understand it, the better off we are."

QUESTIONS

Answer the following questions and then compare your responses with the suggested answers at the end of this chapter.

1. In the study by Reynolds and Kaplan, what was the important factor that increased the chance of cancer in women?

2. According to recent research, what physical change occurs in lonely people?

3. Why does Pearsall object to defining loneliness as a negative state?

ANSWERS

Correct Answers to Self-Test Exercises

Multiple-Choice   Matching

1. a   11. d   1. e
2. d   12. c   2. c
3. b   13. b   3. b
4. c   14. d   4. a
5. c   15. b   5. d
6. c   16. b
7. c   17. a
8. b   18. c
9. a   19. a
10. c   20. c

Suggested Answers to Application Exercises

1. a. Alarm stage: At the sight of the abductors, Selby's blood pressure and temperature probably dropped, his heartbeat quickened, and his muscles went slack. However, his body soon rebounded to mobilize its defenses.

    b. Resistance stage: In this stage, Selby's complete attention was directed toward resisting the three men. He undoubtedly had extra energy at this point because his body's adrenaline production was increasing to meet the demands of his stressful situation. Along with other physiological changes, this increased energy allowed him to put up a good struggle even though he was outnumbered.

    c. Exhaustion stage: Selby's ability to resist his captors couldn't be maintained. It eventually diminished and he became too exhausted to continue his struggle.

2. According to Lazarus, event B would probably be a better predictor of Laura's subsequent health than event A. While learning that her mother had been placed in a nursing home would undoubtedly be sad news for Laura, this would have little impact on her daily life. Losing her housekeeper and baby-sitter, on the other hand, would have an immediate and dramatic impact on both her personal and professional life. She would have to care for her children and her house until a suitable replacement was found and perhaps neglect her law practice in the meantime.

3. a. Dawn's situation would be more stressful because she cannot predict the occurrence of the stressors. She never knows when the emergency room will suddenly fill up with people needing care. Lan, on the other hand, can predict the time each month when she will experience the most stress.

    b. Jose's situation would be more stressful than Keith's. Keith has control over the stressor in question. He can tell his teenagers to turn down the volume on the stereo. Jose, of course, has no control over the noise of the airplanes.

4. a. Positive self-statement: "I can get through that speech tomorrow if I'm really prepared. Stop worrying and think about what you're going to say."
    b. Positive self-statement: "This tension is only natural. Take a deep breath and begin the speech."
    c. Positive self-statement: "I can't remember what I'm going to say next, but I'm not going to panic. I'm going to pause and glance at my note cards."
    d. Positive self-statement: "I didn't do too badly for my first speech. I'll bet I won't be as nervous next time."

5. You should have circled the following:
    a. Eating in one place
    b. Using a small plate
    c. Eating slowly
    d. Avoiding rich-tasting "dietetic" foods
    e. Concentrating on your food without distraction
    f. Keeping some variety in your diet
    g. Eating with others
    h. Doing aerobic exercise at least three times a week

6. The Bensons should eat moderately, avoid snacks, drink alcohol moderately or not at all, participate in a moderate exercise program, and sleep for 7 or 8 hours each night.

7. a. Type A
    b. Type B
    c. Type B
    d. Type A
    e. Type B

Suggested Answers to Reading Questions

1. The important factor was *perceived* isolation or feelings of loneliness rather than actual lack of social contact.

2. They will have lower levels of NK (natural killer) cells.

3. Pearsall sees loneliness as an adaptive response that causes others to respond and attempt to alleviate our loneliness.

Chapter 17:

SOCIAL INFLUENCE

CHAPTER OUTLINE

I. People in groups
   A. Norms and roles: Defining our place in the group
      1. What are roles?
      2. How much of our behavior is determined by norms and roles?
   B. Conformity and groupthink: Why we go along with the group
      1. Conformity
         a. What is conformity?
         b. What affects conformity?
            (1) Differences among people
            (2) Differences in situations
         c. Conformity versus independence
      2. Groupthink
   C. Obedience: Why we comply with demands of authority figures
      1. Milgram's studies
      2. Critiques of Milgram's studies

II. Altruism
   A. When do we help others?
      1. Factors affecting altruism
         a. Recognition that an emergency exists
         b. Number of people on the scene
         c. Characteristics of the victim
         d. Characteristics of the bystander
      2. Predicting altruistic behavior
   B. Why do we help others?
      1. We inherit a tendency toward altruism
      2. We learn to be altruistic
      3. Being altruistic makes us feel good
   C. How can we encourage altruism?

III. Attitudes
   A. Components of attitudes
   B. Measurement of attitudes
   C. Formation of attitudes
      1. Learning theories
      2. Cognitive-consistency theories
      3. Self-perception theory
   D. Changing attitudes: Persuasive communication
      1. Where does the message come from?
      2. How is the message stated?
      3. Who is listening to the message?
   E. Attitudes and behavior

F. Prejudice
　　1. What is prejudice?
　　2. How do we become prejudiced?
　　　　a. Prejudice and competition
　　　　b. Prejudice and learning
　　　　c. Prejudice and personality
　　　　d. Prejudice and stereotypes
　　3. How can we reduce prejudice?
　　　　a. Encouraging cooperation
　　　　b. Preventing the learning of prejudice
　　　　c. Teaching "mindful" discrimination
　　　　d. Raising independent, fair-minded children

Boxes
　　Psychology in your life: What makes people willing to go against the crowd?
　　In the forefront: Why people become regular, committed blood donors
　　Psychology in your life: Should we legislate helping behavior?

LEARNING OBJECTIVES

After you study Chapter 17, you should be able to do the tasks outlined in the following objectives.

1. Define and describe the focus of social psychology.

2. Define norms and roles.

3. Describe Zimbardo's study on prison life.

4. Define conformity.

5. Describe Asch's study of conformity.

6. Define groupthink.

7. Cite techniques for preventing groupthink.

8. Describe Milgram's experiments on obedience to authority.

9. Define altruism.

10. Discuss four factors which affect a person's willingness to help a stranger in distress.

11. Discuss four explanations of why people behave altruistically.

12. Describe two approaches to encouraging altruism.

13. Cite the three elements which make up an attitude.

14. Discuss the use of self-reports in measuring attitudes.

15. Describe how, according to four theories, attitudes are formed and changed.

16. Describe three basic factors which determine the effectiveness of a communication in changing attitudes.

17. Discuss the relationship between attitudes and behavior.

18. Define prejudice.

19. Discuss four major theories that explain prejudice.

20. Cite three possible ways of reducing discrimination.

KEY CONCEPTS

As you read Chapter 17 in your text, look for each of the following concepts. You should understand each concept.

1. Social Psychology

This branch of psychology focuses on how we feel and think about, are affected by, and act toward other people. Social psychologists conduct experiments both in the laboratory and in the field.

2. What Is a Group?

Two or more people who are interacting constitute a group, according to psychologists. In order to be interacting, the individuals must be aware of each other, take one another into account, and have a relationship with some continuity, involving the past or an anticipated future.

3. Norms and Roles

A role is a set of behavioral expectations for people of particular social positions. A role is made up of a group of norms, which are society's definitions of the way we should behave. Norms are positive in that they guide our behavior in many different situations. At the same time, they are negative in that they stifle our independence.

4. Experiment Demonstrating the Power of Roles to Shape Behavior

Philip G. Zimbardo used law-abiding college students as subjects in a study on prison life. The students were randomly assigned parts as prisoners or guards and were to spend 2 weeks in a prisonlike setting. The guards all became authoritarian and abusive to varying degrees. The prisoners became increasingly passive, behaving according to the classic cases of learned helplessness. The subjects played their roles so intensely that the experiment was ended early.

5. Asch's Experiments on Conformity

Solomon Asch conducted a series of experiments in which the true subjects were placed in groups with people posing as subjects. The group members were then asked to respond aloud to simple perceptual questions. About one out of three of the real subjects went along with the majority when the fake subjects gave obviously incorrect answers. Overall, about three out of four subjects gave incorrect, conforming answers at least once.

6. Independent Thinking

At least one study has found a relationship between independent thinking and self-concept. The subjects most likely to go against unanimous peer opinions had high self-esteem and were willing to be conspicuous in public.

7. Groupthink

Groupthink is an uncritical acceptance by members of a closely knit group of an unwise course of action. Groupthink occurs when the group members' loyalty and desire for unanimity prevent them from thinking critically about group decisions.

8. Milgram's Experiments on Obedience to Authority

Stanley Milgram conducted a series of experiments to study ordinary people's willingness to hurt other people if ordered to do so by a legitimate authority figure. In these experiments, subjects were ordered to deliver electric shocks ranging from slight to dangerously severe to a person who they thought was another subject. (This person was actually an actor.) A high proportion of the subjects obeyed orders and administered what they thought were painful shocks to an innocent person. Situational variables seemed to have a greater effect on whether the subjects obeyed orders than did the personal characteristics of the subjects.

9. Definition of Altruism

Altruism is defined as *behavior performed for the benefit of someone other than the person doing it, with no anticipation of reward.*

10. Factors in Helping a Stranger

A number of factors help explain why we will or will not help a stranger in an emergency situation. Our willingness to help may depend on how certain we are that an emergency exists. It may also depend on how many other people are present. When other people are around, we may assume that someone else has or will take responsibility. The characteristics of the person in distress may also influence our behavior. Research indicates that failure to help a victim may be caused by fear or disgust toward the person. Finally, our stopping to help someone may also depend on such factors as whether we are in a hurry, whether we are confident of our own ability to help, and whether we stand to gain or lose by acting or not acting.

11. Altruism as Inherited Tendency

The large amount of prosocial behavior found in various animal species,

including the human species, suggests some hereditary, biologically adaptive reason for it. Many sociobiologists have concluded that there is some kind of genetic programming which makes us act altruistically.

12. Altruism as Learned Behavior

A great deal of research indicates that people learn to be altruistic. This learning is thought to take place at an early age, with parents playing a key role in modeling and teaching altruistic behavior.

13. Altruism as Intrinsically Rewarding

We may behave altruistically because this makes us feel good about ourselves. When we are sad, we may help others because this makes us feel as if we are better people. When we are happy, we may be inspired to treat others well.

14. Altruism and Donating Blood

Donating blood is a special instance of altruism. Researchers have identified the following motivations behind this practice: external social motives, community or social-group responsibility, personal moral obligation, self-based humanitarian concerns, and addiction to the experience.

15. Encouraging Altruism

Researchers are exploring a number of ways to encourage the level of altruism needed in today's increasingly interdependent world. These approaches include teaching children to be less aggressive and more altruistic, attempting to develop chemical substances which will help people master antisocial aggression, and developing positive solutions to individual and group problems.

16. Attitudes

An attitude consists of a cognitive, an emotional, and a behavioral component. These three components may contradict each other. For example, you may think and feel one way but act in a way that contradicts these thoughts and feelings.

17. Measuring Attitudes

Social scientists usually measure attitudes by asking people a number of questions about their beliefs through interviews or questionnaires. Two popular paper-and-pencil attitude scales are the Likert scale and the semantic differential. One problem with using self-reports to measure attitudes is that the phrasing of the questions may influence the answers given. Another problem is that people may not be honest with researchers, or even themselves, concerning their true attitudes.

18. Learning Theories and Attitude Formation

According to learning theory, we learn attitudes the same way we learn everything else. We learn and retain those attitudes that are associated with reinforcement.

19. Cognitive-Consistency Theories and Attitude Formation

One of the most influential of the cognitive-consistency theories is Leon Festinger's cognitive-dissonance theory. Festinger maintains that we find it uncomfortable to hold two ideas, attitudes, or opinions that contradict each other, and so we do something to reduce the dissonance. We may make a choice between the two alternatives and then assure ourselves that the alternative we selected was really the more desirable one. Cognitive dissonance can also be produced when we do something contrary to our ideas about right and wrong, when our beliefs seem to defy logic, when present events contradict past experience, and when we do something "out of character." Dissonance theory can be modified in several ways. Some people can tolerate more dissonance than others; what's dissonant for one person may be consonant for another; and dissonance-arousing information can be useful to us. Another consistency theory, known as self-perception theory, maintains that attitudes follow behavior. In other words, to figure out what our own attitudes are we consider our own behavior.

20. How We are Persuaded to Change Our Attitudes

A number of factors influence the effectiveness of a communication designed to change attitudes. One factor is the source of the communication. We are more likely to be influenced by messages coming from people who are experts on the topic they are talking about, who are demonstrably trustworthy, who are personally unbiased, who are not trying to win us over, and who are similar to ourselves. A second factor is the nature of the message. In many cases, messages which appeal to our emotions, especially the emotion of fear, seem more effective than those which appeal to logic. With intelligent or hostile audiences, messages which present both sides of an argument and refute one viewpoint are more effective than one-sided messages. A third factor is the nature of the audience. Audience characteristics which increase receptivity to a message include feelings of poor self-esteem among the members, the belief that they are being allowed to form their own opinions, and a sense of personal involvement.

21. Relationship between Attitudes and Behavior

A review of several dozen studies on attitudes and behavior concluded that knowing what people say their attitudes are allows us to predict with less than 10 percent accuracy what they will actually do. This may be true because we often don't know what our attitudes are until we are forced to take action. Furthermore, our behavior may determine our attitudes instead of our attitudes determining our behavior.

22. Definitions of Prejudice, Stereotypes, and Discrimination

According to the text, prejudice is a *negative attitude held toward people solely because of their membership in some group;* stereotypes are *oversimplified beliefs about the characteristics of members of a group, with no allowance for individual differences;* and discrimination is *behavior aimed at the person one is prejudiced toward.*

23. How We Become Prejudiced

According to one theory of prejudice, members of an ethnic or racial group become prejudiced against members of another group when they have to compete for the same jobs. Another theory holds that prejudice is a social norm which children learn from the adults around them and from the mass media. A third theory of prejudice views some people as having prejudice-prone personalities. Finally, a fourth theory maintains that prejudice results from using stereotypes to process information.

24. Reducing Prejudice

A variety of means exist for reducing prejudice. We can encourage cooperation among people of different ethnic and racial backgrounds, eliminate prejudicial messages from the mass media, create laws which protect the rights of all people, teach "mindful" discrimination to our children, and rear them to be fair-minded.

TERMS TO KNOW

Define each of the terms listed. You can check your definitions in the text Glossary or on the text pages listed in parentheses.

Social psychology   (p. 598)

Group   (p. 599)

Role   (p. 601)

Norms   (p. 601)

Social role   (p. 601)

Conformity	(p. 602)	Cognitive-consistency theories	(p. 617)
Groupthink	(p. 604)	Cognitive dissonance	(p. 618)
Obedience	(p. 606)	Self-perception theory	(p. 620)
Altruism	(p. 608)	Prejudice	(p. 623)
Cost-benefit analysis	(p. 611)	Stereotypes	(p. 623)
Sociobiologist	(p. 611)	Discrimination	(p. 623)
Attitude	(p. 615)	F scale	(p. 624)
Likert scale	(p. 616)	Authoritarian personality	(p. 624)
Semantic differential	(p. 616)	Jigsaw technique	(p. 626)

SELF-TEST

Multiple-Choice

Choose the one best response to each question. An answer key is provided at the end of this chapter.

1. What is the name of the scientific study of how we feel, think, are affected by, and act toward other people?

   a. Experimental psychology
   b. Sociology
   c. Social psychology
   d. Clinical psychology

2. You are in your first year of high school teaching. For the sake of comfort and informality, you are conducting classes in your bare feet. Which of the following best describes your behavior?

   a. You are violating the norms of your role.
   b. You are violating the role of your norms.
   c. The violation is of norms but not of role.
   d. The violation is of role but not of norms.

3. How do the majority of people respond to norms?

   a. They resist them.
   b. They are indifferent to them.
   c. They modify them.
   d. They follow them.

4. The "prisoners" in Zimbardo's experiment tended to become passive, increasingly doing and saying less that would bring attention to themselves. In effect, which of the following classic cases did their behavior resemble?

   a. Confederates
   b. Learned helplessness
   c. Groupthink
   d. Authoritarian personalities

5. What did Asch's study of conformity reveal about the size of the majority opinion?

   a. The size of the opposition was of little consequence.
   b. One differing opinion was sufficient to induce conformity.
   c. Three differing opinions were necessary to induce conformity.
   d. Five differing opinions were necessary to induce conformity.

6. What do people engaging in groupthink tend to be overly concerned with?

   a. Critical thought
   b. Unanimity
   c. Rationality
   d. Moral consequences

7. In which of the following situations were subjects in Stanley Milgram's obedience studies most likely to obey the experimenter's orders?

   a. When in the same room with the "victim" but not touching the "victim"
   b. When placing the "victim's" hand on the shock plate
   c. When in the same room with the experimenter
   d. When receiving orders over the phone

8. Which of the following seemed to have the most effect on whether or not a subject would obey the experimenter in the Milgram study?

    a. How the situation was structured
    b. Sex of the subject
    c. Subject's level of depression
    d. Subject's age

9. How did those who defined the Milgram experimenter tend to perceive themselves in relation to the other members of the experiment?

    a. They felt less responsible than the experimenter.
    b. They attributed responsibility for the "victim's" suffering to the "victim" himself or herself.
    c. They saw themselves as mainly responsible for the suffering of the "victim."
    d. They saw themselves as better educated than the "victim."

10. Which of the following often explains the failure of people to come to the aid of a person in great distress?

    a. Indifference
    b. Recognition that an emergency exists
    c. Fear of or disgust toward the victim
    d. Being alone

11. Under which of the following conditions are people most likely to come to the aid of someone in distress?

    a. When the situation is ambiguous
    b. When they have plenty of time
    c. When responsibility can be diffused
    d. When others are nearby

12. Which of the following explanations of why you might help someone best fits the cost-benefit analysis of altruism?

    a. There is no risk to your life, and you could be a hero.
    b. You are the only bystander at the scene.
    c. You inherited altruistic tendencies.
    d. You learned altruistic behavior from your parents.

13. To which of the following are sociobiologists inclined to attribute altruistic behavior?

    a. Environmental factors
    b. Situational factors
    c. Genetic programming
    d. Learning

14. A man at the next table lights a cigarette just as you begin to eat. Angered by his lack of consideration, you are unable to enjoy your meal. Which of the following components now dominates your negative attitude toward smoking?

    a. Cognitive
    b. Behavioral
    c. Perceptual
    d. Emotional

15. Although you think that everyone should exercise regularly, you have decided to delay your workouts until the weather is warmer. In terms of attitudes, which of the following best describes your situation?

    a. The emotional component dominates.
    b. The behavioral and cognitive components are in conflict.
    c. The cognitive and emotional components are in conflict.
    d. The behavioral and emotional components are in conflict.

16. Which of the following measures attitudes by listing a number of statements and asking the subject to respond on a continuum from "strongly agree" to "strongly disagree"?

    a. Likert scale
    b. Cost-benefit analysis
    c. Semantic differential
    d. F scale

17. Which measure focuses on what a word or concept means to a person?

    a. Likert scale
    b. Cost-benefit analysis
    c. Semantic differential
    d. F scale

18. If you were primarily interested in measuring a person's tendencies toward authoritarian thinking, which of the following would you use?

    a. Likert scale
    b. Cost-benefit analysis
    c. Semantic differential
    d. F scale

19. Which of the following best reflects a learning-theory explanation of the formation of attitudes?

    a. Reacting to positive and negative experiences
    b. Reducing inconsistencies between thoughts and actions.
    c. Enhancing the value of whatever we have chosen
    d. Rejecting the conventional view

20. Which of the following statements best characterizes Festinger's cognitive-dissonance theory?

    a. We are primarily passive beings.
    b. We are psychologically uncomfortable with basic inconsistencies between our thoughts and actions.
    c. We learn to tolerate basic incompatibilities between our thoughts and actions.
    d. We come to understand our attitudes by observing our own behaviors.

21. In trivial matters, which of the following persuaders is most likely to influence us?

    a. An expert on the topic
    b. Someone proven to be trustworthy
    c. Someone we identify with and find attractive
    d. Someone who is not deliberately trying to win us over

22. Which characteristic of an audience makes it most receptive to a message?

    a. High intelligence
    b. High self-esteem
    c. Low intelligence
    d. Low self-esteem

23. Under which of the following conditions do predictions about our behavior based on our attitudes tend to be fairly accurate?

    a. When we are conscious of our attitudes at the time we act
    b. When outside influences are exerted on our behavior
    c. When we say we believe in judging each situation on its own merits
    d. When the measured attitude does not correspond with the situation being considered

24. Which of the following theories of prejudice did the "Robbers Cave" experiment tend to substantiate?

    a. Prejudice has genetic origins.
    b. Prejudice is a societal by-product of competition over scarce resources.
    c. Prejudice is an attitude we learn from our parents.
    d. Prejudice is the manifestation of a certain kind of personality.

25. To which of the following do Adorno and his colleagues trace authoritarian personality traits?

    a. Competition over scarce resources
    b. Tendency of children to identify with and imitate their parents
    c. Patterns of child rearing
    d. Genetic origins

Matching

Match each research psychologist in column A with the statement in column B that is most suggestive of the researcher's work.

Column A

_____ 1. Philip Zimbardo

_____ 2. Solomon Asch

_____ 3. Stanley Milgram

_____ 4. Jane Piliavin

_____ 5. Leon Festinger

_____ 6. Daryl Bem

_____ 7. T. W. Adorno

Column B

a. "I was just doing what I was told."
b. "I must like California; I keep going back each summer."
c. "When I wear reflector sunglasses and carry a club, it makes me feel tough."
d. "My parents used to beat me a lot; they taught me to respect authority."
e. "Everyone else said the lines were equal, so they must have been."
f. "Why not help the guy? I've got nothing to lose."
g. "I'm glad I didn't ask her out. She probably would have been a bore."

APPLICATION EXERCISES

These application exercises will test your understanding of and ability to apply the material you have read in your text. Suggested answers are provided at the end of the chapter so that you can check your responses.

1. As your text explains, a role is a set of behavioral expectations for people occupying a particular

social position. A role is made up of many norms, which are society's definitions of the way we should behave. For a position to be considered a social role, it must have a number of norms associated with it. Indicate which of the following positions would be regarded as social roles.

a. _____ Member of a movie audience
b. _____ Doctor
c. _____ Minister
d. _____ Pedestrian
e. _____ Sunbather
f. _____ Grandmother
g. _____ Socialite
h. _____ Blood donor

2. Solomon Asch's experiments on conformity demonstrated the power of social pressure. Assume that Dave, a college student, takes part in an experiment in which he and other group members must select the correctly spelled word from a series of alternatives and give their answers aloud, each in turn. The alternatives for one trial are as follows: *nife, knife, knif, knief*. In this experiment, as in Asch's experiments, Dave is the only true subject and the other group members are confederates of the experimenter. Assuming that Dave will react as the subjects in Asch's experiments did, indicate in which of the following situations he would be more likely to give an incorrect answer.

a. Dave is in a group of four and is the last person to answer. The other three people have said that *nife* is correct.
b. Dave is in a group of seven and is the sixth person to answer. Four people have said *knif* is correct and one person has said *knife* is correct.

"Wait! Wait! Listen to me! . . . We don't HAVE to be just sheep!"

Figure 17-1 The "Far Side" cartoon by Gary Larson is reprinted by permission of Chronicle Features, San Francisco.

3. The freethinking sheep in Figure 17-1 appears willing to buck the crowd. Santee and Maslach tried to find out what makes some people willing to speak up against majority opinion. What did they discover about the relationship between independent thinking and self-concept?

4. Your text discusses a number of factors that help explain why people do or do not help a stranger in an emergency situation. In each of the following situations, an individual fails to lend a helping hand. Discuss the probable key factor affecting the person's decision in each case.

a. Sharon is driving to a 9 A.M. appointment for a job interview when she is forced to stop at a red light. She casually glances at an empty parking lot to her right and is surprised to see a toddler walking across the lot crying. Sharon looks around for the adult or older child who must be with the toddler but sees no one. The light changes. She looks at her watch, which says 8:55, and pulls away. Probable reason for not helping:

_____

_____

b. Just as Rob approaches an intersection, the car in front of him slams into an oncoming car. The terrible crunching noise brings a half-dozen people running from their homes to see what has happened. After surveying the crowded scene for a few seconds, Rob swings around the wrecked cars and drives on. Probable reason for not helping:

_____

_____

c. Kitty is lying on the beach sunbathing when she spots someone floating by on a raft far out in the ocean. She can't tell whether the person is a man or a woman, but she can see that the person is wildly waving his or her arms. Kitty looks around at the other sunbathers on the beach. The group of people on her left wave back to the figure on the raft. The couple on her right are smiling and pointing toward the figure. Kitty turns over on her back to continue her sunbathing. Probable reason for not helping:

_____

_____

d. Richard is cutting through an alley on his way to his favorite Cuban restaurant when he comes upon a man lying face down in some broken glass. The man is wearing a filthy pair of jeans, a vest with no shirt, and a spiked collar around his neck. His short hair is dyed orange and green. Blood is trickling from the man's face and hands. Richard hurries past the man and goes to the nearest phone booth to call for help. After calling for an ambulance, Richard goes on to the restaurant instead of returning to the man. Probable reason for not helping:

_____

_____

5. Leon Festinger's cognitive-dissonance theory provides one explanation of how attitudes are formed. Assume that the teachers in two different high schools are requested but not ordered to attend three teacher-training sessions to be held on consecutive Saturdays. One principal has enough money remaining in the budget to pay the teachers from his school who attend the sessions. The other principal does not have the funds to pay the teachers. The training sessions do not prove to be very helpful to the teachers. The leader of the sessions is inexperienced, and the topics covered are not particularly relevant to the needs of the teachers. At the end of the third training session, the teachers are asked to evaluate the sessions. Overall, the teachers who will not be paid for their attendance evaluate the training session more favorably than those who will be compensated. Use cognitive-dissonance theory to explain the

different attitudes of the two
groups.

_____
_____
_____
_____

6. Daryl Bem's self-perception theory
explains attitude formation more
simply than does cognitive-
dissonance theory. Assume that
someone comes to your door
soliciting funds for a mayoral
candidate named Tom Riley, whom you
know very little about.
Nevertheless, you contribute $5 to
the man's campaign. After the
solicitor leaves, a friend who
happens to be visiting remarks, "I
guess you think Riley is the best
man for the job." You pause and
then reply, "Yes, I guess I do."
Use self-perception theory to
explain your response.

_____
_____
_____
_____

7. A variety of factors make some
communications designed to change
attitudes more effective than
others. In each of the following
cases, explain why the message is
likely to be persuasive.

a. Ms. A., fund-raiser for a
charitable organization,
delivers a speech to a group of
office workers. She assures them
that her purpose is not to

pressure them into making
contributions but simply to
explain the community activities
and projects which are supported
by her organization.
Explanation _____

_____
_____

b. Mr. B., Mexican-American lawyer,
makes a speech before a group of
Mexican-Americans, urging them
to oppose legislation which
would require all Texas
residents to carry
identification cards.
Explanation _____

_____
_____

c. Mr. C., an opponent of
unionization for college
faculties, addresses a group of
professors who have expressed a
desire to unionize. Mr. C.
presents both sides of the
issue, criticizing the arguments
in favor of unionization.
Explanation _____

_____
_____

d. A film designed to generate
public support for a nuclear
freeze avoids presenting facts,
figures, and arguments. Instead,
it graphically depicts the
horrifying consequences of
nuclear war.
Explanation _____

_____
_____

READING EXERCISE

Your text describes Stanley Milgram's experiments on obedience to authority. In the following article from *Psychology Today,* Janice Gibson and Mika Haritos-Fatouros explain how ordinary people, outside a laboratory, can be taught to follow orders slavishly--even when those orders call for brutalizing others.

The Education of a Torturer

Torture--for whatever purpose and in whatever name--requires a torturer, an individual responsible for planning and causing pain to others. "A man's hands are shackled behind him, his eyes blindfolded," wrote Argentine journalist Jacobo Timerman about his torture by Argentine army extremists. "No one says a word. Blows are showered. . . . [He is] stripped, doused with water, tied . . . . And the application of electric shocks begins. It's impossible to shout--you howl." The governments of at least 90 countries use similar methods to torture people all over the world, Amnesty International reports.

What kind of person can behave so monstrously to another human being? A sadist or a sexual deviant? Someone with an authoritarian upbringing or who was abused by parents? A disturbed personality affected somehow by hereditary characteristics?

On the contrary, the Nazis who tortured and killed millions during World War II "weren't sadists or killers by nature," Hannah Arendt reported in her book *Eichmann In Jerusalem*. Many studies of Nazi behavior concluded that monstrous acts, despite their horrors, were often simply a matter of faithful bureaucrats slavishly following orders.

In a 1976 study, University of Florida psychologist Molly Harrower asked 15 Rorschach experts to examine

Reprinted from *Psychology Today* magazine by permission of the publisher. Copyright (c) 1986 by the American Psychological Association.

inkblot test reports from Adolph Eichmann, Rudolf Hess, Hermann Goering and five other Nazi war criminals, made just before their trials at Nuremberg. She also sent the specialists Rorschach reports from eight Americans, some with well-adjusted personalities and some who were severely disturbed, without revealing the individuals' identities. The experts were unable to distinguish the Nazis from the Americans and judged an equal number of both to be well-adjusted. The horror that emerges is the likelihood that torturers are not freaks; they are ordinary people.

Obedience to what we call the "authority of violence" often plays an important role in pushing ordinary people to commit cruel, violent and even fatal acts. During wartime, for example, soldiers will follow orders to kill unarmed civilians. Here we will look at the way obedience and other factors combine to produce willing torturers.

Twenty-five years ago, the late psychologist Stanley Milgram demonstrated convincingly that people unlikely to be cruel in everyday life will administer pain if they are told to by someone in authority. In a famous experiment, Milgram had men wearing laboratory coats direct average American adults to inflict a series of electric shocks on other people. No real shocks were given and the "victims" were acting, but the people didn't know this. They were told that the purpose of the study was to measure the effects of punishment on learning. Obediently, 65 percent of them used what they thought were dangerously high levels of shocks when the experimenter told them to. While they were less likely to administer these supposed shocks as they were moved closer to their victims, almost one-third of them continued to shock when they were close enough to touch.

This readiness to torture is not limited to Americans. Following Milgram's lead, other researchers found that people of all ages, from a wide range of countries, were willing to shock others even when they had nothing to gain by complying with the command or nothing to lose by refusing it. So long as someone else, an authority figure, was responsible for the final outcome of the experiment, almost no one absolutely refused to administer shocks. Each study also found, as Milgram had, that some people would give shocks even when the decision was left up to them.

Milgram proposed that the reasons people obey or disobey authority fall into three categories. The first is personal history: family or school backgrounds that encourage obedience or defiance. The second, which he called "binding," is made up of ongoing experiences that make people feel comfortable when they obey authority. Strain, the third category, consists of bad feelings from unpleasant experiences connected with obedience. Milgram argued that when the binding factors are more powerful than the strain of cooperating, people will do as they are told. When the strain is greater, they are more likely to disobey.

This may explain short-term obedience in the laboratory, but it doesn't explain prolonged patterns of torture during wartime or under some political regimes. Repeatedly, torturers in Argentina and elsewhere performed acts that most of us consider repugnant, and in time this should have placed enough strain on them to prevent their obedience. It didn't. Nor does Milgram's theory explain undirected cruel or violent acts, which occur even when no authority orders them. For this, we have developed a more comprehensive learning model; for torture, we discovered, can be taught.

We studied the procedures used to train Greek military police as torturers during that country's military regime from 1967 through 1974. We examined the official testimonies of 21 former soldiers in the ESA (Army Police Corps) given at their 1975 criminal trials in Athens; in addition, Haritos-Fatouros conducted in-depth interviews with 16 of them after their trials. In many cases, these men had been convicted and had completed prison sentences. They were all leading normal lives when interviewed. One was a university graduate, five were graduates of higher technical institutes, nine had completed at least their second year of high school and only one had no more than a primary school education.

All of these men had been drafted, first into regular military service and then into specialized units that required servicement to torture prisoners. We found no record of delinquent or disturbed behavior before their military service. However, we did find several features of the soldiers' training that helped to turn them into willing and able torturers.

The initial screening for torturers was primarily based on physical strength and "appropriate" political beliefs, which simply meant that the recruits and their families were anticommunists. This ensured that the men had hostile attitudes toward potential victims from the very beginning.

Once they were actually serving as military police, the men were also screened for other attributes. According to former torturer Michaelis Petrou, "The most important criterion was that you had to keep your mouth shut. Second, you had to show aggression. Third, you had to be intelligent and strong. Fourth, you had to be 'their man,' which meant that you would report on the others serving with you, that [the officers] could trust you and that you would follow their orders blindly."

Binding the recruits to the authority of ESA began in basic training, with physically brutal initiation rites. Recruits themselves were cursed, punched, kicked and flogged. They were forced to run until they collapsed and prevented from relieving themselves for long stretches of time. They were required to swear allegiance to a symbol of authority used by the regime (a poster of a soldier superimposed on a large phoenix rising from its own ashes), and they had to promise on their knees to obey their commander-in-chief and the military revolution.

While being harassed and beaten by their officers, servicemen were repeatedly told how fortunate they were to have joined the ESA, the strongest and most important support of the regime. They were told that an ESA serviceman's action is never questioned: "You can even flog a major." In-group language helped the men to develop elitist attitudes. Servicemen used nicknames for one another and, later, they used them for victims and for the different methods of torture. "Tea party" meant the beating of a prisoner by a group of military police using their fists, and "tea party with toast" meant more severe group beatings using clubs. Gradually, the recruits came to speak of all people who were not in their group, parents and families included, as belonging to the "outside world."

The strain of obedience on the recruits was reduced in several ways. During basic training, they were given daily "national ethical education" lectures that included indoctrination against communism and enemies of the state. During more advanced training, the recruits were constantly reminded that the prisoners were "worms," and that they had to "crush" them. One man reported that when he was torturing

prisoners later, he caught himself repeating phrases like "bloody communists!" that he had heard in the lectures.

The military police used a carrot-and-stick method to further diminish the recruits' uneasiness about torture. There were many rewards, such as relaxed military rules after training was completed, and torturers often weren't punished for leaving camp without permission. They were allowed to wear civilian clothes, to keep their hair long and to drive military police cars for their personal use. Torturers were frequently given a leave of absence after they forced a confession from a prisoner. They had many economic benefits as well, including free bus rides and restaurant meals and job placement when military service was over. These were the carrots.

The sticks consisted of the constant harassment, threats and punishment for disobedience. The men were threatened and intimidated, first by their trainers, then later by senior servicemen. "An officer used to tell us that if a warder helps a prisoner, he will take the prisoner's place and the whole platoon will flog him," one man recalled. Soldiers spied on one another, and even the most successful torturers said that they were constantly afraid.

"You will learn to love pain," one officer promised a recruit. Sensitivity to torture was blunted in several steps. First, the men had to endure it themselves, as if torture were a normal act. The beatings and other torments inflicted on them continued and became worse. Next, the servicemen chosen for the Persecution Section, the unit that tortured political prisoners, were brought into contact with the prisoners by carrying food to their cells. The new men watched veteran soldiers torture prisoners, while they stood guard. Occasionally, the veterans would order them to give the prisoners "some blows."

At the next step, the men were required to participate in group beatings. Later, they were told to use a variety of torture methods on the prisoners. The final step, the appointment to prison warder or chief torturer, was announced suddenly by the commander-in-chief, leaving the men no time to reflect on their new duties.

The Greek example illustrates how the ability to torture can be taught. Training that increases binding and reduces strain can cause decent people to commit acts, often over long periods of time, that otherwise would be unthinkable for them. Similar techniques can be found in military training all over the world, when the intent is to teach soldiers to kill or perform some other repellent act. We conducted extensive interviews with soldiers and exsoldiers in the U.S. Marines and the Green Berets, and we found that all the steps in our training model were part and parcel of elite American military training. Soldiers are screened for intellectual and physical ability, achievement and mental health. Binding begins in basic training, with initiation rites that isolate trainees from society, introduce them to new rules and values and leave them little time for clear thinking after exhausting physical exercise and scant sleep. Harassment plays an important role, and soldiers are severely punished for disobedience, with demerits, verbal abuse, hours of calisthenics and loss of eating, sleeping and other privileges.

Military training gradually desensitizes soldiers to violence and reduces the strain normally created by repugnant acts. Their revulsion is diminished by screaming chants and songs about violence and killing during marches and runs. The enemy is given derogatory names and portrayed as less than human; this makes it easier to kill them. Completing the toughest possible training and being rewarded by "making it" in an elite corps bring the soldiers confidence and pride, and those who accomplish this feel they can do anything. "Although I tried to avoid killing, I learned to have confidence in myself and was never afraid," said a former Green Beret who served in Vietnam. "It was part of the job. . . . Anyone who goes through that kind of training could do it."

The effectiveness of these techniques, as several researchers have shown, is not limited to the army. History teacher Ronald Jones started what he called the Third Wave movement as a classroom experiment to show his high school students how people might have become Nazis in World War II. Jones began the Third Wave demonstration by requiring students to stand at attention in a unique new posture and follow strict new rules. He required students to stand beside their desks when asking or answering questions and to begin each statement by saying, "Mr. Jones." The students obeyed. He then required them to shout slogans, "Strength through discipline!" and "Strength through community!" Jones created a salute for class members that he called the Third Wave: the right hand raised to the shoulder with fingers curled. The salute had no meaning, but it served as a symbol of group belonging and a way of isolating members from outsiders.

The organization expanded quickly from 20 original members to 100. The teacher issued membership cards and assigned students to report members who didn't comply with the new rules. Dutifully, 20 students pointed accusing fingers at their classmates.

Then Jones announced that the Third Wave was a "nationwide movement to find students willing to fight for political change," and he organized a rally which drew a crowd of 200 students. At the rally, after getting students to salute and shout slogans on command, Jones explained the true reasons behind the Third Wave demonstration. Like the Nazis before them, Jones pointed out, "You bargained your freedom for the comfort of discipline."

The students, at an age when group belonging was very important to them, made good candidates for training. Jones didn't teach his students to commit atrocities, and the Third Wave lasted for only five days; in that time, however, Jones created an obedient group that resembled in many ways the Nazi youth groups of World War II.

Psychologists Craig Haney, W. Curtis Banks and Philip Zimbardo went even further in a remarkable simulation of prison life done at Stanford University. With no special training and in only six days' time, they changed typical university students into controlling, abusive guards and servile prisoners.

The students who agreed to participate were chosen randomly to be guards or prisoners. The mock guards were given uniforms and nightsticks and told to act as guards. Prisoners were treated as dangerous criminals: Local police rounded them up, fingerprinted and booked them and brought them to a simulated cellblock in the basement of the university psychology department. Uniformed guards made them remove their clothing, deloused them, gave them prison uniforms and put them in cells.

The two groups of students, originally found to be very similar in most respects, showed striking changes within one week. Prisoners became passive, dependent and helpless. In contrast, guards expressed feelings of power, status and group belonging. They were aggressive and abusive within the prison, insulting and bullying the prisoners. Some guards reported later that they had enjoyed their power, while others said they had not thought they were capable of behaving as they had. They were surprised and dismayed at what they had done: "It was degrading. . . . To me those things are sick. But they [the prisoners] did everything I said. They abused each other because I requested them to. No one questioned my authority at all."

The guards' behavior was similar in two important ways to that of the Greek torturers. First, they dehumanized their victims. Second, like the torturers, the guards were abusive only when they were within the prison walls. They could act reasonably outside the prisons because the two prison influences of binding and reduced strain were absent.

All these changes at Stanford occurred with no special training, but the techniques we have outlined were still present. Even without training, the student guards "knew" from television and movies that they were supposed to punish prisoners; they "knew" they were supposed to feel superior; and they "knew" they were supposed to blame their victims. Their own behavior and that of their peers gradually numbed their sensitivity to what they were doing, and they were rewarded by the power they had over their prisoners.

There is no evidence that such short-term experiments produce lasting effects. None were reported from either the Third Wave demonstration or the Stanford University simulation. The Stanford study, however, was cut short when depression, crying and psychosomatic illnesses began to appear among the students. And studies of Vietnam veterans have revealed that committing abhorrent acts, even under the extreme conditions of war, can lead to long-term problems. In one study of 130 Vietnam veterans who came to a therapist for help, almost 30 percent of them were concerned about violent acts they had committed while in the service. The veterans reported feelings of anxiety, guilt, depression and an inability to carry on intimate relationships. In a similar fashion, after the fall of the Greek dictatorship in 1974, former torturers began to report nightmares, irritability and episodes of depression.

"Torturing became a job," said former Greek torturer Petrou. "If the officers ordered you to beat, you beat.

If they ordered you to stop, you stopped. You never thought you could do otherwise." His comments bear a disturbing resemblance to the feelings expressed by a Stanford guard: "When I was doing it, I didn't feel regret . . . didn't feel guilt. Only afterwards, when I began to reflect . . . did it begin to dawn on me that this was a part of me I hadn't known before."

We do not believe that torture came naturally to any of these young men. Haritos-Fatouros found no evidence of sadistic, abusive or authoritarian behavior in the Greek soldiers' histories prior to their training. This, together with our study of Marine training and the Stanford and Third Wave studies, leads to the conclusion that torturers have normal personalities. Any of us, in a similar situation, might be capable of the same cruelty. One probably cannot train a deranged sadist to be an effective torturer or killer. He must be in complete control of himself while on the job.

QUESTIONS

Answer the following questions and then compare your responses with the suggested answers at the end of this chapter.

1. According to the article, are torturers mentally ill?

2. Identify two training techniques used to increase binding.

3. What are some of the training methods that reduce the strain of obedience?

ANSWERS

Correct Answers to Self-Test Exercises

Multiple-Choice			Matching
1. c	10. c	19. a	1. c
2. a	11. b	20. b	2. e
3. d	12. a	21. c	3. a
4. b	13. c	22. d	4. f
5. c	14. d	23. a	5. g
6. b	15. b	24. b	6. b
7. c	16. a	25. c	7. d
8. a	17. c		
9. c	18. d		

Suggested Answers to Application Exercises

1. b; c; f; g

2. Dave would be more likely to give an incorrect answer in situation a than in situation b, in spite of the fact that the opposition is greater in situation b. In Asch's experiments, if only one other person agreed with the subject, the subject was likely to resist the pressure to conform.

3. The study by Santee and Maslach found that students with high self-esteem and students who were willing to call attention to themselves were more likely to go against the crowd than those who were self-conscious, anxious, and shy.

4. a. The fact that Sharon was in a hurry to get to an important engagement may explain why she didn't stop. Had she not been pressed for time, she probably would have pulled into the lot and made certain the child wasn't alone.
    b. In this situation, there were so many other people around that Rob probably didn't feel personally responsible for helping the accident victims. Had he been the only person on the scene of the accident, he might have behaved differently.
    c. This situation was ambiguous. Kitty was not sure whether the person on the raft was in trouble. Since no one else seemed to be concerned, Kitty probably concluded that the individual didn't need her help.

    d. In a sense, Richard did help the man by calling for an ambulance. His failure to minister to the man personally was probably due to the disgust or fear aroused by the man's appearance.

5. The teachers who will be paid for attending can tell themselves that they participated for the money. Those who will not be compensated must come up with another rationale for why they voluntarily attended the sessions. If their attitudes toward the sessions are unfavorable, they will experience cognitive dissonance. If their attitudes are favorable, however, they can feel comfortable about having attended the sessions because they were worthwhile.

6. From the point of view of self-perception theory, you relied on an external cue (your own behavior) to figure out what your own attitude toward the candidate was. You concluded that since you had voluntarily contributed money to Riley's campaign, you must think he's the best man for the job.

7. a. The soft-sell approach used in this message is likely to be more effective than a hard-sell approach would have been. If the fund-raiser had tried to pressure the workers into making contributions, their resistance might have been greater.
    b. This message is likely to be effective for two reasons. First, the person delivering the message is similar to the members of his audience in that he is a Mexican-American and so are they. Second, as a lawyer, the speaker is an expert on the legal issue in question.
    c. The two-sided message presented by this speaker is likely to be effective with this particular audience. This audience is

intelligent and also already opposed to the position of the speaker. Presenting both sides won't confuse them, and it may persuade them that their side is wrong.

d. This film's appeal to the emotion of fear is likely to be more effective than an appeal to logic would have been.

SUGGESTED ANSWERS TO READING QUESTIONS

1. Studies of Nazi war criminals and Greek soldiers indicate that torturers are not mentally disturbed, unbalanced people. To the contrary, they have been found to be normal, ordinary individuals.

2. Initiation rites are used to isolate recruits from society. These rites often include strenuous physical exercise and harassment. Trainees are also introduced to a new social order complete with elitist attitudes, an in-group language, and its own set of values.

3. Trainees are taught to view their victims as less than human. Thus the reality of their torture is diminished. Trainees are rewarded for obedience and punished for not cooperating. New members learn to model their behavior after other group members who demonstrate violent acts. Finally, the trainees are introduced to violent acts gradually. In this way, they are systematically desensitized.

Chapter 18:

INTERPERSONAL ATTRACTION
AND RELATIONSHIPS

CHAPTER OUTLINE

I. Studying attraction and relationships
   A. Research
   B. Measuring attraction
      1. Asking people how they feel
      2. Looking at what people do

II. Forming relationships
   A. How do we make decisions about other people?
      1. Perceiving others
      2. Attribution theory
         a. Dispositional and situational explanations of behavior
         b. The fundamental attribution error
            (1) What causes the fundamental attribution error?
            (2) What does the fundamental attribution error imply about
                intimate relationships?
   B. What attracts us to other people?
      1. Proximity: "The nearness of you"
         a. Research on proximity
         b. Why is there a relationship between proximity and attraction?
      2. Physical appearance: "The way you look tonight"
      3. Other personal characteristics: "That certain something"
         a. Warmth
         b. Competence
      4. Similarity: "We think alike"
   C. Why do we enter and stay in relationships?
      1. Exchange theory: We calculate the value of a relationship
      2. Equity theory: We give and we get

III. Intimate relationships
   A. Friendship
   B. Love
      1. Passionate love and companionate love
      2. Triangular theory of love
   C. Marriage and divorce
      1. How we choose someone to marry
      2. How marriage affects us
      3. Breaking up
         a. Breaking up before marriage
         b. Breaking up after marriage

Boxes
   In the forefront: Loneliness
   Psychology in your life: Power in marriage

LEARNING OBJECTIVES

After you study Chapter 18, you should be able to do the tasks outlined in the following objectives.

1. Define interpersonal attraction.

2. Describe two basic approaches to measuring interpersonal attraction.

3. Describe and recognize dispositional and situational attributions.

4. Discuss the role of distinctiveness, consensus, and consistency in determining how we interpret behavior.

5. Define the fundamental attribution error.

6. Explain how the following factors affect attraction: proximity, physical appearance, warmth, competence, and similarity.

7. Describe the following theories which attempt to explain why people are drawn to and stay in relationships: exchange theory and equity theory.

8. Discuss the relationship between time and the building of friendships.

9. Describe three basic ways of explaining loneliness.

10. Identify four means of helping people cope with loneliness.

11. Describe companionate and passionate love.

12. Explain Sternberg's triangular theory of love.

13. Explain the relationship between marriage and physical health.

14. Discuss the relationship between power and marital satisfaction.

15. Describe several societal trends which have reduced the barriers to divorce.

KEY CONCEPTS

As you read Chapter 18 in your text, look for each of the following concepts. You should understand each concept.

1. Interpersonal Attraction

In psychological terms, interpersonal attraction is the tendency to evaluate another person in a positive way. While it may seem that certain people attract us because of their attributes, social psychologists have found that there are no attributes which absolutely predict attraction. Instead, attraction depends on the interaction between our traits and the other person's traits, as well as on the situation in which we get to know the person.

2. Studying Attraction

Because much research on attraction has been laboratory-based, the applicability of the results to real-life situations is questionable. Recently, more social scientists have incorporated survey procedures in their research in order to increase the validity of their studies.

3. Measuring Attraction by Asking People How They Feel

To measure attraction psychologists may use various self-report measures in which people are questioned about specific feelings they have toward designated persons and/or specific characteristics of those people. Two widely used measures of attraction are the Interpersonal Judgment Scale developed by Donn Byrne and the liking and loving scales developed by Zick Rubin. Rubin's scales indicate that liking and loving scores are only moderately correlated.

4. Measuring Attraction by Looking at What People Do

Using unobtrusive measures, psychologists measure attraction between people by observing behaviors which indicate attraction. Little research has been done on the relationship between self-report scales and behavioral measures of attraction.

5. How We Make Decisions about Other People

Our perceptions of a person's attributes and motivations largely determine whether we like or dislike the person. In forming perceptions about people, we actively interpret and draw inferences about their behavior. According to attribution theory, we explain people's behavior either dispositionally or situationally. In deciding whether a particular behavior should be attributed to personal or situational variables, we consider three factors: distinctiveness, consensus, and consistency.

6. Fundamental Attribution Error

Most of us tend to overestimate dispositional factors and to underestimate situational factors in accounting for someone else's behavior. This tendency may be explained by the fact that we know about the situational variables influencing our own behavior, but we often do not know when such variables are affecting another person's behavior, and we may not take the time to look for these hidden factors. By attributing our own failures to the situation and our successes to ourselves, we protect our egos.

7. What Attracts Us to Other People

While some research on attraction has explored the development of relationships in the real world, most research has focused on first impressions of college students in laboratory settings. Attraction is largely determined by the interaction between another person's characteristics and our appraisal of those traits.

8. Proximity and Attraction

There is a strong correlation between physical proximity and attraction. One possible explanation for this relationship is that proximity leads to familiarity, and familiarity leads to comfortable feelings about a relationship. Another explanation is that we are motivated to like someone by the knowledge that we will continue to have contact with that person. Finally, we may like better those people to whom we have been continually exposed.

9. Physical Appearance and Attraction

In recent years, many studies have shown that observers make similar judgments about people's attractiveness and that attractive people are more sought after, more highly regarded, and generally treated better than people who are not as attractive. An early study of attraction conducted by Elaine Walster found that people tend to like and seek out other people who are physically attractive as opposed to people similar in attractiveness to themselves. She also found that physical attractiveness was more important than compatibility of personality or intelligence in drawing people to each other.

10. Four Explanations for the Importance of Physical Attractiveness

First, we may seek out attractive people for aesthetic reasons; we may value their beauty for itself. Second, we tend to assume that attractive people have other desirable characteristics and we may be drawn to them for this reason. Third, we may want to associate with attractive people to enhance our own status by demonstrating that we are capable of attracting them. Fourth, as a result of having received favorable treatment throughout their lives, attractive people may, in fact, have developed desirable characteristics which draw us to them.

11. Warmth and Competence as Characteristics Which Influence Attraction

We are drawn to people whom we perceive to be warm. Warmth is generally thought to consist of such qualities as considerateness, informality, sociability, humanity, generosity, sense of humor, and good nature. People are also attracted by competence. However, too much competence may decrease a person's attractiveness, especially if we view the person as a rival.

12. Similarity and Attraction

Many studies have shown that attitudinal similarity attracts people to each other. In addition, research has shown that similarities of race, age, socioeconomic status, religion, education, intelligence, values, and leisure activities are also a basis for attraction. These findings contradict the theory of complementarity, which asserts that opposite personalities attract. The attraction value of similarity does not hold for people with low self-esteem. Such people are not attracted to others who are similar to themselves.

13. Why Similarity Attracts

We may like to be with people who are similar to ourselves because this reinforces us for being the way we are, because we admire them for being like us, and because we assume that they will like us.

14. Rewards and Punishments

Theories of attraction are generally indebted to the idea that we are drawn to and stay in relationships that are rewarding rather than punishing. The types of rewards provided may differ from one relationship to another. In some cases, we may like people who are near us when we are having an enjoyable time, even if they are not responsible in any way for our enjoyment.

15. Exchange Theory

This theory, which is actually a more complex variant of basic reward theory, states that we consider both the rewards and the costs of a relationship. Costs in a relationship can consist of negative aspects of the relationship itself or the rewards given up to have it, such as the rewards we would gain from another relationship or from being alone. We enter into or stay in relationships when the rewards outweigh the costs, and we avoid or get out of relationships when the costs are greater than the rewards.

16. Equity Theory

The basic premise of equity theory is that people feel most comfortable in relationships in which there is a fair distribution of rewards and costs, and that people will try to restore equity to relationships which they feel are unbalanced. Actual equity can be restored by changing what we are giving to or getting from a relationship. Psychological equity can be restored by changing our thinking to the point where we believe a relationship to be fair.

17. Friendship

To meet different needs, we have different kinds of friends, including friends to do things with, friends to help us, and friends to confide in. Factors which seem to affect the development of friendships are (in order of importance) proximity, similarity of background characteristics, shared role relationships, and similarity of values and attitudes. Current research is attempting to explain the development of friendships and what makes some friendships endure.

18. Loneliness

Loneliness, as opposed to aloneness, is an unpleasant condition resulting from deficiencies in a person's social relationships. These deficiencies can be explained in emotional, social, and cognitive terms, and are most common among adolescents, young single adults, those recently divorced, the unemployed, the housebound, and the handicapped. Programs dealing with loneliness attempt to help people establish personal relationships, to keep loneliness from degenerating into depression and suicide, and to prevent it from occurring in the first place.

19. Love

There seem to be two basic kinds of romantic love--companionate and passionate. Companionate love is like a loving friendship between a man and a woman that includes affection, deep attachment, trust, respect, appreciation, loyalty, and close knowledge of each other. Passionate love is a short-lived, wildly emotional state involving many conflicting feelings.

20. Triangular Theory of Love

Sternberg's triangular theory divides love into three components. The emotional component is intimacy, which involves self-disclosure. The motivational component is passion, which underlies physical attraction and sexual desire. Finally, the cognitive component, commitment, involves the decision to love and to make that love endure. Sternberg outlines eight different love relationships based on various combinations of these basic components.

21. Marriage and Divorce

There is a positive correlation between health and marital status. Research has confirmed that divorce is more painful than ending a premarital affair. In both dating and marriage, women are more likely to initiate breakups than men. Divorce brings about healthier psychological functioning for only one spouse more often than it benefits both marriage partners.

22. Power

Power, as it relates to interpersonal relationships, refers to one person's ability to make another act, think, or feel a certain way. In the past, the male has typically enjoyed more power within marriage because of his cultural and economic advantages. Today, however, the cultural ideal seems to favor more egalitarian marriages in which the power is equally distributed and the decisions are made jointly.

Consensus (p. 636)

Consistency (p. 636)

TERMS TO KNOW

Define each of the terms listed. You can check your definitions in the text Glossary or on the text pages listed in parentheses.

Fundamental attribution error (p. 637)

Interpersonal attraction (p. 633)

Proximity (p. 629)

Close relationships (p. 633)

Mere-exposure effect (p. 640)

Self-report measures (p. 634)

Pratfall effect (p. 642)

Synchrony (p. 635)

"Phantom other" procedure (p. 642)

Attribution theory (p. 636)

Self-disclosure (p. 643)

Distinctiveness (p. 636)

Exchange theory (p. 644)

Comparison level   (p. 644)   Power   (p. 652)

Comparison level
for alternatives   (p. 644)

SELF-TEST

Multiple-Choice

Choose the one best response to each question. An answer key is provided at the end of this chapter.

Equity theory   (p. 645)

1. Which of the following mainly determines your attraction to another person?

Actual equity   (p. 645)

    a. Your characteristics
    b. Other person's characteristics
    c. Other person's actions
    d. How you interpret the other person's characteristics

Psychological equity   (p. 645)

2. What is the most widely used measure of attraction?

    a. Interpersonal Judgment Scale
    b. Friends and Lovers Scale
    c. Love Scale
    d. Friendship Index

Loneliness   (p. 647)

3. A combat veteran from the Vietnamese war returns home and becomes criminally involved with drugs. According to attribution theory, how would most people tend to explain the veteran's behavior?

Companionate love   (p. 649)

    a. Situationally
    b. Systematically
    c. Dispositionally
    d. Distinctively

Passionate love   (p. 649)

Triangular theory of love   (p. 649)

4. If you've liked every musical you've ever seen, which of the following would people say your behavior lacks?

    a. Synchrony
    b. Distinctiveness
    c. Consensus
    d. Consistency

5. If you burst into knee-slapping laughter every time you hear a phone ring, what would people say your behavior lacks?

    a. Synchrony
    b. Distinctiveness
    c. Consensus
    d. Consistency

6. When we commit the fundamental attribution error in explaining the behavior of another person, what do we do?

    a. Underestimate both dispositional and situational factors
    b. Underestimate dispositional factors and overestimate situational factors
    c. Overestimate both dispositional and situational factors
    d. Overestimate dispositional factors and underestimate situational factors

7. Under what circumstances are we unlikely to make the fundamental attribution error?

    a. When explaining the behavior of an enemy
    b. When explaining our own behavior
    c. When explaining the behavior of a friend
    d. When explaining the behavior of our ex-spouse

8. The people living in end houses at Westgate West had fewer than half as many friends as did those whose houses faced the courtyard. What principle of attraction best explains this?

    a. Proximity
    b. Physical appearance
    c. Personality
    d. Similarity

9. Research documenting the advantages of being physically attractive indicates that preferential treatment begins as early as which of the following levels of schooling?

    a. College
    b. High school
    c. Elementary school
    d. Nursery school

10. Which of the following can best explain the fact that people often act the way we expect?

    a. Their physical attractiveness suggests what their behavior will be.
    b. We can make fairly accurate predictions based on the context in which we find them.
    c. They respond to our own cues.
    d. Their proximity to us suggests that they will be like us.

11. If you are viewed as a highly competent person and you want to be found likable, which of the following strategies should you use?

    a. Strive to maintain your "perfect" image.
    b. Make an occasional mistake to prove that you are "only human."
    c. Pretend to be mediocre.
    d. Emphasize your sensitivity to the "real world."

12. The "phantom other" is a research technique used in measuring which of the following factors that draw people together?

    a. Physical attractiveness
    b. Proximity
    c. Warmth
    d. Attitudinal similarity

13. Under what circumstances is attitudinal similarity not a positive attraction factor?

    a. When people are forced to live together in confinement
    b. When people are rivals
    c. When people have low self-esteem
    d. When people have high self-esteem

14. Assume that your self-esteem is low and you hear that an acquaintance has been saying complimentary things about you. According to research findings, how will you be most likely to react?

    a. You will be indifferent to the compliments.
    b. You will be suspicious of the compliments.
    c. You will be impressed by that person's good judgment.
    d. You will be drawn to that person.

15. If you are an insurance salesperson, by whom would you most probably want to be complimented?

    a. Lawyer
    b. Mechanic
    c. Bank teller
    d. Gardener

16. What is the status of the complementarity theory which maintains that we choose mates whose psychological characteristics meet our needs?

    a. It is increasing in popularity but is not universally accepted.
    b. It is universally accepted.
    c. It still needs to be tested.
    d. Testing has not upheld it.

17. Which of the following can best explain the fact that we like people associated with our good feelings and don't like people associated with our bad ones?

    a. Pratfall effect
    b. Rewards and punishment
    c. Equity theory
    d. Self-esteem

18. What does the comparison level in a relationship refer to?

    a. Minimum benefit a person expects from it
    b. Average benefit a person expects from it
    c. Maximum benefit a person expects from it
    d. Attractiveness of other possible ties

19. If your spouse was being unfaithful to you, what could you do to restore psychological equity without restoring actual equity?

    a. Have an affair of your own.
    b. Refuse to sleep with your spouse.
    c. Criticize your spouse in public.
    d. Convince yourself that your own excess weight is the real cause of the problem.

20. At what stage of the family life cycle does the greatest increase in the equitability of the roles of cooking, homemaking, and providing income occur?

    a. When there is a child under 6
    b. When there are school-age children
    c. When children leave home
    d. When the wife is over 60

21. What is one of the most frequently cited costs of friendship?

    a. Monetary expenditures
    b. Loss of freedom to associate with certain people
    c. Loss of freedom to express certain opinions
    d. Time expenditures

22. What view of loneliness stresses as its cause the discrepancy between level of social involvement expected and level experienced?

    a. Emotional
    b. Cognitive
    c. Social
    d. Physiological

23. The emotional component of Sternberg's triangular theory of love is related to which of the following?

    a. Intimacy
    b. Passion
    c. Commitment
    d. Both intimacy and commitment

24. According to Sternberg, which of the following types of love consists of both intimacy and passion but is lacking commitment?

    a. Infatuation
    b. Romantic love
    c. Fatuous love
    d. Companionate love

25. Approximately how many Americans marry at some time in their lives?

    a. 5 out of 10
    b. 7 out of 10
    c. 8 out of 10
    d. 9 out of 10

Matching

Match the theory in column A with the appropriate sentence in column B.

Column A

_____ 1. Equity theory
_____ 2. Attribution theory

_____ 3. Theory of complementarity

_____ 4. Reward theory

_____ 5. Exchange theory

_____ 6. Triangular theory

Column B

a. Opposite personalities attract.
b. We consider the costs and rewards in everything we do.
c. We like to be with people who make us feel good.
d. Love consists of intimacy, passion, and commitment.
e. We want relationships in which there is a fair distribution of rewards and costs.
f. We tend to explain other people's behavior by looking for either internal or external causes.

APPLICATION EXERCISES

These application exercises will test your understanding of and ability to apply the material you have read in your text. Suggested answers are provided at the end of the chapter so that you can check your responses.

1. According to attribution theory, we attribute behavior either to inherent personal qualities or to situational variables. In making this type of inference about behavior, we usually consider three factors: distinctiveness, consensus, and consistency. Read the following description of a person's behavior and then answer the questions concerning the process of attribution as it would relate to this.

   It is near the end of the semester, and Beth has a D average in a linear algebra course. She is a math major in her sophomore year. Her cumulative grade-point average in her major is 3.5. Out of 25 students in Beth's algebra class, 10 are flunking, 9 have a D average, and 6 have a C average. No one expects to make an A or B in the course.

   a. Is Beth's D average due to personal factors or situational factors? _____
   _____
   _____

   b. How did the factor of distinctiveness influence the decision you just made about Beth's behavior? _____
   _____
   _____

   c. How did the factor of consensus influence your decision? _____
   _____
   _____

   d. How did the factor of consistency influence your decision? _____
   _____
   _____

2. Your text describes an error which we frequently make in accounting for behavior—the *fundamental attribution* error. For each of the following situations, indicate whether the person is attributing behavior to dispositional or situational causes. Then explain why the person tended to make this type of attribution.

   a. Mary recently finished last in a 2-mile swimming race. She believes that she performed so poorly because her responsibilities at work kept her from training adequately for the race.

   Type of attribution: _____
   Explanation: _____
   _____
   _____
   _____

   b. One of John's coworkers has not been very productive lately. John assumes that this man is just not the type of person who can maintain a high level of productivity over a long period of time.

   Type of attribution: _____
   Explanation: _____
   _____
   _____
   _____

3. Your text discusses a number of principles which govern our attraction to other people. Apply these principles in answering the following questions about attraction. (Answer as research studies indicate the average person would.)

a. Under what circumstances would you be more likely to enjoy a blind date?

_____ Your roommate has assured you that the person is a lot of fun.

_____ Your roommate hasn't commented on the person in any way.

b. If you consider yourself to be an excellent tennis player, whom would you find more likable?

_____ Another excellent tennis player whom you've seen playing a perfect game

_____ Another excellent tennis player whom you've seen making a few mistakes in an otherwise outstanding game

c. Whom would you be more likely to end up dating?

_____ Someone who lives in the same apartment building as you do

_____ Someone who lives in the same town as you do

d. Whom would you be more likely to ask for a second date?

_____ Someone you consider to be more attractive than you

_____ Someone you consider to be your intellectual equal

e. If you are an extroverted, middle-class, sports-loving college graduate with high self-esteem, who is more likely to be your friend?

_____ Wealthy lawyer who loves opera and reading and hates loud parties

_____ Physical education teacher whose attitude concerning people is "the more the merrier"

4. Exchange theory offers an explanation of why we might decide to either continue or end a relationship. Imagine that Geraldine is experiencing some dissatisfaction in her marriage to Bill. Bill spends most of his spare time fixing old cars, playing basketball, and fishing. Since none of these activities involves Geraldine, she often feels neglected. She is happy, however, that Bill has a good relationship with their two sons, who are often included in Bill's activities. Bill and Geraldine's combined income allows the family to live comfortably. Finally, Geraldine knows that she can count on Bill for emotional support in times of severe stress. Geraldine has no intention of ending her marriage to Bill.

How might an exchange theorist explain Geraldine's remaining in this relationship? _____
_____
_____
_____
_____

5. Equity theory can help explain why we behave as we do in certain relationships. Imagine that Pat and Mary have been married for 9 years. They have two children, aged 6 and 4. During the early years of their

marriage, they shared all household chores, and when the children were born, Pat and Mary also took equal responsibility for their care. Pat and Mary have both had full-time jobs since they graduated from college. While Mary has worked at the same low-paying job for many years, Pat has been promoted several times and now occupies a high-status, high-salary position with a prestigious company. In recent years, Mary has willingly assumed more responsibility for taking care of the children and the house. Use equity theory to explain Mary's behavior. _____

_____

_____

_____

_____

_____

6. According to Sternberg, eight different types of love relationships result from different blends of the three basic components of love: intimacy, passion, and commitment. These range from nonlove (a relationship in which all three components are missing) to consummate love (a relationship in which all three components are present). In Figure 18-1, which of the eight types of love seems to be portrayed?

_____

_____

_____

_____

_____

"There was a time when you indulged in a little tenderness during the commercials."

Figure 18-1 Reprinted from *Punch* Magazine by permission of the publisher. Cartoon by W. Scully. Copyright (c) 1987 by *Punch* magazine.

READING EXERCISE

Your text introduced Sternberg's triangular theory of love. According to Sternberg, the three fundamental aspects of love are emotion, passion, and commitment. In the following article, which appeared in *Psychology Today,* Sternberg's research on love is described by Robert J. Trotter. The article includes some suprising findings concerning what predicts happiness in a relationship and what factors are important in a long-term relationship.

The Three Faces of Love

Brains and sex are the only things in life that matter. Robert J. Sternberg picked up that bit of wisdom from a cynical high school classmate and appears to have taken it to heart. "I spent the first part of my career studying brains, and now along comes sex," he says, claiming to be only partly facetious.

Sternberg, IBM Professor of Psychology and Education at Yale University, has, in fact, made a name for himself as one of the foremost theoreticians and researchers in the field of human intelligence, but in recent years he has turned a good deal of his attention to the study of love. Why? Because it's an understudied topic that is extremely important to people's lives. "It's important to my own life," he says. "I want to understand what's happening."

Sternberg began his attempt to understand love with a study for which he and graduate student Susan Grajek recruited 35 men and 50 women between 18 and 70 years old who had been in at least one love relationship. Participants rated their most recent significant love affair using the well-tested scales of loving and liking developed by psychologist Zick Rubin and the interpersonal involvement scale developed by psychologist George Levinger. The participants also rated their love for their mothers, fathers,

Reprinted from *Psychology Today* magazine by permission of the publisher. Copyright (c) 1986 by the American Psychological Association.

siblings closest in age and best friends of the same sex.

Sternberg and Grajek found that men generally love and like their lover the most and their sibling the least. Women tend to love their lover and best friend about the same, but they like the best friend more than they like the lover. Sternberg thinks he knows why. "Women are better at achieving intimacy and value it more than do men, so if women don't get the intimacy they crave in a relationship with a man, they try to find it with other women. They establish close friendships. They can say things to another woman they can't say to a man."

Sternberg and Grajek concluded that, while the exact emotions, motivations and cognitions involved in various kinds of loving relationships differ, "the various loves one experiences are not, strictly speaking, different." In other words, they thought they had proved that love, as different as it feels from situation to situation, is actually a common entity. They thought they had discovered the basis of love in interpersonal communication, sharing and support.

This research generated a lot of publicity in 1984, especially around St. Valentine's Day, and earned Sternberg the appellation "love professor." It also generated a lot of phone calls from reporters saying things like, "You mean to tell me the way you love your lover is the same as the way you love your 5-year-old kid? What about sex?" Sternberg had to rethink his position.

He analyzed various relationships to figure out what differentiates romantic love from companionate love, from liking, from infatuation and from various other types of love. He finally concluded that his original theory accounted for the emotional component of love but left out two other important aspects. According to Sternberg's new triangular theory, love has motivational and cognitive components as well. And different aspects of love can be explained in terms of these components.

Sternberg calls the emotional aspect of his love triangle intimacy. It includes such things as closeness, sharing, communication and support. Intimacy increases rather steadily at first, then at a slower rate until it eventually levels off and goes beneath the surface. Sternberg explains this course of development in terms of psychologist Ellen Berscheid's theory of emotions in close relationships.

According to Berscheid, people in close relationships feel increased emotion when there is some kind of disruption. This is common early in a relationship primarily because of uncertainty. Since you don't know what the other person is going to do, you are constantly learning and experiencing new things. This uncertainty keeps you guessing but also generates new levels of emotion and intimacy. As the other person becomes more predictable, there are fewer disruptions and less expressed, or manifest, intimacy.

An apparent lack of intimacy could mean that the relationship and the intimacy are dying out. Or, says Sternberg, the intimacy may still be there in latent form. The relationship may even be thriving, with the couple growing together so smoothly that they are hardly aware of their interdependence. It may take some kind of disruption—time apart, a death in the family, even a divorce—for them to find out just how they feel about each other. "Is it any wonder," Sternberg asks, "that some couples realize only after a divorce that they were very close to and dependent on each other?"

The motivational side of the triangle is passion, which leads to physiological arousal and an intense desire to be united with the loved one. Unlike intimacy, passion develops quickly. "Initially you have this rapidly growing, hot, heavy passion," Sternberg says, "but after a while it no longer does for you what you want it to—you get used to it, you habituate."

Passion is like an addiction, Sternberg says. He explains it according to psychologist Richard Solomon's opponent process theory of motivation, which says that desire for a person or substance involves two opposing forces. The first is a positive motivational force that attracts you to the person. It is quick to develop and quick to level off. The negative motivational force, the one that works against the attraction, is slow to develop and slow to fade. The result is an initial rapid growth in passion, followed by habituation when the more slowly developing negative force kicks in. "It's like with coffee, cigarettes or alcohol," Sternberg says. "Addiction can be rapid, but once habituation sets in, even an increased amount of exposure to the person or substance no longer stimulates the motivational arousal that was once possible.

"And then when the person dumps you, it's even worse. You don't go back to the way you were before you met the person," Sternberg explains. "You end up much worse off. You get depressed, irritable, you lose your appetite. You get these withdrawal symptoms, just as if you had quit drinking coffee or smoking, and it takes a while to get over it." The slow-starting, slow-fading negative force is still there after the person or the substance is gone.

The cognitive side of Sternberg's love triangle is commitment, both a short-term decision to love another person and a long-term commitment to maintain that love. Its developmental course is more straightforward and easier to explain than that of intimacy or passion. Essentially, commitment starts at zero when you first meet the other person and grows as you get to know each other. If the relationship is destined to be long-term, Sternberg says, the level of commitment will usually increase gradually at first and then speed up. As the relationship continues, the amount of commitment will generally level off. If the relationship begins to flag, the level of commitment will decline, and if the relationship fails, the level of commitment falls back to zero. According to Sternberg, the love of a parent for a child is often distinguished by a high and unconditional level of commitment.

Levels of intimacy, passion and commitment change over time, and so do relationships. You can visualize this, says Sternberg, by considering how the love triangle changes in size and shape as the three components of love increase and decrease. The triangle's area represents the amount of love and its shape the style. Large amounts of intimacy, passion and commitment, for example, yield a large triangle. And in general, Sternberg says, the larger the triangle, the more love.

Changing the length of the individual sides yields four differently shaped triangles, or styles of love. A triangle with three equal sides represents what Sternberg calls a "balanced" love in which all three components are equally matched. A scalene triangle (three unequal sides) in which the longest leg is passion represents a relationship in which physical attraction plays a larger role than either emotional intimacy or cognitive commitment. A scalene triangle with commitment as its longest leg depicts a relationship in which the intimacy and passion have waned or were never there in the first place. An isosceles triangle (two equal sides)

with intimacy as its longest leg shows a relationship in which emotional involvement is more important than either passion or commitment. It's more like a high-grade friendship than a romance.

Sternberg admits that this triangle is a simplification of a complex and subtle phenomenon. There can be a variety of emotions, motivations and types of commitment in a loving relationship, and each would have to be examined to completely diagnose a relationship. Beyond that, he says, every relationship involves several triangles: In addition to their own triangles, both people have an ideal triangle (the way you would like to feel about the person you love) and a perceived triangle (the way you think the other person feels about you).

Sternberg and graduate student Michael Barnes studied the effects these triangles have on a relationship by administering the liking and loving scales to 24 couples. Participants were asked to rate their relationship in terms of how they feel about the other person, how they think the other person feels about them, how they would feel about an ideal person and how they would want an ideal person to feel about them. They found that satisfaction is closely related to the similarity between these real, ideal and perceived triangles. In general, the closer they are in shape and size, the more satisfying the relationship.

The best single predictor of happiness in a relationship is not how you feel about the other person but the difference between how you would ideally like the other person to feel about you and how you think he or she actually feels about you. "In other words," Sternberg says, "relationships tend to go bad when there is a mismatch between what you want from the other person and what you think you are getting.

"Were you ever the overinvolved person in a relationship? That can be very dissatisfying. What usually happens is that the more involved person tries to think up schemes to get the other person up to his or her level of involvement. But the other person usually sees what's going on and backs off. That just makes the overinvolved person try harder and the other person back off more until it tears the relationship apart. The good advice in such a situation is for the overinvolved person to scale down, but that advice is hard to follow."

An underlying question in Sternberg's love research is: Why do so many relationships fail? Almost half the marriages in the United States end in divorce, and many couples who don't get divorced aren't all that happy. "Are people really so dumb that they pick wrong most of the time? Probably not," he suggests. "What they're doing is picking on the basis of what matters to them in the short run. But what matters in the long run may be different. The factors that count change, people change, relationships change."

Sternberg can't predict how people or situations will change, but he and his assistant Sandra Wright recently completed a study that suggests what will and won't be important in the long run. They put this question, what's important in a relationship, to 80 men and women from 17 to 69 years old, and divided them into three groups according to the length of their most recent relationship. The short-term group had been involved for up to two years, the mid-term group between two and five years, the others for more than five years.

Among the things that increase in importance as a relationship grows are willingness to change in response to each other and willingness to tolerate each other's imperfections. "These are things you can't judge at the beginning of a relationship," Sternberg says. "In the beginning," he explains, "some of the other person's flaws might not seem important. They may even seem kind of cute, but over the long term they may

begin to grate on you. You both have to be willing to make some changes to make the relationship work and you both have to be willing to tolerate some flaws."

Another thing that becomes increasingly important is the sharing of values, especially religious values. "When you first meet," says Sternberg, "you have this love-overcomes-all-obstacles attitude, but when the kids come along you have to make some hard decisions about the religion issue. All of a sudden something that wasn't so important is important."

Among the things that tend to decrease in importance is how interesting you find your partner. "In the beginning," Sternberg says, "it's almost as if the other person has to keep you interested or the relationship will go nowhere. Later on, it's not quite as critical because there are other things in your life that matter."

In addition to asking what is important at different times, Sternberg and Wright asked how much of these various things people had at different times in their relationships. The answers were not encouraging. The ability to make love, for example, often goes just at the time when it is becoming more important. In fact, Sternberg says, almost everything except matching religious beliefs decreased over time. The ability to communicate, physical attractiveness, having good times, sharing interests, the ability to listen, respect for each other, romantic love—they all went down. "That may be depressing," says Sternberg, "but it's important to know at the beginning of a relationship what to expect over time, to have realistic expectations for what you can get and what is going to be important in a relationship."

And Sternberg feels that his triangular theory of love can help people in other ways. "Just analyzing your relationship in terms of the three components can be useful," he says. "Are you more romantic and your partner more companionate? It's helpful to know where you and your partner are well-matched and where you are not and then start thinking about what you can do to make yourselves more alike in what you want out of the relationship."

If you decide to take steps to improve a relationship, Sternberg offers a final triangle, the action triangle. "Often there's quite a gap between thought or feeling and action," he explains. "Your actions don't always reflect the way you feel, so it could help to know just what actions are associated with each component of love."

Intimacy, he suggests, might be expressed by communicating inner feelings; sharing one's possessions, time and self; and offering emotional support. Passion, obviously, is expressed by kissing, hugging, touching and making love. Commitment can be expressed by fidelity, by staying with the relationship through the hard times that occur in any relationship or by getting engaged or married. Which actions are most important and helpful

will vary from person to person and from relationship to relationship. But Sternberg feels it is important to consider the triangle of love as it is expressed through action because action has so many effects on a relationship.

Citing psychologist Daryl Bem's theory of self-perception, Sternberg describes how actions can affect emotions, motivations and cognitions. "The way we act shapes the way we feel and think, possibly as much as the way we think and feel shapes the way we act." Also, he says, certain actions can lead to other actions; expressions of love, for example, encourage further expressions of love. Furthermore, your actions affect the way the other person thinks and feels about you and behaves toward you, leading to a mutually reinforcing series of actions.

"The point," Sternberg concludes, "is that it is necessary to take into account the ways in which people express their love. Without expression, even the greatest of loves can die."

QUESTIONS

1. Describe the typical progression of each of the three components of love in a successful, long-term relationship.

2. What is the single best predictor of happiness in a relationship?

3. What seem to be two key factors in the success of a relationship that increase in importance over time?

4. According to Sternberg, how can the triangular theory of love help people improve their relationships?

ANSWERS

Correct Answers to Self-Test Exercises

Multiple-Choice

1. d	10. c	19. d
2. a	11. b	20. c
3. c	12. d	21. d
4. b	13. c	22. b
5. c	14. b	23. a
6. d	15. a	24. b
7. b	16. d	25. d
8. a	17. b	
9. d	18. a	

Matching

1. e
2. f
3. a
4. c
5. b
6. d

Suggested Answers to Application Exercises

1. a   You probably attributed Beth's having a D average to situational factors.
    b. Beth's behavior in this class is distinctive in that she is making a poor grade. Her 3.5 cumulative grade-point average in her major indicates that she usually makes good grades in math courses. This high level of distinctiveness made you more likely to attribute her low grade to situational factors.
    c. There is a high degree of consensus in this situation in that most of her classmates are also making poor grades. This fact also made you more likely to infer that her low grade was a result of situational variables.
    d. Beth's behavior must have been fairly consistent in the class in order for her to be ending up with such a low grade. The consistency of her behavior in this particular situation influenced you to make a situational attribution.

2. a. Attribution: Situational cause. Explanation: By attributing her behavior to a situational variable--her lack of opportunity to train for the race--Mary was able to protect her ego.
    b. Attribution: Dispositional cause. Explanation: John probably is not aware of situational variables which may be affecting his coworker's productivity, so the explanation most convenient to him is a dispositional one--the type of person the coworker is.

3. a. You would be more likely to enjoy a blind date if you have been assured by your roommate that the person is a lot of fun. Your expectation about the person would determine to some degree how you perceive the person. In addition, your expectations might create a self-fulfilling prophecy.
    b. You would probably find the tennis player who made a few mistakes more likable because the person would seem more fallible and more human. This is especially true in view of the fact that you might view the

person as a rival, since you are both excellent tennis players.

c. You would be more likely to end up dating someone who lives in the same apartment building as you do. Proximity has a powerful impact on attraction.

d. You would be more likely to ask the person you consider to be more attractive than you are for a second date. Research indicates that, in terms of initial attraction, good looks are more important than compatibility of personalities or intelligence levels.

e. You would be more likely to select as a friend the physical education teacher whose attitude toward people is "the more the merrier." Many research studies have shown that we are drawn to people who are similar to ourselves. In this example, you and the teacher would share the personality characteristic of extroversion and an interest in sports as a leisure activity.

4. According to exchange theory, we weigh the benefits and costs of our relationships. If the benefits outweigh the costs, we remain in a relationship. For Geraldine, the benefits of being married to Bill include her satisfaction concerning Bill's relationship with their two sons, financial security, and emotional support in times of severe stress. The cost of the relationship is lack of day-to-day companionship. An exchange theorist would conclude that the benefits of this relationship evidently outweigh the costs.

5. According to equity theory, we feel most comfortable in relationships in which rewards and costs are distributed fairly. If we feel that a relationship has become unbalanced, we will try to restore equity. Mary may be trying to compensate for the fact that Paul now has a higher-paying, higher-status job by assuming greater responsibility for taking care of the children and the house. She may perceive this as a means of keeping the relationship equitable.

6. Figure 18-1 seems to portray empty love, a long-term relationship in which there is still commitment, but no intimacy or passion. The relationship has deteriorated to the point where there are no tender exchanges--even during television commercials.

Suggested Answers to Reading Questions

1. Intimacy grows steadily at first and then tends to level off. Passion develops much more quickly than intimacy, and it is also quick to level off. Commitment increases gradually at first, then speeds up, and finally levels off.

2. The single best predictor of happiness in a relationship is the difference between how a person would like the other partner to feel about him or her and how the person thinks the partner actually feels. The smaller the difference, the better the chance for a satisfying relationship.

3. Willingness to adjust to each other and to tolerate each other's imperfections seem to be key factors in relationships of more than 5 years' duration.

4. Sternberg believes that by analyzing a relationship in terms of the three components and by figuring out where one is and isn't well matched with one's partner, a person can determine what needs to be done to improve the relationship. The person might then take action associated with one or more of the three components of love. Such actions can affect not only the thoughts and feelings of the partner, but also those of the person taking action.

Appendix:

STATISTICS

OUTLINE

 I. Branches of statistics

 II. Descriptive statistics
    A. Central tendency
        1. Mode
        2. Median
        3. Mean
    B. Variability
        1. Range
        2. Variance
        3. Standard deviation
    C. Normal distributions
    D. Skewed distributions
    E. Correlation

 III. Inferential statistics
    A. Sampling methods
    B. Testing research hypotheses
        1. t test
        2. Analysis of variance

LEARNING OBJECTIVES

After you study the Appendix, you should be able to do the tasks outlined in the following objectives.

1. Describe the two branches of statistics.

2. Explain the uses of frequency distributions, histograms, and frequency polygons.

3. Calculate the mean, median, and mode and explain their uses.

4. Identify two variability measures and explain why the standard deviation is considered a more accurate measure of variability.

5. Define a normal distribution and explain the uses of standard scores.

6. Describe the characteristics of a skewed distribution.

7. Explain how correlation coefficients are used to describe relationships; recognize the purpose of scatterplots.

8. Describe the characteristics of random and stratified samples.

9. Explain the uses of *t* tests and *F* tests in hypothesis testing.

KEY CONCEPTS

As you read the Appendix, look for each of the following concepts. You should understand each concept.

1. Branches of Statistics

The two branches of statistics are descriptive statistics (summarizing data) and inferential statistics (generalizing and predicting from data). Both types of statistics are used by psychologists.

2. Organizing Descriptive Statistics

Descriptive statistics can be organized in frequency distributions, histograms (bar graphs), and frequency polygons.

3. Central Tendency

Central tendency refers to the most typical or representative score in a distribution. The three measures of central tendency are the mode, median, and mean. The mode is the score that occurs most frequently. The median is the midpoint or score that ranks in the center of a distribution. The mean is the arithmetic average and is affected by extreme scores.

4. Variability

The spread of scores in a distribution is called variability. The easiest variability measure to compute is the range. The standard deviation is the best measure of variability since it takes every score into account and can be used for further statistical interpretation.

5. Normal Distributions

A normal distribution is a symmetrical bell-shaped curve where the mean, median, and mode are equal and are located in the center of the curve. Almost all scores in a normal distribution are within 3 standard deviations on either side of the mean.

6. Standard Scores

Standard deviation units are referred to as *z* scores, or standard scores. Standard scores can be used to compare scores on tests with different means and standard deviations.

7. Skewed Distributions

Skewed distributions are not distributed normally; the mean, median, and mode fall in different locations. As a result, assumptions about the percentage distribution of standard scores are inappropriate.

8. Correlation

Correlation is the study of the relationship between two variables. Correlation can be represented graphically on a scatterplot. The strength and direction of relationships are represented by a decimal value called a correlation coefficient. Values of correlation coefficients vary from +1 (perfect positive correlation) to -1 (perfect negative correlation). Values near zero indicate that there is no relationship between the variables. Correlation indicates only the strength and direction of a relationship; it does not imply causation.

9. Sampling Methods

A good sample should be representative of an entire population. In a random sample, every member of the population should have the same chance of being selected. Stratification helps ensure that a random sample will have the correct proportions of important and relevant elements in the population.

10. Testing Research Hypotheses

Psychological experiments are designed to reject a null hypothesis and find significant differences between experimental and control groups. Statistical tests are used to be certain that differences are not likely to be caused by chance. If there are only two groups in the experiment (an experimental group and a control group), a t test is used. If the experiment involves three or more groups, an F ratio test must be used.

TERMS TO KNOW

Define each of the terms listed. You can check your definitions in the text Glossary or on the text pages listed in parentheses.

Statistics   (p. 658)

Descriptive statistics   (p. 658)

Inferential statistics   (p. 658)

Frequency distribution   (p. 658)

Histogram   (p. 658)

Abscissa   (p. 658)

Ordinate	(p. 658)	Standard deviation (σ)	(p. 662)
Frequency polygon	(p. 659)	Normal distribution	(p. 663)
Central tendency	(p. 660)	Standard score (z score)	(p. 664)
Mode (M_O)	(p. 660)	Skewed distribution	(p. 666)
Median (M)	(p. 660)	Correlation	(p. 666)
Mean ($\overline{X}$)	(p. 661)	Scatterplot	(p. 666)
Variability	(p. 662)	Positive correlation	(p. 666)
Range	(p. 662)	Negative (inverse) correlation	(p. 666)
Variance (σ^2)	(p. 662)	Correlation coefficient	(p. 667)

"Man on the street" technique (p. 668)

Biased sample   (p. 668)

Random sample   (p. 668)

Stratified random sample   (p. 668)

Null hypothesis   (p. 669)

Experimental group   (p. 669)

Control group   (p. 669)

Independent variable   (p. 669)

Significance   (p. 669)

Analysis of variance
(F test)   (p. 670)

t test   (p. 670)

SELF-TEST

Multiple-Choice

Choose the one best response to each question. An answer key is provided at the end of this Appendix.

1. What is the purpose of descriptive statistics?

   a. To summarize research
   b. To make inferences from research
   c. To make inferences from samples
   d. To test hypotheses

2. Suppose that you have the IQ scores of a representative sample of a group of students and you want to use these scores to draw general conclusions about the total group of students. What type of statistics would you use to make your conclusions?

   a. Descriptive
   b. Correlational
   c. Inferential
   d. Graphic

3. Which of the following illustrations is most useful in comparing two or more distributions?

   a. Histogram
   b. Frequency polygon
   c. Bar graph
   d. Table of raw data

4. Imagine that you scored psychology examinations for a college class. Of twenty students, four scored 68 percent; six scored 72 percent; eight scored 81 percent; and two scored 93 percent. What is the modal score for this test?

    a. 68 percent
    b. 72 percent
    c. 81 percent
    d. 93 percent

5. The mode of a set of scores is 74. Which of the following statements is true?

    a. A majority of the people received a score of 74.
    b. More people received a score of 74 than any other score.
    c. The mean score is 74.
    d. The median cannot be 74.

6. If you add up a set of test scores and divide by the number of scores, what do you get?

    a. Mode
    b. Median
    c. Mean
    d. Range

7. Assume that on a particular test most people scored only 60 points, but two people scored 100 points. Which of the following is a measure of central tendency and would be most affected by the two high scores?

    a. Mode
    b. Standard deviation
    c. Median
    d. Mean

8. What is the main disadvantage of using the range of a set of test scores to measure variability?

    a. It requires lengthy computations.
    b. It requires the use of computers.
    c. It is based on only two scores.
    d. It relies heavily on the mode.

9. Which of the following is the best measure of variability?

    a. Range
    b. Correlation
    c. Standard deviation
    d. Variance

10. Assume that the grades on an examination are normally distributed and all students scoring within 1 standard deviation (plus or minus) of the mean receive grades of C. What percentage of students would receive a C grade?

    a. 5 percent
    b. 10 percent
    c. 50 percent
    d. 68 percent

11. Assume that a corporation asks everyone who applies for its executive training program to take a test. The scores for this test are normally distributed, and the program will accept only those applicants who score in the top 5 percent. If someone's score was exactly 1 standard deviation above the mean, would the person be accepted?

    a. Yes.
    b. No.
    c. It would depend on the value of the mean.
    d. It would depend on how many people took the test.

12. On an examination for which scores were distributed normally, your score was 3 standard deviations below the mean. How would you probably feel?

a. Pleased because your score was better than average
b. Very disappointed, since almost no one had a lower score
c. Delighted that you had one of the best scores
d. Satisfied that you had performed average work on the examination

13. The mean of a distribution is 77, the median is 90, and the mode is 93. What can you conclude about the distribution?

   a. It is a normal distribution.
   b. It is a skewed distribution.
   c. The range and the standard deviation will be equal.
   d. The distribution cannot be plotted on a graph.

14. A psychologist believes that there is a strong relationship between the amount of hours a child spends watching television and the amount of time the child spends "grinding teeth" at night. Which of the following would be most useful in determining the accuracy of this belief?

   a. Standard deviation
   b. Analysis of variance
   c. Range
   d. Correlation coefficient

15. What will a scatterplot of a set of data help you determine?

   a. Significance
   b. Variability
   c. Correlation
   d. Standard deviation

16. Assume that you have just computed the correlation between foot size and success in psychology courses. Your computations resulted in a correlation of −2.72. What can you conclude?

a. There is a high positive correlation between foot size and success in psychology.
b. There is a high negative correlation between foot size and success in psychology.
c. There is a low negative correlation between foot size and success in psychology.
d. You have made an error in computation.

17. Suppose that a researcher finds that the more time people spend in a foreign country, the greater will be their ability to speak the language of the country. Which of the following coefficients of correlation reflects this relationship?

   a. −1.0
   b. +.86
   c. 0.0
   d. −.20

18. A study shows a high correlation between two factors. What can you conclude from this result?

   a. One factor causes the other.
   b. An external factor influences the two factors in the study.
   c. The two factors are probably not related.
   d. You cannot conclude anything about the cause of the relationship.

19. Assume that in order to find out whether Americans favor gun control, a research team surveyed 10,000 customers in sporting goods stores all over the country. Did this research team use random sampling?

a. No, because not all Americans were surveyed
b. No, because not all Americans had a chance to be in the survey
c. Yes, because people were surveyed from all over the country
d. Yes, because the sample size was large

20. Which of the following approaches are used in inferential statistics?

   a. Bias and interpretation
   b. Plotting and graphing
   c. Sampling and hypothesis testing
   d. Control and dependence

21. Which of the following is a correctly stated null hypothesis?

   a. If you eat a good breakfast, then this will not affect your school achievement.
   b. If you eat a good breakfast, then this will affect your school environment.
   c. Breakfast is important for school success.
   d. Lack of nutrition can cause failure.

22. A study indicated that students in a self-paced psychology course scored higher on a final examination than students in a traditional lecture course. The results show a "significant" difference. What does this mean?

   a. The difference was caused by chance.
   b. The difference probably was not caused by chance.
   c. The experimental group influenced the control group.
   d. The study probably cannot be replicated.

23. If there is a significant difference between the results of two treatments in an experiment, what does this indicate about the null hypothesis?

a. The null hypothesis cannot be accepted.
b. The null hypothesis can be accepted.
c. The null hypothesis is unnecessary.
d. The null hypothesis is irrelevant.

24. You have completed an experiment and want to compare the resulting motivation scores of your experimental group and control group. Which technique would you use to determine the significance of any differences between the two groups?

   a. F test
   b. Correlation coefficient
   c. t test
   d. Histogram

25. You have completed an experiment to determine the best method for improving the reading ability of fifth-grade children. You used a different method on each of five groups of children. What statistical technique would you use to determine the difference in reading levels among the five groups?

   a. t test
   b. Correlation coefficient
   c. F ratio
   d. Range

APPLICATION EXERCISES

These application exercises will test your understanding of and ability to apply the material you have read in your text. Suggested answers are provided at the end of this Appendix so that you can check your responses.

Exercises 1 through 4 will all refer to the following scenario.

Imagine that you took a midterm in psychology along with nine other students. You are delighted because your score on the test was 100. You are unaware of the scores of other students and are extremely curious. The scores of the students follow.

Abe	40	Fran	30
Bob	50	Gigi	40
Carl	40	Hank	50
Dick	40	Irene	60
Eve	50	You	100

1. a. You are interested in learning the average score on the test. You ask your professor to compute the mean (X) by adding the scores and dividing by the total number of students.

$$\frac{\Sigma X}{N} = X$$

40
50
40
40
50
30
40
50
60
<u>100</u>

$$X =$$
$$N = \underline{\hspace{1cm}}$$
$$X = \frac{\Sigma X}{N} \qquad = \underline{\hspace{1cm}} = \underline{\hspace{1cm}}$$

   b. You announce the average score of 50 to your classmates, and Carl feels dejected. He states that most people have scores higher than his. You explain that this claim may not be valid and ask the instructor to compute the median (M) score. To compute the median score, the instructor ranks the scores from highest to lowest. The median will divide the group exactly in half. Rank your classmates from highest to lowest and answer the questions that follow.

Rank	Score	Name
1		
2		
3		
4		
5		< Median
6		
7		
8		
9		
10		

What is the median? _____
Is Carl's dejection justified?
_____
Why or why not? _____

   c. You are concerned about Carl's attitude and ask your professor to compute the mode (M_o). How might knowledge of the mode console Carl?

_____
_____

2. In your computations in question 1, you found a 5-point difference between the mean and median. What might account for this difference?

_____
_____

3. Carl is now somewhat consoled but is interested in the variability of the scores. The instructor quickly computes the range:

Highest score - lowest score = range
    100   -   30   = 70

Carl expresses concern that the range included only two scores. Identify the expression which would better describe the variability on this test. Explain why it is more descriptive than the range.

_____
_____
_____
_____

4. On the basis of your calculations of central tendency in the group scores, would you describe the distribution as normal or skewed? Why?

_____
_____
_____
_____

5. Imagine that you are a judge in rock-dancing contests. Contestants are scored on a scale of 1 to 12. After scoring hundreds of dancers, you find that their scores are forming a normal curve like the one in Figure A-1.

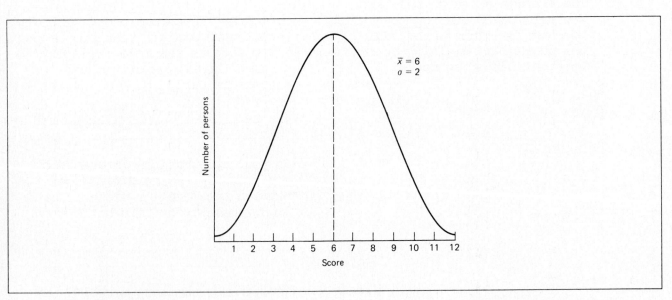

Figure A-1

One characteristic of a normal distribution is the fixed percentages associated with each standard deviation unit. Divide the curve into 3 standard deviation units above and 3 standard deviation units below the mean. Indicate the percentage of rock-dancers that would fall within each unit. Assuming that the director of a video program wants only dancers who score in the top 2 percent, what score would a dancer need to qualify?

_____

6. Assume that you find that all rock-dancers who qualify are under age 17. You wonder whether there is a correlation between age and rock-dancing skill. You survey six persons of different ages and ask them to dance to rock music. Table A-1 summarizes the results:

Table A-1 Rock-Dancing Scores by Age

Name	Age	Rock-Dancing Score
Burl	70	1
Merv	60	3
Eva	50	5
Carol	40	6
Fred	30	8
Michael	20	12

A scatterplot will help to show correlation graphically. Each score is marked as a position or location on a graph. Using the matrix shown in Figure A-2, construct a scatterplot of age and rock-dancing ability. Dancing ability is on the horizontal axis (abscissa) and age is on the vertical axis (ordinate). The first position on the scatterplot has been done for you.

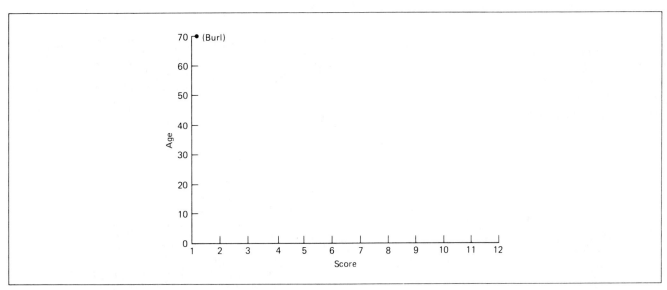

Figure A-2

What can you conclude from the scatterplot?

_____

_____

_____

_____

"Now think carefully. The answer you give will represent the opinion of millions of Americans."

Figure A-3   Reprinted with permission of The Saturday Evening Post Society, Div. of B.F.L. & M.S., Inc. Copyright (c) 1987.

7. a. In Figure A-3, what type of statistics is the pollster using?

_____

_____

b. If this woman is to represent millions of Americans, what type of sampling should the pollster be using?

_____

_____

c. Why would it be inappropriate for the pollster to choose his sample from a telephone directory?

_____

_____

8. Both the t test and the F test (analysis of variance) compare the means and standard deviations of groups and determine whether differences are significant or can be attributed to mere chance. What is the key difference between the t test and the F test?

_____

_____

_____

ANSWERS

Correct Answers to Self-Test Exercises

Multiple-Choice

1.	a	10.	d	19.	b
2.	c	11.	b	20.	c
3.	b	12.	b	21.	a
4.	c	13.	b	22.	b
5.	b	14.	d	23.	a
6.	c	15.	c	24.	c
7.	d	16.	d	25.	c
8.	c	17.	b		
9.	c	18.	d		

Suggested Answers to Application Exercises

1. a.
$$\Sigma X = 500$$
$$N = 10$$
$$\overline{X} = 50$$

b.

Rank	Score	Name	
1	100	You	
2	60	Irene	
3	50	Bob	
4	50	Eve	
5	50	Hank	< Median
6	40	Abe	
7	40	Carl	
8	40	Dick	
9	40	Gigi	
10	30	Fran	

Median is between 40 and 50.

$$\text{Median} = \frac{40 + 50}{2} = 45$$

Carl's dejection may be justified, since half the students scored above him.

c. $M_o = 40$. Carl may be consoled because more students had a score of 40 than any other score.

2. The difference between the values of the mean and median is caused by your extremely high score. In computing the median, only the rank of your score is considered. The full value of your score is used in computing the mean.

3. The standard deviation is the expression that best describes the variability of scores. The standard deviation is computed using each score. The range uses only two scores, the highest and the lowest, and is therefore less descriptive than the standard deviation.

4. This set of scores forms a skewed distribution; the mean, median, and mode have different values:

$$\overline{X} = 50$$
$$M = 45$$
$$M_o = 40$$

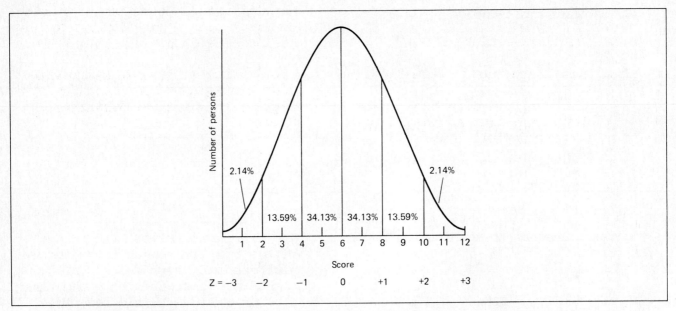

Figure A-4

5. Figure A-4 shows that a score of 10 would be needed to qualify.

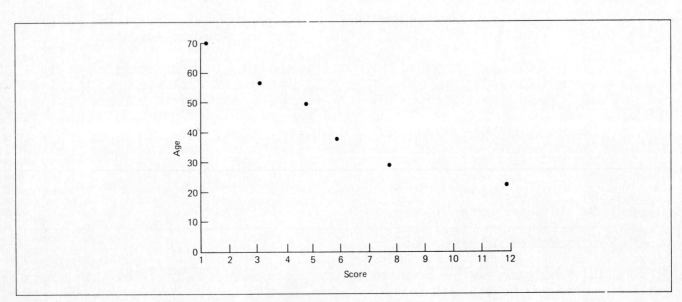

Figure A-5

6. According to Figure A-5, there appears to be a negative correlation between age and rock-dancing ability. However, we can reach no conclusion about the cause of the negative relationship.

7. a. Inferential statistics

   b. Stratified random sampling

   c. The telephone directory is not a good source for sample selection because not all members of the population are listed. The sample would not be truly random. Many people do not have telephones; others have unlisted numbers or share telephones with other people in their households. None of these people could be selected.

8. The t test can be used to compare only two groups. The F test is appropriate for more than two groups.